FEMALE
INFANTICIDE
IN INDIA

FEMALE INFANTICIDE IN INDIA

A Feminist Cultural History

Rashmi Dube Bhatnagar,
Renu Dube,
and
Reena Dube

State University of New York Press

Published by
State University of New York Press, Albany

For information, address State University of New York Press,
90 State Street, Suite 700, Albany, NY 12207

Production by Diane Ganeles
Marketing by Susan Petrie

Library of Congress Cataloging-in-Publication Data

Bhatnagar, Rashmi Dube, 1954–
    Female infanticide in India : a feminist cultural history / Rashmi Dube Bhatnagar, Renu
Dube & Reena Dube.
        p. cm.
    Includes bibliographical references and index.
    ISBN 0-7914-6327-3 (alk. paper) — ISBN 0-7914-6328-1 (pbk. : alk. paper)
        1. Infant girls—Violence against—India—History. 2. Infanticide—India—History. 3.
Women—Violence against—India—History. 4. Women—India—Social conditions. I. Dube,
Renu, 1958– II. Dube, Reena, 1961– III. Title.

HV6541.I5B53 2005
392.1'2—dc22

                                                                                2004045253

10 9 8 7 6 5 4 3 2 1

To Saroj Rani Pathak,
Rekha Dube, and Carol Kay

Inspired by the work
inaugurated by Ranajit Guha

Contents

Preface

This book emerges from our years of combined scholarship as well as from our own lived experience of growing up, living, and studying in postcolonial India as women of a recently decolonized nation-state. We had always been aware that the phenomenon of woman-devaluation was pervasive in our society and that most girls and women were socialized to accept the seeming naturalness of son-preference and its corollary, the devaluation of the life of the girl child. Yet as women scholars we could not help but recoil in horror when we recalled the multitude of allusions in novels, films, and everyday conversations that casually referred to girl child murder. We then began a journey to uncover the coded ways in which talk about female infanticide was socially sanctioned. The initial horror we felt was an important critical subject position with which to begin our journey because it forced us to acknowledge and deal with how we were implicated as women and as scholars in the sanctioned ignorance of the widespread postcolonial Indian practice of femicide.

Our critical and scholarly interest in the phenomenon of female infanticide and femicide leads us from the present into the past. Instead of offering a sensational account of violence on women in the third world, we have tried to understand this issue discursively. This means firstly, that we see this phenomenon as part of a larger continuum of violence on women and of a piece with the worldwide phenomenon of the devaluation of women. Secondly this means that our approach to the issue of female infanticide and femicide is discursive, historical, as well as theoretical: we trace the history of the practice of female infanticide in colonial India, critically evaluate the British efforts at reform, and theoretically examine the ferocious re-emergence of this formerly localized practice across contemporary India. Our approach is guided not only by the important question of how and why female infanticide and femicide take place, but by the more important question of how does this practice become productive for families and communities so that it continues to re-emerge despite legal governmental measures against it.

In the first chapter of the book we examine the national and global implications of femicide in postcolonial India by focusing on the nexus between First World reproductive technologies and the discourse of population control and development within the nation-state. We inaugurate our discussion of femicide by analyzing the present situation regarding femicide

ix

because we think it is important for our readers to understand and appreciate the contemporary genocidal proportions of the situation, as well as the true dimensions of this issue.

In the second chapter we move from the present into the past. We do so in order to understand how the crime of female infanticide was "discovered" by the British in colonial India, and the politics involved in the way this crime was named and discussed. We argue that the colonial politics of naming had an enormous impact on the way the British colonial administrators treated this crime within the imperial center and the way they dealt with it in the colony. Child murder is a capital offense in nineteenth-century England but female child murder is penalized by fines in the British colony of India.

From the politics of discovery and naming and the unequal relations between center and periphery, we move in chapter 3 to the question of how the colonial administrators profile the paradigmatic infanticidal communities in British India in purely racial terms. We critique this racialist profiling because we contend that it contributed to the fabrication of a motive for the crime. Therefore, instead of unquestioningly accepting the colonial hypothesis that this crime was committed and commissioned by a racially proud, feudal, barbaric community in order to ensure racial purity, we explore how and why this repressive practice was productive for the infanticidal community. We put forward the proposition that it was productive because it was part of a network of practices of social violence on Rajput women for the purposes of primitive accumulation of wealth and upward mobility.

In order to appreciate how the crime of female infanticide came to be aligned and associated with the dowry system and continues to be read off as an unfortunate consequence of the dowry system, we examine and analyze in detail the history of infanticide reform carried out by the British administrators in nineteenth-century colonial India. Therefore two chapters, chapters 4 and 5 of the book are devoted to a critical analyses of the British efforts at infanticide reform.

In chapter 4 we look at the administrative history of a "successful" case of British infanticide reform in the Kutch and Kathiawar regions of colonial Gujarat. We conclude that the discursive inscription of daughters as economic burdens emerges in the British colonial discourse of infanticide reform. We name this powerfully persuasive discursive inscription the colonialist-economistic explanation for infanticide. We show how the British grafted infanticide reform onto revenue collection in order to create legitimacy for their revenue collection from the Jhareja Rajputs in Kathiawar. Thus in the absence of an established right to rule, infanticide reform gave the British trading company the appearance of legitimacy as the civilizing, morally superior power.

In chapter 5 we deal with the historical emergence of the first colonial census at the site of female infanticide reform. We argue that it is this fundamental linkage of female infanticide with the first census taking in colonial India that forges the discursive inscription of female infanticide within the overpopulation discourse in contemporary postcolonial India. In the second half of the chapter we reconstruct a fragment of women's history by focusing on the 1854 case against Baee Nathee, a tribal woman in Kathiawar who was accused of killing her newborn twin daughters. The Baee Nathee case was used by the British reformers to discipline the wealthy and powerful infanticidal clans by making an example of the tribal woman who unlike the Jhareja Rajputs, belonged to the most politically powerless community. The Baee Nathee case becomes emblematic for the ways in which it reveals the politics of race, class, and gender in the colonial administration of the British.

In this book we have tried to approach the issue of female infanticide and femicide by circling the issue from various discursive incision points that are available to us as scholars and as women and we have tried to move beyond what Edward Said has called "the politics of blame" in order to map out what makes this social practice productive and therefore persistent in postcolonial societies. However, we did not design this book only as a critical requiem to the missing millions of women in India. We were invested in addressing the issues surrounding femicide with a view to opposing it. One of the questions that has often come up in the course of reviewing and discussing this book with friends and colleagues has been the question of solutions. What is the solution to this problem? Our own meditated answer has been that instead of quickly formulated, programmatic solutions that may or may not work, we are interested in the question of resistance and opposition to this practice.

Consequently the last two chapters of our book are devoted to just such resistance carried out by ordinary women, men, and the subaltern classes under the name of Meera, a woman poet in fifteenth-sixteenth-century Rajasthan. We argue for a recognition of the precolonial modes of dissent that have been inherited from medieval times, and continue to fuel dissent at heterogeneous sites despite assaults by dominant cultures, and in spite of the domestication of these forms by colonial and nationalist writers. Chapters 6 and 7 examine traditions of female dissent, which are opposed to the idioms and material practices of woman devaluation. We argue that Meera's poetry engenders traditions of coauthoring that makes it possible for generations of the poor and dispossessed to articulate their resistance. We focus on the Meera tradition because her poetry inaugurated a woman-centered critique of Rajput patriarchy from within the community. Meera's poetic codes and encoded comments on Rajput daughter-killing contrast women's ecologically centered way of being (as sower, planter, and nurturer) to the elite male Rajput cult of violence and the commodification of women as exchange.

Our book is dedicated to celebrating the girl child as a full human being capable of contributing to the community, the nation, and the world. We oppose a world view that contributes to woman devaluation and treats the girl child as an unproductive consumer of family wealth. Therefore, throughout this book we have been keenly attuned to the ways in which the practice of female infanticide and the phenomenon of woman devaluation has been resisted historically and continues to be opposed in the present times. The practice of femicide in our own times has to be addressed not only by laws and legislation but by the active opposition and resistance of all the women and men who are concerned with the issues of equality and equal opportunity.

Acknowledgments

Spectral and living influences shape my contributions to the present book. My contribution to this co-authored book bears the impress of the graffiti on the college wall in the late 1970s by Naxal members of Indraprastha Hostel for women that read, "Women are not chapatti-making machines." I am indebted to teachers and colleagues at two women's colleges at Delhi University, Indraprastha College for Women, and Miranda House, particularly the latter's year-long seminar on feminist theory in 1985–1986 that gave me the friendship of V. Krishna, Zakia Pathak, Uma Chakravorty, Angela Koreth, Swati Joshi, and Rajeswari Sunderajan. I was privileged to attend the first meeting of the Delhi-based women's periodical Manushi in a room at the women's hostel of Miranda House. The editor Madhu Kishwar was always willing at meetings, processions, or guest lectures to discuss women's issues with me.

I acknowledge my debts to the writings by Chandra Talpade Mohanty and Gayatri Chakrovorty Spivak, especially the latter's lectures at JawaharLal Nehru University in the spring of 1987, as well as her graduate courses at the University of Pittsburgh. The esteem and support of American academic feminists, especially Sharon E. Harris and Alpana S. Knippling, and of my students in my women's studies classes at the University of Pittsburgh and at the University of Nebraska at Lincoln, sustained me in the long and difficult years of co-writing this book. I would also like to pay my debt of gratitude to my colleagues at the University of Nebraska at Lincoln for arranging and attending my lecture, "A Personal Journey: Female Infanticide and the Women's Movement in the 70s and 80s in Modern India" as part of the Women's Studies International Colloquium series in February 26, 1997. Gender exclusion is against the grain of the present book, consequently I acknowledge the intellectual and political support of Satya P. Mohanty, Dipesh Chakravorty, and Jonathan Arac in reading, commenting on and believing in our book project. I acknowledge my debt to my father Jagdish Prasad Dube who wrote a story for me when I asked him to tell me about his life. That story about his sisters written in exquisite calligraphy is a blessing for this book.

Last but not least, I would like to thank my co-authors Renu and Reena, and to the high school student who brought computer printouts from her school library and thus inaugurated the research for this book, my daughter Pankhuree. Her birth at Gangaram Hospital at Delhi was greeted with sympathy and condolences by the staff of the hospital ward because I had given birth to a daughter instead of a son. My contribution to this book is a protest against such practices.

—R. D. B.

We would like to thank our teachers and mentors who made the long and difficult journey to and of this book a voyage of discovery and dedication. First we wish to thank the missing women in our lives: Saroj, our first, best, and enduring teacher, who also happens to be our mother; Rekha, our sister who taught us the discipline and practice of patience, and other-directed love; Carol who believed in us and gave us the message of hope and idealism. We wish to thank Jonathan Arac for taking up where Carol left off, and being a wonderfully positive presence in our lives. We wish to acknowledge Vijay Sheth of Bombay Emporium for being our cultural guide and resource in diaspora. We wish to thank our editor Jane Bunker and Senior Production Editor, Diane Ganeles, at SUNY Press for their help, support, and guidance in bringing this work to fruition. To Rashmi and Pankhuree, our fellow travelers, our debt is bigger than words. Alan O'Connor, Judith Mayne, Jim Knapp, and Colin McCabe, all of whom have shaped this project by their invaluable role as teachers, mentors, and enduring sources of inspiration. Trevor Melia, Henry Krips, and Dilip Gaonkar, with their guidance, help, and friendship; Mavin Cox and the Communication Department at Boise State University as well as Shelton Woods, Associate Dean at the College of Social Sciences and Public Affairs, all have offered unstinting help and support to make the dream a reality.

—R.D. & R.D.

CHAPTER 1

The Practice of Femicide in Postcolonial India and the Discourse of Population Control within the Nation State

The world is going to hell if those people don't stop breeding.
—*National Geographic*, October 1998

I will keep this one only if it is a son.
—An Usilampatti woman, *The Hindu*, November 1994

The selective killing of the female fetus in postcolonial India has received serious commitment from activists in the Indian women's movement(s) but scant rhetorical and theoretical analysis. This omission in postcolonial feminist theory is curious given the fact that the Indian women's movements were the first organized groups in the 1970s and 1980s to call attention to the use of new reproductive technologies for feticide and the selective breeding/nurturing of male fetuses in modern India.[1]

Our objective in this chapter is to attempt a rhetorical and discursive analysis of the violence visited on Indian women. Therefore, our discursive analysis begins by foregrounding the conjunctions between the discourses of femicide and the rhetoric of overpopulation, and examines the ways in which femicide is inscribed, rationalized, and co-opted into the rhetoric of population control in postcolonial India. We argue that the discourses of modernity, development, population control, and new reproductive technologies work together to claim the Indian woman's body as object and to name femicide as informed choice and family planning.

This women's collective eschews the ahistorical, simplified, and colonialist explanations that trace present day femicide in an unmediated manner to nineteenth-century practices of female infanticide in colonial India. The telos of such explanations is a continuist history of femicide in terms of the anti-woman bias of Indian traditions. In refusing to see tradition as the overarching explanatory framework for female infanticide in the past and its resurgence as femicide in the present, we are in conversation with Lata Mani's pioneering work on the practice of sati in colonial India. Lata Mani has

1

conclusively shown that explanations concerning the oppression of Indian women that center on Indian traditions are in fact a product of colonialist discourses (*EPW* 21.7, 26 April 1986). Thus, feminist analyses that focus exclusively on Indian traditions run the risk of omitting and eliding histories of resistances, heterogeneous locations, and discontinuity in history.

Our scholarly commitment is to the study of the condition of postcolonial modernity in its specificity. We understand femicide as a specifically postcolonial violence, which is facilitated by the patriarchal family, reproductive technologies, the nation-state, and the discourses of global agencies and international organizations. The first section addresses conceptual errors that are in wide circulation concerning female infanticide in India; we suggest that it is in and through the conjunctions between the discourse of modern femicide in India and the rhetoric of overpopulation that these conceptual errors come into play. The second section examines the political text of the Emergency in the 1970s in India in order to demonstrate that the effect of the conjuncture between the overt rhetoric of overpopulation and the covert discourse of femicide is that female populations are targeted for extermination. The third section analyzes alternative paradigms and possible solutions.

It is symptomatic of this crime of gendered violence that the available statistics for female infanticide are conflicting. In 1998 the Indian Association for Women's Studies reports that 10,000 female fetuses are killed every year in India. The editorial of a national daily puts the annual figure at 50,000 female fetuses (*Times of India*, August 6 1994). Yet another study determines that from 1978 to 1983, 78,000 female fetuses were reported killed, or 13,000 female fetuses annually were aborted, following the use of amniocentesis as a sex determination test. These conflicting statistics indicate that this violence has become the undetectable crime against women and at the same time, the estimated numbers indicate the proportion of a genocide.

Another indicator of this genocide is the declining sex ratio in India. In colonial India the gender imbalance indicated by the 1901 census is a sex ratio of 972 females per 1,000 males. After India's independence this gender imbalance is exacerbated rather than redressed: the 1981 census shows that the female to male ratio drops to 935 females per 1,000 males. The number of missing women increased to 22 million in independent India from 3 million under colonial rule. This trend continues unabated, currently the female to male ratio is 933 females per 1,000 males. While the world over women outnumber men, India is unique in that here men outnumber women. The normal sex ratio favors the birth of female babies; however, India has a steadily declining sex ratio skewed in favor of male births. This phenomena of missing women is proof that it is not only the female fetus that is endangered but the overall conditions for many Indian women are life-threatening.

In our view exclusive analytical attention to the female fetus does not illuminate the real nature of the problem. Instead we relate the violence of femicide to the birthing mother, the surviving sibling sisters, and to other forms of violence perpetuated on women in postcolonial India like rape (every 54 minutes in India), dowry deaths (every 102 minutes) and the estimated 500 "accidental" suicides of housewives that occur in major cities annually (*India Abroad*, July 1998). By situating the problem in this continuum, we argue that the modern holocaust of femicide signifies not only the serial killing of female fetuses but also girl-child murder by negligence through discriminatory practices such as uneven food allocation causing nutritional deficiencies, uneven access to medical care, family resources, and minimum survival needs. These traditional forms of gendered neglect have increasingly been recognized by feminist scholars as a weeding out process and as virtually undetectable infanticide. Many studies have demonstrated that the girl-child is at risk not only at birth but also in infancy. For example, one writer notes, "The significant decrease in the female population occurs after birth and before the age of four. From 1978 to 1983 . . . of the twelve million girls born each year, only nine million will live to be fifteen" (Balakrishnan 1994, 276). The victims of female infanticide are not only the aborted female fetus, the girl child, the birthing mother, and the infanticide survivors who grow up with the knowledge that they and their female siblings survived attempts to murder them. The list of casualties include the large population of women who are disciplined by the violence visited on other women.

Some Pedagogic Issues Concerning Femicide in Postcolonial India

As teachers and scholars our concern is with the distortions that occur when students and colleagues discuss femicide in India within the rhetorical framework of overpopulation. The chief anthropological misconception is that femicide is a traditional method of population control in Asiatic societies. This misconception has to be dismantled discursively and empirically. The discursive logic of this belief is to portray femicide simply as the resurgence of age-old practices of female infanticide, thus reinforcing the popular belief that the social problem of femicide is facilitated by ancient customs of population control, not by the discourses and institutions of the postcolonial nation state.[2] Furthermore, this perception is ahistorical and is not borne out by women's history. Feminist scholars have shown that in the indigenous cultures of the South (Asia, Africa, Latin America) women knew and had access to a variety of sophisticated and noninvasive contraception to limit pregnancy and for the purposes of spacing children. These methods fell into disuse and were not communicated intergenerationally because women were forced to forget their traditional body-knowledges with the advent of colonialism and neocolonialism. In these indigenous cultures of the South infanticide and feticide was one practice coexisting with a variety of methods, child murder was certainly not the dominant method of population control.[3]

Teaching about the violence against Indian women involves battling the persistent Orientalism wherein Indian women are viewed as passive victims of absolute and undifferentiated customs of patriarchal oppression. Our extensive historical and literary research enables our understanding that female infanticide was never uniformly or universally practiced in India. For example, in nineteenth-century colonial India female infanticide was confined to select landowning propertied families and communities in certain regions in northwest India and with the exception of one tribe, female infanticide was unknown in southern India. Even in these infanticide-endemic districts female infant killing was a discontinuous practice. The paradoxical fact about India's social and cultural traditions vis-à-vis women is the heterogeneity of practices. Historically women-related practices in India were plural and contentious; for example, traditions of cherishing daughters were always in conflict with traditions of daughter-devaluation and daughter-murder.[4]

The British perspective that the commission of female infanticide in India is causally related to the family's burden of providing excessive dowry for the daughter is a viewpoint shared by many in India. Nineteenth-century colonialist female infanticide reform efforts in Gujarat addressed the problem posed by the daughter's dowry by instituting a dowry fund. Colonial administrators promised landowners exemption from land tax for one year on condition that they preserve their daughters. Official documents reveal that the measure failed to have any effect on the incidence of the crime. Our own view is that in contemporary India the dowry system is not so much a hallowed tradition as a patriarchal capitalist means of devaluing daughters and daughters-in-law as worthless objects, a means by which the natal family rids itself of a female claimant on family wealth, and a quick and easy way of acquiring capital for the marital family. Thus in the natal and marital family the system of dowry works within the femicidal logic of woman devaluation. Femicide and dowry deaths are on a continuum because the former requires reproductive technology to destroy the daughter within and outside the womb, and the latter functions in the private sphere as a way of destroying the adult daughter and daughter-in-law. In effect dowry deaths are yet another contemporary aspect of femicidal logic of treating women as valueless consumers.

Family poverty is mistakenly perceived as the source of the problem of female infanticide, in accordance with the popular belief that daughters are neglected because their parents are too poor to take care of them. Our study of the infanticidal clans and communities in nineteenth-century India has shown that infanticidal families had no dearth of money and in many cases owned property in land. Contrary to the economistic reasoning, the serial killing of female fetuses and infants is not a function of the class and wealth-status of the family but rather an index of the totality of women's condition, status, and value in family and society.[5]

The solutions to female fetus killing, hypothesized by current research on modern femicide, also tend toward economism. The economistic solution is family affluence on the principle that it is natural for a rich family to value all its children, including its female children. For instance, Vaasanthi's recent case study of femicide amongst the infanticidal tribe of Kallars in Usilampatti taluk in Madurai district concludes that to prevent female infanticide the Indian Government should deposit 1,000 Rupees at the birth of a girl child for her marriage dowry (*The Hindu,* November 20, 1994). Dr. K. J. Kurian's observations on the Kallars in Usilampatti concur with Vaasanthi's econo-mistic solution to modern female infanticide, "The main point is that a girl needs to be married, which needs a few thousand Rupees which poor villagers cannot afford" (*Eubios Ethics Institute Newsletter 3,* 1993, 3).

A similar economistic solution to female infanticide was attempted in nineteenth-century India by British colonial administrators. The British solu-tion was three-pronged: penalize infanticidal families with fines and land seizure, establish a British-administered Infanticide Fund from these fines, and offer to pay the dowries of surviving daughters from the fund in order to encourage infanticidal families to preserve their daughters. Our research shows that despite regular census by the colonial government to monitor female infant deaths, the economistic solution was a complete failure.

The failure stemmed in part from British collusion with the infanticidal logic wherein daughters are viewed as financial burdens. We discern a funda-mental contradiction between the British analysis of the problem of female infanticide in terms of tradition/custom and their solution in economistic terms. If we are to take the economistic solution seriously then we must sup-pose that customs and traditions can be changed by the simple logic of eco-nomics. Conversely, if we take the British analysis of the problem of female infanticide as Indian custom seriously, then we must suppose that a woman-related custom cannot be eradicated by economics because the custom of female infanticide survives despite family affluence. The fundamental contra-diction we have noted in British analysis continues to be reproduced by post-colonial analysts like Vaasanthi and Kurian. We designate this particular kind of analysis the colonialist-economistic approach to female infanticide. Colo-nialist-economistic solutions do not address the fundamental problem of inequality between the sexes nor challenge the fundamental premises of woman devaluation, instead they offer a stop-gap solution.

We believe in a woman's choice and her ability to be self-determining; we recognize that the small family norm is generally less oppressive on the wife/mother, and generally speaking fewer pregnancies are conducive to the health and longevity of the childbearing mother. We nevertheless take into account the fact that in postcolonial India the small family norm lacks class specificity. The sociopsychology of childbearing of the rural poor woman is markedly different from middle-class woman's discourse about children. While the latter is concerned about the effect of frequent pregnancies on maternal health, childbirth, and child rearing, the poor woman has many children in the hope that some of them will survive the high infant mortality rate. For the poor woman the period of pregnancy is often the only period when her diet, her health, and need for rest has priority. The poor woman cannot buy into the middle-class woman's dream of fewer children, more leisure, health and self-cultivation, and greater family resources for the children.

Western feminists fought long and hard for the choice to have fewer children so that daughters could have more opportunities for education and self-cultivation than their mothers and grandmothers.[6] This narrative of First World emancipation becomes an obstacle in understanding the imperatives for the rural poor women in India who wish to preserve the right to have children. The poor woman's reasoning is explored in Deepa Dhanraj's film *Something like a War* (1991) where the rural women of Rajasthan repeatedly point out that the wealth of the poor inheres in children *(garib ka dhan uske bacche)*. Therefore, more children means more labor power for the poor woman and her family. We do not endorse child labor nor do we advocate large families. Nevertheless, we have to recognize that for the poor woman her children are her support structure and her only resource against total destitution, while middle-class children require long-term investments of education to make them productive members of the family.

The economistic perspective on female infanticide tends to delink the economic factor from classed attitudes to women and children, thereby occluding the fact that the laboring classes value women and children as producers while the upper classes generally regard their women and children primarily as consumers. From an early age the rural poor woman's children work as laboring members of the family; the eldest daughter often assumes the maternal role of childrearing younger siblings; children relieve the mother of labor intensive household chores like collecting firewood, bringing water from far-off places, tending livestock, cooking and cleaning; the children also take care of the mother in times of illness and in old age, often substituting for the male or female parent on the days that either of them is too ill to work. The children of the poor are earning members in their own right, contributing to the mother's subsistence production in the household or in the field, in addition to taking up part-time jobs to augment the family resources.[7]

At the present time this distinction between the attitudes of the middle class and the poor working class toward their children is in danger of being lost as the poor working class as well as the rural poor begin to adopt middle-class values and attitudes toward women and children. The adoption of these values and attitudes have been materially facilitated by displacements of people from their traditional occupations and lifestyles by development projects like the building of dams, mining, and the creation of factories. These displaced populations face alienation at all levels and at the same time are subjected to the pressures of patriarchal capitalism, which is disseminated as a homogenized national culture.

Therefore, the heterogeneity of class- and community-specific gender practices are in danger of being swallowed by the anti-woman capitalist logic. For example, in western and southern India female infanticide was virtually unknown; instead there existed strong traditions of matriarchal organization of the family; women's labor was valued both in the natal and marital family and women had property rights. At the present time in the rural areas of southern and parts of western India, like Usilampatti taluk of Madurai district, the practice of female infanticide has become widespread. In these remote areas where reproductive technology for sex determination is not yet widely available, capitalist patriarchal devaluation of women has become so pervasive that long-forgotten methods of child murder are being revived in order to commit female infanticide. We believe that a persistent colonialist patriarchal devaluation of women, accompanied by the capitalist logic of accumulation through violence, and an increasing emphasis on privatizing of property at the cost of the general community leads to socially sanctioned female infanticide and daughter killing. Under global capitalism it is commodity-relations between men and women that take precedence over earlier heterogeneous modes of upward mobility in India, facilitating the devaluation of women's labor and productivity and finally devaluing women as daughters.[8]

In the capitalist discourse of development the cliché that the poor are poor because there are too many of them implies that it is the poor of the world who rapidly consume the planet's resources while giving nothing back to society and the environment, while rich nations and peoples of the world work hard at producing wealth and conserving the environment. These slogans are resuscitated in a speech by Ted Turner, the American media magnate, at a real estate development conference. The context of Turner's remarks is his billion dollar gift to the United Nations, which the latter intends to channel into the U.N. population programs. Turner suggests that globally families should practice a one-child-only norm. Turner's public statement exemplifies First World thinking about world population, therefore it is instructive to examine it more closely:

> If you have two billion people you could have automobiles, and everybody could have a good standard of living. I've got to worry about the totality of

the planet because there are some people who think we can build a wall around the United States and keep the misery out. (They think) we can just let Africa and Central and South America and parts of Asia stew in their own juices. I don't agree with that at all. A lot of people will stay in India and Bangladesh and Africa and El Salvador. A lot of them will stay there and starve. There's no question about that. But a lot of them won't. They're going to come to where the prosperity is—and they know where the prosperity is, baby. We need to have a one-child family (policy) globally. People who abhor the China one-child policy are dumb-dumb, because if China hadn't had that policy, there would be 300 million more people in China right now. (*India Abroad, 38,* September 25 1998)

Turner's philantrophic, democratic, and conservationist posture dismantles as he speaks. Turner first confesses that even though he is a spokesperson for the small family he himself has a large family. Turner asserts "a personal responsibility to worry about overpopulation" in order to underline his dis-interested concern for the future of humankind. The claim that he is wor-ried about "the totality of the planet" is contradicted by his exclusive focus on Third World populations in Africa, Central and South America, and parts of Asia. Turner's statement, "People who abhor the China one-child policy are dumb-dumbs" makes it clear that he is in favor of coercive mea-sures for population control although his speech appears to support democ-ratic persuasion. Turner's admiring reference to China's population policies implies an endorsement of China's human rights violations and coercive state apparatus. In effect Turner's implication is that democracy and demo-cratic procedures are appropriate in United States but coercive population control policies used exclusively in the Third World, are necessary to con-trol those populations.

Turner's appeal continually shifts grounds because he cannot find the one convincing appeal that will convert his audience to work toward and sup-port the control of the poor in the Third World. He observes that a small fam-ily improves the "quality of life" so that everyone can have "automobiles" and "a good standard of living." This blatant consumerism changes into a concern for the totality of the planet. When that is not enough the rhetorical appeal changes from disinterested philantrophy toward the Third World to xeno-phobia: according to Turner it is not possible to build a wall round the United States to ward off the starving millions from invading America. Quite apart from the cultural imperialism of assuming that all of the people in the Third World desire the American Dream, Turner also commits the fallacy of sur-mising that it is possible and even ecologically desirable that the South aspire to the same level of affluence as the North. The shifting and changing rhetor-ical grounds of the speech reflects the sanctioned ignorance in the First World of the unequal exchange between the North and the South and the damaging impact of unfettered development on the environment.

The causal link between affluence and the small family norm in the North and poverty and the large family in the South has to be radically rethought in the context of global capitalism and the international division of labor. From the 1970s critics like Samir Amin have made us aware that capitalist accumulation and continued development in the North is made possible by the growth of underdevelopment in the South (*Unequal Development: An Essay on the Social Formations of Peripheral Capitalism,* 1976). The North is enriched through collaboration with indigenous elites of the South, and the most damaging consequences of this collaboration are visited on women and environment in the South.[9] Therefore, a study of the relationship between poverty and family size in a country like India needs to be complicated by considering the unequal exchange between the North and the South and the role of international agencies like the United Nations, World Bank, and the International Monetary Fund in this unequal exchange.

The capitalist model of development adopted by India is inspired by the North and is anti-poor, anti-woman, and anti-environment, contributing to the prosperity of the North and the native elites of the South. This development model excludes the poorest classes in India from the material benefits of the nation state, displaces them from their homelands and destroys their life-sustaining natural environment.[10] Within this model of development the Indian nation-state promises affluence for all. However, the unequal exchange in global capitalism means that the prosperity of the First World is predicated on the poverty of the poor in the Third World. In fact, the wealth, accumulation, and affluence of the North is only possible, given the limited nature of the planet's natural resources, on the continuing impoverishment of the poor of the South.

Unable to deliver on its promise of prosperity for the poor the Indian nation-state offers, with the help of international agencies, the palliative of family planning. The poor are told that their eligibility for a share in the nation state's prosperity is dependent on their acceptance of population control. They are asked to voluntarily reduce their numbers even as they are being displaced and further impoverished by development projects. It is in the interstices of these persuasive/coercive strategies that femicide emerges in postcolonial India as the underbelly of the discourses of development and the official version of ecological conservation.[11] Modern femicide is inserted into the global frame of reference through the international discourses of development and the official version of ecological conservation operating as population control.

Our first epigraph from the *National Geographic* represents the popular cliché that the world is going to hell because "those people" are having children or "breeding." In the discourses of development and the official version of ecological conservation the poor, the dispossessed and disenfranchised female population of the South is subject to and blamed for the destruction and depletion of the environment. "In global terms," notes a United Nations report, "the impact of a drastic decrease of population in the poorest areas of Asia, Africa, and Latin America would be immeasurably smaller than a decrease of only 5 percent of the richest countries at present consumption levels" (*UNICEF, Children and the Environment*, 1990). Even though this report acknowledges the error in the blame-the-poor population policies of the governments of the South, there is no attempt to reconceptualize United Nations programs and take effective action.

The large abstractions of development discourse and population theory become concrete everyday realities in Indian women's lives through the notion that to be progressive and desire prosperity for the family, it is necessary that they accept reproductive technology in their lives. It is widely and erroneously believed that the techniques of amniocentesis and ultrasound for sex-selection purposes is a regrettable side effect in the transformation of an underdeveloped nation. In short, there is nothing inherently wrong with the new reproductive technologies. If the Third World misuses these material-discursive practices to visit violence on their own women, that is simply their problem. Thus, the gender bias of invasive fertility control technologies and the violence visited on Indian women are often perceived as incidental and aberrant misuse of gender-neutral science. In contradistinction we argue that the role of new reproductive technologies evolved in the North and exported to the South functions to control Third World women's reproductive choices even at the cost of their health and life expectancy.

The postcolonial state's population program strips the rural poor woman of her only resource and without changing any of the material economic conditions that causes her poverty, persuades her that the simple fact of less children and less labor power will result in more prosperity and better conditions for her. Thus, the state ignores the root cause (her poverty) and attacks the symptom (her many children). She is correct in perceiving that the family planning program is of a piece with the inroads made into her resources of water, soil, seed, and forest by depriving her of firewood through deforestation, sale of pasture land, and the systematic destruction of her living environment. The state's family planning and family welfare programs do nothing about the health of women; when they ask for contraception they are given sterilization.

In unpacking the different strands of discourse that function to keep femicide a rational and national choice in postcolonial India we come to the counterintuitive insight that development and modernization have not always enabled the emancipation of all women in all parts of the world. Madhu Kishwar suggests that in postcolonial societies like India, "progress and economic development can have very differential impacts on women's and men's lives, and sometimes can even have a harmful impact on women's lives" (*Man-Made Woman*, 1985, 33). This is certainly true in the area of femicide: three decades of political independence from colonial rule has meant that the heterogeneity of familial-social attitudes toward the girl-child are marginalized and modernity ushers in scientifically efficient methods of femicide.

It is social forces of our own modern times that introduce the practice of female infanticide in regions and communities that hitherto had no traditions of girl-child murder. It is in the 1970s, 1980s, and 1990s that the violence of femicide is generalized and universalized among all classes, regions, and communities of postcolonial India. History teaches us the profoundly anti-modern and anti-progressivist lesson that political independence and modernization means further attrition of the survival conditions for postcolonial Indian women.

Femicide in the Public Domain:
The Nationalist Populist Rhetoric of Family Planning

Exactly a century passes between the ineffective abolition of female infanticide in British India in the 1870s and the re-emergence of a new and far more generalized form of scientific genocide of female fetuses in the 1970s. Female infanticide (traditional methods of killing new-born female infants practiced in northwest India) reappears as modern femicide (scientific methods of aborting female fetus combined with traditional methods of killing through neglect and discrimination). Our focus is on the function of nationalist populist rhetoric of family planning in this re-emergent and modernized discourse of femicide.

We deploy the term "nationalist populist rhetoric of family planning" in this section to prevent readers from interpreting family planning in India in Western terms. Family planning connotes to First World women choice, planned parenthood, care of maternal health, choice of contraception, and control over their bodies. Family planning carries a very different set of connotations for most Indian women—state coercion instead of affirmation of a woman's individual choice, disregard of maternal health rather than care of maternal health, women selected for experimentation with unsafe contraception rather than an informed choice of contraception. The political issues around family planning for many women in United States may well be the right to life versus the right to choice, however the political issues concerning family planning for an Indian woman involve discourses of development, over-population, and the fact of state coercion. Therefore, we examine family planning not merely as an accepted value-free norm but in the discursive context of state intervention and the dominant political rhetoric of the 1970s, namely nationalist populism in the Indira Gandhi era.

Nationalist populism has its discursive roots in the First World, in the notion shared by corporate America, the U.S. government, the United Nations, and Third World governments that all the problems of underdevelopment stem from overpopulation in the Third World. In the nationalist populist vocabulary national interest connotes the larger good of the greatest number of citizens as well as the imperative for swift development in order to compete with advanced countries of the world in the global market. The corollary to this populism is the notion that coercion is justified as means for the desirable goal of population decrease. This rhetoric is neo-imperialist because it covers over the nexus between the international community and indigenous governments both of which colonize the poor. The indigenous governments are "persuaded" by international interests to buy reproductive technologies and services, which keep the big multinational pharmaceutical companies in business. The forms of coercion adopted by this international conglomerate of interests consists in linking foreign aid and credit to Third World countries with the level of performance in the field of population control. Instead of resisting this carrot-and-stick approach of the North, nascent democracies of the South like India attempt to jump-start development by undemocratic programs of population control.

The nationalist populist analysis of underdevelopment is predicated on the center/periphery binary and carries profound implications for Indian women. First World women's rights over their bodies—their right to maternal health, right to contraception and abortion, their informed choices about, as well as their free access to, a variety of scientific means for determining if and when they wish to be pregnant—coexists alongside Third World women's lack of rights over their bodies. At the very time that American women organize themselves around issues like the environment, nuclear proliferation, women's rights over their bodies and reproductive choice, elsewhere in the world First World scientists and private corporate interests in the U.S. cooperate with the postcolonial state to unleash new and untested reproductive technologies that deprive Third World women of their right over their own bodies and reproductive choice. This combine consisting of corporate and scientific First World interests and the Indian government discover their ideal subjects for trying out new untested contraception among the poor women population of the Third World. Third World rural and urban women are perceived as guinea pigs who can be easily coerced and need not be informed about the side effects of new contraceptive devices, partly because it is assumed that these women do not know that they have a right to refuse and consequently can be intimidated by the medical profession into accepting injections or pills or surgery, and partly because they are unorganized and politically powerless.[12]

The chief rhetorical feature of nationalist populism is a narrative of the "nation" within which alternative visions and political dissent is disallowed and delegitimated. Indeed, the nationalist populist rhetor speaks alone because there is no debate or dialogue in this rhetorical situation. This is true of the 1970s in India; after two decades of political independence the 1970s is marked by social upheaval and economic crisis; many intellectuals, activists, and cultural workers raise doubts about the social justice in India's chosen development model and offer alternative visions. It is precisely at such a politically dynamic moment that the ruling Congress party declares the Emergency. The Emergency of 1974–1977, declared by the then Prime Minister Indira Gandhi, mark the watershed years of unprecedented state terrorism through suspension of all democratic institutions, repression of dissent, and large-scale arrests of political dissidents as well as a media blackout on all forms of reportage on state excesses.

Nation and democracy are no longer coeval in the Indian nation-state's political discourses in the 1970s, thus the imaginary construction of the nation does not include democracy/democratic procedures and institutions. As a direct result the powerful new discourse of family planning does not denote counseling and advising the family, instead family planning in India comes to mean social engineering of the postcolonial family.[13] The watershed years of state terrorism also mark, in our view, the period of social engineering of the postcolonial Indian family through the nation's coercive and persuasive apparatus. For the first time a spectrum of coercive strategies are evolved to limit family size. The euphemism for state coercion is "motivating" and every branch of the government, national media, and youth organizations are involved in "family planning motivation." In the mid-1970s an employee's certificate of sterilization and the number of people "motivated" is a precondition for promotions, loans, housing, licenses, and permits. State employees are required to undergo vasectomy as well as meet sterilization targets by forcibly "motivating" the poor to undergo vasectomies in mass sterilization camps. These camps are set up in railway stations, slums, villages, and some areas with a high density of the minority Muslim population.

Populist slogans that overpopulation is the single source of India's underdevelopment and poverty are internalized by the middle-class intelligentsia as part of their everyday speech and political discussion. Contemporary political discourse of the urban elite has a unidimensional view of national problems and solutions: the urban elite espouses the notion that overpopulation is the source of all national ills and population control is the efficient route to development and national prosperity. While the middle-class patriarchal family's political engagement with nation building lies in consenting to the Prime Minister's call for a small family, the middle classes also come to believe that the recalcitrant poor need not have a voice in determining their family size and must be coerced for their own good.[14]

The political pieties about overpopulation are not subject to debate and question. Instead, the coining of a phrase suffices for genuine political debate in the nationalist populist simulacrum of the public sphere. The state embarks upon a sustained multimedia propaganda about the small family norm. Large billboards, radio jingles, television and cinema advertisements, puppet shows, politicians' speeches all counsel the Indian couple that happiness and prosperity is defined by numbers. The nationalist slogans of the times are, "A small family is a happy family" *(Chhota parivaar sukhi parivaar)* and catch phrases like, "We are two and we have two" *(Hum doe hamare doe),* "Stop at two or three" *(Do ya teen bus)* and "Wait after one and none after two" *(Ek ke baad abhi nahin, doe ke baad kabhi nahin).* Contemporary films include set situations and dialogues deriding the traditional large family and expounding the benefits of a small family. These slogans and set pieces scold, shame, exhort, and silence the citizenry and in so doing have long-term effects on the subjectivity of the postcolonial family.

Collective resistance first appears as people's fear; rumor and unofficial grapevines serve as the channel for people's information about, and anger against, governmental excesses.[15] Nationalist populist slogans are parodied on the streets, for instance Indira Gandhi's election slogan "Remove poverty" *(Garibi hatao)* is parodied as "In the process of removing poverty they removed/ exterminated the poor" *(Garibi hatate hatate garibon ko hi hata diya).* This slogan refers to the combination strategy by the government of setting up sterilization camps as well as removing the poor from the cities and resettling them outside the city in resettlement colonies. The subsequent political overthrow of the Indira Gandhi government in the elections is widely interpreted as people's rejection of coercive male sterilization. In the post-Emergency electoral campaign the anti-poor politics of Indira Gandhi's "family planning" and prodevelopment policies are exposed by populist slogans coined by the opposition, "Denounce mass male sterilizations" *(Nasbandi hai! hai!).* However, the rhetoric of this oppositional critique, being populist in nature, does not address the anti-woman bias of family planning policies, and it is this omission that predetermines the aftermath of the Emergency.

We do not simplify the discourse of modern femicide in India by suggesting that female fetus killing is merely the outcome of a top-down change imposed in the 1970s on a passive people who fall prey to the coercive and persuasive apparatus of the government. In our view the discursive connection between the Emergency and modern femicide is that under conditions of extraordinary state coercion, femicide is the patriarchal family's invested decoding of the official nationalist populist rhetoric. This decoding is a far more complex process than the passive internalizing of state directives by the people. The patriarchal family is faced with a dilemma, they are anxious to stake their claim on the economic opportunities offered to a few by the state so they wish to comply with family-planning directives for a small family, and at the same time they are equally determined to preserve and continue their own patriarchal interests through having one or more sons. However, the traditional method of having a male child through large families is a source of social shame in the 1970s. Nationalist-populist messages—prosperity is accessible to all people if they achieve the perfect small family—is reinterpreted by upwardly mobile households to accommodate son-preference. Thus the postcolonial family deciphers the slogan "Stop at two or three" *(Do ya teen bus)* to mean "Stop at two or three sons." It is in this crisis that many families negotiate between traditional son-preference and the modern small family norm by deploying new, available reproductive technologies like amniocentesis and using them for sex determination and sex selection.

Reproductive technologies imported from the West not only solve the problem of the unwanted female child for individual families, science also quick-fixes the nation's problem of overpopulation through mass female sterilizations. Referring to the immediate post-Emergency years Alaka M. Basu notes, "In 1977–1978 female sterilizations suddenly made up as much as 80 percent of all sterilizations"(*EPW,* vol. xx, no. 10, 1985, 422). The long-term effects of the Emergency on women in general, and the twentieth-century resurgence of female infanticide in particular, only gradually became evident. Family planning in the Emergency mainly targeted poor men. Post-1977 family-planning policies exclusively target poor women in urban and rural India. The targeting of men in the Emergency causes a government to fall, the targeting of women by the state in the post-1977 years causes no political repercussions. Unlike the Emergency period, the targeting of women in the 1980s and 1990s family planning remains unresisted by the postcolonial family because the patriarchal family is willing to submit their women for sterilization so long as their men are protected. The patriarchal family sanctions female sterilizations despite the fact that the female sterilization operation is more complicated, unsafe, and expensive than male sterilizations. The post-Emergency family-planning focus on female sterilizations is premised on the cynical assumption that women constitute the one group in society against whom violence carries no repercussions. Therefore, this collusion among the international agencies, the state, and the patriarchal family in mass tubectomies does not by any means offer reproductive "choice" to women, instead these mass sterilizations constitute yet another mechanism whereby state-sponsored violence is unleashed on women.

The postcolonial family did not suddenly become a conscienceless predator of women, especially since the majority of families practicing modern femicide do not belong to the traditionally infanticidal families of northwest India. The predatory behavior of the post-1977 Indian family toward its own women is the cumulative effect of the criminal negligence of state planners. From the first Five-Year Plan these planners do not concern themselves with how population-control measures, in the context of the untransformed feudal-patriarchal necessity for a male child, put increased pressure on the birthing mother and the female child. Modern femicide could not have reached its present genocidal proportions if the nation state had not turned a blind eye toward new forms of violence on women.[16] It is precisely when the state wages war on the postcolonial family that the patriarchal family retaliates by turning predatory on its own women.

The infringement of civil liberties by the state in the Emergency period as well as the forms of state coercion on the postcolonial family triggers a major discursive shift in the Indian women's movements. Women's resistances are cohesively organized around the issue of family and the violence perpetrated on women by the state via the patriarchal family. In the words of a leading activist Brinda Karat, "The [women's] movement became more focused in the post-emergency period. . . . It was only after the emergency that the movement's focus was directed toward the family" (*India Abroad,* December 27, 1996). In 1974–1975 at the very outset of the phenomenon of modern femicide, women's groups call attention to the fact that scientific technology meant for the detection of genetic disorders in a premier research hospital in Delhi (All India Institute of Medical Sciences) is misused by seven out of eight couples to abort the female fetus.[17] In the 1980s and 1990s the ultrasound test is the most widely used method for facilitating female infanticide. Ultrasound technology is hawked by charlatans in private clinics that do not require patients to produce a doctor's permission for the test. These clinics mushroom in every Indian city and reach small towns and villages in mobile vans and many gynecologists habitually require pregnant women to undergo this test.

From the late 1970s, despite growing criticism and information-gathering by women's organizations about this scientific weeding out of female fetuses, no governmental legislation was enacted to monitor or prevent it. The law of 1994 that prohibits the administering of prenatal tests for the purpose of femicide and threatens those who take or administer the test with a three-year prison term and fine comes too late and offers too little to combat this epidemic.[18] Nationalist populist rhetoric of the 1970s has a lasting effect on the ways the postcolonial family justifies female infanticide. The fusing of the nationalist populist rhetoric of family planning with the patriarchal interests of the postcolonial family has the following effects: within the postcolonial family femicide is named as the practice of the small family norm and femicide exacerbates the violence on all women in general.

Femicide and the Condition of Women in the
Private-Familial Sphere: Lalli's Suicide/Murder

Manjira Dutta's 1995 documentary film *Relationships (Rishte)* deals with the contemporary problem of femicide. The film documents the 1993 case of Lalli Goel and the subsequent efforts of the woman activist Shyamkali to raise the community's awareness in order to organize collective resistance by women. Lalli Goel was a Delhi housewife who fatally poisoned two of her four daughters and committed suicide on June 8, 1993, because she was misled, after several sex-determination tests, into aborting her male fetus. Throughout the film most of the characters display enormous confusion about whether Lalli's death is a criminal offense for which they should seek legal redress or whether Lalli's death can be written off as a suicide. Amidst all this confusion there are no questions raised about Lalli's murder of her two daughters, which is accepted as a "natural" impulse of a desperate mother.

Dutta's film does not isolate the female fetus as the victim of gendered violence. Instead the film visually constructs a chain of female victims—Lalli, her two dead and two surviving daughters, Lalli's mother-in-law, the new wife, and the neighboring women of the community. In Lalli's case three females pay with their lives for the death of one male fetus, thus the numerical ratio between male and female casualties is three women to one male fetus. The violence does not stop there but continues to spiral forward. Five months after Lalli's death, her husband Gopal marries again. A new list of potential victims springs up in the wake of the earlier death toll. The list comprises Gopal's second wife who is submissive because she has come from a poor family and still has to face the family abuse if she does not give birth to the male heir. The list also includes Lalli's two remaining daughters who are constantly reminded that their siblings' cause of death is due to the fact that they are daughters and not sons.

As Indian women viewers we find it remarkable how the film captures an essential ingredient in the phenomenon of femicide: men constantly speak for women and about women. Many of the women in Manjira Dutta's film do not speak with the exception of Shyamkali the activist. Lalli's female relatives do not speak at all. Her mother is reported as saying that it is too late to seek legal justice. Lalli's mother-in-law moves silently before the camera performing her household chores. Lalli's female neighbors listen with somber expressions to Shyamkali who says, "Today it has happened to this one, tomorrow the same thing can happen to another." Thus visually and discursively the film allows us to come to our own conclusion that it is the male members of the family who make decisions about women's reproductivity.

Lalli is the victim of the most widespread and socially sanctioned abuse in postcolonial Indian families, a form of abuse that can be described without exaggeration as the colonization of the Third World women's womb. As a child-bearing mother Lalli faces a variety of psychological, physical, social, and economic abuse because she does not give birth to a son. There are no laws, institutions, governmental or nongovernmental agencies, or women's shelters that can offer Lalli protection from the violence visited on her due to son-preference. Lalli is more educated than her husband but despite her higher level of education the passive collusion of her natal family and her economic powerlessness as a housewife combine to severely limit her options. Lalli and her daughters are at the mercy of her married family and unable to walk away. Infact Indian women's education and employment alone cannot ensure that their status will automatically improve to the degree that they will no longer be subject to the sorts of abuse visited on Lalli. In the postcolonial patriarchal family, the educated and employed married woman is subject to the same sorts of controls as the uneducated, unemployed, or underemployed married woman as is obvious from the dowry death killings in India.

A program of resistance to the systemic violence of femicide involves, in our view, a debate and discussion on the discourses and popular idioms in which that violence is enacted, interpreted, and sanctioned. Each character in the documentary offers their own version of the reasons for the suicide/murder. The filmic text constructs Lalli's victimage in such a way that as spectators we are impelled to focus on the ways in which tradition enmeshes with modernity in making Lalli a victim.

In India the abuser and the female victim's subjectivity is produced and shaped by the material and discursive apparatus of overpopulation theory. Each character in Manjira Duttas' film situates female infanticide in the discursive concepts and terminology of Malthusian population theory. The dead woman's husband Gopal Goel explains the reasoning for the mistaken abortion in terms of numbers, "My Mrs. felt mental *tension* because we already have four daughters and this fifth daughter will add to the numbers." In contemporary India the "numbers game" as we term it, constitutes the popular idiom for the Malthusian connection between a nation's population and the state of national prosperity.[19] In this popular idiom the numbers game refers to the *number of expendable females* because postcolonial modernity ushers in the view that women are not producers but consumers and destroyers of family prosperity.

Gopal attributes the numbers game to his dead wife. Nevertheless the vocabulary in which he describes his own thoughts after his wife's abortion reveals that he habitually thinks in the binary of women as expendable numbers versus men as cherished members of the family. For instance, Gopal refers to the male fetus as his *umeed* or hope, revealing his belief that male children are the family's hope and are never counted in the "numbers game" among the unmourned female casualties. In front of the camera Gopal refers to his new wife as being on "trial," he uses the English word in the idiom of spoken Hindi-English to openly admit before the filmmaker that the new wife's ability to please him and produce sons will determine her fate as a replaceable number.

In a similar rhetorical maneuver Goel's father uses population theory indirectly by attributing it to the victim. Lalli, he claims, killed her two eldest daughters because she wished to save the family ten lakhs in dowry. He says, "She wanted to save us ten lakhs for our profit *(faida)*" thus outlining the Malthusian idea that children are a drain on the nation's resources and their accidental death or murder adds profit to the family and nation. Both men, Gopal and his father, speak before the camera in a relaxed body posture; the state's discourse of population and the popular idiom of the numbers game has made it possible for them to talk about the woman who was an integral part of their family for ten years, as well as the murdered daughters who had claims on their affections, in a dehumanizing and instrumentalized terminology of four numbers who should not become five and are now reduced to two.[20] Thus, male perpetrators argue that female fetus killing is a form of population control when it is actually gender discrimination.

The film uses montage to intercut Gopal's statements with the film-maker's interviews with the medical establishment. Dutta's montage shocks the viewer into realizing that the educated medical establishment echoes, endorses, and completely concurs with Gopal in rationalizing femicide through popula-tion theory. The cinematic text presents us with three characters who analyze the Lalli case through their professional vocabulary. The psychologist Indrani Guha uses the family-planning terminology to describe a mother's desire for a male child as a societal "goal." Ms. Guha's analysis erases the social-familial violence on Lalli by describing her suicide/murder as the psychological effect of failing in a societal goal. These educated urban professionals are not impelled by the Lalli case and the growing statistics of femicide to review, reevaluate, or reflect on the imperialism and gender-bias in the discourse of population control, which they have imbibed from state propaganda.

The educated elite are no different from the marketing professionals who seek to popularize ultrasound technology as a boon for both the Indian couple and the nation. An advertisement in a national newspaper in the early 1980s openly sold the facilities of a private clinic for detecting female fetuses, "Amniocentesis and ante-natal sex determination has come to our rescue and can help in keeping some check over the accelerating population as well as give relief to the couples requiring a male child" (*Indian Express,* June 27, 1982). This advertisement was commissioned by the New Bhandari Hospital in the city of Amritsar, Punjab, and was widely criticized by feminist groups and the national press. The Bhandari Hospital gained national recognition in 1982 when a male fetus was mistakenly aborted by this antenatal sex determination clinic. Note how the language of the advertisement couches the sale of a service to the client in terms of national goals ("keeping some check over the accelerating population"), and moreover aligns the national goal of reduced population growth with the patriarchal goal of male progeny ("give relief to the couples requiring a male child"). There is no perceived dissonance between the two goals: nation and patriarchy have become one, both are the beneficiaries of the genocide of women.

In Gopal's account given below, we can gauge how Indian families respond to state propaganda and the media blitz; the former threatens them with poverty and the latter seductively promises a scientific solution to their problems:

> In 1990 there was an advertisement in the newspaper for an Amrit Clinic in Azadpur which offered "ultrasound." My wife said that she wanted to get an "ultrasound" done. I said there is no profit in such things, forget it. But she did not agree. She kept insisting. I said O.K. I accompanied her to the clinic. The clinic takes one thousand Rupees for an "ultrasound." The first time they did the "ultrasound," they said we have a "doubt," it is not a "confirmed report." We got the "testing" done a second time, they took another thousand Rupees. Then a third, again they took a thousand Rupees. Then after the fourth they said it is "definite" that it is a girl (words used in English are indicated in quotation marks).

Gopal's words show that the money and family resources that can be spent on the birthing mother's health and on the daughters is instead spent on the four ultrasound tests. Lalli is doubly the subject of science: as the reproductive female body she is controlled by science and subjected to intrusive technology; as a modern citizen Lalli comes to believe in the state and medical propaganda that omnipotent science has the answer to her problem of repeated pregnancies in the hope of a son. When the charlatans parading as bonafide medical professionals misdiagnose the ultrasound test Lalli is betrayed by her belief in the infallible god of science. We read a curious anomaly in the fact that for Lalli science enmeshes with woman-hating superstitions in labeling her unlucky *(abhaagin)* and accursed.

The film also introduces us to the radiologists Mr. and Mrs. Garg. Mrs. Garg takes the lead in the ensuing conversation and her views represent the typical response of the educated urban elite to the problem of modern femicide:

> In our country there is an ongoing "controversy" that "female infanticide" is going on. In actuality "infanticide" happens to achieve "population control." From the time that "MTP" (Medical Termination of Pregnancy) has been "legalized," "feticide" happens in any case. Our society already gives more

importance to boys, families insist upon a son. Her mother-in-law, mother put "pressure," her family, mother and mother-in-law put "pressure" that no there must be a son, a son must be born. Then they come to get an ultrasound in order to find out if it is a girl (breaks off). If it is a son they keep the pregnancy, if it is a daughter they (pause) "terminate" the pregnancy (words used in English are indicated in quotation marks).

The idiom of Mrs. Garg's speech is typical of the urban educated Indian. Her switching between Hindi and English words and phrases indicate, in the context of the discussion, that she uses particular English words, phrases and medical vocabulary like "MTP," "terminate" and "pressure" to distance herself from the violence she describes and keep the discussion at the level of clinical abstraction. Mrs. Garg makes an explicit causal connection between modern femicide and the drive for population control. What is troubling about her account is that not only does she accept without question the absolute good of population control, but she naturalizes infanticide as population control, implying that families kill off female children because they want to limit family size. Mrs. Garg speaks within masculinist protocols in the presence of her husband by espousing patriarchal woman-hating logic as common sense.

The film captures how patriarchal and Malthusian discourses from two distinct sites converge in blaming the victim: the psychological battery on Lalli is exemplified by her husband and father-in-law blaming her for the violence meted out to her; in Malthusian theory the poor are blamed for their poverty and poor women and children are told that their oppression is caused by themselves. The two voices dissenting from this pervasive belief within the film belong to the victim's brother and the activist. Lalli's brother repeatedly refers to the multiple deaths as the *Lalli-kand* or crime and insists that it is a crime of violence by Lalli's married family. The activist Shyamkali challenges the very basis of population theory in her opening words to the victim's female neighbors, "It is said that when a nation's population increases the main responsibility and the chief burden *(mukhya zimmedari)* falls on women."

In Manjira Dutta's film we discover that all the characters in the film who are advocates of population theory also end up blaming the female victim for the violence perpetuated on her. Both the psychologist and radiologist insidiously blame the victim by characterizing "such women as Lalli" as ignorant women who commit femicide and suicide. Gopal is far more direct in blaming the victim:

My wife experienced mental "tension" that we already have four daughters, now this fifth daughter will arrive. Mentally she felt burdened. She began creating conflict at home. She then asked what about an abortion? Afterwards, when it was revealed that it was a boy, then I began to feel great sadness in my heart. Mentally the "botheration" arose that things had reached such a pass that it was a matter of killing or being killed? When my wife got the news, her life received a blow that the very hope we were living for had been washed away. Blood began to boil . . .

In the above extract Gopal's rhetoric and self-representation is of the loving, suffering, compliant and passive partner in the marriage who agrees to every unreasonable demand made by his wife to have four sex-determination tests and abortion. In Gopal's rhetoric the dead wife is represented as aggressive, quarrelsome, hysterical, and the killer of his unborn son. Most significantly Gopal characterizes Lalli as desiring a son far more than himself.

A variation of this rhetoric of abuse is deployed by Gopal's father: he represents himself as a loving and doting elder with a special affective bond with his dead daughter-in-law. Both men in Lalli's married family blame her for the mistaken abortion. Both men also make it a point to mention to the filmmaker that they each had, on separate occasions, counseled Lalli against the sex determination tests and abortion. Their version of events is suspicious for the simple reason that in a middle-class Indian family major decisions about the woman's body, especially decisions that involve an outlay of money, are made by the men of the household. The male representation of Lalli as a freely choosing subject is a patriarchal fiction.

To understand how the patriarchal logic of an untransformed feudalism enmeshed with deformed capitalism coalesces into the language of the people, we quote part of an extended speech made by Lalli's father-in-law. In the extract below he explains the patriarchal basis of female infanticide and femicide:

> In our country, our society and way of life *(mulk, samaj, logdari)* girls cannot do without brothers. Why can't they live without brothers? Whose house will married girls go to for their natal home? Here is the family house. This house is the father's and grandfather's ancestral property *(jaidad)*. Daughters mean the dispersion of property *(bat jaigi)*. The house as symbol of our family name *(namonishan)* will perish. Daughters are another's wealth *(beti paraya dhan)*.

The language in the above speech is a perfect example of how two idioms blend inextricably in popular consciousness. For example, Mr. Goel enunciates the feudal axiom of patrilineal property. His use of folklore like daughters are another's wealth, as well as his chosen example of a married daughter's need for a natal home, encourage the film viewer to conclude that Mr. Goel articulates a purely traditional line of thought. However, underlying the feudal values there is also a modernist Malthusian idea, which he has imbibed from the postcolonial nation's twenty-year propaganda. The Malthusian idea is that one claimant results in the consolidation of resources while more claimants result in the dispersal of resources, and furthermore the notion that women as daughters and wives are mere consumers of wealth whereas men are the producers of wealth. Thus, in the above speech the feudal and capitalist elements of violence on women are indistinguishable. Indeed social scientific population theory masquerades as the traditionalism of the family patriarch.

For theoretical and pedagogic clarity, the notion of deformed feudal patriarchies in modern India bears further explanation. Feudal patriarchies under colonialism and neocolonialism are deformed by the discourses of capitalism. The feudal impulse in modern femicide grows out of the feudal-patriarchal traditions of son-preference, patrilineal inheritance customs, property laws, and systems of upward mobility. These feudal features are deformed precisely because modernization under the aegis of colonialism wipes out the countervailing feudal traditions of matriarchies, heterogeneous family structures, and traditional support structures for women from the community and the woman's natal family. Moreover dynamic traditions of social protest in feudal India offered marginal groups, particularly women, avenues of resistance. However, the advance of capitalism in the peripheries robs women of all these traditional avenues.

Traditionally the patriarchal demand for sons has built-in checks and balances against excessive violence on women. Lalli's family can adopt a male child from the extended family or kin. Alternately the family can choose the *ghar jamai* form of daughter's marriage in which the son-in-law lives with his wife's family and performs all the duties and obligations of a son; it was the custom in many communities to invite the *ghar jamai* son-in-law to live with his bride's family at an early age in order that he may bond affectively with the family. In some cases a family without sons rears an orphan boy to fulfill the duties of a son. Among the poorer classes son-preference is modified by the attitude that children of both sexes are labor-power and therefore girls are productive members of the family.

The flexibility of gender roles was another traditional strategy of containment. For instance, in a family without male heirs the eldest daughter assumes the role of an unmarried householder; her earnings sustain the family; she treats her married sisters and their progeny as her own; she lives in the family home and binds the family into a cohesive social unit. A variation of this family structure can be found in many post-Independence traditional Indian families where the solution for the absence of sons is worked out by parents treating the daughter or daughters "like the sons" of the family, including the daughters as productive partners in major family decisions and instilling an indissoluble bond between the siblings. In some instances the family waits and chooses the daughter who seems most likely to benefit from a masculinized child-rearing. These social stratagems do not demolish son preference, as many of us would like to see, but rather work around it; male privilege is sustained while building checks and balances to ensure that life-threatening violence is not meted out to daughters and mothers.

Why did these customary modes fail for Lalli? In the film Lalli's father-in-law suggests that the first of these strategies—adoption of a male child from the extended family—was contemplated. Part of the answer to the question posed above lies in the way the film constructs a portrait of the abuser, Lalli's husband. Gopal Goel is a chilling portrait of the male abuser. He is the urban postcolonial man who views his relations with women like a modern consumer, consequently he applies the consumerist logic to his wife's womb because he expects the best product of a son or sons and feels cheated if he receives damaged products of daughters. This abuser has never been opposed or challenged by the institutions, social forces, or laws in postcolonial society to rethink son-preference or question his male privilege. His forms of abuse derive from his self-confessed capitalist entrepreneurship; he rejects his father's solution of adopting a relative's child on the consumerist logic that he deserves a son with his own genetic makeup. Like a modern consumer Gopal Goel awards himself a new wife, Gopal speaks proudly to the filmmaker of his personal "choice" in his second wife and displays her before the camera. As an entrepreneur Gopal can preserve feudal norms of family property passing from father to son with the help of modern reproductive technologies. Patriarchal capitalism does not, in the majority of post-Independence Indian families, contradict feudal values and family structures. Contrary to the modernity myths, the scientific forces of modernization do not function as an opposing or countervailing force, instead violence on Indian women increases.

The film cannot give us direct access to the deceased Lalli's subjectivity, therefore we do not know how far the victim internalized the abuser's reasoning. Did she value herself only as a son-producing machine? In our reading of the film the silenced Lalli speaks most volubly through the way she assembles the tableau of herself and her two poisoned daughters. We name this death tableau Lalli's suicide note, not because we condone her act of taking life, but because we read Lalli's suicide note as writing-in-death that the living must decipher.

As feminists we read in Lalli's suicide note the impulse to succumb and the equally strong and contradictory impulse to resist. The elements of Lalli's resistance in her suicide note are not easy to read. Women's lives are lived under erasure, therefore the suicide note functions to register the fact that Lalli suffers unbearable psychological abuse from her married family. Lalli's death tableau of mother and daughters spells out the truth that female infanticide and femicide concerns women's survival in relation to each other. The negative side of the suicide note also needs interpretation. In killing two of her eldest daughters Lalli succumbs to the familial-social mode of treating the girl child as excess expenditure, as disposable rubbish and as three female consumers of family wealth. The death tableau reinforces the patriarchal treatment of women as cheap, available, and replaceable.

Perhaps the most evocative shot in Manjira Dutta's film is the still of Lalli's surviving daughters framed by the doorway and staring at the street performance of a vendor and his monkeys. They look neglected and traumatized by the disappearance of their siblings and mother and the arrival of the stepmother. They are infanticide survivors. At one point in the film Lalli's brother says that if Lalli had her way she would have taken all four girls with her. These girls bear the indelible mark of their mother's suicide note. To a greater or lesser degree all the women of the community, including the new bride and Lalli's mother-in-law, are reminded by Lalli's suicide note that they are permitted to survive. The patriarchal productivity of femicide lies not in increasing the prosperity of the family but in subduing the women of the family with reminders of female casualties, thereby reproducing mechanisms within the family to discipline and punish the surviving women.

The postcolonial state colonizes Lalli's womb several times over. The state planners, family planning personnel, doctors, and advertisers put all the weight of state coercion and state propaganda to persuade as well as coerce Lalli into believing that her task is to magically produce a son within the two children family norm. State-organized population theory makes little or no attempt to address the patriarchal issues that Lalli deals with on a day-to-day basis, nor does the state address the very social violence it has created, namely how the small family norm intensifies violence on women. The small family norm enmeshes with son-preference to create multiple victims.[21] In the film Lalli disappears within the population discourse and its variations. The overwhelming dominance of this discourse in the film prevents basic questions from being asked and answered about the crime like the victim's agency. Indeed population discourse speaks the victim.

A public debate and a dialogue needs to be opened up concerning how women can resist the burden of producing male children. In a society where son-preference and daughter discrimination is widely practiced, where state planners are intimately aware that most couples produce large families in order to have a son, the state family planning drive only succeeds in shaming women like Lalli Goel—to the shame of not having a son is added the shame of too many children.

Alternative Paradigms and Possible Solutions

Alternative paradigms for Indian women have necessarily to be located *outside* the capitalist patriarchal logic, because the logic of global capitalism only works by distorting and deforming relations in societies at the periphery like India. Capitalist patriarchy in India devalues women as consumers and destroyers of family wealth and overvalues men as producers and conservers of family wealth. When the Malthusian discourse of few people/more resources is introduced into India by state planners, the scientism of population control transposes into woman control and woman killing.

The discourses that sustain modern femicide in postcolonial India are multiple and complex. The complexity of the issues around femicide derive from the history of this practice in the public sphere as well as the histories in the private-familial sphere. Public and private passions are provoked at the site of female fetus killing. Therefore the solutions to this complex network of violence against women must necessarily be varied, multifaceted, and address the violence against women at multiple levels.

The poor rural Usilampatti woman that we quote in the second epigraph is a woman without choice. Reproductive choice does not mean the same thing for women of all societies. Under the development paradigm Indian women of all classes become victim/consumers of new reproductive technologies, abort their female fetuses, and breed male children by design under the mistaken belief that they are achieving reproductive choice. In fact, they are assenting to, rather than resisting, the femicidal logic of devaluing women. Women without choices commit femicide for the purpose of population control. In order that women have a measure of choice, family planning in India must come to mean local consensual strategies for noninvasive, nontoxic, woman-oriented contraception. Family-planning programs must put more emphasis on maternal health so that the burden of family spacing and family size is not wrecked on women's bodies and women's psyches.

The destructive logic of modern femicide can be opposed and resisted by radically rethinking our basic assumptions about the relations between development and the environment viz-à-viz women. We have to make the choice between development and subsistence: in the development paradigm Third World poverty is often defined as the absence of consumer goods. In our view poverty has to be redefined in culture-specific terms. Further, in the context of Third World, poverty has to be rethought in terms of the absence of a life-sustaining and healthy mode of existence, not the absence of high levels of consumption and ownership. In the subsistence perspective poverty is characterized by the lack of clean air, water, forest, and land through the privatizing of natural resources, the destruction of forests, and the poisoning of land and water resources. By the same token familial and national prosperity, in the subsistence perspective, does not refer to the superabundance of consumer goods and sophisticated consumerism but instead signifies sustainable subsistence predicated on individual and community rights to clean air, water, forest, and land.

We assert that in a sexist patriarchal society the end of girl-child murder is possible only through the affirmation of women as producers, inheritors as well as custodians of ecotraditions, and practitioners of ecological conservation. The nexus between capitalism and patriarchy can and should be resisted by positing the value of women as producers in relation to the environment. The entire Malthusian discourse rests on the notion of the environment as limited resources that human beings plunder and do not regenerate. Throughout history it is women, peasants, and indigenous peoples who have conserved, regenerated, revitalized, and given back to the environment. The Bishnoi community in Rajasthan, led three hundred years ago by a woman Amrita Devi, gave up their lives to save the Khejri trees by clinging to them. The Khejri trees are sacred to the Bishnoi community and this traumatic event began a tradition of protecting animals, the environment, and tree conservation and planting, which continues today. The Bishnoi lifestyle is organized around their role as the protectors of the environment. While population policy makers indiscriminately characterize the rural poor as destroyers of the environment, a closer examination of rural communities reveals that the ecological balance is maintained through the discipline of regeneration traditionally practiced by Bishnoi women and men.

This is not an isolated example of the reciprocity that has traditionally existed between rural poor and indigenous communities and the environment. The two-decades-old Chipko movement in Garhwal is a movement in which principally women fought to preserve their ecological resources—land, water, forests, and hills—which constitute their livelihood and subsistence base. The term "Chipko" literally means embracing trees. Chipko women activists reject development in the form of quarrying of the hillsides and felling of the forest trees that destroys their environment. By refusing monetary compensation for the number of trees felled, Chipko women in effect disavow the capitalist patriarchal industrial system in favor of a subsistence lifestyle, and in so doing these women redefine the notion of what constitutes the good life. The good life for them involves a close reciprocal relationship with the environment where they are in charge of their freedom and choice and manage their environmental resources in accordance with ecologically sound and community based principles.

The anti-femicide affirmation of women as producers and life-sustaining conservationists requires a fundamental change of our world view. In representing and understanding femicide as a postcolonial crisis for Indian women, we have laid particular stress on the discursive aspect of violence on women because the feminist debate on the violence of killing and devaluing daughters has only just begun.

CHAPTER **2**

Center and Periphery in British India: Post-Enlightenment Discursive Construction of Daughters Buried under the Family Room

Colonized women as subjects always appear as a peripheral discursive entity in relation to the central political concerns and policies of the colonial-patriarchal British administration in nineteenth-century India. After several years of reading nineteenth-century British documents on female infanticide, we began to notice that even when a document posited female infanticide as its object of study there was an inexorable logic by which the text veered off into recording conversations and negotiations between brown men and Englishmen, as well as conversations between the English writer of the document and his superiors or his administrative counterparts in other districts. The female subject population simply became the occasion or the starting point for the text to veer off to the central political objective of administering and justifying the empire.

As readers of British documents we trained ourselves to watch out for the invisible compass in colonial discourse, which disallowed women from figuring centrally in the text. Colonized women are positioned as an adjunct to, on the side of, and as a facilitator of the central business of white men politically and economically controlling brown men under the aegis of empire. The difficult lesson that we, as postcolonial feminist scholars, have had to continually relearn is that it is not possible to gain direct and unmediated access to female infanticide in the British colonial period without taking into account the *peripheralization* of colonial women (the same problem occurs in a different form in postcolonial texts where women's issues are at the periphery of the central political concerns of the nation state and the First World).

Therefore our strategy in this chapter is to subvert the center-periphery logic by analyzing a colonial text that is, in a certain sense, peripheral to the issue of female infanticide. It is a text that constructs a powerful image of the room where the newborn female infant is buried by the infanticidal family. In order to understand that representation we examine the politics of the colonial text in which that representation occurs. The text is written by a man who had already become a legend in nineteenth-century India as "Sleeman Sahib" due to his claim of success in wiping out the crime of *thugee* or highway robbery.[1]

29

A Journey Through the Kingdom of Oude in 1849–50 (1858, henceforth JTKO) is without doubt W. H. Sleeman's most ambitious writing project for several reasons. He wrote it at the eve of his appointment as the British Resident in Oudh, a prestigious post that was richly rewarding in terms of money and was granted to him before his retirement in recognition of his services to the East India Company. It is a highly self-conscious text, the activities of observation and judgment are performed in the fullest expectation that the observations and judgments will be respectfully treated as truth by its British readers (Sleeman's employers and fellow officers) and by Indian readers of Sleeman Sahib's official diary. Sleeman is the archetypal colonial administrator—a figure who is memorialized in colonial fiction as the heroic, resourceful, and daring Englishman who arouses fear and respect among the natives in equal measure, a man whose opinions and prejudices in his written work percolate down into the dominant view of events. *A Journey Through the Kingdom of Oude in 1849–50* is an imperial text making its place in history by pronouncing on the civilizing mission of the Englishman in India.

The Politics of the Text: Female Infanticide in Free Oudh Constitutes Sleeman's Proof of Native Maladministration

Sleeman's record of his journey through the Oudh countryside is an ideal text for exploring the ways in which female infant murder is peripheralized in the general argument for the civilizing mission of the East India Company, and the particular argument about colonial expansion. The moral right of the British to rule India is indicated in Ranajit Guha's marvelous phrase "rule of property" (1982). The British empire's rule of right was the rule of property. Yet the Company violated the rights of the indigenous people, and broke treaties they had made with native rulers by capturing Indian territories. The civilizing mission of the Englishman in India was mobilized with a special urgency whenever the Company seized on a profitable slice of territory in order to persuade British and Indians alike that the Company's land grab was not the right of conquest but the rule of right and therefore not to be resisted.

　　The civilizing mission argument of the East India Company foundered in the case of Oudh. It was on this terrain that the Company fought its longest and most inconclusive ideological battle to prove that civilization as represented by Oudh culture was morally inferior to British rule. Oudh represented a problem for the British for several reasons: it played a significant role in the cultural, literary, and political imaginary of North India; for many political pundits ancient Oudh or North-Western Provinces, which were renamed United Provinces during colonial rule or post-Independence, present-day Uttar Pradesh is the political heart of India, winning Oudh means winning

India.[2] Moreover, Oudh had its British supporters in such eminent men of letters as Edmund Burke and William Cowper; the trial of Warren Hastings was a national event in Britain, and Hastings's treatment of the Begums of Oudh was a major source of public scorn, as well as the subject of political cartoons in the English periodicals of the day. The Company's steady accumulation of Indian territories had not entailed such controversy at home and in the colony.

The key political question that preoccupied the East India Company in the 1850s was how to make the annexation of Oudh palatable to British parliament and press at home and the native subjects at the periphery. The pro-annexationist arguments are summed up in the contemporary phrase "native misrule." The phrase condenses the English argument that the Muslim rulers of Oudh are unfit to rule and oppress the people of Oudh, therefore British rule is the greatest good for the greatest number. The anti-annexationist argument was that the people of Oudh should be allowed self-government. Conversely, the pro-annexationists insisted that the people of Oudh wanted British rule. In 1825, three decades before Sleeman wrote his diary, an English evangelist (Bishop Heber) toured Oudh and found that in his personal observation, the pro-annexationist argument was disliked by the Oudh populace:

> I asked also if the people thus oppressed desired, as I had been assured they did, to be placed under English Government? Captain Lockett said that he had heard the same thing; but on his way this year to Lucknow, and conversing, as his admirable knowledge of Hindostanee enables him to do, familiarly with the suwarrs who accompanied him . . . he fairly put the question to them, when the jemautdar, joining his hands, said with great fervency, "miserable as we are, of all miseries keep us from that." (1828, 190–191)

Bishop Heber's travelogue gives us a glimpse of the war of representations at the site of Oudh. A few Englishmen like Heber were unconvinced by the pro-annexationists. In his journey through Oudh, Heber continually noted the discrepancy between what he saw, and what he was told he would see by his compatriots. For example his fellow Englishmen told him that nineteenth-century Oudh was in a state of political anarchy. Bishop Heber did not completely share the imperial gaze, "I cannot but suspect, therefore, that the misfortunes and anarchy of Oude are somewhat overrated" (1828, 190). In the above excerpt Heber and his English companion articulate the pro-annexationist argument, "I asked also if the people thus oppressed desired, as I had been assured they did, to be placed under English Government?" Note that Heber has been "assured" by ideologues of the East India Company that the common people of Oudh wanted British rule. Yet Captain Lockett's knowledge of the language enables him to disrupt the imperial gaze by ascertaining the truth from his Indian servant who says, "miserable as we are, of all miseries keep us from that."

The fact was that for well over a hundred years, the Company had done business with Oudh rulers. To be sure the business had been dishonest and exploitative on the Company's side. The war of representations was exacerbated by the fact that the Oudh territory was divided into free and British-occupied Oudh, in an analogous manner to free- and occupied-France in the Second World War. This state of affairs had come about as a result of numerous treaties, which gave Oudh British military protection in exchange for larger and larger territories ceded to the Company. East India Company officials actively promoted the notion that British-occupied Oudh was the rule of right, political stability, and prosperity, and free Oudh was characterized as native misrule and anarchy. Meanwhile pro- and anti-annexationist arguments were the subject of acrimonious debate in the press and parliament in England and the ruling elites and intelligentsia in India.

The dates for the writing and publishing of Sleeman's journal are of great significance in Indian history because they mark the end of an era and the beginning of a new one in Britain's relation to the Indian colony. The British "annexation of Oudh" is a shorthand for Indian historians and cultural analysts to signify an important event in Indian history; a few years after the limited publication and circulation of JTKO in 1852, Oudh passed into British hands, and a year after the Company's annexation of Oudh, the rebellion of 1857 occurred in India. Many historians have argued that the 1857 rebellion was a direct consequence of British annexation of Oudh. We can gauge the war of representations from the fact that the events of 1857 were named the Mutiny by colonial historians and the first War of Independence by Indian historians.

These major political events had repercussions for colonized women. Until 1856 the colonial authorities represented themselves as a morally and culturally superior force on a civilizing mission in India, and in doing so, attempted a number of unsuccessful reforms like the suppression of sati and female infanticide. After 1857, the first War of Independence where the British suffered losses, they seemed to lose their zeal for reform. The colony passed from the hands of a trading company, the East India Company, into the hands of the British Crown. With the colony in the hands of the British Parliament, British administrators lost all interest in reform measures and were primarily interested in policing the colonial state and creating the administrative infrastructure for increasing their revenues and exploiting the resources of the colony.

Thus JTKO is situated at an important moment in the relationship between empire and colony, center and periphery. The text is not only circumscribed by momentous historical changes, the text wishes to do nothing less than make history. Sleeman's success as a ideologue of the Company had already been established; consequently, he was mobilized by Dalhousie, the

Governor General of India, to provide information that would help to make the case for the annexation of Oudh. Sleeman's own position on the annexation of Oudh is at best ambivalent and at worst disingenuous, his overt statements were anti-annexationist, which has led many scholars to defend Sleeman as an impartial observer.[3] However, most Indian historians agree that it is no accident that *A Journey* became the text par excellence for justifying the annexation of Oudh. It is to this aspect of the text, how it makes the argument for British conquest through emotive images of native maladministration, that we turn our attention.

Colonel Sleeman's journal is a representative colonial document precisely because it does so well what official reports in empire are supposed to do, namely describe the native subjects as savages who cannot rule themselves and need the stern and fair Englishman in order to live in a state of law and order.[4] Sleeman interviews people and writes down his observations. Sleeman's text makes two rhetorical moves to revitalize the civilizing mission of the British in India: first, the text does not directly say that the people of Oudh are barbarians, the ruse of the text is to skirt that issue by suggesting instead that a civilization that had reached a high degree of development was in a state of moral decay. In effect this came to be known as Sleeman's "native misrule" argument for the annexation of Oudh. Second, the text moves imperceptibly from a survey of law and order in Oudh into an investigative report about the incidence of female infanticide in Oudh. Sleeman writes, "That infanticide does still prevail among almost all the Rajpoot tribes in Oude, is unquestionable" (1858, I, 268). There is no separation between the political commentary and the social observations, the text finds evidence for native misrule in the slaying of Rajput daughters in Oudh.

Sleeman inherits a long-standing tradition in the British official document of treating feudal practices of violence on Indian women as proof of native maladministration.[5] District officers found that the perilous business of administering an alien land and collecting revenue was made easier and more politically feasible by naming the feudal practices of violence on women. Consequently, Sleeman's discovery and description of the crime of female infanticide in JTKO appears alongside adverse accounts of land cultivation and the state of law and order in the Oudh territory. The violence against the female child appears in the text as one element in the chaos and anarchy of Muslim rule in Oudh. Sleeman's incessant questioning of native informants at every stop in the journey, as well as his detailed transcription of their responses concerning female infanticide, is driven less by the urge to present a faithful account of the practice and more by the war of representations between empire and Oudh.

The hallmark of British arguments in the political domain was to wage the debate through images. The political effects of colonialist images—like the white man rescuing the Hindu widow on the burning pyre, Englishmen safeguarding Indians from the criminal tribe of thugees, the East India Company rescuing the oppressed population of Oudh from the decadent Asiatic despot—can hardly be overestimated in reinforcing the civilizing mission of the British Empire. Much of the political analysis in a representative official document like JTKO is conducted through the nonscientific literary-rhetorical convention of images. Before Sleeman's report, official reports on female infanticide deployed a variety of textual strategies to convey the horror and brutality of the crime of female infanticide in colonial India. However, none succeeded quite so well as Colonel Sleeman in capturing a precisely detailed account of the house of daughter-murder:

> The infant is destroyed in the room where it is born, and there buried. The floor is then plastered over with cow dung; and, on the thirteenth day, the village or family priest must cook and eat his food in that room . . . by eating it in that place, the priest is supposed to take the whole *huttea*, or sin, upon himself, and to cleanse the family from it . . . after the expiation, the parents again occupy the room, and there receive the visits of their family and friends, and gossip as usual!
>
> Rajah Bukhtawar Sing tells me, that he has heard the whole process frequently described in this way by the midwives who have attended the birth. These midwives are, however, generally sent out of the room, with the mother, when the infant is found to be a girl. (1858, II, 38)

We cannot dismantle the Orientalist politics of Sleeman's room image in particular, and the official documents on female infanticide in general, without an acknowledgment of the power of Sleeman's image. It is an image of a patriarchal formation in which the family's social and material productivity is premised on denying/killing and erasing from family memory the daughters under the family room.

As Indian women whose passage to adulthood occurs in the 1970s and 1980s in postcolonial India when female infanticide was reincarnated as femicide, we read Sleeman's image with contradictory experiences of alienation, estrangement, and the shock of recognition.[6] The critic's detachment is a masculinist model. The postcolonial feminist critic must fall prey to the image of the house of daughter-murder, in order paradoxically to estrange herself from it. Therefore, we receive insight into the economy of the text, both by engaging with the colonial image of female infanticide in Oudh, and by practicing vigilance about the political import of Sleeman's image-making. The question we need to ask as readers is not merely "is this true or false?" This line of questioning is insufficient because it ignores the textuality of the colonial document. We situate the room image in official discourse as an intertextual convention. In the same year that Sleeman's diary was published and read by colonial administrators, another colonial administrator stationed in western Oudh expands Sleeman's room image to portray the house of the Manipuri chief as one where "centuries had passed away and no infant daughter had been known to smile within those walls" (Raikes 1852, 20). A year later the colonial administrator posted in Punjab reports an apocryphal legend of a gold-rush leading to much digging in Burar Jat houses for treasure, however instead of gold the diggers find that every house has the bones of female children buried under the floor (Minute by Montgomery, 16 June 1853, *Selections from the Public Correspondence, Punjab* 1853, I). R. T. Hobart, joint magistrate of Basti in the North-Western Provinces reports a remark made by a Thakur in Amroha pargana that if the floors of the Surajbansi Rajputs and the Babus were dug up, they would be full of skulls of infant daughters (Letter to F. S. Wigram, 18 June 1868, *India Legislative Proceedings*, 5 December 1868). The influence of Sleeman's room image can be judged by the fact that a textual convention came to appear regularly in the official document for the purposes of describing and documenting the incidence, extent and manner of female infanticide.

Sleeman's discursive construction of the room is Orientalist. Orientalist knowledge-formations name the Orient for the West as well as for the non-West precisely because certain recognizable truths and realities are intermingled with half-truths and falsehoods and textualized into visual-aural pictures, narratives, and typologies.[7] The questions we have to ask are—who is gazing on this scene of female infanticide? What is the politics that shapes what he sees and records? How is the scene organized to bear out Sleeman's political agenda? Sleeman's room revolves on the axis of civilized/savage and center/periphery. Sleeman shifts attention away from the fact that it is a patriarchal crime against women, instead the text evokes a barbaric ritual. Sleeman's rhetorical strategy to create this effect is to blur the crime of child-murder with the heinous crime of cannibalism. The muted theme of cannibalism is activated in the following sentence, "The infant is destroyed in the room where it is born, and there buried" (1858, II, 38). The horror of the crime is reinforced by the unnatural way in which the room functions successively as birthing chamber for the unfortunate female infant, subsequently the same room is the site of her murder and burial. Sleeman implies that among civilized people, the bereaved family will inscribe the room where the daughter died with the marks of their grieving and repentance. Instead there is the exotic ritual in which the priest "must cook and eat his food in that room" and mark the space with rituals of purification and expiation.

Nor is this all. The litany of horrors are described with a travel writer's relish. Sleeman intensifies readers' revulsion by recounting how the unrepentant family "again occupy the room, and there receive the visits of their family and friends, and gossip as usual!" Thus in a few words Sleeman evokes a visual tableau of a cannibalistic triad of parents and priests and community, all those who ought to be naturally inclined to prevent and prohibit child-murder in civilized societies. Oudh is a country of savages. In a world turned upside down the priest is hypocritical, the community is complaisant, and affectively bonding parents become cannibals who kill their own offspring.

The rhetorical organization of Sleeman's description of the room precludes the reader's posing an obvious questions. Why does Sleeman question one infanticidal Rajput landowner after another without arresting, prosecuting, and imprisoning these brown men for the crimes they freely confess? There is plenty of moral indignation in JTKO toward the men who commit daughter-murder. Sleeman frequently expresses moral abhorrence, "I bid him leave me, as I could not hold converse with a person guilty of such atrocities" (1858, I, 312). However, there is no legal-administrative or police action taken against those who commit these atrocities. This is all the more surprising given that we are reading the journal of the most powerful administrator in Oudh, the British Resident. Yet Sleeman is curiously silent on the matter of arresting and prosecuting the daughter-murdering father. In asking this question of the text we learn an important aspect of the room. The colonialist image of female infanticide is constructed in such a way that the rhetorical function of the binary civilized/savage and center/periphery, as well as the travelogue feature of expressions of horror and moral indignation, are not designed to protect women and children under law, but rather to shame propertied brown men into acknowledging their cultural inferiority and the moral right of the British to rule Oudh.

The pro-annexationist political argument determines much of the colonialist portrait of the house of daughter-murder. That is why the prominent textual feature of Sleeman's description is the spatial configuration that symbolizes free Oudh. The text plays with the symbolism of the spatial dimension by *splitting* the room. This splitting occurs a few pages after the description of the infanticidal room, when Sleeman alludes to the normative space in British occupied territories of Oudh. In this discursive construction of the room a similar Rajput family occupies an identical room, with the crucial difference that the political order brought by the East India Company's annexation ensures that Rajput parents preserve their daughters. Lest readers miss the point, Sleeman asks his native informants to authenticate the normative space:

> But you know that the crime of murdering female infants, which pervades the whole territory of Oude, and brings the curse of God upon it, has been suppressed in the British territory . . . ? (1858, vol. II, 67)

The natives dutifully supply the right answer to the English sahib, "True, sir, it has been put down in your bordering districts" (1858, vol. II, 67). In the early years of infanticide reform effort in Kathiawar in 1808 Alexander Walker used infanticide reform to make a similar plea for the British conquest of Indian territory, and reported that it was the natives who felt that female infanticide could only be put down by such an extreme measure:

> I entered on this undertaking with sanguine expectations of success, but which were, for a long time, dissapointed; and I must own that the natives had formed much more just opinions on the subject, when they foretold the difficulties that would attend the attempts; which few of them thought could be overcome, but by the Company making a conquest of the country. (Wilson 1855, 74)

Both the Walker document and the Sleeman journal drive the point home, little brown girls survive happily in empire and unprotected female infants are put to death in free Oudh and Kathiawar. Sleeman muses in his journal:

> The government of Oude, as it is at present constituted, will never be able to put down, effectually, the great crimes which now stain almost every acre of land in its dominions. It is painful to pass over a country abounding so much in what the evil propensities of our nature incite men to do, when not duly restrained; and so little in what the good prompt us to perform and create, when duly protected and encouraged, under good government. ([1858]1971, 203)

Note that in the above passage Sleeman's focus is not on prosecuting the offense of child-murder, but on philosophizing about "the evil propensities of our nature." The violence against the girl-child is marginalized and peripheralized by making it a plea for the "good government" as the above passage puts it, of the East India Company.

The composition of Sleeman's representation is worth noting in terms of the positioning of the human figures in Sleeman's description of the room. There is a hierarchy between the person describing the room and the person or persons who relay this information to the Englishman. The text makes it clear that Sleeman's information is solely based on hearsay, and the information is provided by his native informants. If we look carefully at the canvas framing the room, we discern that the conversation is conducted with the figure of Sleeman Sahib standing or on horseback. Sleeman's representation of these conversations makes it clear that his posture betokens moral outrage and chastisement, while the posture of the seated figures of Rajput landlords of Oudh with their heads bowed betokens shame. The framework of the room, the constructedness of the room, helps us to understand that the rhetorical purpose of the room is to evoke shame among the natives and a sense of moral superiority among Company officials. A better way of presenting the civilizing mission of the Company could not have been devised.

Genre Analysis of the Post-Enlightenment Administrative Travelogue

British and Indian histories of female infanticide in colonial India have tended to represent the colonial documents as a linear narrative. Generally speaking, linear history of British India presupposes our political acceptance of the grand narrative of progressivist history within which English colonialism brings emancipation for Indian women. As the Subaltern historian Ranajit Guha (1989) points out, British colonialist historiography presents Indian history as part of the British narrative of progress; British colonizers are aligned to the unfolding narrative of previous conquerors and settlers of India; thus India's past is subordinated to, and represented as the pre-British past of the colony. In our view the linear progressivist model of reading the colonial document glosses over textual-rhetorical features of repetition, circularity, and hearsay dressed up as empirical facts in these nineteenth-century texts.

For example, the official document continues over most of the nineteenth century to employ the literary device of freshly (re)discovering the barbaric custom of daughter-killing, a literary stance that is repeatedly adopted by the dispatches of district officers. Whereas in the ancient world disparate cultures and civilizations traded with each other, travelers journeyed to far and distant lands and documented their journeys, it is only in the age of imperialist capitalist enterprise that such journeys and exchanges are named under the trope of discovery. We argue that the trope of discovery is characteristic of the discourses of colonization; colonial writers refer to their "discovery" of lands, which were inhabited by indigenous people, their "discovery" of sea-routes, which had been navigated before them, their "discovery" of minerals and natural resources, which were known to the people of the region; the colonizers took credit for being the first to discover barbaric rites and customs and bring back the news to the civilized world. Note how a nineteenth-century English writer John Cave Brown emphasizes the originary moment:

> In the year 1789 Mr. Jonathan Duncan . . . first *discovered* the prevalence of the crime in that neighborhood among the Rajkoomars, an important tribe of the great Rajpoot family. (emphasis ours, 1857, 26)

As time goes on the originary moment is reinscribed over and over again. In 1805 Alexander Walker "discovers" that, with the exception of five families, there are no female children among the Jhareja Rajputs of Kathiawar. Three years later the same English officer "discovers" that the Rathor Rajputs of Jaipur and Jodhpur practice sex-selective infanticide.

The modern Indian historian Lalita Panigrahi, in a painstakingly researched book on British documentation of female infanticide, uncritically deploys the trope of discovery in her linear account:

> James Thomason accidentally discovered the practice in 1835, while he was engaged in revising the settlements of the Deogaon and Nizamabad parganas in Azamgarh. (1976, 19)

Fifty years later (in 1885), the British Revenue Collector again "discovers" the infanticide custom among the Lewa Kanbi community of central Gujarat. Seventeen years later (in 1858) Colonel Sleeman is still at the stage of discovery of the same custom in Oudh. Panigrahi resolves the problem of these recurrent discoveries in a chapter titled "The Discovery" by advancing the notion that "It took nearly a hundred years before the extent of the crime could be fully known" (1976, 14).[8] It would seem that whole continents and sea-routes are discovered in a shorter time than it took the British to gauge the full extent of an oppressive custom that was freely acknowledged by propertied brown men!

We argue that the recurrent trope of discovery is less about the material realities of this anti-women practice, and far more about the generic convention of the eighteenth-century travelogue to which the official document faithfully adheres. The circular trope of discovery is part and parcel of the literary pretenses of the eighteenth-century travelogue genre, which invariably posits the traveler as newly discovering a landscape, a people and their social mores. Postcolonial theory names this literary convention the depopulating gaze of the imperial observer/writer. The administrators' repetitive discoveries are not objective facts but are textual conventions by which the official document constitutes its object of study—the domestic crime of murdering female babies at birth among certain propertied landholding social groups in northwest India. To call the official document a travelogue is not to denigrate it, but rather to call attention to the rhetorical construction of the text.

In marked departure from Cave Brown and Panigrahi, we name the genre conventions of the official dispatches about female infanticide from the year 1789 to 1870 as the post-Enlightenment administrative travelogue.[9] This imperial genre is exigent and fluid, evolving in the circumstances of district officers touring the new territorial acquisitions of the East India Company. The travelogue form offers the colonial administrator a loose and motley set of conventions to accommodate the representation of Indian manners and mores. The reason for the choice of genre becomes fairly obvious as one reads

these colonial documents. The bureaucratic travelogues allow for great latitude in the choosing and presenting of "facts" for the perusal of superiors in
the Board of Directors or for correspondence with colleagues in other districts. For example, the English writers of these documents do not need to
explain why they are recording and reporting the deaths of female children or
the statistics on sati in an official dispatch ostensibly concerned with the efficient collection of revenue, precisely because the generic conventions of the
travelogue form allows for great flexibility in administrative reportage. Moreover, these travelogue-like documents carry traces of the Enlightenment tendency of giving a patina of scientific objectivity to unscientific observation and
hearsay. In a moment we shall see how JTKO represents itself as a special type
of travelogue in the preface. Sleeman describes his tour through Oudh as
"more detailed than any similar journey by a European in Oude" (*W. H. Sleeman in Oude* [1858]1971, 14) and describes his authorial intentions with care:

> My object, in writing this Diary of a Tour Through Oude, was, to prepare
> for submission to the Government of India, as fair and full a picture of the
> real state of the country, condition and feeling of the people of all classes, and
> character of the government under which they at present live, as the oppor-
> tunities which the tour afforded me might enable me to draw.
>
>   . . . I can hardly hope that [the lay reader] . . . will ever find much to
> interest or amuse him in the perusal of the Diary of a Tour, without adven-
> tures through a country so devoid as Oude is of commerce and manufac-
> tures, of works of ornament or utility, and above all of persons places and
> things associated in the mind of the reader with religious, poetical, or his-
> torical recollections. The Diary must, for the present, be considered as an
> official document. (ibid., 51)

Sleeman finds it necessary to evacuate the landscape and inscribe it with lack.
Toward this end the preface cautions its nonofficial readership that his new
travelogue about Oudh will not offer the garden variety of travelogue sensa-
tions of adventures, exotic architecture, or the commerce of the East because
the landscape is "so devoid as Oudh is" of such exotic spectacle.[10] The function of the depopulating imperial gaze is that the observer can fill up the canvas with his thoughts, his desire, his hierarchy of needs.

The traveler writes, "The Diary must, for the present, be considered as
an official document." In other words we are asked to believe that this unsys-
tematic meandering tour through the Oudh countryside—its collection of
first impressions and prejudices, its anecdotes and hearsay that masquerade as
scientific facts, its images that function as political analysis—must "be considered" as if we are reading a dry and formal bureaucratic dispatch. Readers
of the fictional travelogues of Daniel Defoe and Jonathan Swift will readily

recognize a nineteenth-century avatar in the prefatory material, which activates readerly expectation, not by promising exotic sights and sounds, but sternly admonishing the reader that he will not "find much to interest or amuse him in the perusal of the Diary of a Tour, without adventures." [11] In eighteenth-century fictional travelogues the function of the admonishing gesture is to establish the text's claim to verisimilitude. Similarly Sleeman, the chronicler of the rites and customs of the criminal tribe of Thugs, will not cater to the taste for the exotic, nevertheless if he finds barbaric rites and rituals he intends to report them with a disinterested objectivity. The preface takes pains to compose the imperial gaze at the Oudh landscape. Although Sleeman readily admits that his gaze is circumscribed by "the opportunities which the tour afforded me might enable me to draw " he nevertheless claims disinterestedness, "as fair and full a picture of the real state of the country" of Oudh not in spite of his bias as the incoming British Resident of Oudh, but precisely because of it. The Diary's reliance on the data from the tour is constructed not as a limitation but as the prerequisite for the scientific gaze of the observer who relies on his sense data alone.

The loose travelogue form allows official documents to simply ignore that which they could not classify, and flatten out that which they document. Thus the effect of the depopulating gaze of JTKO can be judged by the way the text ignores the heterogeneity of the practice of female infanticide in Oudh. Female infanticide is categorized as a custom in the body of the journal. The problem of scientific categorization is that a custom is defined as the practice of a community; if there are individual clans that do not practice the custom or if there are regional variations, then the colonial document must be able to theorize this aberration from the rule in such a way as to prove his category of a uniformly practiced custom. Sleeman's dairy notes:

> Gunga Sing, the zameendar, with whom I was talking, told me, that both the Ditchits and Byses put their infant daughters to death; and that the practice prevailed, more or less, in all families of these and, he believed, all other clans of Rajpoots in Oude, save the Sengers. (1858, vol. I, 312)

In the above excerpt the native informant estimates the uniformity of the custom among the Oudh Rajputs but also carefully points out the exception to the rule, "the practice prevailed, more or less, in all families of these and, he believed, all other clans of Rajpoots in Oude, save the Sengers." Why are the Senger Rajputs the exception to the rule? Sleeman's text records but does not explain the diversity of the social form of the infanticidal family. The journal notes that the same clan of Senger Rajputs practice daughter-killing in Rajpootana, however their migratory branches in Oudh do not adhere to this custom:

> The Sengers are almost the only class of Rajpoots in Bundelkund, and Boghilcund, Rewa, and the Saugor territories, who used to put their female infants to death; and here, in Oude, they are almost the only class who do not. (1858, I, ff 312)

The journal's unexplained documentation of the Senger Rajputs of Oudh jeopardizes the activity of scientific codification. Both the naming of female infanticide as a universal custom, and the naming of the infanticidal social group by clan, community, or region is untenable in Sleeman's journal. What type of custom is this within which one clan branch not only dissents from their clan members in Rajpootana, but also opposes the practice of their fellow Rajputs in Oudh? Clearly daughter-murder in Oudh is not an individual act of criminality, yet the puzzling discrepancy in the custom is that it is not at all clear why one branch of the family is permitted to preserve their daughters while it is decreed that other branches kill their female new born. More importantly, who decides and based on what principle that daughters will be killed? Is it the father, the clan elder, the family's male members, or adults of both sexes?

Sleeman's journal does not attempt to investigate any of these questions. The politics of the imperial gaze at daughter-murder is not scientific data collection or humanitarian rescue of the brown girl child but the limning of the savage native of Oudh.

Infanticide Functions as Enlightenment
Proof of Savagery in Non-European Societies

We trace the emergence in discourse of infanticide in non-European societies to a foundational Enlightenment text, John Locke's *An Essay Concerning Human Understanding* (1689). Our use of Locke in this chapter is a delimited one, we read him not in relation to the philosophical traditions of Europe, but as an enormously influential text whose ideas and rhetorical procedures were popularized and disseminated through his deist disciples and Utilitarian successors.

The revolutionary change inaugurated by Locke's foundational treatise consisted of a new conception of the system of linguistic signs denoting human nature. It is thanks to Locke's influence that from the Enlightenment onwards the sign "man" is henceforth conceived as a living being possessing no inherent claim to innate ideas, an innate moral sense or an innate religious sensibility. Enlightenment philosophy popularized and legitimated the notion that infanticide is proof that non-European societies lack innate morality. This view of non-Western societies was presented by Locke as part and parcel of a radically progressive departure from earlier modes of thought.[12] Locke's discussion of infanticide is an incidental one in a text that is primarily devoted to demolishing innatism and putting forward a new theory of human understanding. A rhetorical and deconstructive reading of a philosophic text makes the incidental references central to the analysis, paying attention to the examples, quotations, asides, and the slippery digressions. It is in these rhetorical devices of the text that we find the citation and the trace of the non-European Other.

In *An Essay Concerning Human Understanding* Locke has an uphill task, he has to persuade his readers that human nature is not naturally inclined to an innate moral poise. In effect Locke has to put forward the notion, while skirting theological controversies, that "moral rules" are not "innate, and stamped upon" the mind at birth. It is worth reflecting on the rhetorical alternatives that were available to Locke to make his philosophy persuasive. Locke could have referred to the numerous and brutal child-murders in England as an example of the lack of innatism in human morality. Moreover Locke could have circumvented the censorship of the religious divines of the day by invoking, as part of his philosophic proofs, the numerous instances of man's inhumanity to man in Europe. The examples of systemic cruelties in Europe were plentiful—the widely condemned Spanish genocide of the Aztec people, the systematic witch-hunts of the seventeenth century, the treatment of the insane and the dispossession of the English poor—and yet the Enlightenment philosopher does not look nearer home. Alternately Locke could have stressed, as writers like Jonathan Swift and Henry Fielding did, that human beings everywhere do not have an automatic claim to moral conscience or spirituality.

Instead Locke chose to prove his avant-garde ideas through a series of examples that unabashedly used spurious travelogues as sources.[13] The use of these dubious sources allowed Locke to blur the distinctions between infanticide and cannibalism, generalize falsely about "whole nations" and "some countries" and "a people," and display pro-colonialist attitudes. It is time to look at the Lockean passage that, we argue, underlies nineteenth-century British documentation of female infanticide in India:

> But I cannot see how any man, should ever transgress those moral rules, with Confidence, and Serenity, were they innate, and stamped upon their minds. . . . Have there not been whole nations, and those of the most civilized people, amongst whom, the exposing their children, and leaving them in the fields, to perish by want or wild beasts, has been the practice, as little condemned or scrupled, as the begetting them? Do they not still, in some countries, put them into the same graves with their mothers, if they die in child-birth; Or dispatch them, if a pretended astrologer declares them to

have unhappy stars? . . . There are places where they eat their own children. The Caribes were wont to geld their children, on purpose to fat and eat them. And Garcilasso de la Vega tells us of a people in Peru, which were wont to fat and eat the children they got on their female captives, whom they kept as concubines for that purpose, and when they were past breeding, the mothers themselves were kill'd too and eaten. ([1689]1975, 70–71)[14]

To a sympathetic reader of Locke, it may well appear that the writer's reference to the barbarism of infanticide is a natural turn of thought. A close reading of the Lockean passage reveals that the reference to the savage Other contains an element of calculation. The delinking of man (signifier) from inherent moral sense (the signified) requires overwhelming proof for a late seventeenth-century readership. Locke's text draws attention away from the arbitrariness of his philosophical proof by unobtrusively activating the binary of savagery versus civilization in his reference to "those of the most civilized people" in the passage above. Locke's late seventeenth-century readership was more likely to believe that people of non-Western societies lack innate moral sense, and less likely to demand rigorous authentication of the philosopher's assertions about exotic, barbaric practices of child-killing in far-off lands.

Locke's style of activating the binary of West/non-West in the passage does not follow well trodden ways but is a distinct Enlightenment reinscription. The binary of barbarian and civilized in the passage does not operate on the mediaeval/religious vocabulary of prejudice, religious intolerance, inherited judgments, respect for authority, and the opposition between heathen/Christian. Instead Locke asks the philosophic observer to approach reality without prejudgment and bring to bear a reflective process on the data gathered by his senses. In contradistinction to the philosophic message of the essay, the rhetorical effect of the passage is to make infanticide in non-European societies signify—not patriarchal violence on the child or the rights of the child or the organization of the patriarchal family—but the savagery of non-European people who lack a belief in God and are devoid of moral feelings.

A more sensationalist litany of exotic rites can scarcely be found in the most debased of contemporary travelogues in Locke's time. The Lockean empiricist in the text invites the reader to observe and draw her or his own conclusions about the amoral infanticidal savages, yet Locke's prose executes a sleight of hand within which hearsay from travelogues is treated as conclusive empirical evidence from sense data. The text hurriedly makes the transition from carefully substantiated and deliberate thought to hearsay. Locke's repeated gesture toward unnamed collectivities of "whole nations" and "some countries" prepares us for the transition to named non-European countries like "the Caribes" and "a people in Peru."

The reader is hardly aware, nor does the text wish the reader to dwell too much upon, the fact that a major discursive change is taking place. *Infanticide in non-European societies acquires an entire new set of connotations in the Enlightenment, child murder and overpopulation marks the binary of barbarism and civilization.* Conscienceless savages who kill their own children also breed many children in the same unthinking and unscrupulous way. The sentiment belongs to Locke:

> Have there not been whole nations, and those of the most civilized people, amongst whom, the exposing their children, and leaving them in the fields, to perish by want or wild beasts, has been the practice, as little condemned or scrupled, as the begetting them? ([1689]1975, 71)

In this sentence Locke characterizes the state of savagery as one where unthinking overbreeding of children (overpopulation) is equated intuitively rather than empirically-rationally with the unscrupulous killing of children. Locke offers no proof of his assertion that non-Europeans breed unthinkingly and kill their children remorselessly, however the text presents this hearsay as scientific proof. Disinterested scientific observation of sense data has been replaced by secular moralizing in the passage above. The phrase "as little condemned" functions rhetorically to resolve abstract philosophic issues of innatism versus Lockean empiricism by the simplified moral formula of denouncing the Other as savage or cannibal.

The final link in this Enlightenment reasoning is to blur the distinction between thoughtless overbreeding, unscrupulous parents who murder their own offspring, and the cannibal's consuming of human flesh.[15] As Jonathan Swift's satire *A Modest Proposal* (1729) was to show, infanticide and overpopulation and cannibalism are all indiscriminately lumped together in Enlightenment reasoning about the colonized Irish. In the place of philosophic argumentation Locke offers us a special type of exotic horror—parents killing and eating their own children—and wins the epistemological argument concerning human nature by invoking the binary of the imperial center viz. à viz. the barbaric practices at the periphery.

Locke constitutes the horizon of ideas for Englishmen in India who concerned themselves with the suppression of girl-child killing—Jonathan Duncan, Alexander Walker, J. P. Willoughby, W. H. Sleeman. In trying to make sense of the alien practices of an alien land, these men drew on the Enlightenment mode of reasoning: first, child-murder is proof of the savagery of non-European people; second, infanticide can be used rhetorically to win political arguments that cannot be made persuasive in any other way; third, Locke's predilection for travelogue data had a lasting influence, the Enlightenment sanctioned the writing of a colonial document in the genre conventions of the

English travelogue, a genre within which it is legitimate to treat hearsay and anecdotal information as scientific fact.

In chapter 1 we traced the discursive association between overpopulation and female infanticide to Malthusian theory. Indeed Malthus merely popularized what were eighteenth-century prejudices and common assumptions of the time. Much before Malthus, the Lockean text draws on the proto-Malthusian association between infanticide and overpopulation. All of these strands culminate in the discourse of population in postcolonial India where the nation state and the official intelligentsia subsume gendered violence on women under the discourse of population.

Center/Periphery Signifies Unequal Value

A child's life has unequal value under law in late eighteenth–nineteenth-century England and the British-administered territories of India. The crime of child-murder is a capital offense in England but not in the British colony of India.[16] Under the aegis of colonial law the brown propertied man's taking of his own daughter's life is punished as a minor infraction of property damage—which is penalized by intermittent fines, threats of land seizure that are rarely carried out, a good deal of talk about the shame and the sinfulness of the deed, and little or no prosecutions of the male offenders—rather than as a criminal offense pertaining to the taking of human life.[17] We are not advocates of the death penalty for child murder, however it is not necessary to subscribe to capital punishment in order to deplore the double standard about child murder and children's rights in the British Empire.

It is in the politics of naming that colonial discourse enacts the center/periphery divide and influences the policies and measures taken by the colonial British administrators to address the practice of female infanticide in nineteenth-century India. It may seem counter-intuitive to our readers that a social practice of such unmitigated oppression—the killing of infants for no other reason than the fact that they are female—is worsened by the colonizer's interpretive language. The violence of colonial naming by no means shifts our attention away from the brown propertied men who commit the crime, however our focus in this chapter is on the politics of the periphery and the construction of a specifically British-colonial gaze on the infanticidal family and clan.

The naming of a social practice of violence against women is not an innocuous matter. Postcolonial theory, recent scholarship on slavery as well as women's studies have shown us that power and domination are always at work in the material-discursive operation of naming, partly because there is a continual cultural conflict in the arena of naming a woman-related practice, and partly because the linguistic enterprise of naming can be a violent and coercive enterprise, erasing and silencing the colonized. The larger agenda of this chapter is to enable feminists and women's studies scholars to understand why female infanticide in India is an issue that is not only patriarchal but also colonialist, why girl-child murder is not only about the violence that men do to women but also the violence that colonial, neocolonial, and capitalist discourses visit on the girl child.

The center/periphery logic is played out in the ways in which the British distinguish between Infanticide Law in England (the center) and the legal punishments and legal definition of the sex-selective crime under British colonial law at the periphery. Describing the political-economic effects of the introduction of colonial capitalism in the colonies, Samir Amin emphasizes the *deforming* political effect of colonial capitalism on feudal societies at the periphery:

> First, the capitalist model was introduced from the outside by political domination. Here pre-capitalist rural relations did not disintegrate but rather were deformed by being subjected to the laws of accumulation of the central capitalist mode that dominated them. (1980, 136)

Amin's insights into the political function of ideas and systems at the periphery is profoundly anti-modernist and anti-Enlightenment. Colonialist documentation of daughter murder in British India functions in terms of the deforming effect of colonialism rather than the civilizing effect of colonialism. The crime is named from the outside, the outsider status of the namer is not that of the spectator but the colonial master. Consequently, the activity of naming occurs within the very processes of political domination.

Our analysis of these relations of domination rejects economic reductionism. Indeed this was the burden of Samir Amin's contention that the logic of center and periphery cannot be understood without leaving the economic field and taking account of the total realm of historical materialism. At another place in his writings Samir Amin warns readers that center and periphery are not to be understood as denoting only economic domination of empire over the colony:

> the social structure of the periphery is a truncated structure that can only be understood when it is situated as an element in a world social structure. (1976, 294)

Under British rule the feudal pre-colonial practice of female infanticide does not wither away or in Amin's words "disintegrate"; rather the social violence of female infanticide is "deformed" by being subjected to official scrutiny. The room of daughter murder in Sleeman's journal revolves on the axis of center and periphery. The view of the room is in terms of three groups of historical players—white men in conversation with brown propertied men, brown men, and silenced brown women who are the subject of the conversation. This conversation about infanticide reform does not occur on a level playing field, but in terms of unequal exchange.

The Public Spectacle of Sati Versus the "Private" Crime of Daughter Murder

We have arrived at last to an answer of how the British administrators justified the double standard of capital punishment for infanticide in England and no serious criminal prosecutions of known daughter-murderers in British India. The colonial justification was skillful, the literary *representation* of female infanticide must be such that it becomes crystal clear to all and sundry that the unequal value of a brown girl child's life versus an English child's life is not the fault of the rulers. The fault lies instead in the vexing nature of realities in India. There is something in the nature of female infant murder in India, colonial officers were to argue, that is so secret, private, and undetectable to the official view, that administrators' hands are tied.[18] We recognize here a characteristic feature of the apparatus of domination by the British empire—blame the colonized for their ills. It is an argument that is not dissimilar to blaming the poor for their poverty and blaming women for being victims.

This rhetorical tactic seems so transparent when we put it baldly—blame the oppressed for their oppression—that it hardly seems possible that this literary representation of female infanticide was accepted by British and Indians alike. It is nevertheless true that the farreaching consequences at the level of colonial and nationalist discourses was that center and periphery were reconfigured to organize the public and private sphere in colonial accounts of female infanticide.

A classic text of eighteenth-century representation of the crime of infanticide is the failed resolution put forward to the British House of Commons by noted figures like Edmund Burke and Charles J. Fox in 1772. The Burke and Fox resolution, as it came to be known, allows us to glimpse the kinds of social and gender issues that to the eighteenth-century mind seemed pertinent to this crime. The failure of the Burke and Fox resolution is of interest to us because it illuminates the pressure points in the dominant discourse about infant killing, the pressure points where enlightened men might agree or disagree about the rationale and effectiveness of English law:

> They [Edmund Burke and Charles Fox] said that in the case of women having bastard children, the common [and] statute laws were inconsistent; that

the common law subjected to a fine, a month's imprisonment, and the fla-
gellation; that this institution necessarily rendered the having of a bastard
child infamous; that the dread of infamy necessarily caused concealment;
that the statute law, in opposition to all this, made concealment capital; that
every mother, who had not at least one witness to prove, that her child, if it
was dead, was born dead, or died naturally, must be hanged; that nothing
could be more unjust, or inconsistent with the principles of all law, than first
to force a woman through modesty to concealment, and then to hang her for
that concealment; that it was infinitely better that ten guilty persons should
escape, than an innocent person should suffer . . . the concealment of the
birth of a bastard might proceed from the best causes, from real modesty and
virtue; that nothing could more strongly prove the absurdity and inexpediency of the law, than the impossibility of putting it in execution. (*Parliamentary History of England* 1771–1774, 1813, 17, 452)

In the above passage we focus on the area of consensus and the area of rational debate. Both the critics and supporters of the Burke-Fox resolution con-
curred on a number of assumptions. The discourse at the center assumed that
infanticide is a crime that necessitates law and punishment, that the typical
victim is an illegitimate child and therefore involves issues concerning the
English bastardy laws. There is not a single British legal reformer who argues
that infanticide should not be treated under law as a criminal offense, the area
of dissension is limited to the plea for leniency in implementing the law.

Note how the passage constructs the patriarchal dimension of the crime.
Burke and Fox agree with lawmakers, judges, and juries that the criminal profile of the child-killer is of a poor, unwed, sexually transgressive English-
woman. The sexism of this assumption is not questioned by the reformers.
Instead they turn their rhetorical skills to painting a contrast between malev-
olent and benevolent patriarchy by pointing out that the infanticide laws
"were inconsistent" and "unjust, or inconsistent with the principles of all law"
and urging their audience to recognize "the absurdity and inexpediency of the
[Infanticide] law." In other words they offer a benevolent patriarchal law that
is lenient rather than harsh to poor Englishwomen, that is sympathetic rather
than inquisitorial in ascertaining the facts, but that is nevertheless unwilling
to question the notion that women are responsible for child death and child
murder, not their male partner nor the male accessories to the crime.

The points of law in arguments for defense and acquittal, as well as the
arguments for prosecution and conviction, tell us a good deal about what is
considered as legitimate discourse about child-killing in late eighteenth-century English society. The modes of argument revolve on the discursive coding
of poor Englishwomen. Legal quibbles circulate around the motivations of
this stereotypical defendant. The discursively coded question in the court of

law concerns the commonly understood and accepted relationship between women, childbirth, and nature. Does the woman's concealment of her newborn show proof of modesty that is natural to her sex, and/or shame that is natural to a woman who is an unwed mother, or postnatal trauma that is natural after a woman gives birth? Is there physical evidence and/or witnesses to prove that she displayed maternal sentiment and if so, can it be proved that the child died of natural causes? The negative side of the same discourse went like this: does concealment of the newborn show the unnatural woman's intent to kill, does concealment show the woman's evil propensity, is it natural to assume that the sin of sexual transgression is followed by the sin of murder, does concealment show that the woman does not have maternal sentiment? In short does this particular woman fit the archetypal European image of the murdering mother?

An entirely different set of issues are invoked in the colonial document to explain why girl-child murder is not a criminal offense in British-administered India. In the excerpt below the motivations of the criminal are not under official scrutiny at the periphery of empire. Instead the *site* where the female child murders take place is under heightened administrative attention and analysis:

> The suppression of Infanticide appears to me by far the most difficult subject that we have ever had to deal with in India: Suttees, or the immolation of children in the Ganges, were nothing when compared to it. They simply required the fiat of the Government to put a stop to them in our own territories; but even to check infanticide we have to oppose not only sentiments which are strong enough to suppress the common feeling of human nature, and, I may even say, of the most savage wild animals, but to interfere in the most secret and sacred affairs among the higher classes of natives, of women; for no one who has been a short time in India, and has used his powers of observation, can have helped perceiving how scrupulously every man pretending to respectability refrain from any allusion to his females, old or young. (James Erskine, Political Agent at Kathiawar, in letter to C. E. Trevelyan, Deputy Secretary to Government, 31 August, 1835; Pakrasi, 1972, 143)

In 1835 the colonial document articulates center and periphery by constructing a binary between two crimes of violence against Hindu women, sati and female infanticide. The tone of self justification in the above passage may well derive from the fact that by 1829 the East India Company claimed to have abolished sati, therefore the document needs to explain why there is a colonial law to punish all those who force the Hindu widow to commit sati, and why there is an absence of such a law for the infanticidal parent or clan. The answer lies in James Erskine's representation of both crimes against women, he classifies sati as the open crime and therefore easier to abolish, conversely female infanticide is described as "the most secret" and "sacred" of activities and therefore impossible to detect and suppress.

In the 1850s several colonial documents reconstruct the public and private sphere in India to explain the difference between the abolition of sati and administrative inaction in female infant-killing crimes.[19] Sleeman also adopts this public (sati) and private (female infanticide) binary when he represents sati as being "essentially a public exhibition" and consequently susceptible to being "put down" by the local authorities in non-occupied Oudh (*W. H. Sleeman in Oude* [1858] 1971, 280). Female infanticide, according to Sleeman, is practiced with impunity by the Rajput landholders because no one dares to openly report on them. This false assertion is contradicted by Sleeman's own journal, his diary shows over and over again that wherever Sleeman tours in Oudh, Rajput men openly admit to killing daughters. Thus the colonial text unravels its own construction, we have noted eight separate instances in *A Journey* where Rajputs freely and forthrightly acknowledge that "they, one and all, destroyed their infant daughters" (ibid., 206). The colonial binary of public crime of sati versus private crime of child-murder reappears in other colonial documents of the 1850s. Montgomery's Minute from Punjab (quoted earlier in the chapter) relates the story of the gold diggers who find, instead of gold, the bones of female children buried under the floor in the Burar Jat houses. Montgomery's image of the house of daughter-murder in Punjab represents female children as equivalent to property, to the gold buried under the living room floor, and therefore connected to the private sphere of the home.

Cave Brown's booklength study of British reform efforts concerning female infanticide (1857) in the 1850s follows the lead of Erskine's official correspondence. The writer is an ideologue of the East India Company, therefore we quote from this colonialist representation of public and private crimes against women:

> They [female infants] were beyond the reach of that merciful law which had rescued so many from a watery grave, which had held back the Hindoo widow from sacrificing herself on her husband's pyre.... In these cases, English rule could vindicate and support the claims of humanity, and check the celebration of such unnatural and unhallowed rites, for they were overt acts, requiring much of preparation, and attended with considerable display, but on the cold-blooded infanticide which is now the bane of India—the destruction of female children at the moment of their birth—what could it effect? It was worse than powerless; for its attempted intervention only drove the perpetrators of this "child murder" into a deeper privacy, and to the use of means of destruction more subtle and secret. The sacred precincts of the

Zenana became more closely secured and guarded; and here "pride, poverty, and avarice" (no longer even sanctioned by, or pretending to a league with, superstition) reigned still, triumphing over and trampling down the heaven-born feeling of parental love, nature's chief connecting link between fallen man and his Divine origins! (1857, 4–5)

Cave Brown describes the ritual of sati as "overt acts" that require a lot of preparation and are attended with "considerable display." According to the logic of this description, the crime of sati is an overt and public criminal act and therefore is amenable to control by British administration, whereas the crime of child-murder in India is characterized as the most "closely secured and guarded" and "secret" activity. The logical conclusion is that secret criminal activities are impossible to detect by the official eye. One is reminded of the fact that when it suited the surveillance apparatus of empire the secret criminal activities of the tribe of Thugs in Madhya Pradesh were recorded and the tribe was hunted down and eradicated. Yet here is document after document lamenting the impossibility of detecting child-killing. Indeed Cave Brown's passage goes a step further. He elaborates Erskine's representation by suggesting that British administrative intervention, far from protecting children and punishing the criminal, will have the deleterious effect of driving the perpetrators into "deeper privacy."

What is taking place in the language of these colonial texts is a discursive configuration of the girl-child within an artifice of space—the Hindu *zenana.* Cave Brown's florid prose repeatedly portrays the room of daughter murder as private and inaccessible, "let us for a moment lift aside the purda which screens from public gaze the Zenana of the Hindoo, and reveal some of the secrets of that prison-house" (1857, 6). The text relies on the travelogue mythology of the *zenana* to persuade readers, making intuitive associations between Hindu women and women's space as secret, mysterious, womb-like, impenetrable, and rife with dark deeds of horror. The ruse of the text is to suggest that the crime is so hushed and secret that it is outside the power of police and the law, and yet paradoxically this most secret of crimes is opened up for the voyeuristic delight of the reader. The imperial gaze maintains the literary fiction of the secret crime while at the same time rendering detailed descriptions of the room of daughter-murder. The literary fiction belongs to the travelogue conventions of promising readers the voyeur's delight of far-off lands and the illusion of direct access into the remotest recesses of these far-off lands. That is why the text creates a skillful impression that readers are being brought well guarded secrets from the most protected and private realms of the Rajput home, the *zenana.* But for the administrative travelogue writer's skill in culling information from native informants, readers would be deprived of eye-witness accounts of secrets inside the veiled and murky realms of the secluded *zenana.*

Instead of focusing on the patriarchal violence perpetrated on women by men, these colonial documents reconstruct the private and the public sphere in order to place female infanticide in the private sphere. We must perforce question rather than accept why it is that the imperial gaze organizes the violence on women into the public and private spheres. *We contend that it is in a specular masculinist economy that sati becomes an open and female infanticide a secret crime.* There is no basis in fact for the textual assertion of secrecy. Sleeman's text tells us over and over again that Rajput men openly and freely acknowledge the crime of daughter-murders committed in their family and community. Thus the imperial gaze of Sleeman is a specular view of the room. The colonial image of the room of daughter murder is not a historical or analytical view. Sleeman does not ask the historical and analytical questions that the British ask of sati: is the woman willing or coerced? Were the women of the house who had to execute the horrific deed willing or coerced? Was the mother asked or told what to do? In colonial documents about female infanticide women are presented as passive victims and/or participants. This has the effect of isolating the murder of the female infant from its effects on the mother, grandmother, aunts, and other female relatives. Furthermore, the structuring of the scene of daughter killing as the most secret, concealed, and private of crimes has the effect of separating the dead infant from the violence that must necessarily be visited on the women in the family, both as actual crime and as disciplinary apparatus.   ·

The public/private binary constructs infanticide as the unnatural severance of affective ties between the male parent and the female child, instead of treating it as of a piece with the pain and suffering that obtains from the denial of women's rights over their children, as well as the erasure of women's relation to each other. Furthermore, the public/private binary represents the crime as involving the male parent against the female child, not as a crime of men against all the women of the family, clan, and community. Sleeman's journal inscribes the room of daughter murder as an uncontested space of private compact between men (father, priest, community) and of men's control over women.

As feminists we know that the private realm is a place of struggle and resistance for women. Our politics precludes us from seeing women as passive victims, therefore it is reasonable to assume that the private realm in the infanticidal family is the site of continual conflict between men and women. What were the material and subjective effects of this violence on the women of infanticidal clans? Did they wonder about their female clanswomen who were allowed to preserve their daughters? Did they look at neighboring communities who showered love on their daughters and mourn their missing daughters? Did they envy lower-class women who possessed the right to have daughters? Patriarchal violence operates arbitrarily and often in contradictory ways, and this arbitrariness generally functions by disciplining women through fear. There was the ever present possibility that discontinuous daughter-killing caused mothers, grandmothers, and aunts to revolt. The colonial documents tell us little or nothing about the conditions of women's lives in the social form of the infanticidal family in British India. We learn little or nothing about notions of childhood vis-à-vis the female child, or the effects of girl-child murder on the conditions for women's productive labor. A total silence prevails over the administrative reports concerning the property rights of daughters. We learn very little about women's self-perceptions, compliances, collusions, and/or resistances to this practice. Female infanticide is named and structured in British official documents as the contestation between the private and the public realm within patriarchy, and colonial reform is articulated in terms of how far the law can penetrate the interior domain of the male householder, rather than about women's rights within patriarchy. The post-colonial legacy of the public/private binary in colonial infanticide documents is that population control is discursively configured by the postcolonial nation state as a public concern, although son-preference is treated as a private family affair, despite the fact that son-preference generally determines the number of children in the Indian family.

Many people believe in the binary of center and periphery in issues concerning the child's rights, children's oppression and child murder. The information retrieval systems of empire tell us that some savage communities murder their offspring, and some Indian communities kill their female infants at birth. At this juncture we see the characteristic Enlightenment impulse to formulate civilizational differences. Heathens do not comprehend the religio-moral sacralizing of the child in Christian Europe. In England the crime of infanticide is sporadic, in India it is systematic. In England the crime is sex neutral, in India it is sex selective. In England child-murder and the child murderess is an index of social disorder, involving the social issues of prostitution, sexuality of the lower orders, bastardy, and the poor law. In India child-murder is openly acknowledged, therefore infanticide concerns the social ordering itself. The social form of the family in eighteenth-century England is late marriages, the affective nuclear domestic group with its normative bonding, the cleaving of parents and children to each other, spacing of children, and equitable resource allocation to each member of the family. Savages do not bond with their children. Therefore, infanticide in non-Western societies is irrefutable proof that the colonized live in a state of savagery. We do not know of a single Indian social reformer, nationalist, or revivalist who questions why the British prescribe capital punishment for sex-neutral infant-murder in England and penalize the gendered crime in the colony with fines, threats of imprisonment, and cajoling. The mode of thinking outlined above seems natural and obvious until we realize that it is through the accumulated power of a century of colonial documentation that these binaries became accepted truths. The naming of female infanticide in British India from 1789 to 1857 was not a progression of the emancipation of Indian women sponsored by the English but part and parcel of the politics of British colonial expansion and the political rhetoric of colonial rule.

The deforming processes of colonial capitalism was the delinking of the crime "female infanticide" from the sign "woman." The traditional feudal character of the crime was distorted by the penetration of capitalist relations. Capitalist colonialism made land, labor, and the girl-child's life an object of private appropriation by the male householder instead of the joint responsibility of both parents, the community, and the state. The effects of colonial naming is that in discourse a child's life is far more precious if the child is English and the mother a poor unwed woman. Conversely, when the criminal is a brown man of property, his daughter's life is, for all practical purposes, treated under colonial law as the male householder's goods or property. Thus the colonial law situates itself as the supervisor who chastises the male householder with slapping fines on him and renames, *violently* renames the act of daughter-murder as poor husbandry of human livestock.

CHAPTER 3

Social Mobility in Relation to Female Infanticide in Rajput Clans: British and Indigenous Contestations about Lineage Purity and Hypergamy

Nineteenth-century British colonial explanations for female infanticide were condensed in the phrase "pride and purse." The colonial explanation was two-pronged. The phrase "pride" indicates that in those elite Rajput communities that were known to practice female infanticide, the motivation lay in race pride and fear of racial contamination through daughters' marriages to a non-Rajput. The colonial reference to "purse" indicates that daughters are killed because of the father's enormous burden of providing an exorbitant dowry in marriage. We bring to bear a discursive analysis upon this colonial explanation. The British codify and propagate an explanation of female infanticide that isolates the practice from its social, economic, historical contexts, and idioms. We call it a self-enclosed and circular explanation because it relates the murder of the female infant singularly to the infanticidal fathers' fears and financial inability. This psychologizing, nondiscursive and self-enclosed move preempts the basic Foucaultian question: how is this repressive and violent practice productive for the infanticidal community, and in what ways does the inter-generational practice benefit the infanticidal community in the long-term? Foucaultian power analysis facilitates the understanding that relationships of power are not simply negative repression, but are productive and creative in multiplying the effects of power. Therefore as postcolonial feminists we ask the question, how does the serial murder of female infants serve to further the father, the clan, and the community's socioeconomic interests?

The economism implicit in the colonialist-economistic explanation for female infanticide and the postcolonial explanations for high female child mortality and femicide, need to be placed in the context of the material and discursive productivity of female infant murder. It is only when we complicate female infanticide with the indigenous idiom of social-economic upward mobility that we get a fuller understanding of the productivity of the practice of female infanticide. The economism of positing the value of the female child in terms of marriage expenses and dowry, or her participation in agricultural production, or the cost of her education and maintenance, cannot theoretically be treated as ahistorical. Instead it has to be seen as a particular historical discourse that develops around the female child in conjunction with a family's desire for accumulation and upward mobility. Therefore, we try to understand and analyze how the fathers, mothers, kinsmen, female elders, and the rest of the neighboring community in nineteenth-century Rajasthan discursively explained the practice of female infanticide to themselves and to others.

The answers given by the infanticidal fathers, the community, the native informants to English officers, the answers embedded in women's folklore and songs, are extraordinarily revealing. These answers do not point to economism (the cost of bringing up a daughter and marrying her) but to the indigenous idiom of social mobility that sociologists call Rajputization.[1] Through a detailed examination of this idiom we provide a refutation of the colonialist-economistic explanation by placing the question of value not on the victim—the daughter—but on the infanticidal parents and their aspirations for higher status. The idiom of Rajputization is not a substitute for economic analysis, rather it situates the cultural-discursive correlatives within which a clan relates the value of daughters to their social aspirations.

Social mobility has not been studied in relation to female infanticide. The anti-colonial politics of the study of social mobility was pioneered by M. N. Srinivas, who debunked the colonial myth of a static, stagnant, and caste-ridden Indian society.[2] In effect Srinivas showed that far from lacking social opportunities for class and caste mobility, Indian society had over the centuries evolved highly sophisticated and heterogenously practiced idioms of social mobility. Thus the term Sanskritization came to signify, in postcolonial theory, opposition to British-colonial nationalist as well as Orientalist approaches to Indian society as a static social organization. Srinivas and other pioneering scholars do not endorse the structures of domination, nor do they valorize Indian culture as superior to the West, instead they provide a theoretical apparatus for the study of class and caste.[3] Through the work of Srinivas it became possible to say that the structures of class and caste domination reproduce themselves in Indian society, not through petrifaction and rigid hierarchy, but rather by a mobile and resilient system by which families, clans, and individuals move up and down the ladder in economic status and ritual status.

The critique that Srinivas accepted from his fellow scholars was that he had "emphasized unduly the Brahmanical model of Sanskritization and ignored the other models—Kshatriya, Vaishya and Shudra" (Srinivas 1969, 7). The excellent fieldwork by several scholars has demonstrated that amongst the hetrogeneous models of social mobility, Rajputization has been one of the most dynamic modes of upward mobility.[4] Rajputization has strong links with Sanskritization but is also distinct from it. Our rhetorical-discursive analysis of Rajputization focuses on Rajputization as an idiom of political power. In our view Rajputization refers neither to a caste nor a race, instead it signifies a highly mobile social process of claiming military-political power and the right to cultivable land as well as the right to rule. Rajputization is unparalleled in traditional Indian society for its inventiveness in ideologies of legitimation and self-invention. The fabrication of a Rajput genealogy in the process of climbing from feudatory to king does not constitute an isolated historical event in the early medieval period. In nineteenth-century India, the village landlord, the Brahmin priest, the tribal chieftain, the local Raja who has recently converted from Islam, the newly wealthy lower caste Sudra, the professional soldier or the member of a community with traditions of military labor, any of these men could Rajputize themselves and their families by adopting the lifestyle traditionally recognized as Rajput. These aspirants deployed Brahmins to compose a genealogy that would retrospectively endow the aspirant's lineage with ritual purity. These social processes get repeated continually and mirrored by communities all over north India that Rajputize themselves to make a bid for political power. With surprising rapidity the newly Rajputized family or clan can gain, over a generation or two, social acceptance of their claim to Rajput status.

Our theoretical intervention into the social mobility debates examines two aspects of the idiom of Rajputization, namely the prohibitions about purity and pollution and the marriage custom of hypergamy. The purity/pollution distinctions specific to Rajputization are socially interactional and dynamic, with the added qualification that the concepts of pure/impure underwent an enormous refinement and elaboration in Rajputization. The same features of resilience and flexibility also obtain in Rajput hypergamy. The general rule concerning marriage as the exchange of women in feudal society needs to be particularized in the case of a group, like the elite Rajputs, which was oriented primarily toward military labor. We suggest that daughters' marriages among the feudal elites of Rajasthan and elite expatriate Rajput clans evolved in response to the upward mobility of the bride's father. We perceive the pure/impure distinctions, as well as hypergamy, as signifying not merely the unstable and fluid "structural distance between various castes" but as primarily signifying the jockeying for power at different levels of society (Srinivas 1969, 120). In the idiom of Rajputization purity and pollution and hypergamy acquire their full meaning in the context of indigenous structures of domination, continual foreign invasions and continual processes of assimilation that characterize medieval Indian history, and the place of women in Rajput feudal patriarchal formation.

Several seminal studies explore the relationship between social mobility and increased constraints on women (Yalman 1968; Das 1976; Srinivas 1977; Liddle and Joshi 1986; Unnithan 1995). Regarding women's relation to the idioms of social mobility Srinivas observes, "Sanskritization results in harshness towards women" (1977, 46). Srinivas's theorizing about the relationship between social mobility and gender lacks a feminist perspective, because as Liddle and Joshi correctly point out, Srinivas treats the relationship between social mobility and gender "descriptively rather than analytically" (1986, 60). Traditionally women have not been the focus of social mobility studies. The disciplinary gender bias results in configuring men as the active agents and proper subjects of traditional Indian society, it is their rise or fall in status that has been theorized. Women figure as objects rather than subjects, as passive recipients of men's upward or downward mobility, as one of the means by which men achieve their desire for social mobility.[5]

Our undertaking the examination of female infanticide in relation to social mobility requires that we sift through several conceptual frameworks. Cultural generalizations about Third World societies or the Western discourses of crime and punishment do not fit the text of female infant murder. The discourse of crime is inapplicable largely because female infanticide in nineteenth-century northwest India was a classed crime, and the discourse of crime rarely penalizes crimes committed by the upper classes. By definition a crime is an act committed by poor and powerless men and women.[6] The discourse of social custom is also inadequate because female infanticide was not a universal practice. Although in feudal societies a man's violence toward his female household was not legislated by law, clearly every father in nineteenth-century northwest India did not devalue or kill his female infants. Therefore, female infanticide in nineteenth-century northwest India was a local rather than universal practice, systemic clan violence rather than individualized pathology, and an elite mode of violence rather than the lower-class vagrant's crime.

The local, systemic, and elite nature of the practice means that we have to logically pose two questions to the text of female infanticide: first, what is the material and discursive productivity of female infant murder for fathers, kinsmen, and female elders, how did these men and women discursively explain the practice to themselves and to others. Secondly, what were the modes and degrees of social assent and social dissent articulated by noninfanticidal communities that lived cheek by jowl with infanticidal clans? What were the modes of dissent socially permissible to women who were either victims, participants, or helpless spectators of this practice? Feminist theorizing in the last twenty years tells us that the private space of the home was never a place of absolute tranquillity and obedience. Instead the home was and has always been the site of gender-role contestation and power struggle. Therefore, we can speculate that there must have been forms of social censure, there must have been oppositional movements and cultural productions that circulated a critique of the practice. We have to keep questions concerning the social sanction and the discursive and extra-discursive productivity of the practice in tension in order to understand the structures of domination that are renewed and perpetuated in the specific patriarchal organization of infanticidal clans.

A Folkloric Nonshastric Woman-Centered
Intervention in the Social Mobility Debate

Without depriveleging the disciplinary tool of fieldwork, we nevertheless argue for a rhetorical-discursive approach to the study of social mobility. M. N. Srinivas and Milton Singer laid the groundwork for linguistic and structural analysis by naming social mobility as *idioms*. In the spirit of their analysis we treat the spoken and written articulations of the idioms of social mobility not simply as ethnographic data, but as texts. It is only by approaching them as texts that we read off the open, exterior, and structural operation of violence against women in the practices of female infanticide. In other words we treat speech and writing as rhetorical constructs in which issues of representation, subject position, genre analysis, discourse formations, and the rhetoricity of the speaker's utterance and the listener's recording is more illuminating of the text than its empirical truth-status.

The patriarchal texts of woman hatred are literal and open texts, daughters are killed because the female child's life is of no consequence. However, that is not the end of the story. The text of daughter-killing must be historicized rather than universalized. That is why our analysis of the relation between female infanticide and social mobility focuses on nineteenth-century Rajasthan. We draw on colonial documents in order to profile the paradigmatic daughter-killing community, while disputing British analysis of the data. According to British data, the group or community that was most likely to authorize and practice intergenerational serial female infanticide in late eighteenth to nineteenth-century India were the male members of the landowning propertied Rajput clan, both in their place of origin in Rajasthan as well as among the expatriate Rajput clans in Kutch, Kathiawar, Oudh, and the Central Provinces.

It is only by treating the colonial documents as text that we make visible the profile of the paradigmatic infanticidal community. We do not treat the colonial document as empirical truth but as a rhetorical construct in which the native informants relay information about the infanticidal community in one way to the colonial officer, and the colonial officer interprets that information quite another way through the interpretive grid of empire. The native informant frequently draws on the indigenous idiom of Rajputization to explain the practice of female infanticide, while British officers consistently interpret these statements through the colonial discourse of race pride. In order to gain access to the infanticidal Rajput man of property, we begin by foregrounding the hidden antagonist of modern sociological studies of Rajputization, namely British-colonial analysis of female infanticide as a leftover from a medieval feudal static and stagnant society.

The value of our rhetorical-discursive approach to social mobility lies in the following areas: it is interdisciplinary, it is committed to the popular, folkloric, and woman-centered understanding of the operation of social mobility rather than the shastric, elitist, and male-defined view of social mobility. Inevitably the exclusion of women and the corollary exclusion of the popular impoverishes and depletes analysis of the very thing that sociologists are looking for, namely the study of culture. For example our texts for hypergamy and purity/pollution are not the *Dharmashastras* but fables, folktales, women's songs, a mediaeval poetess, autobiography as well as statements made by native informants to colonial officers in the nineteenth century, because this community-based critique is more vital to the understanding of culture than the shastric view of Hindu society.

We have culled from the sociological literature, particularly from Srinivas's analysis of Sanskritization, the key differences between the two modes of upward mobility, Sanskritization, and Rajputization. Despite the excellent fieldwork on Rajputization by Sinha (1962) and Kulke (1976), there is no clear theoretical definition of the key features of Rajputization, and its differences and similarities to Sanskritization. We argue that theorizing is as important as fieldwork, principally because of the colonial misreading of the term Rajput and its relation to Rajput history and to Rajputization. As a corrective we demarcate the distinction between Sanskritization and Rajputization in terms of attributional criteria—which denotes a code of living, dietary prohibitions, modes of worship—and socially interactional criteria, which signify rules of marriage, rules pertaining to women, and modes of power. The attributional criteria for Sanskritization are vegetarianism, prohibition against beef eating, teetotalism, and wearing of the sacred thread; the attributional criteria for Rajputized men consists of meat-eating, imbibing alcohol and opuim, and the wearing of the sword; the attributional criteria for Rajputized women are seclusion through purdah or the veil and elaborate rules for women's mobility within the village. The religious code for Sanskritization is a belief in the doctrine of *karma, dharma,* rebirth, and *moksha,* and the *sradda* ceremony for male ancestors. Conversely, the religious code for Rajputization consists of the worship of Mahadeo and Sakto and the patronage of Brahmins through personal family priests (historically the Rajputized rulers gave land grants to Brahmins) and priestly supervision of rites of passage. The socially interactional criteria for Sanskritization is claiming the right to all priestly intellectual and cultural vocations, patronage from the dominant political power, and prohibition against widow remarriage. The interactional criteria for Rajputization consists of claiming the right to all military and political occupations, the right to govern, the right to aggrandize land through wars, sanctioned aggressive behavior, the adoption of the code of violence, compiling of clan genealogies, and the right to coercively police the interactions between castes.

While we draw on pioneering fieldwork on Rajputization, our own approach is neither an apology for the absence of fieldwork nor is it parasitic on fieldwork. The inclusion of women in traditional sociology is via field study, and the disciplinary tool of field study is predicated on the hierarchic distance between the educated sociologist and her field-study of illiterate and oppressed Indian women, and the different fields of discourse they inhabit, which demarcates the distinction between us and them.[7] Our rhetorical-discursive approach to the relation between social mobility and female infanticide is self-implicating and abolishes the distinctions between us and them. For us the critical distance between the fieldworker and the women she interviews and observes is in fact the distance between the fields of discourse each inhabit. In part we inhabit the same field of discourse as our subjects. We share the discourse of those women in the kitchen prescribing the rules of purity and pollution and fighting for power. We share the rhetorical practices of wedding songs sung by women in north Indian weddings, which ritually critique exogamy and hypergamy. We have been silenced by male diatribes about lineage purity. We have been the daughters who have heard family men conversing with other men and lamenting the decline of family prosperity through the birth of too many daughters.

The British Profile of the Intergenerational Serial Daughter-Killer

It is of the utmost importance that, in drawing on British data, we delimit our claims in order that we do not perpetuate a stereotype. All Rajputs did not commit female infanticide, particularly the lower classes in nineteenth-century Rajasthan never practiced this violence. Moreover there were several elite Rajput clans that dissented from this practice. In our view the man who was most likely to commit female infanticide in nineteenth-century northwest India was the upwardly mobile and politically ambitious man of property; he was most likely to have an obsessive interest in land accumulation; thus the infanticidal father is likely to Rajputize himself and his clan in order to make a bid for political and economic power. The distinction between the British profile of the Rajput clan and our own profile of the family or group that Rajputizes itself or undergoes Rajputization will become clearer as the argument unfolds.

It is worth investigating how the British arrived at the caste, class, and gender of the typical daughter-killer. In 1819 Colonel James Walker confirmed the fact that girl-child murder was not a general practice in north India, observing that the crime "is disavowed by the great body of the people, and prevails only among a single tribe" (Wilson 1855, 115). The Political Agent of Marwar, J. Ludlow, noted in 1842 on the basis of information supplied by the Jodhpur Vakil, that the lower classes in Rajasthan did not practice female infanticide, the custom was practiced by the middle ranks in imitation of the upper echleons of Marwar (Letter to J. Sutherland, 29 June 1842, *India Political Consultations* 28 December 1842, 294). By the middle of the nineteenth-century administrative knowledge of the paradigmatic infanticidal community was so well circulated in official circles that John Cave Brown began his book on female infanticide in India by referring openly to this profile:

> This unnatural crime, though not confined exclusively to any one particular class, is proved to exist especially among the Rajputs. . . . Among this race, wherever located, infanticide prevails. (1857, 6–7)

In the above statement Cave Brown moves from classification of the serial killer by "class" to "this race." The colonial emphasis on racial classification functions to de-emphasize the class affiliations of the typical daughter killer, in fact the official colonial document displays a marked unease with the classed nature of the crime. For example in his booklength narrative Cave Brown blurs the classed nature of the crime by suggesting that the men who regret the birth of a daughter are motivated by poverty and the custom of expensive marriages for daughters, "The poor man, whose daily wages rarely exceed four annas (six pence), cannot thus, to celebrate his daughter's marriage, scatter to the winds two or three hundred Rupees . . . without rueing the day that his daughter was born" (17). Oftentimes official texts cover over the information that the typical daughter-killer is an ambitious man of property by sympathetically representing the murderer as a poor Rajput father who will either incur debt to marry his daughters or kill them at birth because he cannot afford their marriage expenses.

By the sheer power of these representations the British tried to blame the crime of female infant-killing on poor or lower class and landless Rajputs. Even when this rhetorical maneuver did not work the official texts succeeded in deflecting attention from the fact that female infanticide was an upper-class crime, specific to the landed elite in Rajasthan and other provinces in northwest India. Upper-class crimes made the British officers uncomfortable, it would simply not do to make much of the fact. The social reforms initiated by the East India Company were designed not to question class domination or patriarchal domination, but to reconfigure class and gender domination in the interests of empire.

That may explain why administrator-writers mentioned the fact that female infanticide was a crime specific to the landed elite of northwest India when it suited the interests of empire. For instance W. H. Sleeman observes, "the Rajputs, among whom alone this crime prevails, are the dominant class in Oude . . . the greater part of the land is held by them" (1858, II, 250). Sleeman's phrase "the dominant class" and "among whom alone this crime prevails" indicates that the British were well aware of the classed nature of the crime. Sleeman refers to the class element of the practice in order to discursively reconfigure it to suit the Company's political purpose of discrediting the ruling classes in Oudh, underline the moral bankruptcy of the Oudh Rajputs and make a case for the British rule of Oudh.

British Explanation for Female Infanticide as Race Pride and Racial Contamination

There is a strong relationship between British race theory about the Rajputs and British analysis of the Rajput practice of female infanticide, therefore the British myth of the pure-blooded Rajput is of central interest to us.[8] Readers may well ask if the British were innocent dupes of the racial theories advanced by the Rajputs. Properly speaking, the race pride and racial contamination explanation for female infanticide came about through a collusion between the elite criminal and the colonizer.

It is quite true that the Rajputs had, over centuries, developed elaborate ideologies of political legitimation, and the pureblooded Rajput was one of them. There is also no doubt that upper-class Rajputs supplied these explanations to Englishmen like James Tod, Charles Metcalfe, and W. H. Sleeman. [9] The British readily accepted and amplified the racial purity and racial contamination explanation for female infanticide, although they discredited many other explanations offered by Indian men concerning practices like sati. It is hard to believe that imperial historians and data collectors did not know that the Rajputs are not a race at all, rather the Rajputs are a particularly telling example of the assimilated and hybridized nature of Indian communities.

British historians and writers-reformers on female infanticide deliberately misrecognized the purity/pollution distinctions made by Rajput native informants and reconfigured the concepts of purity and pollution into Rajput claims of racial purity and racial contamination. A seminal text for the race pride and the racial contamination explanation for female infanticide is James Tod's *Annals and Antiquities of Rajasthan* (1829, 1832). The rhetorical structure of Tod's argument concerning female infanticide exemplifies how colonial discourses inscribed colonized women; in the passage we are about to read race theory is conjoined to masculinist values in order to construct a justificatory framework for the pure-blooded Rajput's violence on daughters.

The wife is the sacrifice to his egotism, and the progeny to his pride. . . . If the female reasoned on her destiny, its hardships were sufficient to stifle all joy, and produce indifference to life. When a female is born, no anxious inquiries await the mother, no greetings welcome the newcomer, who appears an intruder on the scene, which often closes in the hour of its birth. . . . It is, in fact a modification of the same feeling, which characterizes the Rajpoot and the ancient German warrior,—the dread of dishonour to the fair: the former raises the poniard to the breast of his wife rather than witness her captivity, and he gives the opiate to the infant, whom, if he cannot portion and marry to her equal, he dare not see degraded. (1829, I, 504)

At first Tod adopts a benevolent pro-woman position, he criticizes the Rajput men who sanction sati and female infanticide. In the phrase "the progeny to his pride" Tod has managed to linguistically associate female infanticide with the word "pride" although as yet it is not yet clear what is the reason that female children are a threat to the Rajput father's pride. In the same benevolent strain Tod laments the patriarchal oppression on Rajput women, and describes the birth-scene of son preference. Up to this point Tod describes female infanticide both as part and parcel of the general patriarchal oppression on Rajput women, and as integral to the practices of son-preference. Yet these benevolent comments are, rhetorically speaking, merely a preamble to Tod's race pride and racial contamination explanation of female infanticide. As postcolonial theorists of sati have shown, British interest in the Hindu women's oppression did not stem from their alienation from patriarchal domination but rather in their desire to intervene and reconstellate patriarchal discourses and structures (Mani 1989; Spivak 1985, 1999).

At first Tod's benevolence seems to be directed at the Rajput woman and he constructs the scenes of patriarchal oppression: the joyless and suicidal Rajput female, the violence visited on mother and daughter at the birth of a female child. However when we examine Tod's display of benevolence more closely, we perceive that it is directed toward the Rajput male who, caught between his inability to marry his daughter and his fear of her dishonor, nobly chooses to murder her. Tod stops short of inquiring into the productivity of Rajput violence on their own women and instead provides a rhetorical framework justifying female infanticide. In Tod's view the real motive of the Rajput male is a noble one, albeit expressed in an unfortunate form, "he gives the opiate to the infant, whom, if he cannot portion and marry to her equal, he dare not see degraded." It is noteworthy how the motive of "pride" has now been amplified and glorified into the word "degraded" and the suggestion is that the Rajput daughter who marries below her degrades her pure blood, and her degradation reflects back on her pureblooded natal family and her racially pure father.

This is a racialist argument because there is an unambiguous suggestion in the passage from *Annals and Antiquities of Rajasthan* that racial purity is a noble motive, although the action of daughter-killing may be an extreme expression of a laudable objective.[10] Tod achieves this suggestion by rhetorical effects that are more intuitive than rational: this is evident in the way he strengthens the emotive power of degraded blood by associating it with the threat of rape and captivity faced by the German warrior's wife, "It is, in fact a modification of the same feeling, which characterizes the Rajpoot and the ancient German warrior,—the dread of dishonour to the fair." This is a flattering comparison indeed, grafting the European medieval chivalric code on to the Rajput; it is a comparison designed to reinforce Tod's affinity with the Rajput male's obsession with his racial purity.

Even when the historical evidence does not fit the historiographical narrative, the facts are turned inside out to fit the narrative. For example there was incontrovertible evidence that the expatriate Jhareja Rajputs of Kutch and Kathiawar had a mixed Hindu-Muslim lineage, and yet there was a high evidence of female infant-killing among them. Tod's solution was to argue, not from the standpoint of race pride, but from the standpoint of racial contamination. Tod states, "As to the almost universality of this practice [of female infanticide] among the Jarejas, the leading cause . . . [is that] having been contaminated, no Rajpoot will intermarry with them" (1829, I, 507). In many ways it was a circular argument, the racially contaminated Jhareja Rajputs kill their daughters because no pure-blooded Rajput will marry them, and pure-blooded Rajputs kill their daughters because they could be potential sources of racial contamination. It never seemed to have occurred to the British to question why daughters were given this burden of preserving the purity of bloodline of their father, brother, and male kinsmen.

Aijaz Ahmad has commented on the role the Indian colony played in the post-Enlightenment emergence of European racialist theories, "the main European interests (in both senses of the word) shift from Egypt to India, and when the Indo-Aryan linguistic model gets going as the basic explanatory model for cultural unities and mobilities" (1992, 335, ff. 28). In the context of this re-evaluation of India's role in European racialism, we suggest that the colonial historiographical narrative about female infanticide in Rajasthan emerges as one discursive strand of British race theory.

Tod espouses an ill-concealed racialism by arguing that the Rajput motive for daughter-killing is racial degradation and racial contamination. In essence Tod's colonial historiographical narrative went like this: Rajputs believe in the seclusion of their women because women constitute the honor of this pure-blooded race of soldiers; Rajputs practice hypergamy because they have a justifiable obsession with racial purity and can only marry their daughters into a pure-blooded family; consequently they kill their daughters because they have an excessive regard for their daughter's honor, they prefer to put her to death than let her be married into a family of impure blood. Tod's race theory was not an isolated instance, British classification of the paradigmatic infanticidal community was racialist. In the first half of the nineteenth century the empire builders named the infanticidal community a tribe; for instance, Walker states in 1819 that female infanticide "prevails only among a single tribe" (Wilson 1855, 115). By 1857 the official name for the infanticidal community is articulated by Cave Brown as "this race" of Rajputs, "Among this race, wherever located, infanticide prevails" (1857, 7).

Perhaps the most important reason that Tod's thesis is racialist is that like most race theories of the nineteenth century, it is a colonial fiction. The Rajputs were never a race at all. Sociologists have provided convincing evidence that the term "Rajput" denotes neither a race nor a stable class formation, nor a stable caste or *varna* in the fourfold caste system (Brahmin, Kshatriya, Vaishya, and Sudra or priest, warrior-ruler, trader, and lower classes). Rather the term Rajput represents an unstable, socially dynamic, and politically volatile idiom of social mobility called Rajputization. Sociologists like Singer call Rajputization "the kingly or martial life-style" (1964, 101) because this idiom evolved over centuries and eventually became a Rajput claim to secular economic-political power, a claim to military-political occupations and a claim to the right to govern. The term Rajput emerges between seventh- and tenth-century A.D., the point in Indian history when the traditional occupations of the Kshatriyas and the social groups classed as Kshatriya or warrior-rulers are replaced by a motley group of aggressive newcomers. This motley group is as various as foreign invaders of Central Asian descent like the Huns and Scythians, non-Hindu groups, lower-caste rulers, groups with traditions of soldiering, and service occupations like military labor.

The common factor between these groups is their usurpation of the traditional caste occupations and lifestyle of the Kshatriyas consisting of political power, military power, and ownership of land. The term "Rajput" literally denotes a distinctive mode of upward mobility by which diverse groups gained social acceptance for their claims by Sanskritizing themselves and calling themselves *Rajputra* (son of king) and subsequently Rajput. Thus, Rajputization is an idiom of social mobility rather than the description of actual historical groups or social classes, indeed anthropologists have shown how diverse groups and castes claim Rajput status by undergoing the processes of Rajputization.[11]

In JTKO Sleeman meticulously reports his conversations with Raja Bukhtawar Sing, who is his constant companion in his travels through Oudh and a reliable native informant about the customs and manners of the Oudh people. Bukhtawar Sing describes Rajputization to his English companion, he gives the example of the clan of Pausies who "become Rajpoots by giving their daughters to Powars and other Rajpoot families, when by robbery and murder, they have acquired wealth and landed property " (1858, 170). The phrase "become Rajpoots" is a significant one, because the native informant is outlining the social processes by which a clan "becomes" Rajput.

The process of becoming Rajput entails that the non-Rajput clan of Pausies first acquire land capital and money capital by violent and coercive means of "robbery and murder." Then they move upward by associating themselves with that section of society, namely the Rajputs, which legitimates the cult of violence. The process of association is executed by buying Rajput grooms from the Powar clan for their daughters. Bukhtawar Sing implies that this is an exchange in which the wife-giving family Rajputizes itself and the groom's family receives a considerable dowry. Soon the Pausies "call themselves Rawats, and are considered to be Rajpoots, since they have acquired landed possessions, by the murder and ruin of the old proprietors" (1858, 170). This process of name-changing requires the community's consent. Self-invention is not enough for the family to "call themselves Rawats" they must also be able to exert social power over the community so that the newly dubbed Rawats "are considered to be Rajpoots."

The Rajputized clan secures this "by adopting some of the stigmata of the Rajput life style" (Singer 1964, 101). The socially recognizable way of adopting the Rajput lifestyle is to implement woman-related Rajput practices in the newly Rajputized household, practices which include female infanticide.[12] Bukhtawar Sing points out that there is an integral connection between the cult of violence and female infant killing "they all delight in murder and rapine—the curse of God is upon them, sir, for the murder of their own children" (1858, 170). Bukhtawar Sing is an interesting figure for us, because he names the practice of female infanticide in the idiom of social mobility, even though his English companion seems not to understand *this* indigenous explanation.

In JTKO Sleeman also records a conversation with Nowsing, a Rajput landlord of Oudh who openly acknowledges the practice of female infanticide. Nowsing articulates his reasons, not as deriving from race pride, but in the logic of family prosperity, he says, "It is the general belief among us, Sir, that those who preserve their daughters never prosper" (1858, 279). Nowsing's use of the phrase "never prosper" refers to Rajputization, the indigenous idiom of social mobility in which daughters are antithetical to family prosperity. However Sleeman is unable to hear him, he is under the sway of Tod's arguments and often quotes him verbatim from memory, therefore he listens and records carefully but continues to reiterate the official position, "Family pride is the cause of this terrible evil" (1858, 206).[13] The race pride and racial contamination explanation for female infanticide became a self-sustaining textual convention in official documents.

Social Mobility through Purity and Pollution

The infanticidal Rajputs's assertions of purity and his dread of contamination, which seemed to Tod to be inspired by the Rajput obsession with racial purity, were actually the purity/pollution distinctions that are pervasive in traditional India. Purity and pollution are socially interactional concepts in a dynamic social system rather than immutable boundaries in a stagnant and hierarchic society. Srinivas states that "the structural distance between various castes is defined in terms of pollution and purity" (1969, 120). This structural distance between castes is dynamic and flexible rather than static and petrified, therefore the rules of pure and impure are applied with a good deal of flexibility. In other words, the necessity for these distinctions does not change but in actual practice a wide latitude is permitted for the interpretation and application of purity and pollution between actual castes and communities.

We depart from Srinivas inasmuch as we do not conceive of purity/pollution distinctions as exclusive to Hinduism, or as simply signifying intracaste relations.[14] Purity and pollution distinctions in traditional Indian society are not tantamount to racial purity or religious orthodoxy, instead it is both a religious and a secular idiom, which can be creatively deployed by the individual or family to articulate their social aspirations, and these aspirations are ratified or rejected by the family or the community. We call it secular because it is a morphology that is available to all castes, clans, and classes irrespective of their socioeconomic status and distance from Hindu *varna* heirarchy. That is not to say that purity/pollution as concepts do not traffic with religion, but we argue that the mobilization of this concept has more to do with negotiating with power in society than strictly with narrow religious injunctions.

Shahid Amin analyzes how purity and pollution taboos were creatively mobilized by the peasants in Gorakhpur District. He suggests that the populace articulated their own aims and needs through the mythic figure of Gandhi. This was a creative and heterogeneous mobilization of the Gandhi figure; for instance Amin notes the mobilization of purity and pollution prescriptions by high castes, "Observance of proper high-caste rituals were also stressed" (1984, 8) such as reciting the *gayatri* mantra and contributions to the cow-protection fund. Simultaneously the lower castes also mobilized purity and pollution prescriptions as a form of political radicalizing, "in a great many cases lower and middle-caste panchayats imposed novel dietary taboos as a part of the widespread movement of self-assertion which was also exemplified by acts such as the refusal of their women to work as housemaids or the withholding of *begar* (forced labout) both from the *sarkar* and the zamindar" (12). Amin's work contradicts two notions: first, the notion that purity and pollution prescriptions are mobilized solely by the higher castes; second, Amin departs from Srinivas's notion that purity and pollution prescriptions are confined to Hindus; for example, Amin notes that reports of miracles of perfumed water and the discovery of a copy of the Holy Quran in a unopened room were circulated, attesting to the fact that Muslim communities of the region also mobilize the prescriptions for purity (4).

The question remains concerning the exact relation between purity/pollution distinctions and actual economic-political power in the traditional idioms of social mobility. Romila Thapar argues that concepts of pollution date back to pre-Aryan ancient India, and purity/impurity defined the ritual status of a group (1978). In Thapar's view the status of a group was evaluated by actual economic-political status and by ritual status. The two kinds of evaluation were not always identical, ritual status was semi-autonomous from actual political-economic status; for instance a poor priest could assert superior ritual status vis-à-vis the rich landlord. This semi-autonomy of ritual status meant that a group that has won economic or political power asserts its social claim to higher ritual status by reorganizing or Sanskritizing its rules concerning pure and impure, and the pure/impure rules are continually accommodated to the upward or downward mobility of different communities and castes.

There are a number of reasons that purity and pollution are pan-Indian secular concepts signifying power-relations; for example in ancient India, the vocabulary of purity/pollution was evolved by the Indo-Aryan pastoralists to name the indigenous populations as impure barbarians *(mleccha),* and this vocabulary continually accommodated the changing political relations, the cultural exchanges and assimilative processes like mixed castes between the Indo-Aryans and the indigenous populations (Thapar 1978, 152–192). The continually shifting demarcation of people, their language and their lands as impure or *mleccha* not only denoted Aryan dominance and Aryan rules of exclusion, simultaneously the same concept was resilient in interpretation so that it also demarcated selective inclusion of certain indigenous groups as well as the absorption of mixed castes. In other words the *mleccha* had less to do with the professed religion of the excluded group, and everything to do with the relations of power between the Indo-Aryans and the indigenous populations. Thus, it is important to distinguish the concepts of pure and impure from an exclusively religious or narrowly political framework.

In medieval India the concepts of purity and pollution were secularized to a great degree, for instance they not only denoted the rituals of Sanskritization like the death-ritual of *sradda* but also accommodated Islamic prescriptions concerning pure and impure (*paak* and *napaak; halal and haram*), and this syncretism prevented purity/pollution from being exclusively Brahmanical concepts. The creative redeployment of purity/pollution distinctions also occurred in the clash between Brahmanical Hinduism and the *Bhakti* movements on the following question: the former laid down humiliating and degrading prescriptions for the lower classes, especially the *dalits,* in order to continually reinforce the notion that the upper classes have access to purity and the *dalits* are polluted: conversely the *Bhakti* sects, instead of directly questioning the Brahmanical rituals of pure and impure, reinterpreted them to make the point that the lower castes have alternate ways of achieving genuine purity, which are denied to the affluent upper castes.

Thus, in medieval India a man whose labor belonged among the traditionally unclean occupations like tanning, sanitary work, cremation ground workers, or traditionally lower-caste occupations could draw on the *Bhakti* poetry and practices and recode her/his daily work and the materials of her/his daily existence in an alternate conception of purification. For instance s/he could claim that her/his work constitutes an essential service to humanity, thus his work functioned analogically as God's service to humanity, and in this way her/his allegedly unclean work was made sacred. By implication the elites were threatened by pollution because they did not perform service to society or work with their hands, therefore they were denied the tanner or the weaver's proximity to, and direct access to, a life lived in the purity of love for human beings and god. The political significance of these alternate rituals of self-purification and self-pollution varies widely for *Bhakti* followers, for some it facilitated political quietism, for others a parallel social space for dissent or a radical subversion of the Brahmanical social ordering.

Women are centrally involved in the rules of purity and pollution. They have constantly fought against the purity/pollution distinctions that have been imposed upon their daily lives, as well as the continual positioning of them as the site of familial and social pollution, by creatively fashioning their own rituals of self-purification and self-pollution and by negotiating social acceptance for it. "Pollution" notes Thapar "was controlled through the functioning of two taboos—the taboo regarding kinship in the context of marriage and the concern for eating with or taking food from only those ritually permitted" (1978, 126). With regard to the first taboo, clan exogamy, and caste endogamy meant that daughters were the site of purity and pollution; they had to be married away from the clan and village that they knew, and the male elders' primary consideration was to secure themselves from pollution by marrying their daughter into a family that was pure enough to marry their daughters. When this taboo is put in conjunction with the central prescription in Sanskritization against widow remarriage, we can see how patriarchal violence on women as daughters and wives and widows was an inbuilt part of the modes of upward mobility.

Traditionally, Indian women have resisted the artifice of the family's ritual status and the prescriptions of clan exogamy and caste endogamy. The modes of female resistance lie in persuading the natal family to accept a son-in-law from within the village community, or by marrying a distant cousin, or by visiting the natal home as often as possible, or by returning to the father's home or the brother's home as a widow. The north Indian tradition of *ghar jamai* was a skillful way to adhere to the ritual purity of exogamy, while at the same time invite the son-in-law to live with the bride's natal family, and in most cases it was a marriage arrangement that empowered the daughter.

Women's songs in north India decode the purity/pollution prescriptions of clan exogamy and caste endogamy as the original psychic wound on the young woman. These songs, sung at festivals like *teej,* which are oriented toward daughters and on ritual occasions like weddings, record the desolation, powerlessness, and violence inherent in exogamy. For example, the folk genre of *bidaai* songs laments the great distance between *sasural* (the married home) and *naihar* or *maika* (the natal family) and articulates women's longing for the freedom and love that can only be enjoyed in the natal home. *Bidaai* songs are sung either by male or female singers, they are considered to be the test of a vocalist's skill and breadth of emotion, for he or she must be able to evoke the pathos of women's pain for the auditors. Women's lived experience of exogamy is preserved and transmitted in these songs as the originary wound that alienates the young women from her loved ones, the wound through which she relearns her status as a permanently lonely and homeless subject.

Thapar describes the second prescription of purity and pollution as "the concern for eating with or taking food from only those ritually permitted" (1978, 126). Women have a far more aggressive relationship to this form of ritual purity, for the simple reason that this particular prescription concerns a sphere where they can exercise power over men, namely the kitchen. In this sphere women gain power by prescribing what is pure and impure to members of the household, relatives, guests, children, and domestic servants. Most importantly, the contestation of power relations regarding cooked food and dining prohibitions is played out between women. Regarding the pure/impure restrictions on intradining, Srinivas observes that women "are generally more particular about observing the rules of pollution than others" (1969, 122). The reason is that older women exercise power over younger women, like the grown-up daughter or granddaughter or the newly married daughter-in-law, by appointing themselves as arbiters of purity and pollution with regard to food.

Younger women contest this power either by violating the rules of purity and pollution in the kitchen, or by installing alternative rules of their own in a bid to seize power, or even by exemplary practice of the family's rules in a bid to assume ritual purity for themselves. For example, the usurpation of this mode of purity and pollution can be executed by the younger woman's claim that she brings superior rules from the family traditions of her natal family, or by inviting guests who break the dining taboos of the grandmother or mother-in-law, or by showing kindness to domestic servants as a gesture of superior purity in relation to older women's rough treatment of servants, or by representing her education as affording her superior status in the kitchen. Thus with each new generation of women in the family and each new set of power-relations within the family, the necessity for ritual status does not change, it is simply located elsewhere.

The Function of Woman-Related Practices
in Lineage Purity or Rajput *Shaan*

In early medieval India the thirty-six Rajput clans that claimed the purest ritual status did so on the basis of priests constructing royal genealogies of the *Chandravanshi* (Moon-family) and *Suryavanshi* (Sun-family). British writer-administrators like Tod and Sleeman accepted these Rajput genealogies, not as indices of Rajput claims to higher status, but as literal truth. Tod's terms of approbation for the Sisodiya Rajputs of Mewar are that they are the most pure-blooded of all the Rajputs, "[The Rana of Mewar] is universally allowed to be the first of the 'thirty-six royal tribes'; nor has a doubt even been raised respecting his purity of descent" (1829, I, 15). Other English writers followed the official line by describing the Rajputs as pure-blooded, "In Malwa and several Rajpootana states is to be found some of *the purest and proudest blood* of that royal race" (emphasis ours, Cave Brown 1857, 58). Both Tod and Sleeman pinpointed the cause of female infanticide among the Rajputs in the fact that families from superior clans could not intermarry into families of inferior clans.

Contrary to the British view, modern historians tend to treat the "detailed genealogies of ruling [Rajput] clans as a product of upward mobility from an initial feudatory position" (Chattopadhyaya 1976, 70). In medieval India a Rajput feudatory could break away from the parent kingdom and assert political equality by asking Brahmins to construct an appropriate genealogy. The historical evidence for this process of Rajputizing lies in the fact that most of these genealogies "came to be formulated only in the period of change from feudatory to independent status" (ibid.). In essence these genealogies were "charters of validation" (Thapar 1992, 138).

The problem before us is that female infanticide in itself does not endow a Rajput family with ritual purity, unlike sati, which is interpreted as the widow's self-purification that blesses her married family with social prestige and ritual status. Therefore, the question before us is how female child-killing is justified as a means for achieving lineage purity. The answer lies in unpacking the word that is most often associated with Rajputs, both in their self-representations and in the social verdict about them. In north Indian languages it is the word *shaan*, often translated as honor. *Shaan* is a word that the British mistakenly translated as race pride, we suggest instead that Rajput *shaan* denotes the operation of purity and pollution in Rajputization and the specific development of lineage purity among the Rajputs. Thus, ritual status is gained in the idiom of Rajputization, not only through the observance of clan exogamy and dining prohibitions, but predominantly through lineage purity.

The Rajput elaboration of purity and pollution rules in lineage purity or *shaan* results in a network of practices that have certain characteristic features: upward mobility masquerades as lineage purity; the legitimation and preservation of lineage purity is secured by the ruthless supra-exploitation of, and systemic violence on women; Rajput *shaan* also represents the use of direct physical force on women and lower-caste men; lastly, there is a social sanction for direct coercion in the idiom of Rajputization, on the grounds that wife-killing and daughter-killing is necessary to secure lineage purity on the one hand, and on the other that the use of force on lower-caste men is necessary to police the boundaries of ritual purity and impurity.

Lineage purity is derived from a number of practices, all of which have to do with women. The practices are restrictions on women's freedom of movement: the veil or *purdah* and a complex network of prohibitions concerning the veil inside and outside the home; exogamy and hypergamy; widow self-immolation *(sati)* that endows the widow with the highest purity of *sat* and mass self-immolation *(jauhar)*.[15] At this point it is necessary to practice vigilance so that it does not appear as if we are making generalizations about the general oppression of Hindu women, but are addressing a specific idiom of upward mobility. This continual vigilance is necessary in order to alienate female infant killing from the discursive realm of selective population control; the former tends to discursively isolate the practice of female child-killing, whereas we try to restore the patriarchal dimension of female infanticide in the context of Rajput women's lives.

In Rajputization the violence on daughters is on a continuum with the systemic violence on all the women of the family. Rajput women can either be killed at birth (female infanticide); or wrenched from her surroundings by marriage into a geographically distant village (exogamy); she can be married into a higher social strata to further her father's social mobility (hypergamy); or ruthlessly dispensed with by marriage to a political ally or the enemy of the enemy for volatile political alliances (*saga* alliance politics); she becomes part of a household of many wives and concubines (Rajput polygamy); she is trained to take pride in, or be reconciled to, the fact that she has no rights over her sons and daughters; she lives her life under the constant threat of male violence and repudiation if she transgresses the rules of lineage purity imposed on her; she can ascend the funeral pyre of her dead husband *(sati)* or commit mass suicide in the event that her husband is defeated in battle *(jauhar)*. By situating daughter-killing on this continuum we find that the practice of female child-killing becomes intelligible as part of a network of practices. We learn that patriarchal violence toward Rajput women is not an aberration from the norm, nor is it an individual pathology; rather systemic violence is the norm in men's relations to women and in women's positioning in this patriarchal formation.

Lineage purity or Rajput *shaan* is a gendered elaboration of the rules of purity and pollution. For instance an upwardly mobile family that Sanskritizes itself will put the burden of the pure/impure on the female household, nevertheless Sanskritization often entails certain restrictions on the men of the family, like vegetarianism or religious pilgrimages or endowments to religious institutions or male patronage of one member of the family who is allowed to do cultural or religious work. Conversely in the case of Rajputization the lifestyle adopted by men is free of any imputations of pollution and any need for purity; for instance it is demanded of men who Rajputize themselves that they imbibe alcohol, meat, opium, patronize the services of prostitutes and dancing girls and retain mistresses, worship the sword and use force in every dispute concerning lineage purity. Thus the onus of lineage purity or *shaan* is not on men, for Rajput men and their actions are absolved of any imputation of pollution or need for purity. Instead purity and pollution prohibitions are externalized and objectified in women.

It is precisely this absolute gender division in the code of purity and pollution in Rajput *shaan* that endows lineage purity with arbitrariness. Rajput *shaan* is not only defined by men for women, it encompasses any set of restrictions chosen by the father, brother, kinsmen, or the marital family. The men can manipulate the meaning of Rajput *shaan* in any way: for instance the Rajput father can marry his daughter to whoever is most suitable for furthering the family's political ambitions and recode it as his sacrifice for lineage pride; even a marriage that would seem to transgress the prohibitions of purity and pollution, like marrying his daughter to a lower-caste groom, or to a Muslim family, can be recoded in Rajput *shaan* as the invaluable opportunity for mothers and daughters to sacrifice themselves for lineage pride. Rajput daughters and wives are expected to internalize Rajput *shaan* so that they submit to it unquestioningly, and take pride in offering themselves for the sake of family mobility.[16] This feature of arbitrariness is a signal that in this patriarchal formation there is a supra-exploitation of daughters, therefore they are positioned in the pure/impure prohibitions in such a way that fathers and brothers can either overvalue her as the only person who can preserve lineage purity, or devalue her life at birth.

It is important to realize how the particular elaboration of purity and pollution in Rajput *shaan* contributes to social mobility. It is not as if there is a holy grail at the end of the road, where the Rajput family gains social and material rewards for keeping their women in seclusion. *The process itself constitutes a claim to social predominance in the community.* There is a social sanction for the Rajputized male's disciplining women if they transgress the rules of purity and pollution, not only by the Brahmanical method of punishment by making them an outcast, but also through direct physical violence. In many cases Rajput men appoint themselves custodians of the pure conduct of the women of their own family and that of other women, because they gain status by maintaining vigilance over the breaking of caste norms.

When a family Rajputizes itself and lets it be known through their conduct and lifestyle that there is a constant surveillance of the women of the household, then the family paves the way for policing the boundaries between pure and impure in the village as a whole. In his sociological study of a twentieth-century Rajput community in Khalapur in Agra district, John Hitchcock observed that the Rajput male "considers it to be a part of his duty as guardian of the social order to strike a member of the lower castes in order to teach him what to do" (1959, 13).[17] Two characteristics of Rajputization fuse in this bid for social and political power, the systemic violence on the women of the household facilitates the Rajput male's reliance on force to dominate the rest of the community, and the imposition of purity on women legitimates the Rajput male's public role as the guardian of ritual status. It is in this way that systemic violence on daughters is a structural necessity for social mobility rather than an individual pathology or an ancient system of population control.

The violence on women as a result of these prohibitions is considerably increased by the fact that Rajputization signifies a fluid channel of upward mobility. In practice this means that many of the newly Rajputized families forcibly estrange the women of their families from earlier family traditions of greater freedom and mobility. For instance, Surajit Sinha noted in his study of Rajputization in tribal central India that the village headman tried to Rajputize his family by ensuring that "the female inmates of his house could go out to any house in his own village, but would never go as far as the weekly market" (1962, 55). He also found that recent claimants to Rajput status imitated the Rajput architecture for female seclusion "enclosed household compounds where the arenas of the womenfolk were sufficiently excluded from access to outsiders" (1962, 54). The customs affording greater freedom to tribal women—like unrestricted movement, group dancing by women, marriage by elopement and widow remarriage—were demarcated as pollution. Thus, lineage purity puts a greater burden on the women of a newly Rajputized community, alienating them from earlier traditions.

British Anti-Muslim Analysis of Rajput Hypergamy: The Jhareja Rajput Fable of Origins of Female Infanticide in Kathiawar

The Jhareja Rajputs of Gujarat recounted a fable to the English officer Colonel James Walker to explain why marriage customs cause the practice of female infanticide in their community (Kaye 1853, 552). In the Jhareja fable a king who could not find a fitting husband for his exceptionally beautiful daughter, consulted his priest and on his advice put his daughter to death in order to avoid the social disgrace of an unmarried daughter living in her natal home. Thus began the Jhareja custom of female infanticide.

British reformers interpreted such fables and explanations offered by nineteenth-century infanticidal fathers to mean, first, that rigid and arcane marriage customs are the cause of female infanticide; second, that the infanticidal father is a passive and helpless prisoner of social mores; and third, that state intervention in limiting marriage expenditure is the solution to the problem of female infanticide.[18] In the passage below James Tod describes marriage reform as the axe that would cut the root of the problem of female infanticide:

> the laws which regulate marriage amongst the Rajpoots powerfully promote infanticide. . . . Were bonds taken from all the feudal chiefs, and a penal clause inserted, of forfeiture of their fief by all who exceeded a fixed nuptial expenditure, the axe would be laid to the root, the evil would be checked, and the heart of many a mother (and we may add father) be gladdened, by preserving at once the point of honour and their child. (1829, I, 505–506)

Tod's use of the root metaphor for marriage expenses was to echo in official documents concerning female infanticide. In 1887 in the North Western Provinces R. T. Hobart, the Inspector General of Police writing to the Chief Secretary to the Governement of the Province calls prejudice and the blind adherence to custom of expensive marriages "the root cause of the evil (of female infanticide)," which cannot be reformed easily (*North Western Provinces and Oudh Police Proceedings* 1887, file no. 25, serial no. 12). In 1853, Governor General of India, Lord Dalhousie called caste and marriage expenses as, "both (are) the causes of infanticide" (Minute By Dalhousie, 8 August, 1853, *Board's Collection* vol. 2564, no. 151171).

Tod assumes that the infanticidal father welcomes the benevolent intervention of the colonial state in marriage reform, the father's heart would be "gladdened, by preserving at once the point of honor and their child." In terms of the text of the Jhareja fable, Tod's analysis implies that the father in the fable is an overfond father who loves his daughter excessively. The British in India disseminated this view of the infanticidal father as an overfond parent; the colonial myth of the impoverished Rajput father who "would throw away his birthright to celeberate a marriage" (Elliot, 1870) reinforced the sympathetic portrait of the child killer; that myth persisted despite the fact that the father in the Jhareja fable, and in Tod's passage, are wealthy kings or propertied Rajputs, and despite the fact that poor Rajputs neither committed female infanticide nor celebrated expensive marriages for their daughters in nineteenth-century India.

It is possible that the English in India were aware that the tree, to borrow Tod's metaphor for the interconnections between marriage customs and female infanticide, was not in a state of decay but had been flourishing in Rajput political culture for a long time. Indeed a comic pantomime was played out between English officers and landholding Rajput men: the former asks, "Why do you commit the heinous and unnatural crime of killing your own daughters?" and the latter throws up his hands, looks sorrowful and says, "Sir we cannot find a suitable groom for our daughters." The native informants expand on their answer by saying, like the father in the Jhareja fable, that their customs forbid them from considering most of the eligible young men as their potential son-in-law.

In the indigenous protocols of such conversations, the rhetorical purpose of the native informants is to suggest, "If you are so concerned about our daughters why don't you marry them?" Rajputs had good reasons for expecting an affirmative answer to the implied question. For several centuries they had negotiated with the dominant political power in north India by contracting such marriage alliances. In the feudal network of reciprocal duties and obligations between the king/overlord and his feudatories, daughters were treated as the father's property that can, if needed, become part of the exchange between the feudatory and the king. This is the tenor of Thapar's observation that the Rajput father "might also be called upon to give his daughter in marriage to the king" (1966, 242). It is noteworthy that Thapar refers to the feudatory giving his daughter in marriage to the overlord, not giving his son in marriage to the overlord's daughter. Hypergamy functions as an exchange that primarily furthers the interests of the bride's father. The feudal overlord benefits to an extent because such marital alliances bring his feudatories closer to him in ties of loyalty. The bride's father has the most to gain because he can stake a claim on the chieftain as a relative and he can build on that claim with military service, with the additional profit of securing prestigious and lucrative posts for his kinsmen.

English officers did not understand the Rajput's implied question or pretended not to understand it. It was an inconvenient question for the Englishman, the early phase of interracial marriages between Company officials and Indian women was long past. It was social and professional suicide for Company officers to marry an Indian woman, although the company treated the practice of keeping male or female mistresses as a regrettable necessity for their boys away from home. Srinivas makes an acute observation about the relationship between British colonialism and hypergamy, "The establishment of Pax Britannica resulted in freezing the political system and blocked this avenue to mobility" (1966, 32). [19] In other words the British empire's prohibition on interracial marriages and its unwillingness to contract marriage alliances with indigenous rulers froze this mode of upward mobility, although the ceiling imposed by the British colonial power did not prevent hypergamy from occurring at other levels of Indian society.[20]

The Englishman did not openly say no to the native, because he did not want to dash the native's hopes for political collaboration to the ground. The British officer said yes to collaboration and no to the means of collaboration through marriage.[21] He also took the opportunity to distance the East India Company from the assimilative policies of the former rulers of North India, the Mughals, by denigrating the Mughal practice of marrying Rajput daughters. One such encounter took place in 1814 between Sir Charles Metcalfe, British Resident at Delhi, and an elderly Indian official of the Jodhpur state. The extract below is an example of how conversations between the colonizer and the colonized resulted in the official explanation about the connections between female infanticide and hypergamous marriages between the Mughals and Rajput daughters:

> It was first proposed to the Rajpoot Rajahs to form a connexion with the imperial family by taking in marriage imperial princesses; but this proposal was rejected, as such a communication would have polluted the blood of the Rajahs' families, and would have been an utter abomination for ever; they were glad to effect their escape from so alarming a danger by sacrificing their own daughters, who were considered as dead from the time of their connexion with the emperors. After the ice had been broken by the formation of a connexion of this kind, it came to be considered a custom, and ceased to be objectionable. A connection with the emperors was thought desirable for political purposes; and the rivalship of the Rajahs of Jyepore and Joudpore made both occasionally press forward with their daughters, each being jealous when such a connexion was formed by the other. Nevertheless, the daughters were considered dead and gone, though their posthumous influence was an object of desire to their fathers. (Kaye 1858, I, 416–417)

Metcalfe's written report is a classic text of Orientalism because it mixes half truths with anti-Muslim propaganda and conveys what he has learned from the Jodhpur official through the lens of empire-building. Metcalfe is right in noting that there was a connection between Rajputs' hypergamous marriages and female infanticide. He is also perceptive in noting that the infanticidal Rajput family in nineteenth-century India had an absolute gender division concerning the marriage laws that applied to sons and daughters. Rajput men did not want "to form a connexion with the imperial [Mughal] family by taking in marriage imperial princesses" but preferred "sacrificing their own daughters." Metcalfe accurately suggests that such marriages were primarily political in purpose because "a connexion with the emperors was thought desirable for political purposes"; elite Rajput families competed for this political prize because, like the father in the Jhareja fable, the greatest political advantage of hypergamy was secured by the girl's father, consequently this political "influence was an object of desire to their fathers."

The damaging half-truths in Metcalfe's report are first, that hypergamy originated with Rajput-Mughal marriages, "it came to be considered a custom, and ceased to be objectionable." Second, Metcalfe makes the erroneous diagnosis that gender division in Rajput hypergamy, the use of daughters and not sons for profitable marriage alliances, was motivated by the threat that a Muslim son-in-law "polluted the blood of the Rajahs' families, and would have been utter abomination forever." The term "polluted" signifies the hiatus between the indigenous idiom of purity and pollution and the colonial misreading of the idiom as racialist. In Metcalfe's account the chief metaphor for racial assimilation in medieval India—the marriages between Mughal rulers and Rajput princesses—is pathologized as a mutation of female infanticide. Instead of examining the patriarchal violence common to hypergamy and female infanticide, the bad faith in Metcalfe's account lies in using a crime against women for purveying racialist theories of blood pollution.

Resistance to Lineage Purity by Women and by the Community

In JTKO one of the cultural misrecognitions between Sleeman and his Indian companion is the latter's frequent references to the notion of pollution. Bukhtawar Sing denigrates the infanticidal Oudh Rajputs as stained, "there is hardly a family among these proud Rajputs, unstained by such connexions" (1858, 170). Sleeman realizes that his native informant is deploying an idiom of purity and staining, however he misrecognizes it as an idiom denoting race pride. The Englishman fails to understand that Bukhtawar Sing is rhetorically countering the Rajput claims of ritual purity with the notion that the practice of female infanticide has stained them. Both Bukhtawar Sing and the Shahjenapur priests who meet Sleeman on his tour, refute Rajput claims of purity, by asserting in their own turn that the killing of female children irrevocably pollutes or stains the Rajput clan.

In conversation with Sleeman Bukhtawar Sing elaborates one of the ways in which noninfanticidal families and communities discredit the purity/pollution taboos of Rajput *shaan* or lineage purity. He describes the ritual purity gained by *kanyadaan* (the giving away of the daughter in marriage) in these words:

> Sir, we brahmins and other respectable Hindoos feel honored in having daughters; and never feel secure of a happy life hereafter, till we see them respectably married . . . and then, and not till then, do they [the parents of

the daughter] feel, that they have done their duty to their child. What can
men and women, who murder their daughters, as soon as they are born, ever
hope for in this life or in a future state? (1858, 286–287)

The traditional concept of *kanyadaan* is a powerful rhetorical maneuver
drawn from the daughter-affirming strands in the religious vocabulary of
Hindu sects.[22] *Kanyadaan* cannot be oversimplified into the patriarchal prescription concerning the marriage of daughters, for it symbolizes a network
of practices relating to the daughter's material, affective and religious status
in the natal family. It is less about marriage and more about parental, broth-
erly as well as maternal uncle's duty and commitment to daughters, as
Bukhtawar Sing puts it, "their duty to their child." *Kanyadaan* is less about
parents earning religious merit by marrying off their daughters, and more
about sacralizing the female child in such a way as to ensure her survival. The
religious notion of earning entry into heaven functions to motivate fathers
and grandfathers to feel duty-bound and act affectionately toward female
children. When Bukhtawar Sing states that the daughter-killing father is
denied this mode of ritual purity, he is pointing to a powerful mode of dissent by noninfanticidal Hindu communities. This is a mode of dissent from
within religion, not outside religion, and this mode of dissent relocates self-
purification in the preservation of daughters.

The evidence of women's resistance to lineage purity lies in the cultural
texts of folklore and Meera's songs. Women's anger and disillusionment about
the gender division, within which Rajput women carry the burden of purity
and pollution and Rajput men are free of that burden, is preserved and reen-
acted in the women's folklore of Rajasthan compiled by Vijayan Detha (1997).
These folk narratives have to be read not as the naive text of a simple and
unlettered consciousness, but as the distillation of generations of women's
conversations with each other, their laughter, anger and bitterness, and their
lived knowledge of Rajputization.

Unlike the protagonists of other Indian folktales, the female characters
in Detha's collection are not presented in the folk conventions of the virtuous
woman, the trickster, the magician, or the resourceful strategist. The heroines
in the Detha anthology have a common characteristic, they are thinking and
reasoning beings on an ethical quest. The central figures in Detha's collection
are drawn from all classes—a moneylender's daughter, a queen, a cowherd's
wife, a potter's wife, and a gypsy—and that means that the ethical quest is not
a classed activity in these tales. Most of these women do not have the leisure
or social sanction for contemplation and renunciation, consequently they are
an aberration from the folktales concerning the male quest for enlightenment.
These female questers ask and answer their own questions while fulfilling a
heavy load of work everyday, while giving birth to children and sometimes los-

ing them, while being turned out of doors by their natal or married family and moving from a state of prosperity to destitution.[23] As women the ethical quest is not a tranquil exercize for them, everything that they hold dear is at risk, and the material conditions of their everyday life depends on the answers to their questions.

The ethical quest of these folkloric heroines continually gestures to the practices of daughter devaluation and female infanticide. It is not as if other aspects of a woman's life are unimportant, rather women's songs and folktales gesture to a psychosocial truth about women's experience of self-proximity under conditions of domination. For example, in one story the heroine faces a crisis in her married life, she makes a crucial decision about her life by reflecting on her devaluation in her natal home, "A daughter's growth is as unwelcome to her parents' eyes as the accumulation of dust in the house"; she describes her own status as an unwanted child, "Her mother's womb had given her a place but there was no place for her in that house" (1997, 156). The psychosocial truth in this episode of the tale is that when the adult woman encounters patriarchal oppression, her thoughts arc back to that originary moment of devaluation in her childhood, almost as if that originary moment of alienation explains her suffering to herself.

In another story the folkloric heroine articulates women's point of view concerning the pure/impure prohibitions in Rajputization:

> Unless she scrubbed, washed and polished these rotting, decaying norms, she would find it difficult to breathe and live. Yet how could this accumulated filth and rust be removed and a new shine created? By imitating the ways of men? By keeping pure the ways of women? But how long must women keep filling the tilted scales of purity? How long must they alone bear this burden? (Detha, "Double Standards" 1997, 52).

The passage affords us a glimpse of what it was like for Rajput women to be subjected to the conditions of lineage purity, many of them "find it difficult to breathe and live." The purity-seeking Rajput society is named as polluted in the phrase "these rotting, decaying norms" and "this accumulated filth and rust." The folktale draws on popular common sense to unmask lineage purity as the the ideology of men who conceal the rot within themselves and the patriarchal order they inhabit. Drawing on the language of common sense, the folktale states that it is Rajput women who "scrubbed, washed and polished" the pollution caused by men, while elite Rajput men cause pollution through their actions. In the folkloric imagination men put the burden of purity and pollution on women, not because there is an inherent taint in the female sex, but because men are socially gendered into worshipping the forces of violence, hatred, ambition, and greed for wealth.

The queen who utters these thoughts in the folktale does not confine her critique to naming men as the polluters of society. She questions the central premise of Rajputization, namely that women bear the responsibility of the clan's purity. She calls this responsibility a "burden" and mocks the double standards of women "filling the tilted scales of purity." In the folktale there is no doubt in the queen's mind that the "rotten, decaying norms" must be destroyed. The passage moves from an image of unbearable confinement, the Rajput woman unable to live and breathe, to an image of female resistance. The problem occurs when female resistance has to be theorized in the context of extreme devaluation of women. The queen is aware that in thinking about resistance in the trope of washing, scrubbing, polishing, and creating a new shine, she continues to adhere to the idiom of purity and pollution even as she rails against its Rajputized version.

In "Double Standards" the queen suggests that one of the ways female resistance can be accomplished is by manipulating or "imitating the ways of men." The relation between this mode of resistance and the pure/impure prescriptions in Rajputization is explored in another folktale in Detha's collection, "The Crow's Way," a tale that ends in the heroine deliberately and defiantly adopting the ways of men. "The Crow's Way" is a canny satire of Rajputization from the perspective of disaffected and alienated women. The satiric terminology of crows and swans allows the tale to decode the purity/pollution taboos in Rajputization as motivated by "self-interest" in opposition to the interests of the family or the community. The principle of pollution is described as the crows' eating of carrion in the Thar desert, "The air began to rot with the spreading stench" (90) and renaming themselves proudly "We are the swans of Thar" (91). The references to the Thar desert of Rajasthan signify the marginalization of the autochtonous tribes of Rajasthan by the Rajputs who came and settled in the province, and the crows' renaming themselves as the swans of Thar indicate that the tale is satirizing Rajputization. The principle of purity is embodied in the swans who eat pebbles and produce pearls and live at the shores of the Mansoravar lake where "the pure waters rippled in the lap of the Himalaya" (90), a barely concealed personification of the Vedic scriptures.

The two principles are described in the tale as antithetical to each other. The crows are "not pleased" by the swans' lake because they crave the pollution of their homeland where there is "the silence, the empty wastes and the corpses" and the pleasure of devouring animals that are dying from the famine "the helpless animals, their bleeding wounds and entangled entrails" (90). The swans are repelled by the crow's way, "the swans began to feel suffocated by the stench" and they interpret the crow's way as the denial of ecoconservation "Not a sign of a plant anywhere" (91).

The drama properly begins with the entry of the female protagonist who must choose between purity and pollution, the swan's way or the crow's way. She is a rich trader's daughter-in-law *(sethani)*, her natural inclination is to believe in purity and she nurtures the purity-symbolizing swans. Despite the fact that she adheres to all the social norms, the heroine is bewildered by the turn of events that shift her from a devoted wife and daughter-in-law who represents the purity of the family, to the polluted outcast who is turned out of doors by her married family. It is at this point in the tale that she turns into the female quester, for she must understand why she has been excluded from the realm of purity and accused of pollution.

In her journey the heroine of "The Crow's Way" learns about the social dimensions of purity and pollution by encountering both kinds of traditions of daughter-cherishing and daughter devaluation in Rajasthan. When she is turned out of doors from her marital home, she discovers a potter woman who craves the affection of a daughter even though she has seven grown-up sons. In north Indian folktales seven sons is a magicalized number that denotes son-preference. Seven sons are considered a blessing for the patriarchal family. Seven sons or seven brothers also constitute ideal female desire in the popular idioms of north India, because these male children are the guarantee of security for the mother and the sister.

The satire in "The Crow's Way" begins to make sense when we understand the folkloric convention of seven sons. The tale reverses readerly expectations by making the potter woman, who should have been fulfilled and cherished by her seven male children, articulate her desire for a daughter. The character of the potter woman is a vehicle for exploring the daughter-cherishing traditions and communities among the poor people of Rajasthan. The text explains what a daughter means to the women of a noninfanticidal family:

> Three years ago the potter had died. He had fathered seven sons. All of them were married and although the house was filled with their children, it seemed empty without a daughter. Now, the coming of a daughter enriched the house. The mother's joy knew no bounds. As if youth had once again bloomed in her quaking body. (1997, 101)

In these words the folktale puts its finger on an intergenerational knowledge passed down between women, namely that a woman finds the birth and nurture of a daughter her only experience of self-nurturing. Nancy Chowdorow refers to the paradox of woman as the nurturer who is herself never nurtured (1978). In "The Crow's Way" we are asked to imagine an old woman who has spent her life in child-bearing, and lives amidst her married sons who take care of her and the grandchildren who love her, and yet she craves the affection of a daughter. The text makes it clear that the potter woman's wish to have a daughter is not a product of narcissism, for the grown-up woman she shelters is not her daughter by birth.

The folkloric name for this mother-daughter bond is "joy" and the filling of the empty house, "it seemed empty without a daughter." The daughter's place in the family is compared to wealth, "the coming of a daughter enriched the house." The text goes further and suggests that this enriching joy is experienced by the widowed mother as a second youth, as a bloom that comes over "her quaking body." This is an idiom one encounters again and again in the cultural texts of north India, which describe daughter-cherishing families or communities. In this idiom the value of one or several daughters is not defined in terms of exchange, or material-economic terms of prosperity, or as the harbinger of purity. In daughter-cherishing families or communities the female child is magicalized as the source of the psychic-emotional well being of the family, the house is empty without her. The parents experience themselves, not merely as providers in their parent-function, but as the loved subjects with the daughter. Folklore suggests that the daughter has an inherent value, she is valued not for her actions and duties, in herself she is self-delighting for the family.

The heroine of "The Crow's Way" learns this when she steps out of her class, but in order to fully understand her own predicament she has to return to her own class. She encounters the practice of daughter devaluation when, as a destitute married woman, she seeks shelter in her natal home and is not allowed to enter. Her mother repudiates her with these words, "I wish I had given birth to a stone instead of you" (1997, 109). The mother in the folktale uses proverbs that are traditionally associated with female infanticide in north Indian languages, she says, "If you had the least shame and modesty left, you would go and drown yourself in a handful of water" *(agar tumhe jara bhi sharam hoti to chullu bhar paani mein doob marti)*. It is only a little child who can drown in a handful or a pail of water. The proverb refers to one of the methods of killing the newborn female child, the infant was taken away from the birthing mother, and the female members of the household executed the Rajput father's wishes by drowning the newborn child in a basin of water.

It is only after the heroine has lost all her illusions, after she loses everything and tries everything, that she can listen to the prostitute Lakhu, and practice the crow's way taught by her. The text calls Lakhu's teachings "a new Gita," which is a provocative way of reminding the reader that the tale is in dialogue with Sanskritization and Rajputization. In the excerpt below we hear a tone in Lakhu's voice that is different from the tone of the thoughts expressed by the queen in the earlier excerpt. While the queen utters her despair, her idealism, and her readiness for revolt, Lakhu's insights into the pure/impure prohibitions of elite Rajput society stem from a fully alienated and detached perspective:

> Though our life stories are no different from each other's, they appear different to us. All the women in this world have but one life story—they are

robbed by men and bear the consequences of that robbery throughout their lives. No woman is untouched by this experience. But the illusions of home and family prevent them from understanding this truth.

Daughter, all religion, devotion, philanthrophy, meditation, non-violence, ritual, customs, traditions and norms are false illusions. If anything is true, it is the crow's way. Self-interest is the most important thing. . . . When one comes here one must forget the rotten norms of the family. . . . No relations of caste or community, kith or kin, father or son, brother or nephew are acknowledged here. . . . For these men there are no limits and restrictions. These forms of male grossness are our source of wealth. Don't show disgust at such things. Accept them as your wealth. (1997, 110–115)

Lakhu speaks of the end of narrative, a vanishing point in which the tale itself will disappear.[24] She advises the heroine that women's life stories "appear different" in the veil of patriarchal ideology, which she calls "the illusions of home and family." The end of narrative proper occurs when woman as storyteller and listener realize that, "All the women in this world have but one life story." Yet Lakhu's stern words are uttered in the feminine space of the brothel. The brothel is the place in the folktale where women narrate their stories and women are also the audience for those stories. The heroine says to Lakhu, "Till I tell you the story behind these tears my heart will not be lightened" (107). Lakhu is incurious, even bored of women's life stories, "I have heard so many sob stories that I really can't bear them any more" (107). Nevertheless Lakhu permits the storytelling, "Anyway, if you like, you can tell me the story when you come back here" (107). She accords a strict protocol for the telling and hearing of women's stories once, inscribing the brothel as a space where female narratives are recorded "the clerk records all the details in a register" (110).

The telos of the heroine's ethical quest lies in this death of oral storytelling, where it is both recorded in a written form and recognized as "one life story." This death constitutes the condition of the ethical. Lakhu's ethical position is to fully accept, internalize and manipulate the pollution of rich men. She recognizes that the taboos of purity and pollution do not apply to elite Rajput men, "For these men there are no limits or restrictions." She describes the brothel as the socially sanctioned site where the taboos concerning food and marriage are exposed and subverted, "No relations of caste or community . . . are acknowledged here." Lakhu's diagnosis of the pure/impure restrictions is in opposition to the queen's desire to scrub and clean these patriarchal norms until there are no double standards for men and women, Lakhu does not hope for change.

Nor does she agree with the heroine of "The Crow's Way" who believes that all her suffering stems from the pollution-causing crows of Thar desert.

Lakhu blames neither the double standards of society nor the Rajputs, instead she points to the primary organization of patriarchal society within which women are the fundamental mode of exchange between men; she rejects the exchange function of women in the family and adopts the exchange value of the brothel, "When one comes here one must forget the rotten norms of the family." In Lakhu's view the exchange of women in the brothel is far more profitable for women, she exhorts the heroine to discard her former reactions of "disgust" toward polluting activities and regard "male grossness" as her source of wealth.

The tale ends with Lakhu's final lesson concerning a social prohibition that is anterior to, and more fundamental to, the social organization of Rajput society than the purity/impurity restrictions, namely the incest taboo. Claude Levi-Strauss's structural-linguistic analysis of kinship leads him to the notion that, "the basic unit of kinship, as we have defined it, is actually a direct result of the universal presence of an incest taboo" (1963, 46). In Levi-Strauss's view the incest taboo is universal in all patriarchal societies because it insures "the circulation of women in the group" and this circulation constitutes the most basic form of exchange in patriarchal societies because women "are circulated between clans, lineages or families" (61). The folkloric text is canny when it makes Lakhu speak against the incest taboo, "No relations of . . . kith or kin, father or son, brother or nephew are acknowledged here." When the heroine's son visits the brothel as a client, she passes the test of Lakhu's teaching. She says, "I have no faith in any relations now" (116), meaning that she has repudiated the purity/impurity prohibitions for women by embracing the final self-pollution, the rejection of the basic unit of kinship between mother and son.

These folktales demonstrate that absolute gender domination in Rajputization can generate profoundly radical modes of resistance. The question posed by the queen in the folktale "Double Standards" has dogged the cultural history of the women of Rajasthan: should women resist by "imitating the ways of men" or should women resist by asserting the principle of difference and "keeping pure the ways of women." The former alternative was adopted by the Rajput princesses and queens who masculinized themselves and adopted the Rajput cult of violence, as well as by the fictional character of Lakhu and the trader's daughter-in-law. The latter alternative is one to which we turn our attention, the modes of resistance practiced in the heterogenous anti-violence, woman-centered, and ecoconservationist traditions, histories, and communities of Rajasthan.

Dissenting Rajput women often represented themselves, not as outside the prohibitions of purity, but as naming them alternatively. It is precisely because of this flexibility that, as Srinivas notes, every Indian language contains terms for the concepts of purity and pollution and "each of these terms has a certain amount of semantic stretch enabling it to move from one meaning to another as the context requires" (1969, 120). Rajput women named themselves as the purifying, nurturing life-force that not only give birth to children but create a family through love instead of destroying the family through hatred. They named themselves as pacifist in opposition to the Rajput emphasis on violence, as the principle that demolishes interclan violence through the ethics of pacifism, creativity, and ecoconservation, as the sturdy life-force that survives after the depredations of internecine Rajput warfare.

Denial of lineage purity was also effected by the aggressive suggestion, made by female dissenters, that in itself purity does not represent a positive, nor does pollution represent a negative. Thapar speaks of upward mobility gained through the denial of the importance of ritual status. "Social mobility therefore" Thapar states, "did not necessarily mean a change in the actual status of a caste, but perhaps more often the attempt to improve the ritual status or else to deny its importance" (1978, 129). For example, a lower-caste man whose hereditary occupation was regarded as polluting could join the Buddhist orders and disavow the Brahmanical ranking of his social status. Thapar's phrase "or else to deny its importance" implies intriguing possibilities for women's resistance. For instance, a man or woman can deliberately and ritually undertake self-pollution in order to achieve spiritual enlightenment, or Tantric power over self and others.

It is in this sense that dissenting Rajput women defied the pure/impure prescriptions by shifting their forms of worship away from the Rajput religion of the sword, in favor of local deities or local versions of Krishna worship or woman-centered worship of the goddess Durga.[25] The medieval poet Meera (the subject of chapters 6 and 7) is a powerful site of female dissent. She upsets the purity/pollution distinctions of Rajputization by mocking all the marks of Rajput women's purity-seclusion, never being seen in public without *purdah* or the veil, answering to the name of the natal or marital clan, the adornment of jewelry and finery appropriate to an elite Rajput wife, unquestioning obedience to the Rajput male, living for husband and the marital family. Meera's songs play with the concepts of pure and impure by referring repeatedly and obsessively to her deliberate and ritualized self-pollution. Traditionally female modesty or *laaj* is an invocation of women's need to inhabit ritual purity and women's tendency to ritual pollution. Meera's songs poetically enact the rejection of *laaj* as the act of a woman throwing away the veil. Her songs repeat, mockingly reiterate, the reproaches leveled at her for causing familial-social pollution.

For the sake of all other women the songs enact Meera's repudiation of the rules of pure and impure female conduct, rules that are laid down by her parents and her husband and sister-in-law.[26] Some of Meera's rituals of self-pollution consist of publicly dancing before her god with anklets on her feet, of running out of the house and roaming the streets, of eating and praying with lower-caste men and women, and treating a ritually unclean tanner as her spiritual guru. Thus, Meera relocates female purity in the jouissance that is only possible after this self-pollution—namely through the self-purification of love, the ecstasy of pain or *dard divani* (Mishra, 15) and pain in love or *prem divani* (Bhati 1964, 71).

Social Mobility through Daughters' Marriages: Hypergamy as the Other Face of Female Infanticide

We examine the logic of the violence in the Jhareja fable, a logic in which two seemingly incommensurable valuations of women are held together. In the fable the Jhareja daughter is both overvalued as too good for any groom and devalued as not good enough to live. Official histories and empirical disciplines do not help us to write this cultural history of women, it is only by treating the Jhareja fable as our central text that we may be able to uncover how the social form of hypergamous marriages constitutes the other face of female infanticide.

The point of contention between British and indigenous explanations is whether elite men in a traditional society are the prisoners of social customs or the active and successful makers of marriage customs. In the Jhareja fable the patriarchal father is an active agent who decides that there is no fitting groom for his daughter; he also decides that the alternative of an unmarried daughter is unsuited to his rank and prestige; he chooses to consult his priest and follow the priest's advice, he exercises his power as father and king to put his adult daughter to death. The fable shows clearly that infanticidal fathers manipulate the various customs for daughters' marriages, they are not bound by rigid and inflexible customs but construct their own rules.

In our interpretation of the Jhareja fable the father's decision to search far and wide for a suitable groom, as well as his dissatisfaction with the kind of men who were ready to marry his daughter, constitutes a coded allusion to the practice of hypergamy within the idiom of Rajputization. The father's decision has very little to do with the daughter's merits or beauty, the traditional phrase used in the fable "There is no one good enough for my daughter" signifies the upwardly mobile father who is really saying that there is no one good enough to be his son-in-law. The practice of hypergamy or marrying daughters to bridegrooms of superior status or wealth or higher caste, was particularly associated with the idiom of Rajputization. Srinivas describes how the marriage custom of hypergamy became a mode of upward mobility for the father of the girl:

> The giving of girls in marriage to boys from a higher caste or higher section of the same caste added to the prestige of the wife-giving lineage and caste.

> In some cases it also enabled the lower group to claim, eventually, equality with the higher group. Hypergamy was significant for mobility in yet another way. A caste or section of a caste would Sanskritise its way of life and then claim to be superior to its structural neighbors or to the parent section. (1966, 30)

Note the ways in which Srinivas's analysis, in the passage above, differs from Tod. The latter had characterized Rajput marriage customs as an old and decaying tree that must be cut down by the British. In contradistinction Srinivas shows that hypergamy is not a meaningless and static custom, it is a resilient and successful way through which the girl's father, in Srinivas's phrase "the wife giving lineage or caste" gains social prestige and ascends higher in the social rank. Srinivas's analysis accords well with the history of the Jhareja Rajputs, they were expatriate Rajputs in Gujarat who had engaged in intermarriage with the Muslim rulers in Kutch and who, on moving to Kathiawar continued to marry their illegitimate daughters to Muslims, now wanted to increase their political power by marrying their daughters into Rajput clans that were richer and more powerful than them.

Historically the parent custom, from which hypergamy emerged as a social innovation, was exogamy or contracting daughters' marriages outside the immediate neighborhood or village or clan. Srinivas locates exogamy as a central tenet of the idiom of social mobility, which he calls Sanskritisation.[27] Tod explains Rajput exogamy as promoting female infanticide by causing a paucity of eligible grooms for daughters:

> Not only is intermarriage prohibited between families of the same clan, but between those of the same tribe(gote); and though centuries may have intervened since their separation, and branches thus transplanted may have lost their original patronymic, they can never be regrafted on the original stem . . . the Seesodia is yet brother to the Aharya, and regards every female of the race as his sister. Every tribe has therefore to look abroad, to a race distinct from its own, for suitors for the females. (1829, I, 505)

Tod's metaphor for marriage customs as a tree allows him to characterize exogamy as transplanting, "branches thus transplanted have lost their original patronymic, they can never be regrafted on the original stem." In Tod's view the explanation for exogamy is the incest taboo, daughters cannot be married into their natal clan or even the breakaway clan because the primary relationship is of brother and sister.

In our view the logic of exogamy in Sanskritization and Rajputization has much more to do with the systemic severance and denial of daughters' blood relationship to her natal family. It is women who have to live far away from their natal village and visit their parents' home only on ritually prescribed occasions in the year, while sons enjoy the privilege of growing up with and living with the people they have always known.[28] Thus sons' blood relationship with their natal family takes precedence over women's blood relationship with their natal family as well as with their marital family. Exogamy facilitates violence on the married daughter, the strongest safeguard for a woman against the violence of her marital family is to stay close to her natal family and participate in the family life.

Kinship structures contributed in no small measure to the political feasibility of Rajput hypergamy and exogamy. The Rajput clan confers a group identity on individual members, but the clan is not so much a collectivity of cohesive economic-political interests as an internally competitive and contentious group of equals. A girl's marriage within the clan benefits her most, she lives among people she knows best and she strengthens the ties of affection and protection that are forged in her natal home. However, such a marriage among equals has little or no value in advancing the political interests of the bride's father, because his clan members are already his natural allies in war.

Male elites' labor in the Rajput community—waging war for self advancement, supplying a labor pool of common soldiers, hiring themselves out as mercenaries, receiving gifts of land grants in return for their military victories—was an insufficient, volatile, and impermanent power base. Srinivas notes that Rajputization and Kshatrization as a mode of upward mobility thrived in times of political fluidity:

> A potent source of social mobility in pre-British India was the fluidity of the political system. . . . In order to capture political power, however, a caste or its local section had to have a martial tradition, numerical strength, and preferably also ownership of a large quantity of arable land. Once it had captured political power it had to Sanskritise its ritual and style of life and lay claim to being Kshatriya. (1966, 32)

An essential element of Rajputization is the evolution of the Rajput style of gaining political power through hypergamy. The disjunction between the idealized function and nature of Rajput states on the one hand, and the actual practices in Rajput state formation on the other hand, is exacerbated in the case of the infanticidal community's relationship to political power. The political ideal in this idiom is the taking up of arms to defend the people, and the assumption of kingly duties in order to protect the unprotected and rule with justice and equity.

The discontinuities between Kshatriya ideals and actual Rajput practice occurs right here. The claim to be the legitimate ruler of a kingdom in pre-British India was, more often than not, backed up by socially sanctioned aggressive behavior and the adoption of the code of violence rather than a commitment to righteous and just rule. Historians like Thapar do not follow official history's model of continuous evolution of the Rajputs through glorious military campaigns; instead Thapar shows that Rajputs did particularly well in times of great political unstability, whenever land grabbing intensified due to a lack of centralized authority in north India (1978, 154). Rajput political strategies for land-grabbing through war, alliances, and legitimating genealogies became one of the most successful style of politics in pre-British India.

The political history of medieval Rajasthan contains ample evidence that the mode of upward mobility called Rajputization was precarious if it was anchored in warfare alone. The fact of the matter is that political power and land can be captured by violence, legitimated by hiring priests and bards to compose genealogies. However, political power cannot be consolidated by these means alone. This is where the British explanation breaks down. The British suggested that these elite groups spread far and wide in northwest India and carved out a power base simply on the strength of their famed military skills. History indicates otherwise. These groups needed a political style of making alliances, negotiations and collaborations with the dominant power as well as with lesser kingdoms and their political equals.

Rajput alliance politics are unlike the politically expedient marital alliances that were a regular feature of European royalty in two ways: Rajput alliance politics are marked, not by stable and enduring political ties, but by the constant making and unmaking of alliances through betrayals, internecine feuds, competing and oubidding and fresh negotiations.[29] Rajputs needed a type of alliance with rivals or friendly states or the superior political power that would be eminently suited to an unstable political climate where alliances are made and unmade, friendships are followed by betrayals and power can only be enjoyed by outnumbering one's enemies with one's allies. In other words the alliance must be consolidated by an exchange, which quickly cements the relationship between the men of both clans, while also ensuring that there are no damaging consequences to breaking the alliance by forming a new one or by waging war against the erstwhile ally.

This is the second way in which Rajput hypergamy differs from the marital alliances of European royalty, namely Rajput daughters were exclusively chosen to execute this style of alliance politics.[30] Hypergamy was the Rajput answer to their political problems, to their hopes for upward mobility and to their obsession with land accumulation. Elite Rajputs turned to their daughters to fill the lacunae in their political practice, they forged a style of political alliance, which gave fathers, brothers, and male kinsmen maximum advantage, maximum maneuverability, and minimum risk. Daughters were used as pawns to strengthen negotiations with political allies, or to win a favored political status with the foreign colonial power, or to maneuver with the new players in north Indian politics, or secure an alliance with the enemy of the enemy. Rajput daughters' marriages became feudal spectacle through extravagant marriage ceremonies, not because fathers were overfond of their daughters, but rather because extravagant marriage ceremonies served as an index of the father's material status and daughters' marriages were political occasions for inviting and consulting with allies.

It is a mark of how far we still have to go discursively and theoretically for a women's history that this significant fact would never have been apparent from reading official history or sociology. While Srinivas's analysis is hospitable to gender analysis of hypergamy, for instance he notes that it is the "wife-giving" family that increases its prestige, he does not analyze the consequences on women of being married into a family that is superior in caste and wealth to her natal family. Neither does Thapar analyze the gender distinction in the feudatory giving his daughter in marriage to the overlord, not his son in marriage to the overlord's daughter or female relatives (1966, 242). The reason is that even for Srinivas and Thapar the gendered violence of exogamy and hypergamy seems to be the natural order of things.

Indigenous accounts of the Rajput history of marriage alliances, particularly the history of Rajput-Muslim interactions, are markedly different from the British explanation. The historical chronicles of Marwar by indigenous bards provides ample proof that political alliances through hypergamous marriages were a regular feature of medieval Rajput politics long before the Mughals ruled over north India. Moreover the chronicle of elite Rajput marriages by these bards shows that there was a vigorous history of Rajput-Muslim interactions at the social, cultural, political, and literary level, and Rajput-Muslim intermarriages were a standard feature of Rajput society.

While Srinivas and Thapar gloss over the gender distinctions in Rajput hypergamy, the only group that recorded the evidence of the gendered violence in Rajput hypergamy are the indigenous bards of Rajasthan. Bardic literature makes a clear gender distinction between the two terms *saga* and *bhaiyyad* in Rajput society.[31] The term *saga* denotes alliances contracted through daughters' marriages while the latter term *bhaiyyad* denotes male kinsmen through the male bloodline. A Rajput's *bhaiyyad* or male relatives and kinsmen cannot be discarded and must always be respected, however *saga* alliances are expedient and profitable for the natal family.

From the time Rajputs emerged as players in medieval north Indian politics, *saga* alliance politics dominates Rajasthan history.[32] *Saga* alliance politics constitutes gendered violence on daughters, for in an unstable and fluid political scenario the use of daughters is more efficient than the use of sons. Sons cannot be used with the same efficiency in Rajput alliance politics, not only because sons are infinitely more precious than daughters and must not be jeopardized for political gambling, but also because the son's relatives by marriage form a more permanent bond and therefore *sambhandi* alliances through sons' marriages must be made more cautiously. Therefore no restrictions apply to sons' marriages, they can marry across class and caste lines and bestow their caste on their children, or they can adopt a child, or recognize their illegitimate sons as their heirs. Daughters' marriages are quite another thing, the daughter bore the burden of the Rajput claim to racial purity, and the prohibitions on daughter's marriage means that she must be married into an upper-caste or upper-class family.

The daughter's benefits are uncertain in her husband's polygamous household as she competes with other women for her husband's benevolence. In fact such marriages were exceptionally precarious for the married daughter; if the political alliance went well she could expect to be treated well in her married home; however if the political alliance broke down and turned into enmity she had no means of claiming protection from her natal family. Fathers and brothers contracted such marriages for the daughters in the full knowledge that if the political alliance and mutual benefit between the men of both families ended, their daughter was dispensable. Postcolonial films decode hypergamy by exposing the myth that daughters benefit from such alliances (*beti raj karegi* or the daughter will rule like a queen over a rich household).

The autobiographical writings of a twentieth-century elite Rajput, Thakur Amar Singh of Kanota in Rajasthan, which were written between 1898 and 1942, indicate how the political influence of the bride's father accumulates over generations of *saga* alliances. Amar Singh describes how hypergamy helps a girl's father to arrange politically favorable and inexpensive marriages based on his reputation alone, "At present the people [who take our girls] don't ask money [in dowry] of us because we are influential, but we cannot continue so forever" (1942, Rudolph 2002, 362). The symbolic power of *sasur-samdhi* alliances lay principally in the power of reputation—one possesses the power as long as it is not used or overused.

We argue that *saga* alliance politics contradicts the following stereotypes: a married Rajput daughter has no role to play in her natal family; Rajput women are a wasteful and unproductive consumer of property; indulgent and adoring Rajput fathers and brothers expect nothing from their daughters and sisters except the preservation of family honor; a proud and self-respecting Rajput will not even drink water at his daughter's married home *(beti ke yahan to pani bhi peena mana hai)*.

Thus the Jhareja fable is a text that reveals that hypergamy is the other face of female infanticide. The term hypergamy is a euphemism for the most ruthless harnessing of daughters to the father's political project. Hypergamy coexists with female infanticide because the logic is the same in the Jhareja fable, killing daughters because fathers decide that they are valueless and preserving daughters because fathers decide how to maximally exploit their marriages.

Both customs constitute gendered violence against daughters, the latter is premised on the notion that daughters are of no use to a family and are a threat to family prosperity, and the former is premised on the notion of maximum use of the daughter by marrying her into a family whose wealth and status is greater than the natal family.

Postcolonial Perpetrators of Femicide
Draw on the Idiom of Rajputization

In postcolonial India a considerable number of the men and women who commit violence against their daughters explain their actions by drawing on the idiom of Rajputization. In Manjira Datta's film on femicide *Rishte* (see chapter 1 for a detailed analysis of the film) the paternal grandfather of the dead female children deploys the idiom of Rajputization to explain why men force their wives and daughters in law to undergo ultrasound and abort the female fetus. Mr. Goel tells the interviewer that the reason for daughter deval-uation and femicide is that a man wishes to leave his ancestral property to his son, principally because daughters break up ancestral property and take their portion with them to their marital family.

Most of the film viewers we spoke to had a visceral response to the grandfather's interview, viewers rejected what he had to say as sexism. We argue that the umbrella term of sexism is insufficient for building a feminist rhetoric against the grandfather's argument; it is necessary to recognize and counter the logic of Rajputization articulated by Mr. Goel, a logic within which the patriarchal necessity for preserving family property is conjoined to an upper-class idiom for property accumulation through violence on the birthing mother and daughters. It is through the internalization of this logic that men and women rationalize son-preference and femicide.

In *Rishte* the father of the dead daughters, Gopal Goel's aspirations for upward mobility are evident in the way he self-consciously arranges compositions before the camera, riding his scooter or walking hand-in-hand with his daugh-ters or looking at the wedding album with his second wife in the drawing room. Gopal sits and talks in a self-consciously modern manner, in order to distinguish himself from his father who sits in the traditional manner on his haunches, smokes a *bidi* and wears simple clothes. Datta's film constructs a visual contrast between the grandfather and the father, bringing home the fact that Gopal is an upwardly mobile postcolonial man who does not contest his father's belief in property accumulation and daughter devaluation, while at the same time Gopal wishes to distinguish his clothes, manner, and speech from his father.

One of the distinctive features of the idiom of Rajputization is its inven-tiveness in ideologies of self-legitimation and self-invention. Gopal reinvents himself before the camera. For instance, Gopal speaks openly to the interviewer of his rebellion against his father, even though his alleged "rebellion" does not mean that he has no use for his father's property. He also speaks in the same breath of his self-invention as a modern man who contracts a love marriage with his second wife. In effect Gopal has constructed a socially acceptable narrative in which the violence visited on his first wife is caused by the fact that it was a "traditional" marriage according to his father's wishes, and his second marriage is constructed not as a bid for sons but rather as a "love marriage."

Gopal offers several narratives of his social aspirations. These are Rajputized narratives because they justify the violence on his first wife and his daughters. Gopal's devices for self-legitimation consist of blaming his first wife for their inability to have sons, and also blaming her for feeling depressed and committing suicide. The cult of violence in Rajputization facilitated and sanctioned violence on the female household, and the Goel men draw on this idiom when they speak about Lalli and her daughters. In Sanskritization violence on women is justified with reference to shastric texts, while in Rajputization violence on women is justified with reference to the family's property and political ambitions. Like most perpetrators of femicide in postcolonial India, the Goel men continually situate the discussion of unwanted daughters and cherished sons in the context of family prosperity, wealth, and land.

We have argued in this chapter that the deployment of the idiom of Rajputization is a signal for a family's *political* ambitions. This is in marked contrast to the idiom of Sanskritization in postcolonial India within which there is a more generalized aspiration to social preeminence through religious and cultural activities; these activities signal a family's ambition to be thought of as rich, a patron of the arts and of education; the Sanskritized family introduces new intradining taboos concerning who they invite to their home for dinner, in order to be known as well connected and exclusive; the Sanskritized family also wishes it to be known that they possess the means for higher ritual status through marriages for their sons and daughters, which bring in cultural capital or dowry into the family. Srinivas' acute insight is that, in postcolonial India, an upwardly mobile family's Sanskritization is often accompanied by Westernization (1966). Oftentimes the positive result of this fusion of two styles of familial emancipation is that in a family where there are no sons, the daughters are treated as sons, and made into full partners in the production unit of the family. Or a family in which one or more daughters display academic potential, business acumen or talent, the family encourages, supports, and invests in the daughter in order to advance the ritual and cultural status of the family.

It is only in the idiom of Rajputization that families connect political ambition, property, and violence on daughters. Gopal Goel discusses femicide while also telling the interviewer that he has several shops and plans to enroll himself as a candidate in the local elections. His remarks suggest that the deaths of his wife and two daughters are not caused by his inability to financially support his daughters or marry them, but are related to his upwardly mobile plans for a political career on the basis of his several properties. The infanticidal father's property-based political ambitions, and the corollary notion that daughters are destructive of the father's political ambitions, is a hallmark of Rajputization. Unlike the idiom of Sanskritization where a woman's education is often represented as the cultural capital of the family, Gopal has no use for his first wife's educated status, his stated criteria for his second wife is that she should please him. In fact Gopal's statements before the camera imply that now that his first wife has rid him of two burdensome daughters, he is free to invest his money in the local elections. Gopal's father goes one step further in elaborating the idiom of Rajputization, he says that Lalli's suicide pact with her two daughters was a way to rid the family of the burdensome dowries of two daughters.

Journalists and activists have been puzzled by the fact that communities and groups that have no traditions of female infanticide adopt the practice of femicide. In her study of femicide in Uslimapatti taluk in Madurai district, Vaasanti notes that the reason given for killing female children is the dowries for their marriage, and that dowry is a new word adopted by the community as part of their imitation of the higher caste groups (*The Hindu* November 20, 1994). We suggest that Vaasanti describes a social process of Rajputizing in terms of the little traditions rather than the great tradition. That is to say, it is of no consequence whether the infanticidal parents in Uslimapatti know the word Rajput or Rajputization, for the arguments they advance display their awareness of the idiom. Every village or town does not follow a textual and institutionalized model of Sanskritization or Rajputization, instead each region adapts the idioms of social mobility to their own ethnic-cultural specificity.[33]

The fact that Rajputization is not the description of actual historical groups or social classes, but an idiom of social mobility through which diverse groups and castes ascend upwards in society, may go a long way toward explaining the enormous spread of the practice of femicide in postcolonial India. For the people of Uslimapatti, the substance of Rajputization is more important than the historical nomenclature of Rajputs. Femicide retains its connection with Rajputization through the notion that daughters are destructive of the family's upward mobility, therefore upward mobility and family prosperity is premised on reducing or eliminating the female claimants to family resources. The Rajputization of entire communities occurs when families who do not possess wealth explain their adoption of the practice of femicide as an imitation of upper caste and upper class norms. There is the added danger of the coming together of the idiom of Rajputization and the state sponsored discourse of family planning. Son-preference is recoded as the nationalist objective of a small family; and in this way family planning is made to fit the feudal-patriarchal idiom of Rajputization in which a number of sons are required to ensure the family's prosperity and future. In effect the discourse of nationalism rhetorically reinvigorates the discourses of social mobility and woman devaluation.

Examining the relation between social mobility and systemic violence on women is useful for several reasons. There is an inherent and natural impatience in the discourses of feminist activism: we are so appalled by the cruelty of killing newborn infants or the unborn fetus simply because they are female, that we are tempted to confine ourselves to a discussion of political agitation—to laws, legal punishments, speeches and slogans, statistics and horror stories. We call feminist activism a discourse as well as a practice, because we do not subscribe to the opposition between activism and scholarship. There is always an implicit discourse in the Indian women's movements and in their modes of agitation. Indeed theory and activism feed off each other and are put to crisis by each other. Women's scholarship on marriage and inheritance laws feeds into the anti-dowry agitations, conversely the insights of activists and grassroots workers problematizes accepted theory and sets new agendas for research. It is in this context that we suggest that the activist-agitational approach to modern femicide and traditional female infanticide is prey to political correctness unless it takes cognizance of the colonial construction of the race pride and racial contamination explanation for female infanticide on the one hand, and the idiom of upward mobility deployed by the men and women who commit female infanticide and femicide on the other. A feminist rhetoric against the practice of femicide must engage with the discontinuities as well as the continuities between the idioms of Rajputization on the one hand, and the discourse of population on the other, insofar as both discursively configure femicide.

CHAPTER 4

A Critical History of the Colonial Discourse of Infanticide Reform, 1800–1854

Part I: Infanticide Reform as an Extra-Economic Extraction of Surplus

Postcolonial scholars and subaltern historians have successfully established the truism that imperialism used the emancipation of women as an alibi for its conquest, and as the moral rationale of its civilizing mission.[1] In the context of the historiography of colonial reform by historians, it is a singular fact that British infanticide reform continues to be held in high regard by the few who have studied it (Wilson 1855; Pakrasi 1970; Panigrahi 1976; Vishwanath 2000). The chief problem that plagues history writing of British infanticide reform, like the book-length study by Lalita Panigrahi (1976) or the more recent one by L. S. Vishwanath (2000), is the impulse toward a linear account of British reform in terms of a steady progress toward successful abolition of female infanticide in colonial India. We argue that a critical account of British infanticide reform will fall prey to the progressivist fallacy unless it marshals the data in a nonlinear, region-specific narrative. While progressivist histories link the past to the present in terms of steady, cumulative progress, we assert a discontinuous, conflictual, fragmented, nonprogressivist account that marks the discursive erasure of the girl-child and the erosion of her rights under the twin discourses of economism (chapter 4) and population control (chapter 5).

We choose British infanticide reform in Kathiawar for detailed study principally because British administrators and the Jhareja Rajputs of Kathiawar used women and female infanticide to negotiate a revenue arrangement. This linking of revenue and reform earned high acclaim among British reformers and made Kathiawar reform central to the official colonial historiographical narrative concerning infanticide reform (Wilson 1855; Cave Brown 1857; Pakrasi 1970; Panigrahi 1976; Vishwanath 2000). Our focus in the history of infanticide reform is on the discursive yoking of women/daughters and value, in terms of the colonialist-economistic approach to female infanticide and postcolonial femicide.[2]

Throughout the history of British reform efforts in Kathiawar the Jharejas continued to commit murder with impunity, and British officials continued

101

to proclaim and write about their success in letters, dispatches, reports, minutes; contradictorily they also reluctantly acknowledged the failure of their reform. In 1837 Political Agent Erskine characterizes female infant murder in terms of "a domestic misdeed of the Jharejas" thus minimizing the nature of the crime (J. Erskine to Secretary Bombay Government 30 June 1837, *Parliamentary Papers* No. 613 [1843]). In 1840 Political Agent LeGrand Jacob writes: "I can trace eye-service to Government, but no real service to humanity, in the profession of such of the community [of the Jharejas] as pretend to take any interest in the matter"; Jacob concludes that "all the Rajputs who rear their daughters feel a direct interest in the continuance of the crime by others" (L. G. Jacob to Willoughby 23 October 1841, *Papers Relating to the Practice of Infanticide in India 1834–42,* Prepared on the Orders of the House of Commons).[3] These statements offer proof of the fact that it was well known among colonial administrators that British infanticide reform was a failure.

Further proof that the British reform measures were an abysmal failure is furnished by the petition forwarded by six *bhaiyyads* (clans) of Kathiawar in 1836 arguing for leniency in the only case of conviction of Suraji, Chief of Rajkot. The petition stated, "the rich and powerful Jharejas will always be able to conceal their guilt while the rigorous system will tell only against those who have not the power to suppress evidence" (J. Erskine's Report, 30 June 1837, *Selections from Records of Bombay Government*). The Jharejas knew that the British did not have the conviction or the will to adequately carry out the suppression of female infanticide. The inclusion of the statement in the petition functions as a threat by the Jharejas, it reveals both their intention to continue to practice female infanticide as well as their ability to suppress evidence of the crime.

The issues that concern us in the officially documented British colonial history of reform is not simply the evaluation of infanticide reform as success or failure. The tasks that we set ourselves are threefold: the specific material and discursive productivity of infanticide reform; to understand what the colonial history of infanticide reform signifies in terms of women's history; finally, to comprehend the historical emergence of the colonialist-economistic approach to femicide in postcolonial India, which we have argued in chapter 1, is a generalized, powerful, and persuasive discourse in postcolonial India. This chapter circles, traverses, and selects incision points in the documented history of infanticide reform in nineteenth-century Kathiawar in order to understand how the Jhareja Rajput practice of using daughters as an extra-economic means for upward mobility and as pawns in negotiations with the dominant political power in north India (see chapter 3) comes together with British strategy of deploying women and reform as an extra-economic means of coercion/persuasion in the emergence of the colonialist-economistic discourse about female infanticide.

There is no contradiction in our naming the colonialist-economistic discourse a solution, a particular approach, and a discourse formation at various points in this book. The reasons for this are that the colonialist-economistic discourse is deployed both as a diagnosis, a mode of argument, and a solution in postcolonial India. This discourse emerges most clearly in Kathiawar infanticide reform, not (as one might expect) through the suppression of female infanticide, but in the coming together of disparate, contradictory, collusive, and resistant strategies, events, linguistic and legal transactions to form the discourse of economism around the issue of daughters/women. The British colonialist-economistic discourse regarding female infanticide could not have achieved the success it did without the *active participation* of the Jhareja Rajputs. Although the Jharejas continually resisted the imposition of punitive fines for the alleged crime of daughter-murder, they did not oppose or counter the colonial representation of female infanticide as a crime committed by the poor Rajput father who cannot afford to bring up his daughter and marry her according to his status. This representation had no basis in fact, historically propertied Rajputs committed female infanticide when they could not use daughters to further their political ambitions. The Jharejas also participated in the colonial construction of the daughter as valueless consumer rather than producer.

The Rajput-British construction of daughters as consumers depends and draws on the precolonial idiom of Rajputization. Rajputization is an idiom in which a group claiming to be Rajput considers it beneath their dignity to till the soil and engage in agricultural labor. The ideal concerning land in this idiom—the Kshatriya's trusteeship of land on behalf of the people—degenerates in actual practice into a claim on all cultivable land in the territory. Rajput history in north India affords ample evidence of the relationship between son-preference and the Rajput obsession with land accumulation; it is a history marked by constant internecine wars for land, an intergenerational obsession with land accumulation, the dispossession of tribals from their ancient homelands, and the extraction of surplus from the tillers of the soil.[4] The nineteenth-century Rajput-British construction of daughters as valueless consumers covers over two significant historical events in the disinheritance and colonization of Rajput daughters and women. The first historical event occurs when Rajput patriarchy forcibly disconnects their women from laboring on the land through the system of *purdah*, restricting women's productivity and deifying the secluded Rajput woman. The second historical event occurs when the Rajput woman, having been made unproductive through her enforced disconnection with land and labor, is reinserted into production by Rajput patriarchy for the purposes of primitive accumulation.[5]

The central premise of the idiom of Rajputization illuminates the logic of female infanticide; a family or clan rises steadily in political and economic power by ensuring that its property is not divided but accumulates over generations; sons and son-preference facilitates this accumulation, not because sons increase family property through their own deeds, but because they are male. Daughters emerge as a considerable threat to land ownership within this model of social mobility, the daughter's claim to a share in the property interferes with the right of the male heirs to receive the accumulated landed property. Daughters' claims to property must be denied at all costs because daughters are seen as inherently property-dissipating, while sons are seen as inherently property-conserving. Fragmentation of land between the descendants must also be avoided at all costs. Within the idiom of Rajputization daughters were portrayed as annihilators of the father's property and prosperity, unless the vigilant father murdered her at birth or exchanged her in hypergamous marriage to further his political and economic ambitions. Thus the precolonial construction of daughters as inherently property-dissipating in the idiom of Rajputization was overlaid by the colonial British construction of the daughter as consumer.

This is the prehistory of Kathiawar infanticide reform, the historical evolution of the idiom of Rajputization and the two historical events of Rajput women's dispossession within this idiom. It was not in the interest of the East India Company to challenge the indigenous form of primitive accumulation because they required the political and economic collaboration of the Jharejas for their own project of colonial-capitalist primitive accumulation.[6] We contend that colonial infanticide reform signified the political accommodation as well as the jockeying for power between the two forms of accumulation, the indigenous primitive accumulation by Jharejas and the colonial-capitalist primitive accumulation by the East India Company, both of which disenfranchised the daughters of infanticidal clans.[7]

In order to understand why the East India Company attaches infanticide reform to revenue, it is necessary to understand the pre-British history of Jhareja Rajput presence and dominance in Kathiawar. The Jhareja Rajput community was a relatively new settlement in Kathiawar; they were part of the invading tribes of Rajputs who came into Kathiawar via Kutch from Sind. The Kathiawar province was ruled by viceroys of the Mughal Emperors (1572–1705) until the Marathas entered Gujarat and supplanted the imperial Mughal power.[8] The Marathas were never able to fully establish their control and dominance over the rebellious Jhareja Rajputs. The uneasy state of truce between the Jharejas and Marathas was often broken by the former. These political events determined the specific form of tribute arrangements between the Kathiawar Jharejas and the Marathas. When the Marathas collected their annual tribute, they sent a revenue collecting army *(mulkgiri)* to enforce revenue collection. Punitive measures like burning the crops were carried out to punish those Jharejas who reneged on tribute payments.[9] Among the Jharejas there existed the mode of production that Samir Amin characterizes as the tribute-paying mode of agricultural production.[10] The Jharejas were not landlords in the pattern of European feudalism, they were socially and economically organized in terms of extended clans with a complicated system of communal proprietorship of the land by the entire clan; thus, for instance, the chiefs were selected through a combination of election and inherited power; the clan system of social organization meant that the entire Jhareja clan was collectively responsible for paying the tribute.[11]

The Jharejas were recent settlers in the Kathiawar region; they were a self-governing group; historically they had displayed a nominal acceptance of the Maratha right to extract tribute; all these factors play an important role in the East India Company's policies for establishing effective control and rule over the Jharejas.[12] In 1807 the East India Company forces entered Kathiawar, ostensibly to assist the Gaekwar's army in tribute collection. In return the Company secured one-third partnership in the tribute, while two-thirds of the tribute was shared between the Gaekwar, and his overlord, the Peshwa.[13] In the first year of tribute collection itself (1807–1808) the British Resident at Baroda, Alexander Walker, executed a permanent revenue settlement with the Jhareja Rajput chiefs.[14] With characteristic rapacity the Company acquired the tributary rights of the Peshwa in Kathiawar (the 1818 Satara Proclamation), and in 1820 the Gaekwar was forced to concede to the Company forces the collection of his share of the tribute.

In Kathiawar the British do not prove their supremacy by fighting a war, nor do they inherit a stable system of tribute collection from the Maratha guerrillas. The fixed settlement of revenue in the Kathiawar region differs in important respects from the Permanent Settlement in Bengal, Bihar, and Orissa, although there is an analogical relationship between the history writing at the site of the Permanent Settlement and the historiographical narrative about Kathiawar reform.[15] Revenue collection in the colony by the East India Company cannot be understood in functional terms purely as a trading-military-administrative activity, it involved discursive and historiographical enterprises. The subaltern historian Ranajit Guha (1982) has shown how the East India Company's accession to *diwani* in 1765 was not enough to establish their right to rule and collect revenue. Guha argues that in order to understand the intricacies of proprietorship in these provinces within the relations of power that had accumulated over time, the British undertook the function of the historian. Guha characterizes nineteenth-century British scholarship in these terms:

> it investigated, recorded and wrote up the Indian past in a vast corpus which, worked by many hands during the seventy years between Mill's *History of British India* (1812) and Hunter's *Indian Empire* (1881), came to constitute an entirely new kind of knowledge. (1982, 211)

Guha shows how the Indian past was mobilized in order to serve the political ends of the colonizers. Local histories were written to determine inheritance along the lines of descent in the class of landed proprietors in Bengal, Bihar, and Orissa. According to Guha, the skills of nineteenth-century British scholarship were harnessed to the project of reinforcing the British empire's apparatus of ideological control once the empire was secure in its control of the wealth of the land. Thus colonialist historiography was executed under the exigencies of British administrative needs.

Earlier we said that there is an analogical relationship between history writing at the site of the Permanent Settlement and the discursive apparatus harnessed for transformation of tribute in Kathiawar to the revenue system. In Kathiawar the discourse of infanticide reform was grafted on coercive revenue-collection carried out by a small unit of East India Company forces.[16] The grafting of infanticide reform onto revenue was enormously productive for British administrators in the absence of an established right to rule; infanticide reform gave the East India Company the appearance of legitimacy as the civilizing, morally superior power. The British entered Kathiawar as bullies of the extortionist Gaekwar of Baroda whose right to extract tribute was contested by Jhareja Rajputs in 1807. Faced with the prospect of the combined forces of the Gaekwar and the Company, Jhareja chiefs were not conquered but cowed down into signing revenue settlements within which tribute was renamed revenue and this revenue was fixed for perpetuity.

The British entered Kathiawar as mercenaries and tribute collectors and stayed as revenue extractors and reformers. The British Resident at Baroda, Alexander Walker, played mediator and friend to both the Gaekwar (reinforcing his right to extract tribute) and Jhareja chiefs (offering them peace instead of war at the cost of a revenue arrangement). The price Walker had to pay for Jhareja compliance was a fixed revenue settlement that provided limited opportunity to the rapacious Company. Thus for instance in 1808 Walker collected Rupees 51, 95, 550 or 51 lakhs, 95 thousand 550 Rupees as revenue from Kathiawar of which Rupees 9,97,880 was paid as tribute; in 1880 the total revenues of Kathiawar amounted to Rupees 1, 65, 50, 310 or 1 crore, 65 lakhs, 50 thousand 310 Rupees while the tribute only amounted to Rupees 10, 77, 570. This means that while the revenues of the region had more than tripled in approximately 70 years, the sums paid in tribute by the Jhareja Rajput chiefs of Kathiawar had remained more or less stationary.[17] The problem that engaged Walker, given that the Company had taken over the tribute collection from the Gaekwar, was to determine the theoretical principle on which the East India Company could assert their superior right to revenue, and what would serve as the channel for surplus revenue that Walker could promise the Company.

Walker discovered the means for political legitimation and expanded the limited opportunity for surplus revenue by appending the infanticide provision in the revenue settlements. The grafting of the infanticide provision to revenue collection constituted an agreement made exclusively between the Jhareja chiefs and the Company. The Gaekwar, on whose behalf Walker was acting as mediator, vanished from the negotiations at the precise point when this new revenue document, which Walker calls "infanticide engagements," was signed between Jhareja chiefs and the Company (Report of A. Walker 15 March 1808, *Hindoo Widows* 2, part 2). Walker discovered in the infanticide engagements the perfect extra-economic, extra-legal coercive-persuasive leverage over Jhareja Rajput chiefs. In the tradition of nineteenth-century colonial historiography, John Wilson underlines the Company's bid for power through infanticide reform; the colonial historian suggests that Walker, the architect of this strategy, would not have been successful in infanticide reform unless the Company made a "conquest of the country" (Wilson 1855, 74). Thus a historiographical narrative emerged within which revenue and infanticide reform were inextricably yoked together.

The text of Walker's first successful infanticide engagement in 1808 with the Gondul Jharejas deserves detailed examination. Walker uses a spurious religious vocabulary culled from the Hindu scriptures and the Koran to condemn the "heinous sin" of child murder. For our purposes it is the sentence appended at the end of the document that highlights the new discursive formation. The 1808 document states:

> that we [Gondul Jharejas] shall from this day acknowledge ourselves offenders against the Sirkars. Moreover, should anyone in future commit that offense . . . he shall be punished according to the pleasure of the two Governments. (Report of A. Walker 15 March 1808, *Parliamentary Papers* No. 426, 1824)

The phraseology of these sentences is indicative of the specific colonial relation between reform and revenue in Kathiawar. Walker induced the Gondul Jharejas to sign an arrangement in the first person, thus disguising the coercion in the confessional first person singular in phrases like, "we shall from this day acknowledge." The confession is interesting in itself, the Jharejas ostensibly disavow the practice of female infanticide, in reality however the Jharejas commit themselves as "offenders" or subjects of a "Sirkar" or Government that does not yet exist. To cover over the glaring absence of a governmental apparatus in Kathiawar, the text refers to two governments, the nonexistent East India Company Government in Kathiawar and the weakened and contested authority of the Gaekwar. In this way Walker provides legitimacy to the Company's claim to revenue by *borrowing* legality from the Gaekwar.

The text of this document was used by the Company from 1808 to 1834; however, in 1834 the new Political Agent J. P. Willoughby rewrote the text of the engagement. The timing of the revision, as well as the particular alterations in the wording of the document are noteworthy. The 1830s mark the heyday of infanticide reform in its coercive phase; it is precisely in this period of imperial confidence that Willoughby renames the coercive treaty as voluntary engagements, which were "unconditionally entered into with the Government twenty-five years ago" (J. P. Willoughby to C. Norris, Chief Secretary to Bombay Government, 24 September 1834, *Selections from the Records of Bombay Government* op. cit.). Thus between signing of the first engagement in 1808 to the new engagement in 1834, the central text of reform represents the Company as the sole Government and the Jhareja chiefs as voluntary and willing subjects of this government. The imposition of the colonizers' will leaves its mark in the gaps between the first draft and the revised document.

The writings of Company officials show that the yoking of reform and revenue was an emergent and uneasy discourse rather than a fully consolidated discourse. The exigencies of colonial conquest and administration are best characterized by LeGrand Jacob, the Political Agent of Kathiawar in 1841 as "A handful of Englishmen, scattered over a territory as large as Europe" (L. G. Jacob to Secretary to Government Willoughby, 22 March 1842, *Parliamentary Papers* No. 613, 1843). In the early years of the East India Company's takeover of the Kathiawar region, British colonial enterprise was forged through rough-and-ready measures—the seizing of local opportunities, a plethora of expedient and local measures taken by officials in the field—that were later ratified or rejected by the Company's Board of Directors.

The correspondence between Jonathan Duncan, Governor of Bombay Presidency, and the "Supreme Government of India" indicates how officials at the highest rung of the ladder articulated the rationale for infanticide reform in Kathiawar:

> to avoid the necessity for the ever-recurring and coercive progress, by inducing the dependent local rulers in Kathiawad, chiefly through an appeal to their own interests, to accede to an equitable permanent accommodation, ascertaining the amount of their future pecuniary acknowledgments, without the concurrence of force for their realization. Toward the attainment of these salutary ends, it was deemed expedient that one general circuit should be made through the peninsula assisted by the appearance of a detachment from the British subsidiary force; and it was thought a duty of humanity to aim also, on this occasion, at the suppression of female Infanticide. (Letter of Jonathan Duncan, Governor of Bombay to Supreme Government of India, 15 May 1806, *Parliamentary Papers* No. 426, 1824)

In this letter Duncan presents his "hands-on" knowledge of the rebellious Rajputs and the necessity of extracting yearly revenue from them through coercive means. Duncan offers the Company the viable strategy of appealing to the Jharejas' "own interests" in agreeing to an "equitable permanent accommodation" of revenue and promising them an integrated system of revenue extraction by the use of "one general circuit." Duncan's administrative jargon cannot cover over the extortionist extra-legal presence of the East India Company in Kathiawar, nor does Duncan conceal the fact that the British extract revenue by a show of the "British subsidiary force."

The colonial administrator's will to power is displayed in the statement about attaching female infanticide reform to revenue extortion. Attaching reform to revenue extraction endows the Company's demands with the appearance of governmental legality. Legal power was a vexed issue in the Company's history in Kathiawar, the issue of legality was raised by Mountstuart Elphinstone, the Governor of Bombay in 1820. In a dispatch to the Political Agent of Kathiawar, Elphinstone says, "It may also be doubted how far we have a right to interfere to such an extraordinary pitch with the private life of a people with whose civil government and internal police we do not pretend to have any concern" (Minute of M. Elphinstone to Political Agent of Kathiawar Barnewall, 28 March 1821, Kaye [1853] rept. 1966, 561–562). This statement conveys a certain unease concerning reform. Reform is described as the "right to interfere to such an extraordinary pitch with the private life of a people." In characterizing reform as the right to interfere, in effect Elphinstone makes reform discursively proximate to the company's right to extract revenue. The Elphinstone statement gestures at the crux of the colonial dilemma. The East India Company's primary concern was colonialist capitalist accumulation through coercion. However, a handful of Englishmen could not keep the majority of natives in a permanent state of fear, especially the rebellious and warlike Rajputs. Therefore, the Company forged the apparatus of persuasion, backed by the appearance of humanitarian principles, and the *larger* aim of capitalist utilitarian enterprise (the greatest good for the greatest number). While Company officials continued to name female infanticide a *private* crime, their aim was to garner *public* opinion and consent for their own ends.

The East India Company's letter in response to Duncan's proposal regarding revenue collection and suppression of female infanticide is worth quoting in detail:

> We cannot but contemplate with approbation the considerations of humanity which have induced you to combine with the proposed expedition, the project of suppressing the barbarous custom of female Infanticide. But the speculative success even of that benevolent project, cannot be considered to justify the prosecution of measures which may expose to hazard the essential interests of the state; although as a collateral object, the pursuit of it would

be worthy of the benevolence and humanity of the British Government. (Governor General in Council to Bombay Government 31 July 1806, *Parliamentary Papers* No. 426, 1824)

Duncan had proposed to the Company that infanticide reform could be a strategy for essaying the appearance of legality and garnering consensus while the British *tukri* (small military unit) collected revenue through coercive force. The Company's letter reveals the language in which British policy makers articulated the relation between revenue and reform. The significant phrase in the letter "essential interests of the state" refers to the Company's accumulation, which cannot be jeopardized by the "speculative success" of infanticide reform. Therefore the letter suggests that female infanticide reform should be the "collateral object" to revenue collection. In practice this meant that each alleged occurrence of female infanticide should be deployed as a means of extorting more revenue under the guise of punitive fines. The letter suggests that this extortion should be characterized as the pursuit "worthy of the benevolence and humanity of the British Government." This benevolent reformist measure of fines is distinguished from reform through prosecution of other kinds of measures, which would "expose to hazard the essential interests of the state." The British policy statement encapsulates the administrative rhetoric and reasoning by which the colonialist-economistic discourse about female infanticide was forged.

The colonial notion that daughter-killing can be eradicated by fines inscribed the link between economism and female infanticide. In Kathiawar the British diagnosed the cause of female infanticide as Jhareja greed and avarice.[18] Paradoxically the punitive measures imposed for the practice by the Company reformers consisted of individual fines, there is a bad faith in the colonial reasoning that a crime motivated by Jhareja greed can be eradicated by British greed. The individual nature of fines is significant, were the British to fine the entire clan or tribe for sanctioning the custom of daughter murder, the collective fines would resemble further taxation. It suited Company interests to assign individual blame, and describe this form of taxation as a fine for the breach of infanticide agreement with the Company.

The institutionalization of the economistic approach to female infanticide was effected by a reformist institution unique to Kathiawar, the Infanticide Fund. In 1825 the Infanticide Fund was established by the British from a fine imposed on the Raja of Gondul for the amount of Rupees 6000/-. This institution was prepared for by the accumulation of a large sum of money in fines, between 1821 and 1824 the British collect Rupees 40, 000/- from the Jharejas in revenue fines. At its very inception the institution mobilizes its funds for the military-economic interests of the Company: in 1825 Political Agent Barnewall informs the Company that the fund had been spent to cover military expenses incurred in putting down the Khuman insurgency in Gujarat (Letter of Barnewall to Chief Secretary Bombay Government, 7 June 1825, *Parliamentary Papers* No. 548, 1828). The stated objective of establishing the Infanticide Fund (to reward and help poor Jhareja fathers arrange the marriages of their daughters) is disparate from the actual practice of using the Fund to further the Company's political-military campaigns in Gujarat.[19]

The Jhareja Rajputs are not compliant partners of Walker's infanticide engagements. They negotiate—with the fact that the East India Company establishes effective control over the Gaekwar who was their direct overlord, and with the fact that the Company is the dominant political player in Kathiawar—by deploying their time-tested strategy for political alliances with the dominant political power. In chapter 3 we named this the idiom of upward mobility through hypergamous marriages. Here we elaborate on the Jhareja Rajput use of that idiom in infanticide reform. Within the tributary mode of production operative in the Jhareja clans, daughters were used as an extra-economic means for accumulation, protection against excessive taxation, and for making and cementing alliances with the dominant political power in the region.

In our view the Jhareja Rajputs make a historic misrecognition in the case of the British colonizers. Operating on the alliances they had made in Sind with the Mughal rulers in the past, the Jharejas perceived Walker's infanticide engagements as an invitation to form *saga* alliance. In the absence of such marital alliances, the Jharejas were willing to employ (to use the British term for infanticide survivors) the "preservation" of daughters in exchange for British promises against the levying of excessive taxation. For example, the Jhareja Chief of Murvi Jehaji sent a written promise to voluntarily renounce female infanticide, on the condition that Walker help him to repossess the lands seized by the Gaekwar.[20] Walker's reaction to the letter is illuminating, he describes Jehaji's request in these words:

> [I]discovered the selfish and mercenary motives, that attached the Jadejas to Infanticide. I preserved it [the letter] as a testimony which refuted their pretenses of the inviolability of the practice, as a custom of the caste; and destroyed every argument they attempted to found on principle. (Report on Infanticide in Kattywar, A. Walker 15 March 1798, *Selections from the Records of the Bombay Government* 1856)

This exchange shows that the infanticidal elite male decodes infanticide reform as a site of political negotiations about landed property and revenue payments, and that Company officials did not want infanticide reform to work in the Jhareja's interest. In Walker's view the letter Jehaji sends is a testimony of Jhareja criminality and greed. Walker's response to the Jhareja initiative brings home to the Jhareja chiefs the fundamental difference between the previous Mughal rulers who operated on the principle of assimilation, and the new conditions of coloniality under the East India Company. The Jhareja response to the new conditions was to refuse submission to the infanticide engagements, unless the British negotiated revenue abatements for them. Faced with the united refusal of the Jhareja chiefs, the British decided to break up the unity of the chiefs through the time-tested legal ploy of individual crime and responsibility. Thus, the Jam of Nowanugger was singled out and accused of an *infringement of the infanticide engagement* that he did not sign in the first place. The British did not punish the Jam for his alleged act of daughter-killing, instead the British intimidated the Jam with the threat of the British army, extracted a fine of 5,000 Rupees and made the Jam sign a fresh engagement with the Company on February 25, 1812. The fact of the matter was that the infanticide engagements were never meant for the criminal prosecution for the crime of female infanticide. Throughout the history of Kathiawar reform the infanticide engagements were used precisely for the purpose that Walker had designed them, the extraction of surplus wealth that the Company was not legally entitled to within the terms of the revenue settlement.

We foreground and textualize a minor incident at the margins of colonial history of infanticide reform in order to show how a discourse of economism emerges and comes into being in the very interstices of Jhareja-British negotiations and conflicts, and the push and shove between Englishmen and the indigenous elite male.[21] In this minor episode Jadeja Raydhanji was a particularly unappealing and minor actor in stage of history. He belonged to the Gracias community, which are an intermixture of Rajputs and tribal Bhils, and are traditionally perceived as a fierce and rebellious group, which captured land by force. Raydhanji appears in official history as a self-confessed reformed subject, however there is a prior text of the seizure and dispossession of his small landholding by the Company. His negotiations with Company reformers were dictated by his poverty, and his dispossession.

We retrieve this minor figure from the colonial document to illustrate the difficulty, indeed the sheer intransigence of the colonial documents available to us, to illuminate the cultural history of women. In this dry, laconic narrative by the Political Agent we are not afforded access to Raydhanji's two daughters, all we know is that they are represented by the father as infanticide survivors, as the alleged beneficiaries of Alexander Walker's accidental encounter with the father. This representation of the girl-child is made suspect by the fact that it is at two removes, the author of this pro-British representation Raydhanji, and Political Agent T. G. Gardiner, British Resident at Kutch, who writes down this oral representation and inserts the incident into the colonial history of infanticide reform. We give below the official 1823 account of the Raydhanji-Gardiner negotiations:

Jadeja Raydhanji, residing at the village of Dhamarka, who had some years since voluntarily preserved two of his female children, owing to the casual circumstances of meeting with Lieut. Col. Walker at Murvi. . . . Disappointed in obtaining any satisfactory arrangement in regard to some giras [mouthful inheritable rights to his lands] due to his family, which had been seized by the Government . . . this person and his family had been living at his village, on the produce of their own labor and exertions, but from a wish to preserve appearances, and to maintain his daughters suitably to their rank and birth, Raydhanji had incurred expenses, which obliged him at length to appear at Bhuj, and to apply to Mr. Gardiner's predecessor for relief, when temporary allowance of grain was given to him.

Having consumed this supply . . . Raydhanji came a second time to Bhuj with his daughters, alighted at the gates of the palace, soliciting support. The Jadeja chiefs being at Bhuj, Mr. Gardiner regretted that such a display . . . might have a bad effect on the minds of the Jadejas who would perhaps attribute his distress more to the circumstances of his helpless family, than to the unsatisfactory state in which the arrangements about his giras claim had been allowed to remain. To remove this feeling as soon as possible Mr. Gardiner directed the same allowance of food to be issued to him during his stay, as to other Jadejas in the habit of visiting Bhuj. (Report of Gardiner, 23 March 1823, Wilson 1855, 151)

The letter ends at this point and the colonial historian John Wilson provides a postscript to the Raydhanji case. Gardiner recommended that a donation be made for the purposes of performing the marriages of the two daughters of Raydhanji, to which the Court of Directors agreed and a sum of two thousand Rupees was given to Raydhanji. Subsequently it was learned by the Bombay Government that Raydhanji sold his elder daughter in marriage for 5, 000 koris to an 80-year old, blind and bed-ridden relation of the Rao of Kutch. As a preventive measure the Company officials deposited the sum of 1,000 Rupees, the share of the younger daughter, to be used for the purpose of her marriage.

The incident is a text of the many ways in which indigenous men like Raydhanji bartered, threatened, and embarrassed British administrators because both sides understood that infanticide reform was nothing more or less than a site of continuous political negotiations and accommodations. The incident encapsulates the misrecognition by Jhareja Rajputs regarding the possibility of the British marrying Jhareja daughters. Raydhanji's actions show that he wishes to contract a *saga* alliance with Gardiner's predecessor. Raydhanji is refused; instead he is given an allowance of grain. If Raydhanji had not appeared in Bhuj with his two daughters, even this grain would not have been available to him. Having secured something from the British through the public appearance of his two daughters, Raydhanji is motivated to try the same strategy a second time. In order to make a beneficial alliance with Gardiner Raydhanji is a decoder of the high-flown British rhetoric of reform, he decodes reformers' needs for an indigenous reformed subject who can be used to discipline others. Raydhanji has spent time to think through how he will make the case for a marital alliance with the Company officer. His story of a chance meeting with the legendary Alexander Walker at Murvi, which led to his "voluntarily" preserving two daughters is a patently sycophantic story of the reformed subject, and is designed to generate affect in Political Agent Gardiner. Gardiner is being nudged into perceiving Raydhanji as a Rajput father who has so completely converted to the principles of British infanticide reform that he empathizes with the colonial administrator's sensibilities and takes initiative in changing his clan's custom. Raydhanji uses the presence of the Jhareja chiefs at Bhuj to negotiate with Gardiner; he counts on the Jhareja chiefs' understanding his motivation for publicly parading his daughters. Raydhanji also counts on Gardiner's political embarrassment and the jeopardy of his negotiations with Jhareja chiefs.

We do not know, because Gardiner's report does not tell us the reasons for the Company's seizure of Raydhanji's lands. Land seizures are the prior text of coercion. In Raydhanji's case the prior text of land seizure is erased by the colonial document. The Company's takeover of his minor landholding would not have merited attention in the colonial document, and been consigned to the refuse heap of history. It is only when Raydhanji decodes, manipulates, and negotiates the rhetoric of reform that he is inserted into the official correspondence of the political agent and history by John Wilson. The Gardiner letter mentions that Raydhanji's lands were taken away from him because they were in an "unsatisfactory state." The phrase "unsatisfactory state" implies mismanagement of lands, and mismanagement of lands was an umbrella term used by the British and could be employed to imply a range of transgressions. We speculate that Raydhanji's lands were seized by the Company for either of two reasons: he was not willing to pay more revenue; alternately it was alleged that he practiced female infanticide. At any rate in the British administrative lexicon, a lapse in revenue payment could be usefully exchanged for allegations of female infanticide.

Feudal and colonial capitalist modes of exchange collide and accommodate each other in the Raydhanji-Gardiner interactions. Feudal exploitation of daughters is manifested in the fact that Raydhanji preserves two of his daughters in order to profit from them. The British Resident refuses the adequate exchange, that is marriage to both daughters in exchange for the return of his lands and a powerful and profitable alliance for Raydhanji. Instead the exchange rate set by Gardiner is to grant Raydhanji grain and 2,000 Rupees. The way is clear for Raydhanji to profit from both the colonial capitalist exchange as well as the earlier mode of feudal exchange. In effect British colonial reform has made Raydhanji's two daughters doubly profitable for him; he can petition the Company because daughters are expensive to maintain, and sell them off in marriage to the highest bidder, because colonial marriage reform was unconcerned about the fate of infanticide survivors. That Gardiner and his predecessor were well aware that Raydhanji wished to contract *saga* alliance with them is evident from the text; there is no other reason why they would otherwise compensate Raydhanji. Gardiner's subsequent actions also bear out our analysis; he makes it Company policy that grain be issued to "other Jadejas in the habit of visiting Bhuj." Gardiner's message is clear, the Company policy disallows marriage between the Englishmen and native women, therefore applying to him for the purpose of an alliance is futile, however the Company is willing to concede a pittance for the poor Rajput father of daughters.

The Raydhanji anecdote is a perfect exemplification of how collaboration between colonial administrators and the indigenous elite brought about the colonialist-economistic discourse around the issue of daughter/women. Grafting the Company's revenue extortion onto reform gave the British the perfect alibi for the economistic approach to daughter-killing. If the British had addressed the social issues that relate to female infant-murder, they would necessarily have had to fine the entire clan; the Jharejas could name the fine as further revenue extortion, and Jhareja rebellion could be premised on the Company's violation of the revenue settlement fixed for perpetuity. By personalizing the issue of female infanticide and making it a matter of individual responsibility and choice, the British set up a system in which they renege on their revenue agreements and gain the power to seize land.[22] British reform names the cause of female infanticide among Jhareja Rajputs as greed and avariciousness, and then uses Jhareja greed to negotiate monetary transactions with Jharejas (remissions of revenue to those who married their daughters, small amounts dispensed for preserving daughters and performing marriages of the daughters). It is through these processes that the British insert the female child into global colonial monetary exchange, and name her within the distortion of the colonialist-economistic discourse, while the not-yet subject Jhareja Rajputs are active and willing participants in this distortion. Henceforth, until the late 1980s we encounter the colonialist-economistic discourse regarding daughter rights.

Dowry as Monetized Exchange:
British Intervention in Indigenous Marriage Customs

It is in the nineteenth century that for the first time the colonial argument is made that family ruin is caused by exorbitant dowries for daughters. This argument constitutes the second link (the first link is revenue-related reform) in the colonialist construction of the economistic solution to female infanticide through marriage reform. We critique the economism in this argument; anti-dowry colonial reform assumes a narrowly restricted approach to the economic dimension of women's lives by ignoring the range of economic issues (women's inheritance rights, the social controls on women owning property, her participation in agricultural production, her household labor, the social opportunities for woman's economic self determination, a woman's right over her children) and focusing exclusively on the expense incurred for a daughter in terms of her dowry at marriage.

The tendency toward economism in British anti-dowry reform had far-reaching results. It disseminates an apolitical approach to female infanticide by overemphasizing a narrowly conceived economic determinant of women's devaluation, at the expense of the political, social, and cultural determinants. Economism substitutes a radical political critique of patriarchal formations with piecemeal reform of marriage customs. This apolitical and narrowly economic view of a daughter's value in terms of dowry tends to distort the cultural aspects of marriage customs. Colonial reform ignored the heterogeneity of marriage practices of infanticidal clans, which ranged from dowry marriages to brideprice and exchange marriages, and isolated one embedded practice in a culture—dowry marriages—without seeing dowry in relation to all the cultural practices that endow it with meaning in a society.

The consequences of an apolitical and distorted emphasis on dowry reform is evident in the enormous error that the British perpetuate, namely that infanticidal clans practice female infanticide because of the expense of dowry marriages for daughters. In the specific case of the Kathiawar Jhareja Rajputs, British reform was so off the mark that they ascribed dowry marriages to an infanticidal community that solely practiced brideprice. Nor was this ascription a result of cultural misrecognition or ignorance of an alien culture; text after text in the British administration provides damning proof that the British knew only too well that dowry was not the cause of female infanticide. The deliberate ideological inversion in the British reference to brideprice as dowry marriage in Kutch and Kathiawar is produced by the tendency in colonial capitalism to deform all feudal systems of human exchange. With repetition the colonial ideological inversion gains in strength and conviction, and becomes a self-sustaining argument about marriage reform. Even when there was no evidence in British data that marriage reform decreases the incidence of female infant killing, the yoked-together discourse is steadily more persuasive and self-sustaining.[23] The colonial discourse of dowry marriage reform became the most discursively successful and uncontested of the East India Company discourses of reform.

By misrepresenting a diversity of marriage customs as dowry marriage and by disseminating the notion that dowry is the root of all evil, colonial marriage reform monetizes the heterogeneous feudal exchanges between the families and clans of the bride and bridegroom. The colonial interpretation of dowry monetizes the complex exchanges that transpired between the two families of the bride and bridegroom. Without advocating the exploitative forms of feudal marriage systems, we nevertheless take the position that there were diverse and fluid forms of exchange that took place between the two families. The daughter could be gifted as exchange between the feudatory (the bride's father) and the feudal chief (her husband or father-in-law) in order to get greater political and economic advantage; the bride's family could secure upward mobility in return for cash and land; the exchange could enlarge the bride-giving family's sphere of political influence or win allies in war. By reducing these complex sets of exchanges to the money economy of dowry marriages, the colonial marriage reformers served to further disenfranchise the Rajput daughter who had already been removed from participation in all forms of production. The Rajput daughter was now only configured as a drain on the family's resources, without any advantage accruing to the bride's family. The reduction of all forms of daughter's marriages to dowry marriages does not inaugurate a public debate by British reformers about Rajput daughters' inheritance rights or her fair share of the family wealth as her dowry. Instead British reform reduces all daughters' marriages to dowry marriages only to propagate the abolition of dowry and thus further disinherit the Rajput daughter.

We offer a nonprogressivist, nonlinear account of marriage reform that begins at the end of Kathiawar marriage reform, in order to highlight the repetitions and discursive links that yoke female infanticide to marriage reform.[24] The first and most fully elaborated model of marriage reform as a panacea for female infanticide was implemented in the province of Kathiawar, Gujarat. British reformers insisted that female infanticide could be eradicated among the Jhareja clans by lowering marriage expenses. This insistence was erroneous because the predominant marriage custom for nineteenth-century Jhareja daughters was brideprice. The custom of brideprice meant that the marriage expenses were chiefly borne by the bridegroom's family; furthermore the father of the daughter was given cash as well as symbolic presents of a sword and horse by the bridegroom's family. None of the forms of daughter's marriage amongst Jhareja Rajput clans in Kutch and Kathiawar involved the giving of dowry by the father.

Native informants from the highest echelons of the Jhareja community informed the British that dowry was not part of the marriage customs of infanticidal clans in Kathiawar and Kutch. An official report relays the explanations offered by the head of the Jhareja clans in Kutch and Kathiawar, the Rao of Kutch, in which the native ruler explicitly and unambiguously points out that the rationale for daughters' marriages in his community was not dowry but the political advantages accruing to the bride's father:

He (Rao of Kutch) is ambitious that his tribe should ally itself in marriage with the numerous and high caste Rajput families of Jaudpur and Marwad. To this end he has broken off the custom of intermarrying with Muhammadans, which was formerly very prevalent among the Jadejas, stimulated, as he asserts, by the consideration that there are comparatively few great Muhammadan families, and therefore few advantages to be expected from their alliance . . .

An additional reason which might be supposed to act as check upon marriage, by deterring the Rajputs of the neighbouring countries from contracting alliances with Kachh, was the amount of the customary expenses always heavy among Rajputs, but nowhere more so than among the Jadejas, and falling principally upon the father of the bridegroom. (Political Agent of Kutch, J. G. Lumsden, in his report of 1842, Wilson 1855, 360–362)

This is an important document because the native informant outlines the political processes by which infanticidal clans exploit their daughters' marriages. For instance, migration brought a new set of political issues for the migrant clans, and these changes were reflected in the alterations in marriage customs. The Jharejas who migrated to Kutch and Kathiawar from Sind discovered that it was no longer politically advantageous to contract hypergamous marriages for their daughters with Muslim families, as they had done formerly with the ruling Muslim clans of Sind.[25] In the new political climate in Kathiawar there were "few advantages to be expected from their alliance" with the Muslims. The term "advantages" and "ambitious" used by the native ruler emphasizes that in this community daughters are grist to the fathers' political ambitions. The extract makes it clear that indigenous marriage customs are not engraved in stone, they can be changed in response to political exigency. We find it significant that the head of the clans discredits the colonial discourse of dowry, which had become a major theme of British reform in the 1840s, by stating that all the expenses of hypergamous marriages were borne by "the father of the bridegroom" and not the father of the bride.

Low cost marriages were advanced as the British reformist solution to female infanticide. British tenacity on this issue can be gauged by their recommendation of *dhola marriages*. In the British view the fact that dhola marriages were inexpensive was a primary consideration. Dhola marriages were a particularly cynical and exploitative arrangement, little better than a socially sanctioned form of getting rid of daughters of marriageable age for profit, in terms of furthering the father's political alliance or promises of friendship with the ruler who was sent daughters in dhola marriages. Dhola marriages were a means of getting rid of the daughter and gaining political and social favor at the same time. We argue that these marriage customs were not alternatives to female infanticide, they were on the same continuum of gendered violence, killing female infants because they are valueless, or getting rid of the daughter through dhola marriage for profit.

Indigenous resistance to the colonial reformers' recommendations that dhola marriages should become the predominant mode of daughters' marriages came from the highest levels. The head of the Jhareja clans explains his reasons for disliking British reform in a letter to the East India Company:

> But the matter of taking *Pudloo* and marrying by *Dhola* (by *"taking Pudloo" is meant the sum of money given to the parents of the girl about to be married by the parents of the bridegroom*. By "marrying by Dhola" is meant the sending of the bride to the bridegroom, who does not come to receive her; this happens when the rank of the bridegroom is greater than that of the bride) is in opposition to the Shasters and the custom of kings, and I cannot consent to it; and as it is the custom for the Kattywar Chiefs both to take *Pudloo* and to marry their daughters by *Dhola,* they do not make any objections to it. (Translation of a Yad from His Highness the Rao of Kutch to Colonel Trevelyan, Acting Political Agent in Kutch, 2 July 1855, *Selections from the Records of the Bombay Government* Nos. 39–40, 1856)

The exploitation of the daughter was never an issue between the reformer and the reformed, nor was the issue the change of marriage customs. In the above extract the grounds on which the Rao contests the reformers' imposition of dhola marriages is political advantage. The primary consideration for daughters' marriages was political advantage; therefore it follows that he could marry his daughters to Muslim rulers of Sind when the Jharejas resided in Sind because it signified immediate political advantages. By the same token he could marry his daughters to the British, had the British been so inclined, because there would be political benefit in aligning himself and his clan with the new dominant power in the region. But there was no political mileage in offering his daughter in hypergamous alliance to a Rajput of superior rank because that would have been an admission of the Rao's subordination in terms of rank and genealogy, and jeopardize his distinction as the leading Jhareja Chief. He could not give his assent to a custom that was founded on the superior political ranking of the bridegroom's family; in effect that would mean that he had accepted a politically inferior position as the bride's family.

British codification of Jhareja Rajput marriage customs begins in 1816 when the Bombay Government requests information from Political Agents on the matter. From its very inception this line of reform wove dowry into the very formulation of their request for information. They did not ask for data on marriage customs, instead they requested information regarding marriage expenses.[26] As the codification proceeded, a certain linguistic usage appeared in reports like the one titled "intermarrying groups of Kathiawar" (Report of

Political Agent of Kathiawar, James Erskine, 30 June 1837, *Parliamentary Papers* No. 613, 1843). Throughout the document, the writer carefully abstains from ever using the word marriage in connection with daughters' marriages. Instead the document uses the euphemism "giving" the daughter. This is not a mere slip of the pen because the word marriage is used twice in the document and, remarkably, in both instances the word is used to describe the marriage between Jhareja daughters and Muslims.[27] The official distinction between marriages and "giving the daughter" indicates that British officers were aware, even as they vigorously promoted dhola marriages, that dhola marriages were not marriages at all but arrangements devised for the exploitation of Jhareja daughters, who were not disposed through infanticide, but instead were offered to chiefs who were superior and more powerful than the father.[28] Thus the 1842 Lumsden report, the 1855 Trevelyan transcription, and 1837 Erskine document are texts that exemplify the ideological inversion in British marriage reform.

Institutionalized coercion was deployed to lend force to the British perspective on Jhareja customs on daughters' marriages. A key coercive measure was the Infanticide Fund established in 1825 by Elphinstone, Governor of Bombay Government. The political agent at Kathiawar was instructed by Elphinstone to first grant Jhareja fathers postponement in the payment of the tribute in the year of a daughter's marriage: second, to credit all revenue fines under Rupees 20,000/- to an Infanticide Fund (Minute of Elphinstone, 28 March 1825, ibid.). In effect the Fund systematically wove in economism and linked company subsidies to female-child murder.

In the later decades the institution of the fund was elaborated and developed, not by linking it to a decrease in the deaths of female infants, but by combining coercive and persuasive measures to disseminate the colonialist-economistic discourse of marriage reform. In 1834 Willoughby suggested that the expense of marrying poor Jhareja daughters in Kathiawar should come from the Fund (Report of Willoughby to C. Norris, Chief Secretary to Bombay Government, 24 September 1843, *Selections from Records of Bombay Government* op. cit.). Thus the fund came to represent the institutional route by which money that was extracted as fines from Jhareja revenue payers was redistributed, albeit in a small trickle, as financial rewards to those fathers who preserved their daughters, as well as to those Jharejas who arranged the marriage of their daughters. For instance, the Infanticide Fund records for a period of sixteen years (1834–1854) show that an approximate number of 291 Jhareja daughters received marriage assistance from the Fund. This assistance ranged from Rupees 75/- to Rupees 200/- depending on the rank and class of the Jhareja father. Consequently the daughter of a lowly Grasia was advanced the sum of Rupees 75/- from the fund, while for the dhola marriage of the sister of the Jam of Nowanugger Rupees 5000/- was sanctioned from the Fund to pay for the expense of an elephant and other gifts. It is clear that the British persuasion followed class distinctions, discriminating between what would be an inexpensive marriage depending on the rank and class of the Jhareja father. Therefore the Fund served to further the monetization of daughters' marriages and reinforced class hierarchies.

Marriage reform through the Infanticide Fund facilitated the Company's extortion and accumulation; ostensibly the money in the Infanticide Fund was meant for the marriages of all the Jhareja daughters preserved in Kathiawar; by actually paying for a fraction of the total number of daughters, the Fund diverted and absorbed revenue fines by the Company. We have already noted the use of the money collected in the Fund in 1825 to pay for the Company's military expenses in putting down the Khuman rebellion. In 1837 Political Agent Erskine suggested that the East India Company rethink its policy regarding the abolition of female infanticide through marriage assistance, since the Fund was incapable of supporting the expenses of all marriages of Jhareja daughters preserved as a result of infanticide engagements in Kathiawar (Report of J. Erskine to Secretary Bombay Government, 30 June 1837, ibid.). Yet applications from Jhareja fathers for marriage assistance had been so few in the intervening years that in 1842 the Political Agent in Kathiawar reported that the large sum of Rupees 1, 16,786 or 1 lakh, 16 thousand and 786 Rupees had accumulated in the Fund.

Despite suggestions from successive Political Agents like Erskine (1837), Jacob (1840), and Malet (1842), money from the Fund was not sanctioned for funding any social improvement schemes such as the establishment of a school in the Kathiawar region. Finally in 1847 the money in the Fund had grown large enough that the Bombay Government put Rupees one lakh from the Fund on 5% loan with the interest to be used for the purposes of education.[29] By the close of infanticide reform era in Kathiawar in 1854 the Fund had accumulated Rupees 1,05,348 (*Selections from the Records of the Bombay Government* [New Series] 1875, No. 147).

The official critique of Company marriage reform was that the colonial state's subsidizing of every Jhareja daughter's marriage, through the institution of the Infanticide Fund, constituted a financial absurdity. In 1837 Political Agent Erskine argues that the Bombay Government's approach to marriage reform is inefficacious and needs rethinking. He reminds the Court of Directors that in 1825 Political Agent Barnewall had estimated that by the year 1837, 183 Jhareja daughters would become eligible for marriage in Kathiawar amongst the lowest rank of Jharejas, and as the minimum expense incurred for the marriage of a daughter was Rupees 1500/-, the total cost to the Jharejas would amount to Rupees 2,74,500/-. Erskine makes it clear that the Infanticide Fund cannot support the marriage of all the Jhareja daughters preserved through infanticide engagements. Instead he suggests that the government should follow his recommendation, which is to concentrate on eradicating expensive marriages that were the root cause of infanticide. Erskine is either unaware or doesn't care that both the proof he employs and the alternative solution he offers to improve the efficacy of British infanticide reform measures are premised on the ideological inversion of the colonial formula for marriage reform. Neither did the Jhareja Rajputs follow the practice of dowry marriages for daughters, nor were the majority of the marriage expenses borne by the bride's father.

Erskine shores up his argument with further proof; he reasons that the Company policy of giving financial rewards to Jhareja fathers who preserved a daughter or married a daughter, while benevolent in intent, was ineffective because in effect the Company was aiding in the "presumptuous arrogance" of the Jharejas by advancing to each Jhareja an amount "more than 3 times" the amount that was approved for the marriage of Rajputs higher in rank than the Jharejas (the Jhala, Waghela, or Gohel Rajput). Erskine concludes, "these sumptuary measures appear to me to lead to the perpetuation of the custom by showing sympathy with the perpetrators . . . why should we acknowledge the necessity for a Jhareja spending five to six times the amount on his daughter's marriage than any other Rajpoot does?" (J. Erskine to Secretary Bombay Government, 30 June 1837, ibid.). Far from strengthening Erskine's argument, his second line of reasoning shows how the Jhareja Rajputs resisted and used the coercive/persuasive colonial institution of the Infanticide Fund to reappropriate the funds extorted by the Company to maintain their pre-eminence in the Kathiawar community.

Mobilization of Jhareja men in large-scale meetings in Kathiawar and Kutch marked the last decades of marriage reform.[30] These mobilization strategies were an ingenious move; these meetings served as forums where indigenous elite men internalized British perspectives and arguments on Hindu marriages, and rearticulated them as their own initiative in social reform. In 1837 Erskine proposed that Jhareja chiefs enter into "a stipulation that the expenses of the marriages of the daughters of their bhayad shall not exceed the amount to be fixed at a general meeting of the caste" (Erskine to Secretary Bombay Government, 30 June 1837, *Selections from the Records of of the Bombay Government*, No. xxxix, part II). However no meeting was held and as a result no stipulation was adopted.[31] In 1850 a meeting proposed between Rajput chiefs to adopt a resolution for the reduction of marriage expenses, by giving daughters into the same families from which wives were received, failed to fructify due to the death of the Jam, and the refusal of his son and successor to do anything independently of the Rao of Kutch, the leading Rajput Chief of the region (Report of Political Agent Barr, 18 December, 1852, *Selection of the Records of the Bombay Government* no. 39–40 [1856]).

In 1854 a general meeting of Rajput chiefs was held at Rajkot to discuss lowering of marriage expenses. But the Political Agent declared that the meeting "was unsatisfactory" and no agreement was signed. However he was very hopeful since the Rao of Kutch had decided that in the future he would seek alliances for his family near home rather than at a distance, and the Jam of Nowanugger had indicated that if the Rao sanctioned the practice, he would be willing to seek alliances for his daughters from the same ranks from which wives were taken. In the same letter the Political Agent notes that, "the Rajpoot Grasias and landholders having, for some time past, very generally given daughters into families from which they have taken wives" (the Political Agent of Kathiawar to Bombay Government 1855, Pakrasi 1970, 297).

The decision of the Rao was communicated to all Rajput chiefs in Kathiawar, and its approval by all Rajputs allowed the Political Agent to conclude, "thus the first and what may be regarded as the crowning point in our efforts, has been attained" (Letter of Captain Barr, Political Agent of Kathiawar to H. L. Anderson, Acting Secretary to Government of Bombay 23 August 1855, *Selection of the Records of the Bombay Government* no. 39–40 [1856]). In the same year the Political Agent in Kutch informed his counterpart in Kathiawar that the Rao of Kutch had recently performed the marriage of his daughter to a minor chief, the Raja of Edur, and therefore all inferior Rajputs were now free to reduce marriage expenses by marrying their daughters to families of equal or lower rank. The Political Agent concludes, "I am not aware that anything is further required to be done in the way of promoting marriages among them" (Letter of Acting Political Agent in Kutch, Colonel Trevelyan to Captain J. T. Barr 9 July 1855, *Selections from the Records of the Bombay Government* Nos. 39–40 1856; Pakrasi 1970, 719).[32]

The British solution of marriage reform could not have achieved the success it did, without the enthusiastic support from nationalists and indigenous social reformist discourse concerning the link between female infanticide and marriage customs, as can be gauged from the extract below:

> the practice of female infanticide . . . must in the beginning have arisen from family pride. One's daughter should not be married into a family possessing no importance or distinction. To marry her into a high family requires a heavy expenditure of money, which the father cannot afford. . . . Hence rather than suffer the disgrace of allying himself with a low family, he allowed his daughter to be destroyed. . . . Here again you will see that the motive of action was not under the guidance of the higher feelings of love and tenderness for a human being and especially for one's own child. (R. G. Bhandarkar, "Why Social Reforms?" Address at the Ninth Social Conference, 1895, K. P. Karunakaran, *Religion and Political Awakening in India* 1965, 159)

As postcolonial feminists we read this excerpt as a salutary lesson about the collaborationist impulses in the Indian social reform movements. This statement requires qualification. Indigenous reformers contested the objectives and even the right of the British to reform Indian society; moreover Indian reformers, revivalists, and nationalists disputed many of the arguments made by British reformers on reformist issues like widow self immolation, the Hindu religions, widow remarriage, Age of Consent Bill. Keeping in view these necessary qualifications, we nevertheless argue that it is precisely in Bhandarkar's uncritical acceptance of the British discourse about female infanticide, as well as his acceptance of the colonial solution of marriage reform, that the collaborationist impulses in nationalism are manifested. The passage functions like a citation of imperial texts, it begins with the rhetorical strategy that is characteristic of the imperial text, namely the speculation about the origins of the practice of female infanticide. The passage faithfully echoes Sleeman's "pride and purse" formulation as well as Tod's observation that infanticidal parents lack the "higher feelings."

Bhandarkar's participation in the colonial discourse concerning marriage reform as the solution to female infanticide shows that British anti-dowry campaigns at the site of female infanticide reform had a harmful effect on nineteenth-century debates about women's oppression. The passage links three colonial formulations concerning the marriage customs of infanticidal clans. Hypergamy is characterized as a custom originating in the false pride of wishing to marry the daughter "into a high family." In chapter 3 we dispute this colonial formulation, suggesting instead that hypergamy in infanticidal clans is part of an indigenous idiom of upward mobility, the father is motivated not by race pride but by the desire for maximum political advantage and status through his daughter's marriage. Second, Bhandarkar accepts unquestioningly the colonial myth that the infanticidal father "cannot afford" his daughter's marriage, although British and Indian reformers were well aware that the infanticidal father was a man of considerable property.

Third, Bhandarkar disseminates the colonial myth about dowry; he states that the daughter's marriage "requires a heavy expenditure of money." The flaws in this colonialist-nationalist myth are that the rationale for marriage expenditures, or the lack of it, was the father's political and social ambitions; for instance in Kutch and Kathiawar, we have shown that the marriage expenses were borne by the bridegroom's family; in Rajasthan the father determined the extent and scale of expenditures at his daughter's wedding according to this criteria, the wedding's political function for making allies and declaring enmities. Bhandarkar's wholesale endorsement of the language, the arguments, the myths about marriage reform in British texts reveals the collaborationist impulses in indigenous nationalist reform.

The innovative impulses of nationalism and indigenous social reform movements were located in the following directions. Social reformers like Bhandarkar challenged the British notion of the civilizing mission by contending that Indians were fully capable of initiating their own reform of marriage customs. Religious reformers like Dayanand Saraswati contested the British critique of the Hindu religions by demonstrating that the Hindu religion had the vitality and vigor for internal reform. The test of this reformed, rational, and semiticised Hindu religion, which came to be known as the Arya Samaj and took root in the infanticide endemic provinces of north-west India like Punjab and Uttar Pradesh, was the Arya Samaj marriage. The Arya Samaj constructed the model of a simple, inexpensive marriage in which rituals were kept to a bare minimum, the restrictions of caste and clan were discouraged, widow remarriages were encouraged, and an indigenized version of the companionate marriage was advocated. Thus marriage reform became central to the Hindu male's religious identity, to his confidence in self-reform and the reform of the imagined community of the nation.

It is only by distinguishing between the collusive and innovative strands in Indian reformers' speeches and pamphlets about marriage reform that we can comprehend the new set of meanings attached to marriage reform. These new sets of meanings demarcated men and male interests in marriage reform as distinct from women and women's issues in relation to marriage reform. To women the social reformers' and nationalist message was that the marriage reform was the all embracing and all inclusive solution for all forms of violence on women. Thus the social reformers conjoined female infanticide with sati, by positing one solution for both forms of gendered violence. To men the social reformers' message was simply this: marriage reform was necessary to produce mature, educated, and companionate wives and enlightened mothers for Indian men. The British solution was readily accommodated within the modes of bourgeois male nationalist thought, because marriage reform did not entail questioning the structure of the patriarchal family or the patriarchal structural controls over the economic resources of the family and the women of the household. Marriage reform also did not entail that Indian men should rethink their patriarchal power in their role as husband.[33] Most importantly, marriage reform did not impose any legal or social obligation on the father, brother or male members of a girl's natal family to give daughters their rightful inheritance in the family property.

Postcolonial analysts, state reformers, and journalists articulate the colonialist-economistic approach to female infanticide in the discourse of economism. The British solution of the Infanticide Fund for daughter's marriages in colonial Kathiawar continues to be echoed by modern Indians. Postcolonial reformers propose that daughter killing can be eliminated by state subsidies for the economic cost of rearing a female child, particularly the cost incurred in a daughter's dowry and marriage celebrations. Dr. Kurien says, "The main point is that a girl needs to be married. . . . Society should start taking these unwanted girl babies and bring them up, educate them, and set them up in self employment" (*Eubois Ethics Institute Newsletter* 3 1993, 3). Similarly Vaasanthi, herself a fiction writer and researcher, proposes that the Indian Government deposit a thousand Rupees at the birth of a girl for her marriage dowry (*The Hindu,* November 20, 1994). These two examples are characteristic of the proposals and arguments made by state officials, the intelligentsia, and concerned citizens. The problem with these postcolonial explanations is not only that they revive British explanations for female infanticide, but that they are unsuccessful precisely because they do not address the true dimension of the problem. Families do not stop the practice of femicide and daughter devaluation even if they are given money to rear and educate their daughters, nor do they rethink femicide even if the daughters are the most economically productive members of the household. Patriarchal violence against the female child is not solved by economism.

There is a strong connection between the gender bias in inheritance laws for woman and the practice of female infanticide and femicide in postcolonial India. Under the Prime Ministership of Indira Gandhi, public concern about land fragmentation led to the passing of a new law that daughters cannot inherit ancestral landed property. Thus, the postcolonial state reinforced the bias against daughters, favored landed and propertied men and perpetuated son-preference. A related issue raised by the Indian women's movements is rethinking dowry as *stridhan* or women's wealth, this reassessment of dowry means that it should not be treated as a transfer of money or goods from the males of the natal family to the males of the girl's marital family, rather dowry should be treated as an investment in the daughter's future through education and a recognized stake in her natal home that cannot be denied.

A fair example of the arguments and counter-arguments about marriage reform in postcolonial India consist in the writings of Barbara Miller (1980) and Kalpana Bardhan (1986). Miller begins her article concerning female neglect in rural India by reiterating the colonial argument that "pride and purse" are responsible for female infanticide. She writes, "Like this theory of one hundred years ago, my understanding of the current practice of female neglect in rural India also draws on the custom of giving large dowries" (1980, 95). This is an unexamined position, Miller aligns herself with a nineteenth-century colonial theory without examining the imperial implications of that theory. There is an assumption here that theory, in Miller's case "this theory of one hundred years ago," is free of its historical and political moorings.

She argues that there is a strong correlation between expensive dowries for daughters and son-preference and low survival rates for girls amongst northern propertied groups, and a greater variation in marriage customs and therefore a more equal sex ratio between boys and girls in the south. Like the colonial administrators of Kutch and Kathiawar, Miller fails to appreciate that marriage customs are a symptom rather than the cause of female child neglect. Miller's solution for female child neglect in the north is the substitution of the dowry marriage with low-cost marriages such as cousin marriages and exchange marriages of the south. We critique Miller's solution for reintroducing the colonialist tendency towards economism. It is our position that in the context of the complete absence of daughter's rights of inheritance, simplifying and reducing expense of marriage does not address the basic issue of daughter devaluation. Instead, it serves to further the father's monetary interests and promotes the patriarchal argument that daughters should be disposed of at little or no expense and with no hope of a share in the father's property.

Kalpana Bardhan contests Miller's thesis that expensive dowries are the cause of female child neglect, by suggesting that femicide and violence against women is a symptom of patriarchal control of economic resources. Instead of an exclusive and distorted emphasis on dowry, Bardhan contextualizes female child neglect and violence against women through a number of covariables like female exclusion or inclusion in terms of economically important work, property rights, the custom of village/clan exogamy or endogamy, the location of marital residence, the pattern of marriage payments, and the ways in which these factors "follow the divisions of caste, class and landholding" (1986, 9). In her discussion of exogamous marriage customs in north India, Bardhan points to a far greater correlation between exogamy and female child neglect than marriage payments. Bardhan states, "Son preference tends to be more lethal for female babies where marriage customs are more oppressive for the in-marrying women, in terms of isolation and distance from natal village and kin relations" (9). While Miller valorizes the cousin and exchange marriages in the south for being low-cost arrangements, we locate the pro-woman traditions and equitable sex ratio in the south in the support systems provided to the married daughter in cousin and exchange marriages.[34] In this sense we concur with Bardhan that it is geographical and affective closeness of the daughter to her natal family that ensures the well being of her female children and herself.

In postcolonial India daughters' dowry and marriage custom is a very important question for Indian women's movements, every time there is a public debate about the high incidence of femicide there is a considerable section of influential voices that suggest that the root cause of, and the solution for, female infanticide and femicide lies in the anti-dowry campaign. Madhu Kishwar's thoughts on dowry present an interesting case of work in progress in the feminist-activist thinking concerning the role of dowry in the violence on women. Kishwar is an activist feminist and the founding co-editor of the feminist journal *Manushi;* she has documented and participated in street protests against dowry demands as well as written extensively about the phenomena of dowry and dowry deaths. Through the late 1970s and 1980s *Manushi* was a forum for discussion about women's rights. Kishwar's earlier anti-dowry position was combined with activist work in helping the families of victims of dowry deaths or broken marriages retrieve the dowries of their daughters from the marital family. In her most recent article on the subject, Kishwar observes that all forms of violence against daughters, including female infanticide and foeticide, are ascribed to dowry payments. However, Kishwar notes that this is a colonial inheritance because there is little mention in pre-British history and literature of exorbitant dowries causing the ruin of families. She writes, "Ruin due to exorbitant dowry payments became a major theme in nineteenth-century literature" (1993, 9). In the process Kishwar moves away from her earlier anti-dowry position (1986) and states "Today, I find it irrelevant to talk of abolishing dowry" (1988, 13). She reassesses marriage payments as "in itself, [this] is neither good nor evil" and concludes that, "there is no evidence that this [dowry] always in all societies led to the woman's maltreatment. It may even have enhanced her status under certain circumstances" (1988, 10–11). The evolution of her position from this earlier colonialist-economistic position has led to the opening up of the question of daughter rights in the 1990s in *Manushi*. In the 1990s *Manushi* editors reopened the question of the girl child in terms of her rights in the natal home, in the natal property and the life-long continuance of those rights even after marriage. We see this as a significant move away from the colonialist-economistic discourse about daughter rights.

CHAPTER 5

A Critical History of the Colonial Discourse of Infanticide Reform, 1800–1854

Part II: The Erasure of the Female Child under Population Discourse

The history of British-colonial reform of female infanticide in nineteenth-century Western India illuminates the postcolonial phenomena of the disproportionate sex ratio that exists in India today (the current overall sex ratio is 933 females per 1,000 males). The full significance of the phrase "disproportionate sex ratio" cannot be grasped by the reader unless we appreciate that in terms of India's population, this means that there are millions of women missing in India. How did reformist measures concerning the disproportionate sex ratio in nineteenth-century western India facilitate postcolonial discourses that circulate around femicide? Chapter 4 provides part of our answer in the discursive yoking of revenue and reform. Here we explicate the second half of our argument concerning the discursive relation between British colonial infanticide reform, census, and population discourse.

To understand the relation between women, census, and population discourse in postcolonial India, it is necessary to comprehend the specific historical development of the colonial census in nineteenth-century India. *The colonial census comes into being at the site of female infanticide.* The emergence of the census as a tool of population study under the auspices of female infanticide meant that population discourse, from its very inception, was the imperial discourse deployed for women and violence against women. The discursive association between population study and violence against women is not the only legacy of the colonial census. The colonial census mapped Malthusian discourse onto the terrain of the feudal practice of female infant killing. Therein lies the interpretive problem: British reformers claimed that female infanticide was an indigenous mode of population control, yet they could not produce a single recorded statement by infanticidal clans as proof of their claim. Despite this lack of evidence colonial discourse successfully configured female infanticide as the efficient disposal of the redundant population of daughters amongst the indigenous elite of western India. Population discourse in nineteenth-century Kathiawar

129

was a specifically post-Enlightenment colonial discourse in which female infanticide is discursively located as the selective killing of a target group—daughters of upper-class families who are implicitly defined as socially and economically unproductive and dispensable—within a traditional Asiatic mode of population control.

In making the discursive connections between colonial census-taking in Kathiawar and postcolonial population discourse, we take cognizance of the work by postcolonial scholars, which theorizes the relation between the past and the present in the field of female child neglect in northwest India. In her anthropological study of female infant mortality in rural north India, Barbara Miller notes that in nineteenth-century India there was "a regional and social pattern of infanticide . . . in the Northwest and among the higher castes," which correlates to the regional and social pattern in "sex ratio imbalances in twentieth-century India" (1981, 14). Miller suggests that there is "a link" between the nineteenth-century practice of female infant killing and the twentieth-century practice of systematic neglect of, and discrimination toward, the female child.

Several explanations have been offered for the "link" between female infanticide and northwest India. It has been suggested, for instance, that the female child is valued in those areas where there is female-intensive agricultural production, conversely the female child is devalued in male-intensive crop production and economic activity in general in northwest India (Pranabh Bardhan 1974, 1982). Miller follows suit by locating female participation in agricultural production as the key factor for female child survival rates (1981). Kalpana Bardhan disagrees with Miller and suggests instead that class, patriarchy, and social hierarchy (caste/ethnic strata, religious differences) or the caste and landowning status of a peasant community are all factors that determine the value or devaluation of women (1986). We intervene in this debate by suggesting that the question concerning female child neglect in northwest India cannot be addressed without an examination of the colonial discourse within which the girl-child in nineteenth-century western India was erased. The deferment of the rights of the colonized subaltern sexed subject is productive for the colonizer as well as the indigenous elite male. In the story of British reform of female infanticide, we encounter the continually shifting and marginalized female subject whose erasure stands as guarantee for the productivity of the British civilizing mission, and the elite Jhareja male's assertion of the inviolability of his home.

In order to understand the specific historical development of the colonial census, the reader of our book has to estrange herself from the assumption that the census is a neutral tool of population study. For First World citizens the census has historically signified individual political voluntarism, democratic process, and an impartial state apparatus. For postcolonial Indian women, the census apparatus has a different set of political significances. On the one hand the census enables the nationalist-populist rhetoric of population explosion and state coercion in population control programs; census figures add fuel to the political rhetoric concerning Third World overpopulation circulated by developed countries and international agencies like the United Nations Population Fund. On the other hand the census is a gauge of the missing millions of women in India's disproportionate sex ratio. As postcolonial feminists we associate the census with the twin social issues of the disproportionate sex ratio in India and state coercion in the sphere of population control.

Census-taking is introduced for the first time in colonial India in order to discover the extent and incidence of female infanticide among the Jhareja Rajput population in Kathiawar. British-colonial census takers perform a systemic manipulation and interpretation of the results of their shoddy, anecdotal, and unreliable census data, in order to make the question of the female child disappear. To put it in Lacanian terms, the female child becomes the *objet petit a* whose repression is the productivity of the post-Enlightenment discourse of population control.[1] We trace in Kathiawar the beginnings of what we name as demonic demography, which continues to the present. In the 1970s in postcolonial India the female child is continually aborted and erased under the exigencies of the national problem of exploding population.

We analyze the discursive displacement of female infanticide, from a region-specific and class/clan specific practice to the more generalized population discourse, in the 1819 dispatch by the principal architect of infanticide reform in Kathiawar, Alexander Walker. The dispatch executes the rhetorical stratagem by which official writings of the East India Company attributed British perceptions of population control to indigenous people. Walker is a transitional figure in the context of population discourse, his earlier writings of 1808 indicate that he was persuaded by the mercantilist theory of population. Gazing at the sparsely populated region of Kathiawar, Walker had drawn connections between increased population, greater productivity, and maximum revenue. At that point Walker believed that the saving of female children would contribute toward greater productivity and increase in revenue from the Kathiawar region ("Report on Infanticide in Kattywar" (1808) *Selections from the Records of the Bombay Government* [1856]). By 1819 however, Walker observes: "This revolting practice may have begun among these people from want, fear of future evil, and *a redundant population;* it has been continued from prejudice and habit" (italics ours, Wilson 1855, 129). In this statement Walker has decisively switched from mercantilism to Malthusian population theory: female children are no longer included among the productive part of the population, instead they are characterized as a redundant and useless section of society.

Walker deploys a myth of origin: he suggests that the killing of female children was a survival strategy for a migrant martial tribe who did not want their women to fall into the hands of the enemy. This argument is tenuous because Walker has still to explain why a survival practice endures even when the tribe becomes a settled landowning community. He covers over this yawning gap in his explanation by reaching for a favorite colonial stereotype about the colonized, namely that a formerly rational practice continues long after it has outlived its necessity as superstition. In this statement Walker is not expressing an individual viewpoint, but adapting to Indian realities the ideas and philosophies that were current in England at the time. The Enlightenment theorist who is associated with this view of population, Thomas Malthus writes:

> as its [female infanticide] prevalence amongst the higher classes of people has removed from it all odium, all imputation of poverty, it is probably often adopted rather as a fashion than a resort of necessity, and appears to be practiced familiarly and without reserve. (*An Essay on Populations* 1798, I, 116)

The common ground between Walker's observation about the Jharejas and the Malthusian proposition is worth examining in some detail. Female infanticide amongst the elite classes poses a contradiction to Malthus's theory because it limits the growth of the very population that is, in his view, the most productive in society. Note that Malthus makes no reference to the gendered violence of female infanticide. He focuses entirely on the classed nature of the practice. He asserts that female-infant killing is not linked to "poverty" or "necessity." It is precisely here that we see the characteristic elitism in Malthusian theory; in effect he assumes that only the poor are driven by the economic motive and therefore "the higher classes of people" practice violence on their own female children as "a fashion."

In Malthus's theory the upper classes of people are not interrogated in terms of the modes of upward mobility by which they came to be rich, nor does Malthusian theory concern itself with the modes by which the elite population maintain their elite dominance through violence on their own women and the lower classes. In Malthusian theory the "higher classes of people" constitute an ahistorical and static unit of population, they are a pregiven in his theory, and it is for this reason that we call it an elitist philosophy.

Malthus's use of the term fashion is particularly significant: it suggests that rich people practice violence with no regard to their own profit but merely to follow a fashion. The term fashion also carries the implication that, at some point in history, female infanticide was a necessity for the higher classes of people; however that necessity has faded away and it has become a mere fashion. This second sense in which Malthus uses the word fashion links up to Walker's theory about the Jharejas. The deforming effect of colonial capitalist discourses on the feudal practices of female infant killing at the periphery consists in the attribution of Malthusian theory to indigenous people, by suggesting that they destroy female infants as a method of population control. The colonial capitalist discourses superimpose and re-inscribe feudal practice of violence against women.

Discursive Displacement of Female Infanticide onto Population Discourse through Introduction of Census Technologies

Census operations were undertaken by the East India Company in the Kathiawar region of Gujarat in the years 1808–1854. The census reports of this period are sketchy and unreliable at best; they are not the comprehensive census reports we have come to expect and rely on for sex ratios in modern times. The census operations in Kathiawar during the period between 1808 and 1854 are the precursor of the all-India census inaugurated by the colonial government in 1870. The voices of the victims of the practice of female infanticide are irrecoverable; nevertheless the subject position of the female infant victim is essential to the coming into being of the text of colonial infanticide documents, for it is ostensibly on behalf of the Hindu female child as victim that the East India Company finds its rationale for reform.

It is precisely in these sketchy and rudimentary census reports that we track the *naturalizing* of all linguistic references to the girl-child in terms of census figures and numbers. Colonial reform did not end the practice of female infanticide, it simply constructed a bureaucratic and flawed state mechanism for recording it. Twenty-five years after Walker signed anti-infanticide engagements in Kathiawar with the Jharejas, the 1834 census shows that female infanticide continued unabated. The overall sex ratio was 235.8 males per hundred females, males were more than two times the number of females (1,422 males and 696 females).

The census as a specifically colonial apparatus became an end in itself. A discourse of census data analysis accompanied the facts and figures, and this official discourse was continually preoccupied with further refinements, corrections, and elaborations of the census. Report after report worries about "the imperfections of our instruments." Increasingly the language of the documents made it appear that infants girls were being "saved" by the censuses, and the coining of the phrase "save a life by the census" made it appear as if the action of compilation of census figures by itself effected the rescue of female children (Political Agent of Kathiawar, LeGrand Jacob to Bombay Government, 23 Oct. 1841, *Parliamentary Papers* No. 613, 1843; Wilson 1855, 261; Pakrasi 1970, 174). Thus the administrative activities of compiling and analyzing the census came to signify the work of reform in Kathiawar. *It is precisely in the metonymic shift of infanticide reform from female infant killing into the administrative-enumerative discourse of census, that we note the discursive displacement and continual deferment of the question of the missing girl child.* The female victim disappears in the colonial apparatus of the census.

What takes the place of the missing girl-child in the colonial census is the operation of the colonial will. The colonial will operates in census data by making census operations a measure of administrative success, not of the extent to which reform addressed the violence on female children. The place of the murdered girl-child is occupied by the discourse of careerism, a discourse within which individual British officers essay a self-representation of their zeal and success and offer a progressivist narrative of successful reform. Thus the will that animates official texts is not that of the zealous reformer, but the will of the careerist administrator posturing as a zealous reformer. Each one of the Company officials made his career on the basis of infanticide reform, men who were mostly military officers used infanticide reform as their defining career opportunity to secure prestigious diplomatic and administrative appointments.[2] The census became an official measure reflecting the success of the administrative reformer rather than reflecting the conditions of women's oppression.

Operation of the Colonial Will in Willoughby's 1834 Census

In many ways the 1834 census was the East India Company's proudest achievement in western India.[3] The census was always accompanied by an interpretive and explanatory commentary by the political agent. Therefore we treat the census as a rhetorical construction, it is an extraordinarily revealing text for the rhetorical maneuvers through which ambitious colonial reformers claimed success in infanticide reform, and deferred the question of the missing girl-child. J. P. Willoughby's 1834 census became a benchmark for all succeeding censuses, which were compared to Willoughby's census and seen as cementing the good work inaugurated by Willoughby.[4] The Willoughby tenure represents the thorough elaboration of the colonial census apparatus.[5] The birth of the census officer is heralded in 1833 by Willoughby's suggestion that a *Karkun* (clerk) be appointed for the express purpose of visiting every district and conducting a census inquiry about the number of females in a district; the names, ages, marital status, profession, or occupation of each Jhareja male. The Willoughby regime created the appearance of bureaucratic efficiency and successful reform by multiplying the paperwork, the census was augmented by half yearly registers submitted by every Jhareja chief of all marriages, betrothals, births, and deaths. Through the censor as well as the registers, Willoughby claimed that his 1834 census had been repeatedly cross-checked for figures and now was the "most complete" and the "most accurate census" surpassing all previous censuses in quality and accuracy (*Selections from Records of Bombay Government* 1856; Pakrasi 1970, 84).

The 1834 census made a significant advance over previous censuses by computing the sex ratio of the 28 infanticide endemic districts of Kathiawar. For the first time estimates of Jhareja males figures were included along with Jhareja female figures. The sex ratio provided damning evidence of the extent of violence on female infants and women at each age level: the overall sex ratio was 3 males to every female (3:1), the disproportion was far greater at age 20 (4:1) and the sex ratio at age 10 and at age 1 was the same as the overall sex ratio (3:1). In his analysis of this data Willoughby acknowledges that in most districts the number of males far exceeds the female, he states, "the excess is so great as of necessity to lead to the conclusion that the shocking practice still prevails in them to a considerable extent." He cites the example of Rajkot, which was the headquarters of the Infanticide Agency where, "in fifteen years the number of females alive has only been increased by one" (Willoughby to Chief Secretary to Bombay Government, C. Norris, 24 September 1834, *Selections from Records of Bombay Government* 1856; Wilson 1855, 178–179).

The census figures create a hiatus between the continuance of female infanticide and the success of infanticide reform. Willoughby repackages the failure of infanticide reform as administrative success. The glaringly disproportionate sex ratio is reconstructed in such a way as to show the enormous improvements made by Willoughby. The ambitious young official, who would be the *only* Political Agent to be appointed to the Company's Court of Directors, achieves this repackaging of failure as success by deploying the old colonial trick of depopulating the entire landscape and mapping colonial endeavor on it.

Willoughby gives a history of the reform years immediately preceding his tenure as a progressivist narrative, by positing a zero point before the advent of British reform when there were no female children in Jhareja clans. This is simply untrue, there were always a few infanticide survivors in infanticidal clans. One or more daughter was saved in the infanticidal clan for the purpose of hypergamous marriage, which would benefit the father and brother (see our discussion in chapter 4), or the individual wish of the father, or if the father was very wealthy and so inclined. Moreover it was a well known fact that the illegitimate daughters of Jhareja men were not subjected to infanticide. The patriarchal formation functioned precisely by the arbitrariness with which a few daughters were allowed to live and the majority were put to death. Furthermore it was well known that the Jhareja Rajputs who had converted to Jainism, Islam, or had become followers of Kabir, did not murder their female children. These facts militate against Willoughby's technique of depopulating the landscape of female children in the prereform period.

Willoughby's fiction of zero daughters in Jhareja clans before the era of British reform enables him to repopulate the Kathiawar region with an impressive list of female children rescued by British reform (68 in the first five years, then 102, 176, and 225 in each of the next five years) (*Selections from Records of Bombay Government* 1856; Pakrasi 1970, 88). In making this list Willoughby has managed to present village "tittle-tattle" under the rubric of scientific and verifiable data from the prehistory of his regime. A steady progress toward the present of Willoughby's tenure constitutes the rhetorical schema of the 1834 census.[6] Willoughby uses several techniques of statistical manipulation to inflate the numbers of the female population. For instance his overall sex ratio is computed on the basis of a female total that includes the females deceased (93) as well as females known to be above the age of 20 (39) who are therefore disqualified from comparison with males of 20 years. Furthermore we speculate that these 39 women were wives and mothers from non infanticidal clans, who were included along with daughters born as a consequence of the engagements, in order to inflate the figures.

Willoughby's census does not give a districtwise breakdown of the female population by age. Consequently the overall sex ratio hides rather than reveals the shocking disproportion in districts like Murvi (61:7), Drappa (67:10), Veerpoor (52:10), Rajpoora (30:2), Kotra (24:2), and Rajkot (15:3). Willoughby has a particularly ingenious way of demonstrating his success as a reformer. He makes special mention of the districts of Keesura, Mengani, and Satodar, which show an excess of girls, and represents this as a direct outcome of reform which is "so gratifying" that he sent for their reassessment and ascertained that they were "quite correct" (ibid. 143; Wilson 1855, 178). However a closer examination of these allegedly gratifying figures—Keesura (12:16), Mengani (6:6) and Satodar (38:24)—reveals that the population in these three districts is so sparse that it is more to Willoughby's ingenuity that credit must accrue rather than his reformist efforts. The weakest part of Willoughby's analysis of the 1834 census concerns the female infant mortality. He explains away the high rate of female infant mortality (13 % of the total female population) by stating that the majority of these deaths are, "of that description to which infancy is peculiarly liable, such as small pox, measles, convulsions, and fever" (ibid.; Wilson 1855, 177). This general description suffices for 57 deaths and the cause of death of the remaining infants (36) is unspecified. Willoughby does not provide a comparable figure of male infant mortality.

Our own analysis of the causes of female infant mortality in the 1834 census suggests that indigenous euphemisms are being deployed to hide deaths through female child neglect. A majority of these deaths occurred in the age group of 3 months and under, the report specifies 44 deaths as "under 3 [months of age] still born age not specified" (Wilson 1855, 177). We interpret this description of female infant mortality as indigenous euphemisms for the practice of infanticide, it was a common practice in the infanticide endemic districts to refer to female infants who had been murdered as being "still born" (Panigrahi 1976, 176–177). Colonial census and census analysts tended to suggest that female child neglect replaced female infanticide, principally because it was a reconfirmation of the progressivist narrative of British reform. Once reformers declared that female infanticide had been successfully abolished, then any suspicious deaths had to be attributed to the allegedly "new" phenomena of child neglect. We argue that it is far more likely that both practices, female infanticide and female child neglect, co-existed alongside each other.[7]

Perhaps the most effective way that Willoughby represents his achievements as a reformer is to move away from, to use his own phrase, the "shocking" extent of female infanticide and the imbalanced sex ratio, and focus instead on a highly personalist eyewitness account in the colonial idiom of rescue. He paints a narrative of the beginning years of infanticide reform (1817) by making the false claim that in this period there were no known instances of a Jhareja father saving more than one daughter. He contrasts this period with his own tenure in 1834 by providing a cumulative account of reformist progress: Willoughby presents dazzling figures of 80 fathers having saved 2 daughters, 13 instances of 3 daughters and 2 of 4 daughters. These figures sound far better than the bleak sex ratio, for they remap the indigenous landscape entirely through the lens of colonial paternalism. Willoughby's strategy of citing individual cases of Jhareja fathers saving one or more daughters is calculated to reinforce the notion that these rescues are a direct result of his zeal and perseverance.

A certain authenticity is provided to the 1834 census through the rhetorical technique of eyewitness observation; Willoughby writes that he has personally observed that in every talook either the chief or his relatives have preserved a daughter; Willoughby attests to the fact that many of them, "have intermarried into the families of the other Rajput tribes of this province" (Pakrasi 1970, 89; Wilson 1855, 178). We mark the 1834 census as the classic text of the discursive displacement of the missing girl-child with population discourse. The discourse of colonial reform does not examine the social, economic, and cultural milieus that support daughter devaluation; instead it substitutes census figures and numbers as the main focus of the reform.

The Failure of Colonial Coercion:
The Official Argument for Persuasive Reform

Willoughby's reforms were deeply resented by the Jhareja community, which interpreted the census as a mode of surveillance and resisted all attempts by the census-takers to gather information. The official critique of Willoughby's tenure in general, and the 1834 census in particular, was articulated by James Erskine, the Political Agent who succeeded Willoughby and became one of his most vocal critics. Erskine's 1837 census report is a significant example of how the discourse of domination can assimilate its own critique and regroup by disguising coercion as persuasive measures.[8] Like Walker and Willoughby before him, the chief rhetorical technique of Erskine's 1837 census is to review and evaluate the progress of infanticide reform in the years preceding his own tenure in Kathiawar. This history writing provides Erskine with an opportunity to characterize Willoughby's reform as "too partial and superficial" and not "comprehensive and radical" (Erskine to Secretary to Bombay Government, 30 June 1837, *Selections from Records of Bombay Government* [1856]; Pakrasi 1970, 120). A purely coercive approach is characterized as partial in order that Erskine can build a case for his own reformist style, within which coercion is disguised in persuasive measures and represented as a truly radical and comprehensive reform.

Erskine's other strategy is to present his census as reflecting the consequences of Willoughby's brief coercive tenure, which had rebounded on Company officials and caused a reversal in reform efforts. Erskine was subjected to great hostility from the Jhareja population of Kathiawar; he notes in his report to the Government, "it [infanticide] is not a safe subject to investigate and legislate upon" (ibid.; Pakrasi 1970, 120). It is in this light that the following census figures are represented. In less than two years since Willoughby's census, Erskine's census reports a meager increase in the number of female children and an enormous increase in male children. Erskine's report shows a rapid deterioration from the Willoughby years (809:262) to 1837 (1310:337): whereas the female children constituted 24 percent of the total population in Willoughby's time, the failure of Willoughby's reforms was reflected in the fact that this figure had dropped down to 20 percent of the population in Erskine's census. A look at Erskine's census tables shows that while the sex ratio for infants of one year and under was not quite two males to one female (168.5 per 100 female infants), from the age group of 2–4 years, male infants outnumbered female infants by almost 5 to 1, and virtually the same highly imbalanced sex ratio characterized all ages from 5 to 20 years.[9]

Erskine successfully uses the 1837 census figures to demolish Willoughby's claims to success through coercive reform. He deploys the overall sex ratio (4:1) and districtwise sex ratios. The significance of Erskine's participation in reform is double-edged, while he openly criticizes Willoughby, he also singles him out for strategic praise. Erskine's objective is to both discredit his predecessor, and at the same time persuade the Court of Directors and the Bombay Government to allow him to refashion Willoughby's measures. Erskine was aware of Willoughby's meteoric rise in the Company ladder and was not averse to wishing something similar for himself. Erskine suggested two persuasive measures in contrast to Willoughby's coercive strategies. First Erskine suggested a cooling off period of two years in which the Company would undertake no investigation of infanticide cases of the past or the present; this measure was supposed to reassure the Jharejas and win their confidence. Second, Erskine prepared for circulation among the Jharejas an anti-infanticide proclamation that rivaled Willoughby's earlier anti-infanticide proclamation of 1834.

Erskine argued that Willoughby's 1834 anti-infanticide proclamation was directly responsible for saving 123 new born female infants under the age of one. So Erskine's rationale seems to be that if one proclamation can be so effective, a second proclamation (under his own name) should prove doubly effective. The way Erskine demonstrates the effectiveness of Willoughby's 1834 anti-infanticide proclamation is interesting. He notes that of the 73 new born female infants, "upwards of forty . . . would have met with inevitable destruction" had it not been for Willoughby's intervention (Wilson 1855, 223). How Erskine arrived at the figure of 40 infants is itself a mystery, since Erskine does not explain how he gets this figure. We uncover the mystery in the Court's response to Erskine's proposal where they note, "The year before the census has a show of 102 males, and only 20 females, evidencing that nearly 80 infants must have been put to death," (Memorandum of Willoughby, Secretary to Bombay Government, 8 September 1838, *Selections from Records of Bombay Government* [1856]; Wilson 1855, 239). This statement suggests that Erskine's calculation (40 female infants saved as a direct result of Willoughby's 1834 proclamation) is based on the simplistic and false assumption; in Erskine's view, an equal number of males and females must exist; therefore for 20 female infants to have survived in contrast to 102 male infants, he speculates that at least 80 female infants had been killed; for 73 female infants to be alive in 1835, the hypothetical assumption is that 40 of them are directly due to Willoughby's 1834 proclamation.

The tenor of Erskine's analysis suggests that he wishes to create a receptive audience amongst the company's Court of Directors for his own suggestions; consequently he declares that, "there is every hope that the two Talooks of Murvi and Drappa have effected an abolition of the atrocious practice in their respective limits" (ibid.; Pakrasi 1970, 117). Erskine isolates one fact from the rest that in the age group of one year and under Murvi has an infant sex ratio of 20:13, while Drappa has a sex ratio of 11:10 and presents these two sex ratios as a measure of success.[10] He ignores the fact that Murvi boasts of the most disproportional sex ratio (5:1) and in Drappa the sex ratio was only marginally better (4:1). Erskine's plans for a rival proclamation were rejected by the Bombay Government (the Court's reply was written by Willoughby who had become the resident expert on infanticide matters at the

Bombay Government). However, Erskine's strategies for manipulating the census to indicate that the reform objective had been achieved in selective areas met with enthusiastic approval by the Court of Directors and the Bombay Government.[11]

Census Data as Proof of the Successful Eradication of Female Infanticide in Kathiawar

The declaration that female infanticide has been successfully abolished in Kathiawar was the chief driving force behind the censuses of the last decade of reform (1840–1854). The earlier censuses had been driven by the urgency of the political agents in charge to represent their personal success. The 1840–1854 period is characterized by two new factors. First, there are more frequent censuses of the population, as compared to the previous decades, and this frequency means that the Company uses unverified and frequent censuses to create the appearance of greater effectiveness of reform measures. Second, there is an enlargement of the purview of the census through the *discovery* and inclusion of new infanticide practicing communities and districts. These new populations are deployed by Company officials to argue that the success of the Jhareja infanticide reform system is corroborated by the fact that new communities are discovered and speedily reformed. The colonial claim that infanticide has been eradicated completes the processes of erasure of the girl-child from the reform discourse. The final step in the erasure is accomplished through survey techniques and obfuscations, such as the discovery and enumeration of new communities, new demographic trends, and new sampling issues.

After 32 years of reform, the 1840 census constructs results in all districts to reflect the new Company policy and rhetoric of declaring successful abolition of female infanticide through British reform efforts. The aberrant results in Shahpoor where not a single female was reported and Adhoee Parghanas, which had been newly added to the census and had the sex ratio of 17:1 did not deter the British from declaring success (*Parliamentary Papers* No. 613, 1843; Pakrasi 1970, 172). The British found ingenious ways of reconstellating abysmal census results to declare their reform successful. In itself this would merely be a story of colonial bureaucratic manipulation of census data to further their own agendas and not worth investigating. However, in terms of our argument about the colonial legacy of the erasure of the girl-child under population discourse, and its continuance in the postcolonial generalization of female infanticide and femicide, we have to analyze the discursive emergence of bureaucratic erasure that is faithfully followed by postcolonial Indian bureaucracy. *We argue that each statistical manipulation serves as a historical inscription on the discourse of population that repeats and reinscribes the erasure of the girl child.* Therefore, these manipulations cannot be treated with the cynicism that we have come to associate with statistical analysis. Rather in this case they provide us with an invaluable text that performs the historic erasure of the girl-child again and again.

Political Agent LeGrand Jacob's analysis of the 1840 census provides an example of how the missing girl-child is buried under British interpretation of the census data. He ignores the damning imbalanced overall sex ratio (4:1) and instead singles out and concentrates on the complete sex ratio balance in the age group of one to five years (1:1). The *new* demographic feature of the 1840 census, which is the imbalanced sex ratio in the number of dead (1:3) is significant (Pakrasi 1970, 172–173). We speculate that the recording of a greater number of female deaths in the 1840 census is yet another way devised by the Jhareja community to resist the Company. In the 1841 census there is an incredible reversal in the death rates of males and females (3:1) (Jacob to Willoughby, Secretary to Bombay Government *Selections from Records of Bombay Government* 1856). Whereas in 1840 three times more female deaths were recorded than male deaths, just a year later three times more male deaths are recorded than female deaths.

There seems to be a clear indication that the Jharejas had decoded the Company's alarm at the excessive number of female deaths and decided arbitrarily to record a complete turnaround in the female mortality figures. Similar inexplicable and alarming reversals happen in other aspects of the census. In 1840 the overall sex ratio of the population under 20 years was 4:1, however in just a year that changes to 2:1. The miracle of census technology makes it possible for the sex ratio imbalance to drop from four males for every female to two males for every female in a mere twelve months!

In the 1970s we notice similar strategies used by governmental agencies to manipulate census figures to show "satisfactory progress" in family-planning programs by making sterilization a collateral issue to government housing, licenses, and so on (see our discussion in chapter 1). We name the legacy of colonial population discourse as the numbers game in postcolonial India. The numbers game is played out at all levels in the discourse of population in postcolonial India: lived social, political, and economic realities disappear under the weight of alarming numbers. The discourse of population explosion and the need for population control becomes the facilitator, allowing the indigenous elite and the international agencies to talk about human beings, specifically the poor and women, in terms of target groups and numbers.[12] While the poor and women are persistently represented in terms of numbers and phrases like "teeming millions," "hungry hordes" that the planet's limited resources cannot sustain, there is no corollary mention of consumption patterns of the rich versus the poor, and North versus the

South. Statistics and numbers suffice and persuade the majority, statistics become a substitute for debate and discussion.

In this context the colonial census of 1841 is noteworthy, for it marks an upswing by reporting an excess of female infants over male infants in the one year and under age group and this trend carries on for the next decade. By 1849 the Company declared that female infanticide had been abolished in the province of Kathiawar. In our view the excess of females in the one year and under age group is a diversionary and compensatory tactic by the Jhareja community. They record gratifying results at the first age group in order to subvert Company dictates regarding marriage arrangements and expenditures for marriageable daughters. We suggest that daughter-devaluation in infanticidal clans goes alongside the practice of not marrying daughters, thus preventing marriageable daughters from claiming any share in the family property, and effectively ending the female line by ensuring that daughters never have children. In 1841 only a quarter of the total Jhareja female population was married (26%) while the majority remained unbetrothed (58%).

In the 1840–1854 period the official pressure on census officers to reflect the eradication of female infanticide in their census figures is indicated by the comparative analysis done by a member of the Company's Court of Directors, the ubiquitous Willoughby. He compares his own census (1834), Erskine's (1837), Jacob's (1841), and Malet's (1844) in order to show his subordinates how to construct a progressivist narrative about a steadily improving sex ratio in the Jhareja community in the late 1840s and 1850s, even while successive censuses reflect an imbalanced overall sex ratio. Willoughby contends that the consistent increase in the number of Jhareja females over males means that the sex ratio disparities were steadily declining. He bases his contention exclusively on the number of Jhareja female children in the 1 to 10 years age group (9929: 8425, or 118 per hundred, or not quite 1:1).

Willoughby cannot ignore the fact that while newly born female infants continue to outnumber male infants since the census of 1841, the overall sex ratio continues to persist in favor of males (the 1844 sex ratio of the Jharejas was 295 per 100 or about 3:1). Willoughby's rhetorical solution is to raise doubts regarding Malet's census figures (collected for the first time by a husband and wife team of censors):

> the result of your census leads to the very improbable inference, if the number of males and females shown under each age be correct, that the number of male and female births amongst the Jharejas in Kattywar have, for the last ten years, been annually decreasing from natural causes in the ratio from ten to twenty percent. (*Selections from the Records of the Bombay Government* Nos. 39–40, 1856; Pakrasi 1970, 221)

Willoughby's comments are based on the new colonial argument of "inaccuracies." This argument was to become a great favorite for explaining imbalanced sex ratios in colonial censuses of infanticide endemic provinces right upto the end of the nineteenth century. The argument of inaccuracies is flexible: it explains the persistence of an unfavorable sex ratio by either of two sets of conditions: either the excess of males is "only apparent" because of the under-reporting of females due to devaluation of women, "concealment" or "reticence practiced in an Oriental country" (Census of India, 1875, 13); alternately the "inaccuracies" argument is used, as Willoughby does in the extract, to suggest that the absence of coercive measures has facilitated the hoodwinking of British officials by the deceitful Jhareja community. By distributing the blame for inaccurate returns on the lack of forcible measures, competence of census officials, and the untrustworthy character of the Jharejas, the second line of argument elides the commonsensical conclusion that the decreasing number of births reported in the last ten years (1843–1854) is due to the fact that infanticide continued to be practiced unchecked by the Jhareja community.

Colonial Technologies of Surveillance through the Census and Jhareja Resistance

The colonial will manifests itself most clearly in the deployment of the census as a mode of surveillance. Female infanticide reform becomes highly productive for the Company through the information-gathering required by a census of the population. The Company can use the census to gather detailed information about the Jharejas: that is births, deaths, marriages, household size, profession, and income, and the influx of new residents. In short every sort of information becomes grist to the census's mill. Information that would normally be inaccessible to the British becomes available under the rubric of reform. All this information-gathering and frequent census-taking means that the Jharejas are closely monitored. The reason that the Company closely monitors the Jhareja community is that Jharejas had a reputation for being warlike and rebellious, and surveillance is a tool par excellence for creating an atmosphere of intimidation and fear. The yearly census becomes a way for the British to assert the simple maxim—the Company is watching—which is an essential ingredient for a repressive, coercive colonial state. In effect the British suggest the appearance of a state apparatus without in fact possessing the necessary state apparatus, merely on the basis of a few census officers.

   Walter Benjamin, in his study on the French poet Baudelaire (1938) notes the coming into being of the modern state apparatus after the French Revolution. We quote a passage from Benjamin in order to contrast the surveillance techniques of the modern state that are inaugurated in Paris, the other imperial center, with the modalities of surveillance that are introduced in a remote part of the periphery, the sparsely populated region of Kathiawar. Benjamin describes Baudelaire in Paris:

> Since the French Revolution an extensive network of controls had brought bourgeois life ever more tightly into its meshes. The numbering of houses in the big cities may be used to document the progressive standardization. Napoleon's administration had made it obligatory for Paris in 1805. In proletarian sections, to be sure, this simple police measure had encountered resistance. As late as 1864 it was reported about Saint Antoine, the carpenters' section, that 'if one asks an inhabitant of this suburb what his address is, he will always give the name of his house and not its cold, official number'. In the long run, of course, such resistance was of no avail against the endeavour to compensate by means of a multifarious web of registrations for the fact that the disappearance of people in the masses of the big cities leaves no traces. Baudelaire found this endeavour as much of an encroachment as did any criminal. On his flight from his creditors he went to cafes or reading circles. Sometimes he had two domiciles at the same time—but on days when the rent was due, he often spent the night at a third place with friends. ("The Flaneur: The Paris of the Second Empire in Baudelaire" 1973, 47)

In Paris the citizens' anonymity vanishes under what Benjamin calls "a multifarious web of registrations" and the "progressive standardization" of house numbers. Benjamin's brilliant insight is the resistance to such official codification and surveillance encountered by the state and the police from the populace. The "extensive network of controls" in the city of Paris are dictated by the modern government's fear of uprisings by discontented Paris residents. The Parisian residents correctly perceive these controls as the repression of the state, and the state's daily intrusion into their everyday lives. If we turn from the imperial center of Paris to the colonial periphery, we find that in Kathiawar surveillance and intrusion into the everyday lives of Jharejas occurs under the aegis of a deforming and truncated discourse of reform. Like the Parisian populace, the Jharejas were well aware that the British used female infanticide reform as a leverage to extort exorbitant revenue and justify census as a mode of surveillance.

It is precisely when the census performs the surveillance functions of empire that we discern the operation of the resistant will of the native Jharejas. The obstructions, flaws, and defects that mark the census reports provide us with a text of Jhareja resistance. At the same time that the British were discovering that census could be used for surveillance of the natives, the natives were also discovering that the census offered effective means for resisting the

Company's increasing interference into their lives. The Jhareja Rajputs recoded their patriarchal violence on the female child into the entire village's collective resistance to surveillance by the Company authorities. In the colonial regime in Kathiawar, the census became the chosen battle ground between the British and the natives.

The surveillance functions of the colonial census and indigenous resistance to this surveillance through census, which we name as the collusion between the colonizer and a section of the colonized elite, also marks the deferment of the question of the missing girl-child. Both sides much preferred to negotiate at the site of the census data collection, rather than on the issue of female-child murder. The daughter-killing Jharejas found that the census provided eminently suitable grounds for their own objectives, partly because they secured the cooperation of their noninfanticidal neighbors in the village and presented a united front to resist the census officer, and partly because the Jharejas could now say that they object to the colonial scrutiny of their female household through the intrusive questions of the census officer. For instance, in his 1841 census report Political Agent Jacob confesses that the majority of the female population in the census "have no other guarantee for their existence than the word of their male relations." Jacob concludes that this native prejudice is deep rooted and supported by public opinion, therefore it would be inadvisable to use coercion on this issue; he states, "we should err in attempting to force them" (Jacob to Secretary to Bombay Government, Willoughby, 23 October 1841, Wilson 1855, 261; Pakrasi 1970, 174). The colonialists also preferred census operations because it provided the appearance of colonial power through the interplay between coercive and persuasive measures.

The conversations, political negotiations, and conflicts between the reformers and the perpetrators of infanticide revolved around the enormous problems with regard to census operations. The native census officer became a much maligned figure who was resisted, obstructed, misinformed by the Jhareja community and hounded out from villages. [13] While the Company discursively coded female infanticide in census operations, the native population resisted all efforts at being enumerated and branded. Official reports describe these modes of resistance. For example one report of 1816 recounts the difficulties in collecting census facts and figures. The Company appointed several officials or *mehtas* in the principal Jhareja towns to report the birth, preservation, and murder of female children. The official report states that the census officials aroused so much dislike that, "their exertions (were) nearly abortive." Colonial domination required the controlled representation of indigenous resistance, therefore the report represents the census as an indirect means of knowledge necessitated by the fact that direct knowledge of female infanticide is impossible. In chapter 2 we analyzed the colonial naming of female infanticide as the most secret of all crimes. In Kathiawar we can glimpse the productivity of this rhetorical maneuver: by coding it as a secret crime, the report justifies the census as an indirect means of information retrieval. The report states, "We may consider that every attempt to arrive by direct means at a knowledge of the practices of infanticide has been and will be unsuccessful" (Captain Carnac's report to Bombay Government, January 1816, *Selections from Records of Bombay Government* 1856).

Ranajit Guha argues that the discourse of domination, in his words the prose of counter-insurgency, reveals itself in representing insurgency (1983). In an analogous manner, official documents like the 1816 report betray the true intent of the census as an instrument of surveillance. This self-disclosure in the colonial text occurs where the report puts the abortive efforts of the census officers in a positive light, the 1816 report states: "though such officers could gain little information, their presence operated as a check, and made fear of discovery tend to the abolition of female Infanticide" (ibid.). The false premise of the report is that a patriarchal crime can be prevented by adopting the tactics of intimidation. This statement marks the complex processes of deferment, eradicating the practice of female infanticide is deferred for information-gathering; information-gathering is deferred for the higher colonial imperative of creating an atmosphere of fear and intimidation among the communities of Kathiawar. Thus the material and discursive productivity of official thinking lay in fashioning the census as a colonial technology of surveillance.

Far from intimidating infanticidal Jhareja fathers by the presence of the official censor, the censor and the census apparatus served to coalesce native resistance and boosted their confidence. A powerful reason for this was that the men of infanticidal clans found that their noninfanticidal neighbors, who informally disapproved of Jhareja daughter killing but married their own daughters to infanticidal clans, united with them to resist the census officers. One candid letter describes the organized resistance by Jhareja villages in Kutch, "The Mehtas, sent at my request, by the regency, were either cajoled by false returns, or expelled from towns and villages, not only by the classes charged with the crime but by the other inhabitants" (Letter from Major Henry Pottinger, British Resident at Kutch, to Deputy Secretary Trevelyan, Fort Williams August 31, 1835, *Selections No. 167*).[14] The united resistance of the people through the passive-aggressive techniques of bribing the census officer by "false returns" of female population estimates or the openly aggressive tactics of expelling the census officer from the town or village, constituted an unexpected and troubling turn of events for the East India Company.

The reformers had hoped to tap into the disapproval of daughter killing by noninfanticidal communities in order to make schisms between the people and achieve their objective through divisive tactics. Instead the census became a rallying point for resistance in the Kutch and Kathiawar regions of Gujarat. The 1835 letter describes a number of techniques of resistance: the letter notes that in the post-census reform period Jhareja men were openly expressing their refusal, "most of the Jadejas declared their inability to act up to their agreement, even as far as regarded their nearest relations." The letter narrates the abortive attempt by the Company to construct an indigenized system of surveillance, within which tribal feudatories would be forced to inform their chief, the Rao of Kutch, each time that their wives were expecting, and give information regarding the sex of the newborn child. The letter reports that they responded, "with feelings of equal disgust and horror" (*Selections from the Records of the Bombay Government* Nos. 39–40, 1856; Wilson 1855, 283). The proposal was rejected by Jhareja men on the grounds of extreme intrusion into their domestic affairs.

It is apparent from this exchange that the terms of reform have shifted into a debate about the necessity for, and the militant rejection of, a scrutiny of the subject population (in the Foucaultian sense of the term) through census machinery. The daughter-killing men welcome these new terms of debate, because it allows them to speak from a moral high ground about the cultural impropriety of questions regarding pregnancy and child birth. The 1835 letter from Kutch reports on the rhetorical position taken by elite men regarding the indecorum of census type questions, "Several fathers, for instance, assured me that they dare not establish such a scrutiny regarding their grown up sons" (Wilson 1855, 282–283). The report concludes that the census as a reformist strategy is "defective" and "an utter failure" because the census official is not able to elicit information from the natives. With unusual candor the report admits that the company is helpless before the united resistance of the Kutch Jharejas and "the few censuses that were furnished [were] found to have been drawn up by guess work, from what may be termed the tittle-tattle of the village" (Wilson 1855, 282–283). Village gossip seemed to have been the main resource for the census official in Kutch and Kathiawar in the period from 1808 to 1833.

The Indigenous Elite Males' Manipulation of Census Data: Female Infanticide becomes More Entrenched amongst Jharejas

Like the people of Kutch, the Jharejas of Kathiawar learned to manipulate the census to demonstrate their resistance and make the census productive for themselves by discovering techniques for subverting census figures. The 1840 census marks a new way employed by the Jharejas to resist the Company by recording more number of female children deaths. The 1841 census records covert Jhareja resistance to the company's reform efforts by not marrying the majority of the female population: only 26 percent of the total female population was married while 58 percent of the females remained unbetrothed. Even the introduction of a female censor in the census of 1843 proved an abysmal failure; ironically the 1843 census, which used the female censor to gather information, was in fact returned by the Bombay Government for improbable conclusions based on incorrect data and despite the submission of amended returns. In the censuses of the last decade of reform the Jharejas did not register any births, male or female, in many of the districts or talooks. Furthermore, from the census of 1841, the Jharejas manipulate census figures to show a disproportionate increase in the number of male deaths, exceeding the number of female deaths every year.

The censuses of the last decade record a number of new strategies of covert resistance devised by the native elite to inflate female population numbers in the Jhareja community. One of these consisted of recording more male and less female deaths. Beginning with the census of 1841, the recording of more male deaths became a regular feature of all censuses. Jhareja male deaths exceed by 345 the total number of Jhareja female deaths in these years.[15] This demographic trend is unique, these censuses make the improbable suggestion that in the infanticide practicing community of the Jhareja Rajputs, the male is more vulnerable than his female offspring. The census returns show that the Jhareja mortality sex ratio was the only one biased in favor of females (2:1), while the Jetwa (1:3), the Soorma (1:3), and the Mowhur Meena (2:3) mortality sex ratio were all imbalanced in favor of the males (Pakrasi 1970, 264). Another strategy of resistance devised by the Jhareja community to inflate female figures and rectify the sex ratio disparity at birth consisted of failing to record any births, male or female, in many talooks.[16] For instance in 1849 out of 41 districts there were 10 where no births were recorded, in 1850 there were 14 talooks, in 1851 there were 16 and in 1852 there were 17 talooks in which there were no births, male or female, recorded for the year.

Indigenous resistance often blurs into collusion: Jhareja resistance to reform was in effect a collusion with the imperial census officer to provide statistical evidence of the eradication of female infanticide. The native elite registered an inordinate increase in the female Jhareja population by including, from the 1845 census onward, a disproportionate influx of Jhareja female population from outside the province of Kathiawar. This indigenous strategy functioned collusively with the Company's continued inclusion of new areas under surveillance of the census (13 new districts in 1849, making a total of 41 districts) to cloud the fact that female infanticide continued to be practiced in Kathiawar. The increase in female population may have been a natural result of the influx of migrating Jharejas from outside the province each year. But the inflow of female Jharejas as compared to male Jharejas was so excessive that in 1847 Political Agent Lang remarked, "the number of new residents . . . is so great when compared with those for former years as to excite some doubt whether mistakes may not have been committed in the registry" (*Source Book of Selections from the Records of the Bombay Government* Nos. 39–40, 1856; Pakrasi 1970, 237).[17]

By the end of the nineteenth century the discursive reinscription of female infanticide as an indigenous mode of population control was well established in official correspondence among colonial administrators. Writing to his colleague the Collector of Kaira in Gujarat wrote that female infanticide was a "rational" and "commendable form of population control" (Collector of Kaira, J. D. Atkins to Commissioner, Northern Div., G. B. Reid, 8 February 1895, *Selections* No. 296, no. 436). In saying this Atkins was not expressing a personal viewpoint, rather he was participating in the colonial application of Malthusian theory in northwest India. In effect Atkins was reminding his correspondent of Malthus's argument that the elite or "superior" population decreases in number in an overpopulated or densely populated region, while the "inferior" or lower orders continue to produce large numbers of children. In the British empire this Malthusian proposition was adapted for the colony, in order to discursively reinscribe the high incidence of female infanticide among elite groups.

The implications of this discursive inscription is clear in the Atkins letter. The colonial document explicitly states that the community under official scrutiny (the Lewa Kanbis of Gujarat) practice female infanticide. Atkins acknowledges his awareness of this practice in his official capacity as Collector. Nevertheless, Atkins makes an official recommendation that no reform measures should be initiated by the imperial government to stop the practice. The reasons that Atkins advances are that the infanticidal group are efficient land managers and moneylenders, possess large tracts of land and are adept at land accumulation, and most important of all, daughter-killing elites are exemplary payers of revenue to the British empire. Atkins was convinced that the community's efficient revenue payment and elite domination was due to their marriage customs and female infanticide. Atkins concluded that if they kill their infant daughters at birth, official response should be, in the words of the British poet Pope, "whatever is, is right." Thus in the twilight years of colonial reform, the Malthusian population discourse fully consolidated itself as an imperial discourse justifying female infanticide as a traditional method of population control.

The Figure of Woman in the Discourse of Colonial Reform

The single instance in which the East India Company infanticide reform treated female infant killing as murder was in order to criminalize a tribal woman.[18] In 1854 a tribal woman belonging to the Mohwur Meenas tribal community in Mallia district of Kathiawar, was sentenced to one year's imprisonment for causing the death of her newborn twin daughters (*Sourcebook of Selections of the Records of the Bombay Government* Nos. 39–40, 1856; Pakrasi 1970, 265–269, 292–296). Baee Nathee was a 24-year-old woman belonging to the Mohwur Meenas tribe in Mallia district of Kathiawar. Her case was brought to light in 1853 by Nurbeshunkur Hureeshunkur, the company mehta. The mehta is a figure we have discussed earlier in relation to the census surveys in Kathiawar. He was a much despised native informant in the employ of the Company: his task was to provide evidence of births, deaths, marriages, and report on suspected cases of infanticide for investigation by the political agent. The company's case against Baee Nathee was built on the basis of two sets of depositions: the first set of depositions included the information provided by the midwife Baee Hoora, the corroborative evidence given by the defendant's mother also named Baee Hoora, and the statement given by the defendant. The second set of depositions are recorded from the defendant and the two female witnesses in the presence of, and subsequent to interrogation by, the Political Agent of Kathiawar, J. T. Barr. Barr's superiors in the Bombay government rejected the plea for leniency, stating that they do not find it "prudent" to pardon the tribal woman (Letter from Acting Secretary to Government, H. L. Anderson, to Barr, 8th April 1854, *Selections from Records of Bombay Government* 1856). Consequently Baee Nathee was sentenced to one year's imprisonment.

It is at the margins of the official history of infanticide reform that we discover the reported speech of Baee Nathee, the tribal woman accused of the crime of infanticide. Baee Nathee speaks twice, before the mehta and then again before the British officer. Each time she recounts how and why her daughters died just after their birth. However, even before her self-representation is translated into English and inserted into the official text, an entire discourse of infanticide reform has been mobilized to criminalize Baee Nathee. We recover women's history as fragments in these sets of texts consisting of the depositions of the tribal woman as well as the depositions of her mother and the midwife.

From the margins, the fragment of women's history in these depositions or *ikrarnamas* unpacks the gendered punishment by colonial law. The few instances in which reformers prosecuted the daughter-killing male Jhareja Rajput, the punishment was invariably in economic terms as a fine. Contrarily in the case of Baee Nathee, the punishment was one year's imprisonment. The colonial government's rationale for this gendered scale of punishment is worth quoting: the Bombay government wrote back to the Political Agent that it was "unable to accede to any pardon for the guilty woman" because "infanticide was murder and no enlightened Government could permit the perpetrator of murder, if apprehended, to escape without punishment" (Letter from H. L. Anderson to J. T. Barr 8 August, 1854, *Selections from Records of Bombay Government* 1856; Pakrasi 1970, 268). The benevolent paternalism of British infanticide reform, articulated as the protection of mothers and infant girls, is exposed in this official statement. When men sanction female infanticide they are treated as revenue-paying subjects who commit a crime of property, and punished accordingly by fines. When the tribal woman commits female infanticide, she is perceived as "the perpetrator of murder" and her punishment is imprisonment.

This gender distinction for the same crime of female infanticide is accompanied by a hierarchic distinction by caste and class. These distinctions have a great deal to do with the discursive construction of female victimage in colonial reform. British sati reform focused on the unitary figure of the widow, conversely female infanticide reform pluralized the victim, ranging from the dead female infant, the infanticide survivor, the birthing mother, the grandmother, and other members of the female household, and the midwife. The question that was debated by British sati reform concerned the distinction between voluntary self-immolation and coercive self-immolation. In a related sense the issue that was debated by British administrators concern the mother of the murdered female infants in infanticidal clans, whether she was a fellow victim or criminal. Lata Mani describes the discursive construction of the widow's victimage in sati reform, "Women were cast as either pathetic or heroic victims" (1989, 97). We argue that the discursive construction of victimage in British infanticide reform differed from sati reform principally through the hierarchizing of female victimage on caste and class lines.

The subject position of total victimage in British infanticide reform was accorded to the Rajput women belonging to the elite clans of Rajasthan. Colonial writers described her as a devout and resistant victim, "There is the well-known anecdote given by Captain Hall, of the Mairwarra mother whose entreaty 'for Crishna's sake' rescued her babe from death" (Cave-Brown 1857, 198). Alternately colonial accounts configured her as a fellow victim who was gradually disciplined into passivity, "[Rajput] mothers wept and screamed a good deal when their first female infants were torn from them; but after two or three times giving birth to female infants, they became quiet and reconciled to the usage; and said, 'do as you like' "(Sleeman 1858, 208). The reason that the Mewar mother and the Oudh Rajput mother were constructed as pure victims had very little to do with British recognition of their extreme oppression, and everything to do with British construction of them as racially pure-blooded upper class women.

In the colonial calculation women as victims were the natural ally of the East India Company reformers. A good deal of official correspondence discussed ways and means of appealing to the "humanity and tenderness congenial to" the naturally tender-hearted Rajput mother in order that she inform on her husband and male kinsmen (Walker, September 1807; Pakrasi 1970, 43). The framework within which colonial reformers constructed the mother as victim/informer was persuasive reform, "In short reason, persuasion, and the aid of women, who more readily feel then men the cruelty of such a practice, would do much to put a stop to Infanticide" (Walker, 27th August 1819; Wilson 1855, 123). It is only by textualizing a freely confessed practice as the most secret of crimes that colonial discourse of infanticide reform situates women as informers.

British reformers were in possession of considerable data, which contradicted the colonial construction of absolute female subordination in the infanticidal clan. The British anecdotes—of the Krishna worshipping mother who saves her child, Walker's reference to the humanity and tenderness of the Rajput mother, as well as stray data that showed that Rajput mothers saved their infant daughters if they happened to give birth in the natal home—indicates that there were practices and strategies for female resistance in the Rajput household. Historically many Rajput daughters and wives were radically disaffected and alienated from elite Rajput values (see chapters 6 and 7). Moreover patriarchal power circulated unevenly in the Rajput female household, both the female infant and the childbearing wife were the most powerless, followed by the infanticide survivor, while a modicum of patriarchal power was granted to female elders, especially the paternal grandmother. The paternal grandmother could use her power to prevent female infanticide if she wished, however it was often the case that these older women had survived by internalizing and sustaining the patriarchal ethic.[19] These differences in power and powerlessness by age and kinship between members of the female household, as well as the religion-centered practices of resistance by Rajput women, point to the fact that the discursive construction of absolute victimage in the infanticidal clan was a colonial artifice. This artifice required yet another colonial fiction, namely that the female victims could be persuaded to turn informer without severe consequences to her own survival.

At the lower end of this specifically colonial continuum in reform discourse were the Jhareja Rajput wives who, in the British estimation were not victims but active agents and full participants in the killing of their own daughters. In the British view, the principal distinction between the Rajput mother as victim and the Jhareja Rajput child murderess was that the former belonged to the pure-blooded elite clans of Rajasthan and the latter belonged to the Rajput Jhareja clans of Kutch and Kathiawar, which were allegedly contaminated in their bloodline through intermarriage with Muslims. An official letter articulates this colonial racialism by describing the reasons that women are responsible for killing their own female infants in the Jhareja families of Kutch. The letter describes these clans as having "adopted all the vices" of the Muslims; British race theory is coupled with colonial misogyny in the following statement, "I strongly suspect there is hardly one chaste female [in Jhareja families]"; this discursive association between racial contamination and sexual immorality in women is represented as the cause of women committing female infanticide, the letter states, "several instances have been told to me where young mothers, just before married from other tribes, and even brought from distant countries, have strenuously urged the destruction of their own infants, even in opposition to the father's disposition to save them" (Letter of British Resident in Kutch Henry Pottinger to Deputy Secretary to Government C. E. Trevelyan, 31st August, 1835, Wilson 1855, 236; Pakrasi 1970, 143).

Once the hierarchy of racially pure/impure Rajput women was established in reform discourse, stratification by class became operative. We can see this most clearly in the case that most resembles the Baee Nathee case, except that the defendant accused of female infanticide was an elite Jhareja Rajput man of property. The contrast between the two cases illuminates the class and gender hierarchies in British infanticide reform. In the 1834 case the defendant was the Chief of Rajkot Suraji, whose father had functioned as a British native informant and ally.[20] The reason that East India Company administration in Kathiawar chose to prosecute Suraji was the necessity for a scapegoat, Political Agent Willoughby explained this in a letter, "one instance of detection followed by severe punishment, would contribute more to the extinction of the crime than any other measure that can be resorted to" (Report of Willoughby, 1834 in Wilson 1855, 182). Several elements of the Suraji case illuminate the British construction of female infanticide as a class-stratified crime. Even though the colonial reformers were able to prove that the death of Suraji's newborn female infant was a intentional act of murder, the elite male offender was punished by a fine. Moreover the mother of the dead female infant, midwife, and slave girl escaped punishment, partly because it was an upper-class crime and the mother was portrayed as a victim, and partly because the punishment of Suraji was politically exigent. It lent weight to Willoughby's 1834 Proclamation that Jhareja chiefs of Kathiawar would be allowed to hold their lands subject to their compliance to the infanticide engagements.

Through the 1854 Baee Nathee case we make an incision into the discursive history of infanticide reform, an incision that reveals the superimposition of feudal and colonial violence on the Rajputized tribal woman. The tribal organization of the Mohwur Meenas, to which Baee Nathee belonged had egalitarian social customs like women's right to elopement, divorce, and remarriage. When a tribe Rajputizes itself, for a time the communal features coexist alongside the newly adopted practices of violence associated with Rajputization. The Rajputization of the tribals thus represents a community in a state of transition and upward mobility. Older woman-centered customs have not died out, they exist alongside and are losing ground to the gendered violence of adopted customs. Thus, for example, Baee Nathee as a tribal woman exercised her right to elopement, but once she became a child-bearing mother there was great pressure on her from her husband to commit female infanticide.

It is precisely in this transition that colonial capitalism superimposes its own system of gender and class violence. The British reformers did not find it convenient to prosecute the elite Rajput male and female practitioners of female infanticide. The tribal woman who commits female infant killing on the instructions of her husband is the weakest link in the chain. British reform found her an ideal scapegoat for prosecution and punishment in order to make her an example. The scapegoat had to belong to the most politically powerless community, and the tribal woman fits this category.

Colonial-infanticide reform distinguishes the tribal woman's crime of infanticide from the victimage of the pure-blooded wives of the Rajputs in Rajasthan, and the unchaste Jhareja wives. Under colonial law, the tribal woman's infanticide is far worse than the culpability of Rajput women for the same crime because in her case the crime signifies her sexual freedom and immorality. According to the colonial perspective it is because Baee Nathee has the socially sanctioned right to choose her own husband, as well as the right to leave him if she finds the marriage oppressive and elope with a man of her choice, that she commits child-murder.[21] For the British administrators this line of reasoning did not seem at all illogical; they reason that the tribal woman's sexual liberty could not but make her a vicious, profligate, brutalized, and unfeeling woman lacking in maternal sentiments, and liable to murder her children for no other reason than that they pose a threat to her freedom. Therefore reformers felt it was entirely appropriate that honorable motives (the racially proud Rajput male who commits female infanticide to preserve his racial purity, see Tod I 1829, 504) should extenuate the crime to such a degree that the male offender goes unpunished, and dishonorable motives (the sexually unrestrained tribal woman who commits the same crime to preserve her sexual freedom) should be punished.

First, however, the Company officials had to put together a text that proved that the crime (female infanticide) issued from the motive (women's sexual freedom). Five months before Baee Nathee was brought before the mehta, her crime had been reconstructed and labeled by colonial officials with the aid of the midwife. The figure of the midwife is a crucial one in infanticide documents. The class of women who fell prey to the Company reformer's coercive tactics was the economically underprivileged midwife, it was the midwife who was often coerced into the role of informer. The midwife was a politically powerless player in British reform; she was generally poor, a widow, and easily coerced.[22] The post-1870 infanticide reform documents relating to the northwestern provinces indicate that many of these *dayees* or midwives became easy targets and received punishment (including imprisonment) at the hands of the colonial government (Panigrahi 1976, 174–175). As practitioners of traditional female knowledge of childbirth, they would be increasingly marginalized in the succeeding century by Western gynecology.

In the context of infanticide reform, the midwife is a beleaguered figure caught between her indigenous clients and patrons whom she dare not betray and the East India Company officials who bring pressure to bear on her to provide eye-witness evidence of female child murder. In her deposition the 50-year-old Baee Hoora articulates this predicament, she says, "I am a widow, and a poor woman, and should I openly come forward, it would be difficult for me to live with the Meenas" (1st deposition, May, 1853; Pakrasi 1970, 295). By forcing one powerless woman to inform on and indict another woman, the East India Company contrived a case for criminal prosecution.

The midwife's depositions perform a dual task. First, she articulates the British critique of the immoral tribal woman in this statement: "Amongst the Meenas this crime is greatly prevalent, *on account of daughters of their own free will eloping with other men; hence the cause of infanticide*" (italics ours, 2nd deposition, November 1853). In this statement, the midwife has been prompted by company officials to make the discursive link between female infanticide and the practice of tribal women's elopement. The discursive relationship is of cause and effect, tribal women are child murderesses because they exercise free will. The use of the term "daughters" in this statement suggests that women are themselves causing daughter devaluation, Meenas women as daughters run away with any man they like, therefore Meenas women as mothers consider their female children as hindrance and do away with them.

The midwife's second task is to provide hearsay, which proves Baee Nathee's premeditated intention to murder. The midwife executes this task with some difficulty. She contradicts herself several times in her depositions and each time her self-contradiction is designed to make her hearsay evidence doubtful. In May 1853 she states that Baee Nathee told her not to bathe the newborn twins, in her words, "the mother said, 'The infants are to be destroyed, therefore do not bathe them.'" In November of the same year the midwife retracts and states, "That what is written of the infants having been murdered is false, as I did not say that she would destroy them." In her revised story she states that her evidence was based on her suspicion, "She told me not to wash them, as she knew what to do with children born to her." The midwife says, "So saying, I suspected she would destroy them" (2nd deposition, November 1853). This reported statement is obscure compared to the clear intent of the earlier one.

After a period of verbal and physical coercion, which the colonial text refers to as "interrogation" the midwife retreats still further from the role of prime witness. She says, "When the Jupteedar sent for me, I then became aware that she had destroyed her infants. I forget who told me so" (2nd deposition, November 1853). These series of retractions in the depositions constitute the site of a contestation of wills, the colonial will seeks to divide tribal women in order to delegitimate the pro-women customs of tribal communities, and the will of the midwife who resists the processes of interrogation because she does not wish to be the colonial instrument for another woman's disciplining.

The resistant will of the tribal women is even clearer in the depositions by the 40-year-old mother of the defendant. In her first deposition she is noticeably cryptic and refuses to provide eyewitness evidence of her daughter's crime. Despite repeated interrogations, the defendant's mother states that she only heard but did not actually see the death of the children, she says, "I state what I heard rumoured in the town" (1st deposition, September 1853). The mother's second deposition before Political Agent Barr is a significant text because it reveals the operation of the colonial will as well as the degree to which the elderly tribal woman is noncompliant with the wishes of company officials. Through cross-examination and interrogation, Barr constructs the mother as the embodiment of the community's disapproval of Baee Nathee's sexual transgression. The mother is used to bring in her daughter's prior sexual history as the motivation of her crime, it is in this context that the mother is made to say, "Nathee was married to Kajee Raja, whom she deserted and lived with Sangun" (2nd deposition, November 1853). She is made to voice her disapproval of Nathee's alleged licentiousness, "I consequently never unnecessarily spoke to them" (2nd deposition, November 1853).

In the mother's second deposition there is a clear contradiction between her stated disapproval of her daughter and her passionate defense of her daughter before the Political Agent. Her presence at her daughter's time of need contradicts the official construction of her. Baee Hoora rejects the suggestion that her daughter deliberately murdered her newborn; she says, "but, after giving birth, it is unlikely she would knowingly destroy them. . . . Would any woman kill her own offspring? All women would not do so" (2nd deposition, November 1853). She portrays her daughter as a young woman beset with a number of worries, who is anxious about her 3-year-old daughter suffering from small-pox and in the exhaustion of the postpartum period, is guilty only of inadvertently neglecting her newborn twins and unknowingly causing their death.

Barr is not satisfied with the mother's statement. Therefore after a period of interrogation Baee Hoora is compelled to reveal the full extent of her daughter's real crime. The deposition states: "On further interrogation—

[the mother states] Sangun eloped with Nathee while Raja Kajeea was alive, and twelve months after his death Sangun returned to Mallia" (2nd deposition, November 1853). This statement amplifies the full extent of Baee Nathee's immorality—she lives with another man while her first husband is alive—and this action furnishes conclusive evidence that Baee Nathee is an immoral woman lacking in maternal sentiments who willfully and intentionally commits child-murder.

In a certain sense Baee Nathee's own deposition is irrelevant from the perspective of colonial law. Her alleged crime has already been assembled and reconstructed, her motivation has been analyzed much before she is allowed to speak and defend herself. The two depositions (26 September 1853; 9 November 1853) in which the accused tribal woman defends herself do not give us unmediated access to the subaltern woman. The two depositions are, first of all, a function of her positionality and insertion into colonial law as a criminal. Inevitably Baee Nathee's speech is a highly mediated, fragmented, and contradictory pastiche of several discourses, unevenly structured under overlapping censorships and the multiple kinds of violence visited on her. As postcolonial feminists, we take into account these protocols of reading Baee Nathee's position. Between the British Court's investigation and Baee Nathee stands the interrogator and interpreter: between our use of her depositions as a historical document for women's cultural history there intervenes the political administrative structure and the discursive modes of British colonialist historiography.

In her opening words in her first deposition, Baee Nathee refers to the idiom adopted by the Mohwur Meenas tribe, the idiom of Rajputization within which the lives of infant daughters are subject to the will of family men who decide whether or not they will be preserved, she states: "Twin daughters were born to me, and I, having no wish to preserve them, did not suckle them" (22 September, 1853). Later in the same deposition, she reiterates, "as it was not my wish to preserve them, why should I have suckled them?" These two statements of Baee Nathee encapsulate the processes of Rajputization and the tribe's internalization of daughter devaluation. Baee Nathee represents the first generation of Rajputized tribals, therefore she still carries traces of tribal values regarding women's sexual choice. However the idiom of Rajputization and the disciplining of women that is an inherent part of the idiom, is inscribed over the residual traces of tribal custom.

Baee Nathee occupies a fractured position vis-à-vis Rajputization. A tribe Rajputizes itself through the social prohibition against intermarriage within the village, as well as with other tribes of Meenas. This prohibition entails that Meenas daughters, like Rajput daughters, have to be married into a family that is considerably distant from the bride's natal clan. It is clearly acknowledged in the mother's deposition that Baee Nathee had eloped with a fellow tribesman Mohwur Sangun Walanee. This violation of the rules of exogamy in Rajputization was the reason that the couple had to leave the village and were ostracized by Baee Nathee's natal family. Baee Nathee describes her social ostracism in these words:

> I am the married wife [of] a Raja Kajeea, but I deserted him, and lived with Sangun, and after my husband's death I returned to Mallia twelve months ago; until then I kept wandering about.
>
> The daughter now with me and the deceased twin daughters, are Sangun's. About five years ago Sangun eloped with me of my own free will. After the decease of my twin daughters my mother left off visiting my house; she never came when he was present, on account of my elopement with him. (2nd deposition, 9 November 1853)

The above extract shows that Baee Nathee has internalized the social injunction concerning exogamy. The particular words in which Baee Nathee explains her marital status are noteworthy, she states that she is the "married wife" of Kajeea whom she "deserted" and she currently "lives with" Sangun. Her choice of words confirms the colonial proposition that the immorality rampant in tribal society is responsible for the custom of female infanticide. Baee Nathee's statement is factually incorrect, she is not the wife but the widow of Kajeea. By virtue of her live-in status, as well as the fact that all her children are Sangun's, Baee Nathee would be considered by tribal custom to be Sangun's wife. This is clearly indicated in Baee Nathee's mother's deposition, "The wife of Mohwur Sangun is my daughter" (1st deposition, 20 September 1853). Baee Nathee is also referred to as Sangun's wife in the midwife's deposition, as well as by colonial documents.

In the extract above Baee Nathee's words suggest that she has been the victim of the tribal community's ostracism. She characterizes the five years spent with Sangun as "wandering about" and the implication is that these five years have been a period of homelessness, itinerant jobs, and lack of support from the community as well as her natal family. She also states that after her return to the village, her mother is unwilling to accept her elopement, "she never came when he [Sangun] was present on account of my elopement with him." This is corroborated by the mother's second deposition, "I consequently never unnecessarily spoke to them but their eldest daughter having been very ill with the small-pox, I went to see her, but having no wish to remain there, I did not stop to attend upon their eldest daughter" (2nd deposition, November 1853). Baee Nathee is doubly ostracized. The colonial law singles her out for punishment, although both British and indigenous authorities know that there are many families in the tribe that practice female infanticide. We argue that this specifically colonial violence on Baee Nathee is preceded by the prior violence of the Rajputizing tribal community, which condemns her for violating their newly adopted marriage customs.

The colonial document maps the imperfect mis-fit between Baee Nathee's position as a tribal woman subject to different levels of violence, and her desire to successfully coexist with her tribal heritage and the injunctions of the Rajputizing tribe. Baee Nathee's alleged murdering of her twin infant daughters cannot be seen in the same way as the propertied Rajput male's practice of female infanticide. Neither can it be seen as women's resistance to the processes of Rajputization and daughter devaluation. Instead Baee Nathee's prosecution and confession marks a moment of rupture in the seemingly natural process of Rajputization of the Mohwur Meenas tribe and the territorial expansion of the East India Company in Kathiawar.

The powerful censor on Baee Nathee's speech is the injunction on her as well as the midwife and Baee Nathee's mother, to speak the discourse of successful infanticide reform. All three women say by rote, "It was anciently the custom in my caste not to preserve daughters, but at the present time infanticide is extinct" (Baee Nathee's 2nd deposition, November 1853). This statement is identical to the one made by Baee Nathee's mother, "It was customary in my caste to commit Infanticide but from the arrangements made in the last twelve months, no one commits the crime" (1st deposition, September 1853). Tribal women are forced to testify that female infanticide has been suppressed as a direct result of British reform.

It is not difficult to imagine the 24-year-old tribal girl's terror and bewilderment, as she is brought under the spotlight and is made to confess that she acted alone and take the full blame on herself. It is evident from her disclaimers in the second deposition that she has gradually become aware that the mehta has made her indict herself, therefore she says, "It was not my intention to destroy them [the twins] and if the attachment mehta has above stated so, I am not perfectly aware" (2nd deposition, November 1853).

Under colonial law indigenous men or women were forced to occupy the subject position of the informer. Thus, for instance, the midwife escapes punishment only because she informs on Baee Nathee and is ready to inform about yet another case. Even the elite Jhareja Chiefs who preside over the District Court point the finger on the tribal male in order to divert British wrath. However the 24-year-old Baee Nathee is either unaware or unwilling to take recourse to this survival strategy. She understands the most fundamental law of community in the tribal society, which is to create a wall of silence before the outsider, and thus implicate no one other than herself. Baee Nathee does not engage in a war of words and counter accusations against the midwife or her mother, or point the finger at any person in her village; she states, "when they died, no one else besides my husband who buried the four day old baby in a graveyard, therefore none of my caste people or relations attended" (2nd deposition, November 1853). Colonial law contrives to endow Baee Nathee with a false agency, through his cross-examination the mehta elicits from Baee Nathee, "Neither my husband nor anyone else advised me (to deprived[sic] them of life); I did so of my own wish" (1st deposition, 22 September 1853). Colonial law stigmatizes the free will ordained by tribal law in a woman's right to elopement, while paradoxically bestowing the illusion of free will to Baee Nathee precisely in the domain that has been restricted and disciplined by Rajputization, namely her right to have female children.

Even though her speech is a pastiche of indigenous patriarchal and British reformist discourses, Baee Nathee is not the silenced subaltern woman who is spoken by discourse. Colonial law divides the three women by discursively situating the midwife as eyewitness and informer, representing the mother of Baee Nathee as the embodiment of social disapproval, and positioning Baee Nathee as the criminal who is brought before law as a direct result of the depositions of the midwife and mother, which indict her. Language, discourse and the state machinery of law are arrayed against them. The depositions of the three women are recorded under conditions that distort their speech and silence them. They are subject to the capriciousness of a law that does not prosecute the elite but victimizes the disempowered, an alien British law that is not answerable to the community and that was never intended to police the crime but only to profit by it. The women are confronted by a legal apparatus they do not understand, and an English language in which Baee Nathee's speech is translated and recorded by the mehta and read back to her as the confession of a criminal. Despite these odds the three women's depositions are powerful texts, not of tribal women's passive submission, but of tribal women's resistance to colonial patriarchal violence. The power of these texts comes from those elements in their recorded speech that assert their collectivity.

We cannot appreciate the rhetorical efficacy of the three women's depositions, unless we contrast it with the standard account of female infanticide in colonial documents. The scene of Baee Nathee's confinement in no way resembles the account codified in British documents. Conventionally the newborn female infant was taken away from the mother and put to death by the female household with the aid of the midwife. Contrarily Baee Nathee is alone and in the same room with her ill daughter and hungry infants. We can now see why the two women (her mother and the midwife) insist on recording the fact that they do not stay with Baee Nathee in the time period of her confinement or help with the ill child. Both women state that they were not present at the time when the death of the infants occurred, they heard of it much later. It is clear that neither the mehta nor Barr can find any evidence to dispute these facts. The company officials are unable to make Baee Nathee's account conform to the standard colonial representation of female infant murder as an act executed by other members of the female household.

The second rhetorical strategy deployed by the three women is the construction of the spatial and temporal representation of the scene of the childrens' death. The midwife says, "the small cot was close to the large one" (2nd deposition, November 1853). Baee Nathee states:

> These twin daughters were born about three hours after sunrise and on the third day about midday, they died. . . . After the twin daughters were born, I placed them on a separate small cot, as my eldest daughter slept on the same cot with me; the cots were placed close together. The twin daughters were on one cot, and I constantly looked after them, but my not having suckled them, they died. (2nd deposition, 9 November 1853)

The spatial and temporal configuration described by Baee Nathee does not conform to colonial accounts of female infanticide, in the latter the newborn infant was removed from the birthing room and swiftly disposed off right after birth.[23] Baee Nathee's spare description of the day and a half conceals, with the characteristic stoicism of tribal people, the toll it must have taken on her in the postpartum period. Baee Nathee had to endure the torture of hearing the infants, seeing them and remaining in the same room for the thirty-six hours it took the twins to die. The spatiality of the scene, as well as the details about the time of birth and the time of death, tend to bring home the material realities of Baee Nathee's life and militate against the strict, univocal and stereotypical picture of the criminal that Barr wishes to create.

It is conceivable that on their own the three women may not have been able to subvert the language and discourse of colonial law. The role of the native informant and translator gains significance in this regard. The mehta Nurbeshunkur Hureeshunkur is a politically ambivalent figure. He obeys the Company directive to find a scapegoat to drive home the necessity for infanticide reform, however he secretly subverts his English superiors. Much of the detail in the first depositions by the three women is elicited by his cross questioning, and a great many of these details are not relevant or advantageous to the case made by the East India Company against Baee Nathee.

For instance the mehta repeatedly questions the three women about the whereabouts of the husband, Mohwur Sangun, and all three women answer that he was present in the house at all times. As a crucial link in the chain of command, the mehta brings to bear on the case, even in the way he formulates his questions, his own knowledge of the patriarchal nature of the crime. The question points to the patriarchal dimension of the crime; however the Company's representative, Political Agent Barr displays lack of interest in the role of the husband and the patriarchal responsibility for the crime. In our reading of the text of the depositions, it is significant that at all times the husband was present in the house, although not in the room itself. The evidence states that the husband buries the infants in the enclosure. The husband's presence in the house throughout his wife's ordeal means that he was at hand to ensure that the twins were not saved and to remind his wife that her present ordeal would result in benefits of Rajputizing upward mobility for both of them. Baee Nathee in turn negotiates with her torture, pain, and loss by focusing on the discomfort of her three-year-old daughter.

The third and most important rhetorical strategy employed by the three women to resist the colonial legal machinery is by foregrounding the specifically women's domain of nurture and the mutual support by the community of women. Colonial law is indifferent to the manner in which the infants were put to death, it simply requires evidence about the defendant's expressed intention to kill in order to prosecute her. In opposition to this imperative of colonial law, Baee Nathee asserts an alternative reality by continually steering the depositions to the theme of breast feeding. This is a strategic ploy on Baee Nathee's part; she diverts the deposition from the issue of her intentionality to a different register, namely the cause of infant death. She declares that she did not kill her daughters intentionally, because she did not use any of the traditional methods of female infanticide, "I suckled them twice or thrice, which not being sufficient, they died" (1st deposition, September 1853). Some of the traditional methods of female infanticide that were codified in colonial documents consisted of administering opium, strangulation, or smothering.

Having shifted the grounds of the deposition to the fact that she did not nurse the twins, Baee Nathee proceeds to narrativize her predicament as the mother of three daughters. There is a contestation of realities between Baee Nathee, and Political Agent Barr: the reality imposed by colonial authorities is that of a promiscuous tribal woman cold-bloodedly killing her own children: the reality constructed by Baee Nathee, aided by the depositions of her mother, is of a physically exhausted and psychologically bewildered young woman who divides her attention between three daughters who need her. By making the legal case turn on whether the defendant knowingly or unknowingly denied breastfeeding to the newborn twins, Baee Nathee draws attention to the figure in the wings, her three-year-old surviving daughter. Even though British reform masquerades as the paternalistic defender of the girl child, the colonial authorities are curiously uninterested in Baee Nathee's living daughter. The two women re-insert her into the scene, describing her as a three year old who requires constant attention from her mother because she has been recently weaned and is seriously ill with the life-threatening disease of smallpox. Before the invention of the vaccine, smallpox was a disease that disfigured children for life or took their lives. Either possibility would be a source of anxiety for the parents, a girl disfigured with smallpox faced social ostracism and had little chances of marriage in a traditional society.

Baee Nathee describes her maternal solicitude for this daughter, she says:

> My third daughter, who is at present with me, is three years old and as she suffered severely from the small pox, my time was taken up in attending upon her; I was therefore unable to suckle my other twin daughters; they consequently died. . . . My surviving daughter I suckled and ten days prior to the birth of my twin daughters I weaned her. I had not sufficient milk at the time, but to pacify her, I permitted her to suckle, but at present she [is] sufficiently suckled. (2nd deposition, 9 November 1853)

This extract undermines the colonial construction of the scene of birth as a criminal act of child murder. As a mother distressed by her eldest daughter's illness, and as a woman in the throes of postpartum stress, Baee Nathee seems less and less like the cold-blooded child murderess. In her first deposition Baee Nathee says that she refused to nurse the twins. However in the second deposition she amplifies her statement to say that she nursed them a couple of times "which not being sufficient, they died." Through these details Baee Nathee subverts the legal question of her intentionality. She discloses a scene in which the question, did she knowingly or unknowingly deny breastfeeding her newborn twins, metamorphoses into a question concerning nurture, how a woman divides her attention between her three children, all of whom require her complete attention. She says, "my time was taken up in attending upon her[the eldest daughter]" and this is corroborated by her mother. The defendant's mother underscores Baee Nathee's maternal anxiety by stating that she went over to her daughter's home to check on her ill granddaughter.

Together both women's depositions shift the affective center of the scene toward the ill girl child, suffering cruelly from smallpox and needing constant attention, loved by her mother and grandmother. The picture that emerges is much more of a distraught mother who keeps her daughters in close proximity to her, and inadvertently causes the death of the twins. This emotional emphasis militates against the colonial construction of the tribal woman's immorality, criminality, and daughter devaluation.[24]

The public event of the trial of Baee Nathee is precisely the point at which, from the margins of colonial reform discourse, the Baee Nathee text moves toward the center. At the center Political Agent Barr takes over the representation, and it is in the interstices of his official descriptions that we read and recover the negotiations between the indigenous male elite and the colonial authorities at the site of Baee Nathee's trial. The tribal woman's trial does not take place in a *punchayat* (village council) nor is it in the manner of the 1834 Suraji trial in which the East India Company's Political Agent was the prosecutor, judge, and jury. Instead the trial is staged as a public spectacle on 12 July 1854 in Rajkot. In the absence of any legal or political jurisdiction in

Kathiawar, the revenue collecting agency of the East India Company dresses up the paraphernalia of British justice for self-legitimation as a legally appointed government in a civic society. The High Court of Criminal Justice had been in operation since 1831 ostensibly for the purpose of trying criminal cases. Willoughby had proclaimed in 1834 that all cases of infanticide be tried by this court. This court was a deformed institution comprised of the elite and powerful, the political agent served as its president, along with premier Jhareja chiefs and. its sentences were reviewed by the Bombay Government (Wilson 1855, 185).

We quote Political Agent Barr's description of the Baee Nathee trial because it affords a glimpse of the tug of war between elite males and the East India Company:

> Putwaree, the Karbaree of Saela, and three Chiefs, one of them a Jhareja, sat as assessors and the evidence adduced was so clear that they at once found the prisoner guilty; but on weighing the circumstances elicited, they were of[the] opinion that she had left her newly born twin infants to die from want of nourishment in obedience to the command of her husband, whom they consider to have been the greater culprit, and that she did so when she herself was in a state of bewilderment. They have, therefore, passed this lenient sentence of one year's ordinary imprisonment upon her . . . the Chowuttias of Mallia attended this Court, as did all the Chiefs and Grassias who are at present at Rajkot, and the open trial and condemnation of the woman will have an effect in putting a stop to the crime of which she has been found guilty. (Letter of Political Agent Barr to Anderson, Acting Secretary to Bombay Government, July 14, 1853, *Selections* 1856; Pakrasi 1970, 268)

Barr's account refers to the jury as "assessors," the word denotes the fact that the cases tried in the High Court of Criminal Justice were all revenue related cases, in which assessors were required to appraise the property of the defendant and calculate revenue fines. The institutional framework in which British reformers try and sentence Baee Nathee deals with revenue, land, and property. The relationship of the people of Kathiawar as revenue payees to the Company inflects the colonial description of the larger community of Rajkot who attended the tribal woman's trial to express solidarity. Barr designates them in terms of their relationship to land and revenue, "Chowuttias" (one fourth partners in land), "Chiefs and Grassias."

We mark the particular arguments and interventions deployed by indigenous elite men as the place of negotiation in the discourse of colonial reform. The indigenous patriarchal authorities use the three women's textual representation to guide the reaction of the Company authorities. Indigenous men, Barr writes, hold Sangun to be "the greater culprit" than Baee Nathee. This line of reasoning has been prepared for by the mehta who conducted the first depositions of the three women. From the indigenous male perspective, the murder is done at his behest of the father. It is precisely at this point in the text that elite males betray their knowledge of the patriarchal nature of female infanticide, this knowledge is reflected in their judgment that the fate of infant daughter is decided by the father, not the mother, even though she may be the executor of the father's will.

There is an element of self-interest and political calculation in the men revealing just how well they understand the predicament of women like Baee Nathee. Their judgment contained an implicit challenge to colonial law to prosecute the real criminals, the fathers. This challenge was issued in the full knowledge that, after the 1834 Suraji trial, the prosecution of the male offender for the crime of infanticide was too politically risky for the East India Company. It is precisely through these negotiations and threats between men that the sentence of Baee Nathee is mitigated to one year's imprisonment.

The postscript to Barr's hope that, "the open trial and condemnation of the woman will have an effect in putting a stop to the crime of which she has been found guilty" lies in British reformers' lack of interest in Baee Nathee's surviving daughter. A letter from the Bombay government states that the indigenous community requested that the elder daughter of Baee Nathee be allowed to live with her mother for the year of her incarceration. This post-script reveals that the tribal womans' alternative representation was effective in focusing attention on the eldest girl child. The fact that the request was made by Jhareja elite men suggests that these men wished to see how far they could go in the push and shove with the Company.

There is an irony in the fact that the Bombay Government refused the request, the Secretary wrote, "A child at the breast may be allowed to remain with the mother in prison, but not children of advanced age." Instead the Government suggested that if the elder daughter of Baee Nathee fell sick, she should be treated at the Civil Hospital at Rajkot till her health was restored (Letter of Anderson, Acting Secretary to Bombay Government, 8 August 1854, *Selections* 1856; Pakrasi 1970, 269). The Bombay Government's refusal of this innocuous request exposes the ideology of colonial reform, Company reformers feign interest in the girl child's welfare and initiate infanticide reform on her behalf but are indifferent to the welfare of the surviving daughter.[25]

The long-term consequences of the British prosecution of Baee Nathee were two fold. The Meenas tribes in Kathiawar demonstrated their compliance with the Company's infanticide reform by initiating marriage reform and permitting intermarriages amongst the different tribes of Meenas. The second consequence of the Baee Nathee case was that female infanticide was subsumed by colonial authorities in the discourse of the census. The colonial census of the Meenas had disclosed the case of Baee Nathee in 1853 through the attachment mehta who collected and collated census data for the district. Barr's comments make a discursive connection between Baee Nathee's case and census figures of the Mohwur Meenas, "I regret to add that the whole tenor of evidence [of the Baee Nathee case], supported, as it is, by the startling fact which the census discloses, of there being only 24 females in the Mohwur community in Mallia, whilst the number of males is 94, convinces me that the crime must have been prevalent in the tribe" (Letter of Barr to Anderson, Acting Secretary to Bombay Government 23 March, 1854, *Selections* 1856; Pakrasi 1970, 267). In the aftermath of the Baee Nathee case, the company ordered the inclusion of the Mohwur Meenas tribe in the colonial census of Kathiawar.

We gain an invaluable glimpse of tribal women's perspective on infanticide reform at the margins of the Report on the Political Administration of the Rajputanana States for 1865–1867 (RAR). This colonial document records the statement made by a Purriar Meenas woman to a census officer. It is a remarkably critical and contentious statement and displays a sophisticated understanding of the enmeshing of colonial and indigenous patriarchal discourses on female infanticide. The unnamed tribal women in the RAR document articulates her grievance in an entirely secular vocabulary of the law. She tells the Company officials who compile the RAR report that there is a discrepancy in her rights under the law. She can order legal punishment for Meenas men if they rob and steal goods from her. However, she has no legal recourse if the men of her family and community sanction daughter-killing. In effect she has no rights under law for the preservation of her female children (317).

We retrieve this tribal woman's trenchant critique from the colonial archive because she has hit upon the precise contradiction in colonial infanticide reform. The revenue collecting Company instituted female infanticide reform to augment and provide leverage for its revenue collecting activities. The robbery of goods rated greater punishment in the Company's legal discourse than taking the life of daughters. The RAR document does not address the tribal woman's question. Instead the official document configures her and her missing daughters in the sex ratio of the census of all the Meenas villages in Mewar, Jaipur and Bundi (28.88, 29.60).

The Connections between British Infanticide Reform and Postcolonial Femicide

Postcolonial men and women who commit femicide say that they are following state directives for a small family by paying for reproductive technology in order to determine the sex of the child. They call this process of repeated pregnancies and the serial elimination of the female fetuses "trying" and the word indicates the patriarchal direction of their reproductive practices, because they are practicing violence on the family women by trying to beget a son. We textualize this by revisiting briefly a text that we have analyzed in detail in Chapter 1, Datta's film on femicide *Rishte*. In *Rishte* the educated characters in the film like the radiologist and his wife deploy the discourse of population control to explain femicide, thus demonstrating the discursive connections between colonial female infanticide reform and postcolonial femicide.

It is in and through this enmeshing of feudal practices of violence against women and the neocolonial capitalist logic of population control that patriarchy renews and perpetuates itself. The past in nineteenth-century western India leads up to this present. There is a melancholy truth in understanding how patriarchal violence against the female infant does not remain a purely feudal crime in nineteenth-century India. Feudal cruelty toward women was based on absolute domination, however it was the British empire that gave Indian men a certain confidence, a vocabulary of race pride, economism, and population control for the practices of violence toward women. Feudal cruelty gained a new impetus from British colonialism.

CHAPTER 6

Subaltern Traditions of Resistance to Rajput Patriarchy Articulated by Generations of Women within the Meera Tradition

Postcolonial theorizing about women's writing in India has had to operate within the dialectic of elitism and nationalist mobilization.[1] By this we mean that the recovery of pre-Independence women's writing in India has generally been limited to representations of a very narrow elite group of women writers who through benevolent patriarchal patronage and/or family privilege were able to gain prominence. The general tendency of such women writers was to align and subsume their gender politics toward the ideals of nationalism. When the question of pre-Independence women's writing is further complicated with the question of dissent, resistance, and opposition, the field becomes curiously evacuated. Recent critical scholarship has attempted to address this lacunae through work on the writings of female poets and saints (Manushi 1989; Dehejia 1990; Mukta 1994).

In the attempted canon formation by Susie Tharu and K. Lalitha (1993) the first of the two-volume anthology devotes less than one-fourth of the anthology to pre-nationalist women's writing; three-fourths of the volume is devoted to "Literature of Reform and Nationalist Movements." It is quite true that cultural nationalism and the Swadeshi movement marks the emergence of middle-class women's participation in nationalist activities, and a virtual renaissance in nationalism-centered women's writings. It should be clear that we do not devalue either the women's writing that flowered around the Swadeshi movements, nor the critical re-evaluation of these women's texts, for these writings have shaped the critical consciousness of postcolonial men and women. However we do not subscribe to the critical approach typified by Tharu and Lalitha's anthology, which puts elite nationalist movements at the center, and reads off Indian women's literatures from this nucleus. We do not wish to erase the modes of women's writings, and the nonelite domains in which those writings are articulated, that are invisibilized with the privileging of elite nationalism and nationalist-centered canon of women's literature precisely because these writings have also shaped the critical consciousness of women and men in India.

Nationalism-centered canons of Indian women's writings display an elite bias, similar to the elite bias in British and nationalist historiography of

India critiqued by Ranajit Guha. This elite bias should not be read as a personal error of judgment, but a general malaise in the field of postcolonial theory, and shared by none other than Edward Said. In Tharu and Lalitha's case, our critique addresses the nationalism-centered canon formation, we question the exclusions of the genres and periods of women's writings that fall outside the formation. In Said's case our question is broader in scope because we address his stated mode of secular interpretation of cultural and political texts. The problem in Said's writing involves his definition of secular interpretation. Said's location allows him to see the inter-imbrication of religion with nationalism, and he is critical of both nationalism as well as religion. There is a certain continuity in the elite bias of the Tharu and Lalitha canon and Said's essays on secular interpretation. These continuities are, in our view, an indication that the problem is endemic to our disciplines. We link the three critics in order to map out the dimension of the problem; it is not part of our project to undermine the pioneering work by each of these scholars.

In response to the interviewer's question concerning what Edward Said means by the phrase "the politics of secular interpretation," Said replies:

> The notion of secularism. This goes back to actual living human beings. Men and women produce their own history, and therefore it must be possible to interpret that history in secular terms, under which religions are seen, you might say as a token of submerged feelings of identity, of tribal solidarity. . . . But religion has its limits in the secular world . . . you need a secular and humane vision, one based on the idea of human history not being the result of divine intervention but a much slower process than the politics of identity usually allow . . . secular interpretation which argues for historical discrimination and for a certain kind of deliberate scholarship. It implies a certain interpretive sophistication. Above all, it argues, and this is the point, for the potential of a community that is political, cultural, intellectual, and is not geographically and homogeneously defined. . . . But one does have to give a certain attention to the rather dense fabric of secular life, which can't be herded under the rubric of national identity or can't be made entirely to respond to this phony idea of a paranoid frontier separating "us" from "them." . . . The politics of secular interpretation proposes a way of dealing with that problem, a way of avoiding the pitfalls of nationalism I have just outlined, by discriminating between the different "Easts" and "Wests," how differently they were made, maintained, and so on. (Sprinker 1992, 232–233)

Said's intellectual and political commitment to the politics of secular interpretation emerges both from his own situatedness as an exiled Palestinian intellectual actively involved in the Palestinian struggle, and from his position as a First World metropolitan secular academic professional. Said situates his critique of nationalism and national identity within the "larger Islamic context" of the place of Palestinians, Jews, Armenians, Kurds, Christians, and Egyptian Copts within the Middle East; according to Said this geo-political context produces a kind of "desperate religious sentiment."

Edward Said's enormous influence in the field of postcolonial studies makes it possible to cite him as an example of the dominant academic discourse of secular interpretation, even while we note his location as an oppositional academic in the larger field of the humanities. Within this dominant academic discourse, the binary of secular/religious functions such that secular interpretation stands for all that is "deliberative," "sophisticated," "historical," and deals with the "political, cultural and intellectual aspects," where attention is paid to the "dense fabric of secular life." Secular interpretation also stands in for detailed attention to heterogenously constructed histories and difference, while all that is religious denotes a commitment to religious or cultural identity that is ahistorical and naive. Religious identity is submerged to national identity, fundamentalism is then seen as a historically necessary step in the anti-colonial struggle; however its moment is in the past and the attempt to map and understand religion and the formation of religious identity are seen as involved in somewhat simplistic, nostalgic, and futile reconstructions of a past that is usually imaginary and impossible to prove. Commitment to the politics of resistance and opposition to the globalizing tendency of capital in interpretive cultural work seems to become, in this discourse, a *natural* commitment to the politics of secularism. In marking this binary in Said's thought, we are also critiquing religious fundamentalism, the religious right, and the historiography and cultural production of the Hinduvta movement in postcolonial India, which are politically exclusionary and cause historical amnesia. In effect we do not bind ourselves on either side of Said's binary because there is a certain repression implicit in the notion that to be at odds with "secular interpretation" is automatically to be inside religious fundamentalism.

We mark our critical distance from this play of the binary of secular/religious cultural analysis. We suggest that the elitist metropolitan academic and political commitment to the politics of secular interpretation renders certain modes of resistance opaque. An example of this is the resistance articulated from within a religious vocabulary by women and the poor to patriarchal domination. Unless we are able to bring to bear deliberative and critical attention and a commitment to feminism to the seemingly religious text of Meera's poetry and the legends around Meera's life (1498–1546), in short the Meera tradition, we cannot appreciate the process of subaltern dissent. Unless we are able to discard the critical assumption that secular politics is all that is outside of and around religion, and that the religious text is always and already a naive text of medieval, feudal consciousness and accept instead the radical premise that a secular critique is possible from within the religious vocabulary and sensibility, when the religion is a syncretic coming together of Hindu and Muslim, Sufi and Bhakti traditions that have historically been articulated by women, we cannot understand the Meera tradition.

In medieval India Meera's poetry through the use of a dissenting religious idiom essays a secular (anti-casteist, anti-class, women-centered) critique of Rajput patriarchal values and Rajput accumulation. We do not propose that the Meera tradition embodies the notion of secular in the same way as we understand it in our own times. We do however suggest that Meera's seemingly religious poetry has to be evaluated not in terms of a patronizing dismissal of its simple, rural, folk religious idiom, which can then be dismissed as naive nostalgia for divine intervention in the affairs of human beings and a transhistorical understanding of the history that men and women create. Rather Meera's poetry has to be evaluated in terms of the subaltern protest, dissent, and resistance it gives voice to and keeps alive through four centuries of oral intergenerational transmissions.[2]

Meera's poetry alludes to the custom of female infanticide among rich families in Rajasthan in several ways. The most clear and consistent reference to female infanticide is signified in her self-naming as the daughter and wife who rejects natal and marital relationships as laid down in the norms of Rajput clan identity.[3] In a song sung all over India Meera says, "of father, mother, brother, kinsmen I have none" (Chaturvedi 1983, 240). There is a still, almost cruel detachment of the truly estranged woman in this poetic formulation of self-orphaning. For Meera the condition of being female in Rajput society is to be under the constant threat of annihilation. We argue that at the heart of Meera's rejection of her Rajput inheritance lies a refusal of the practice of female infanticide. So complete is her refusal of the treatment meted out to women in the Rajput community that Meera rejects her family, community, and country. When she is exiled from her marital home, she takes to the life of a wanderer in protest. She would rather embrace poverty, humiliation, threats to her survival, and banishment than subject herself to the militaristic, anti-women logic of Rajput aristocracy.

Meera's early life in the royal house of Merta in fifteenth-century Rajasthan is atypical. The only narrative of girlhood celebrated by bards in medieval Rajasthan is the masculinized girl-child who learns the art of warfare from her father and dresses in masculine gear. Meera's childhood is described in terms of one telling incident: Meera's mother tells her daughter that she is betrothed to the god Krishna (Chaturvedi 1983, 19). We interpret this as a folkloric convention for the transmission of survival knowledge from mother to daughter, arming her daughter against the violence she is certain to encounter as a girl and as a wife.

Meera's refusal to marry the groom chosen for her, and her family's coercion in forcing her to marry into the royal Sisodiya family of Mewar is celebrated in popular verse.[4] Meera conducts a civil war against her politically powerful marital family despite their life-long persecution of her. This part of Meera's life concludes, not with her submission or her death, but with her leaving home and wandering through northwest India. This is the period when the majority of Meera's verses are composed, as her message is disseminated far and wide among the people. Meera's life is brutally terminated. As a rallying point for resistance to elite Rajput hegemony Meera cannot be allowed to live, although the exact mode of her death is shrouded in mystery. In some legends Meera was unaffected even after drinking the cup of poison sent by her husband Rana, and lived and traveled as a widow after her husband's death (Kinsley 1980; Sangari 1990). In other legends her marital family sends brahmins to bring her back, brahmins who vow to fast to death until she accompanies them. Meera is reputed to have solved her dilemma by disappearing into a temple and merging with an idol of Krishna and never reappearing in human form (Kinsley 1980; Sangari 1990; see Harlan for an interesting take on this incident [1992, 211, 220]). Thus in the Meera figure we read and locate female resistance to Rajput patriarchal norms from *within* the community.

The wealth of recent scholarship on Meera (Desai 1984; Sangari 1990; Harlan 1992; Mukta 1994) has ignored and passed over in silence the critical possibility that Meera's poetry obliquely comments on and opposes daughter-killing. This is all the more surprising given that British administrators meticulously document the incidence of female infanticide among the elite families in Rajasthan. Among recent scholars it is only Kishwar and Vanita (1989) who refer to the prevailing practices of female infanticide, son-preference, sati / *johar* as the conditions under which Meera composes her poetry.[5] However Kishwar and Vanita do not directly connect the critique in Meera's *bhajans* (religious songs sung collectively) to her opposition to these anti-women practices in Rajasthan; instead Kishwar and Vanita concentrate on how Meera opposes the pressure put upon women to uphold the family honor by remaining under purdah.

Author as Meera: Indigenous Practices of Co-authoring

Meera as an individual authorial figure has always been an issue of controversy. Scholarly debates about the historical accuracy concerning the details of Meera's life (1498–1546) have included speculations that this fifteenth-century poetess of Rajasthan may never have existed. Added to this is the question of the authenticity of her poetry. How much of Meera's poetry is her own

and how much has been added to by Meera *bhaktas?*[6] These debates and speculations are not germane to our own argument concerning Meera. Our critical interest is in how the author as Meera is an indigenous practice of co-
authoring. Therefore, we are interested in the ways in which Meera as a figure
of female resistance has been deployed all over India for the past four centuries. The circulations and accretions of meanings that accumulate to Meera
the real historical figure and Rajput princess, and Meera as a figure of legends
and myths, and Meera as author interest us all. In our reading, the historical
figure, the legend, and the author together tell us about the ways in which
Meera has remained a live, vibrant tradition of protest and resistance. We also
do not read Meera within the larger *Bhakti* movement. While this may be a
valid, scholarly route to her poetry, it is a route that subsumes the radically
subversive anti-patriarchal critique within a generalized framework of the
Bhakti movement.[7] The fact that Meera poetry recitations and bhajan singing
are primarily an oral tradition means that, for our purpose, it is not relevant
what is the authentic Meera poem or song and what has been added to and
interpellated by various followers and fellow-composers of Meera.

Rather than submit to the dichotomy of the authentic/ inauthentic
Meera, we read the accumulations, additions, revisions, and versions of the
Meera corpus as evidence that Meera is a continually compelling site for
women's critique and creativity.[8] In Meera's case we move away from the
Western notion of author as an individual person whose "I" carries the power
of individual authorship, personality, creativity, and opinions. Instead we
choose the more complex idea of Meera as the name of a social text of patriarchal critique.[9] This means that individuals and groups deploy the name
Meera in their compositions in order to release certain implicit cultural meanings in their audiences and thereby unite the writer/singer and reader/audi-
ence in what Barthes has called a "single signifying practice" (1977, 162).
Meera as social text in our reading is not the author-poet but the collectivity
of bhajans that have been composed and orally disseminated in north India.
Meera is the putative name under which subaltern expressions, articulations,
and political agitations are waged. Even though we redefine authorship in
Meera as co-authorship, for the sake of convenience we continue to refer to
this co-authorship in the first person singular and as Meera's writing.

A Meera scholar was told by a librarian in Udaipur that written history
has no interest in authenticating a historical figure that exposes the underbelly
of official Rajput history. (Mukta 1994, 1, 69–70).[10] The range of emotional
and political significance that is invested in bio-graphing Meera is significant
precisely because most women's lives are unrecorded in official history. The
details of Meera's life are constantly biographed, in the Derridean sense of
graphing/fabricating/writing a biography, by different groups like the epic
about her life composed and sung by the Bauri tribe (Mukta 1994, 112–113).[11]

Meera as a figure of resistance is heterogenously configured in women's protest against female infanticide. We are invested in those aspects of Meera's life that have been appropriated by generations of professional bards and singers, peasant women, lower-caste women, middle-class married women, and women artists.

Meera as Social Text: The Codes in Meera's Poetry

Some of the Meera bhajans provide us with a clue regarding the possibility for appropriation by the subaltern classes. In a song Meera's sister-in-law Uda challenges Meera by reminding her of her high caste birth and marriage into a princely family and asserts that Meera belongs within the confines of the palace. Meera responds that she has forsaken her husband Rana for her God and her body cannot be confined within the palace walls but belongs to the wider world (Sekhavat 1974, 222–223). In another poem Meera claims that she will only be remembered through her work, she has neither produced a son nor left a legacy with disciples or formed a sect (Sekhavat 1974, 242).[12] Meera's refusal to be part of a sect or tradition, her desire to belong to the world, and her desire to leave her work to the world rather than to a lineage, opens up the possibility of appropriations by diverse sections of the subaltern classes.

Meera's bhajans are generally sung, thus the individual singer inserts himself or herself in the activity of co-authorship through the act of musical interpretation. This is the reason why there is such an enormous variation in Meera songs and poems across different regions. Singers interpret her songs musically by emphasizing a particular line or word, repeating a phrase and subtly altering its meaning. Singers also change and add words, phrases, and translate her songs into different regional dialects. For a person who wishes to compose a Meera song, the possibility exists of taking up a well known refrain or a couplet and then adding fresh stanzas, thus altering and adding to Meera's critique.

This possibility of participating and co-composing is a special gift of Meera's poetry. It is a radical possibility that is not available in other Bhakti poets like Kabir, Tulsi, and Surdas. We argue that this possibility exists in Meera's poetry because it consists of several codes of subaltern protest. When a singer or listener identifies a particular code, they insert themselves into the activity of writing, inscribing, revising, and adding to the tradition of subaltern protest of patriarchal and elite practices that marginalize and disempower women and the poor. We have identified some of the major codes in Meera's poetry as 1) code of renunciation—subversion and sublation of marriage, 2) code of mock servitude, 3) anti-patriarchal mapping of agricultural/life metaphors—Meera's ecological code 4) code of fakiri or subsistence, and 5) code of biographing. We devote a section to the analysis of each code. However, these codes in no way exhaust Meera's poetry. The unlocking of any code in Meera is always in relation to the subject position of, and the understanding of protest by the reader/writer or critic. The practice of the bhajan *mandali* (informal gathering to sing and discuss Meera) is essential to our theory of Meera's codes. Meera bhajans are not sung passively in a bhajan mandali, rather the singing of Meera bhajans inevitably generates discussion and analysis of one of these codes.

The codes function as a coded message that the subaltern singer/listener identifies. At the more general level, the codes function as an open secret. That is to say Meera's codes function like the purloined letter in Edgar Alan Poe's famous short story by the same name (1982). There is an exchange between Dupin and the Prefect, indeed their very first conversation in the text, where the status of the problem and the method of detection is debated. Dupin invites the Prefect to entertain the notion that the activity of detection, which signifies the activity of interpretation, can run into difficulties if the interpreter/ detective is too enamored of his own intellectual powers. Later in the text Dupin names this error in interpretation as "consider(ing) only their *own* ideas of ingenuity" because "when the cunning of the individual felon is diverse in character from their own, the felon foils them, of course" (118). The critic or interpreter who treats the text as signifying her/his own ingenuity falls prey to the danger of not being able to decode a Meera poem that is historically distant, and alien in sensibility and language. Instead Dupin advocates a different approach to detection/interpretation, which he elaborates in the following exchange:

> "The fact is, we have all been a good deal puzzled because the affair *is* so simple, and yet baffles us altogether."
> "Perhaps it is the very simplicity of the thing which puts you at fault," said my friend.
> "What nonsense you *do* talk!" replied the Prefect, laughing heartily.
> "Perhaps the mystery is a little *too* plain," said Dupin.
> "Oh, good heavens! who ever heard of such an idea?"
> "A little *too* self-evident."
> "Ha! ha! ha!—ha! ha! ha!—ho! ho! ho!" roared our visitor, profoundly amused, "oh, Dupin, you will be the death of me yet!" (109–10)

Dupin names this alternate way of approaching the interpretive problem as "The very simplicity of the thing" and as "the mystery is a little *too* plain" and "*too* self-evident." The rest of the story unravels and explains Dupin's theory of interpretation. The interpretive problem, Dupin suggests, is the literalness and exteriority of the text. At two points in Poe's story, the letter is hidden in full view, the secret remains concealed because in fact it is open and plainly in sight.

This has a direct bearing on the codes in Meera's poetry. The critic or scholar who approaches the Meera poem with the problem of egotistical love for her own ingenuity is in peril. For example, if we try to approach Meera's poetry with the expectation that there is some hidden message about the Rajput practice of female infanticide, the text slams the door in our face. Instead we have to learn to approach the Meera poem in humility and openness, we have to surrender to its imagery, the logic of its metaphor, we have to orient ourselves to the characteristic obliqueness and surprising directness of her address. It is only then that we learn to read and listen to the Meera song, to actually learn to comprehend that it says what it says. Once we lose our fear that our understanding is a little "*too* self-evident" because it is faithful to the literalness of the Meera poem, then we find that a magical process starts to happen. A Meera code begins to unfold before us. This is not a moment of passivity, we do not simply transcribe the information. Dupin finds that the activity of understanding the intricate and complex processes of the Minister's mind taxes him to the fullest. The Minister is a poet and a mathematician, and the Prefect's cognitive error lies in assuming that a man with a poetic talent is a fool. As Dupin says, "the remote source of his (the Prefect's) defeat lies in the supposition that the Minister is a fool, because he has acquired renown as a poet" (119).

In an analogous manner the critic or interpreter of a Meera poem must maintain a vigilance about underestimating Meera because she is a poet. The Meera poem demands that the listener should neither deify nor deride the poem. It is only by the listener/reader inhabiting her own subject position, psycho-sexual history and her own moment in history that she can become an active participant in co-authoring the Meera poem. Thus, the Meera code is an open secret, it is open because the meaning lies on the surface, it is secret because the surface meaning will not be disclosed by itself, the Meera poem is a code precisely because it requires our participation to receive and decode it.[13]

We refer to Meera's codes as subaltern critique and not a poetic discursive formation because we want to maintain a necessary and vigilant separateness of these poetic codes of dissent from the hegemonizing tendencies of scholarly discourse. Scholarly academic discourse with its hegemonizing tendencies always attempts to make dissent and resistance assimilable and by extension co-opts subaltern resistance to capitalist logic and discourse. While our desire to maintain a separateness between Meera's poetic codes of resistance and academic discourse may, to some extent, be a theoretical fiction; we feel that it is an important and necessary fiction because it is between the language of hegemony and subaltern dialects that Meera's poetic codes continue to function. Subaltern speech and speech acts transact with hegemonic language. Yet the multiplicity of dialects in Meera's poetry construct, dissolve, and reconfigure dissent, in conversation with hegemonic linguistic constructs (marriage, family, women's duties, etc.) and everyday lived experiences of oppression, disempowerment, and deprivation that are expressed in dialect languages. Dialect languages are, to use Bakhtin's words a "social phenomenon" with a "social life . . . in the open spaces of public squares, streets, cities and villages, of social groups, generations and epochs" (1981, 259).

Meera's several codes embody resistance to female infanticide. The codes function in several ways. We foreground the referential and rhetorical dimension of the codes by insisting that Meera is unintelligible unless the reader comprehends the forces that she and her followers oppose. Her poetry acquires its full range of meaning in terms of what she resists and subverts, therefore there is always in her poetry an empty space for the antagonist. Sometimes that space is filled up by her princely husband, "Rana" or by the tyrant ruler "Raja" or by the disapproving herd *"log kahe"* and sometimes that space is left empty for the listener to fill.[14]

The notion of codes allows us to distinguish popular and elite decodings of Meera. We question the dichotomies established by Bhakti scholars between elite/subaltern, written/oral and authentic/inauthentic.[15] In our own work on Meera we try to make visible the nonhegemonic resistant readings of Meera. Meera's codes are not univocal, they are polyvocal in that they address the concerns of different groups and classes. The codes are unlocked differently by different groups and adherents, the code is mobilized by the subject position of the interpreter/singer. These poetic codes are not static riddles. They are elaborated by readers/singers; each person or group adds to and expands the Meera code by the way he or she lives that code and by the way she interpellates herself in those codes. There is an integral relation between our concept of Meera as co-author and the codes in her poetry—every time the *bhajniks* sing the codes unfold, and the unfolding text holds the Meera text.

Meera's Use of Dialects

The ideologically invested representation of north Indian dialect poetry is that it induces nostalgia and political passivity because dialects are premodern, lack social-reformist content, and are irrelevant to a modernist critical consciousness. This is the tenor of the celebrated comment by a major twentieth-century Hindi poet Sumitranandan Pant, that in dialect literatures "there was the sweetness of sleep" (1967, 22). Pant spoke not with hostility but as a lover of dialect poetry, nevertheless Pant felt that dialect poetry was a feudal obsolescence. Pant's definition of dialect poetry plays into one of the Orientalist myths about native cultures. The association of sleep with dialect carries the undertones of laziness, slowness, and pleasure-seeking. This scholarly and critical verdict has inevitably inflected the modern reception of Meera's dialect poetry as a naive text. Dialect languages and literatures are in conflict with the nationalist hegemony of state-sponsored Sanskritized Hindi, and with the print and translation industries of the West; both erase the oral performative aspects of dialect and retrieve it as exotic obsolescence.

We dispute this judgment by examining three aspects of north Indian dialects, and Meera's particular contributions to them: the potential in dialects to destabilize and continually reconfigure elite/popular hierarchies; the critical possibilities in dialects' multilingual polyphony; the distinctive relation between language and literature in dialect, as opposed to languages like Sanskrit or the modern Hindi language. The historical evolution of north Indian dialects is proof that the charge of regressiveness is inaccurate. Historically Hindi dialects were a contested site between state ideology and subaltern voices. Dialects did not blossom in royal courts, or with the patronage of wealthy traders in the market place or in the writings of the priestly class of Brahmins.

The post-Vedic period was characterized by an elite/popular linguistic division: Sanskrit and Pali were the languages of the scriptures and the court, while *Shaursaini* (a dialect that evolved in military camps) and Prakrit were the languages of the people. This linguistic hierarchy was destabilized in the period between the tenth and twelfth centuries, a period that is generally recognized as formative in the development of north Indian dialects. An instance of this linguistic destabilization is the historical shift of bardic literature from Sanskrit to Brajbhasha, from a learned language to the vernacular, that corresponds to the shift from the Brahmanical Bhats to the low-caste Charans. Therefore Brajbhasha in particular, and the north Indian dialects in general, carry the diacritical mark of the shifting boundaries between elite and subaltern communities. It is the everyday language of the people, on the street, the argot of the artisanal professions that fertilizes and reinvigorates dialect, although it is the elite classes that appropriate this enriched language. Thus, one of the noticeable characteristics of north Indian dialects is the continually shifting and unpredictable traffic between elite and popular cultures.

Scholars acknowledge Meera's enormous contribution to Hindi dialects but fail to highlight the essentially political relationship between Meera and nonstandard Hindi. The Rajput was a powerful and all pervasive linguistic construction by Meera's time. Rajput feudal militaristic ideology had been disseminated far and wide over north and central India over several centuries through the Bhats and Charans. The bardic critique of Rajput ideology of daughter devaluation was indirect, characteristically they accomplished this through comparing the present to the chivalry and glory of the Rajput past and thus initiating debate about true Rajput values of protecting and cherishing women. Meera's great innovation is to deploy the bardic dialect of Brajbhasha far more assertively and contentiously than the bards, to articulate the disaffected Rajput woman's perspective. Brajbhasha had never been used in this way, it is with Meera that we hear for the first time in dialect a distinctively female enunciation of anti-patriarchal anti-Rajput opposition. Scholars of Bhakti literature have tended to list Meera alongside her male counterparts, in the process they have not posed the question concerning the disequilibrium and reorganization that occurs in a dialect literature when it is broken open in order to articulate female disaffection. Clearly one of the changes is that instead of the long narrative poems favored by the bards, Meera prefers the brief lyric form of the *pad*. Yet another linguistic innovation of Meera's Rajasthani poetry is the mixture of bardic Brajbhasha with Rajasthani dialects (Merwari, Dundhadi, Malwi, Mewati, Bagri), especially the Mewari dialect. The Bhakti literature scholar Padmavati Shabnam describes Meera's Rajasthani padas as *lokik* by which she means that they use the folk language and literary style (1976, 117). Meera's Rajasthani padas in Brajbhasha and Mewari subvert elite/subaltern linguistic distinctions.

Another chief characteristic of north Indian dialects is that they are porous and absorb a variety of cultural-linguistic influences. There is an explosion of linguistic traffic in the period from tenth to twelfth century in north India; part of the reason for this is the influx of ideas, images, verse forms, and words from Arabic and Persian into the north Indian dialects as a result of the coming together of Hindu and Muslim communities. It is precisely this feature of north Indian dialects that make them resistant to linguistic fundamentalism and monolinguality. North Indian dialects simply do not obey the boundaries between Hindu and Muslim religions, or between upper castes and lower castes. Indeed these dialects are living embodiments of the unofficial history of Hindu-Muslim assimilation and the anti-Brahmanical movements from the tenth to twelfth centuries in north India. Therefore north Indian dialects are intrinsically polyphonous, overlapping, and possess a linguistic fluidity.

Meera enters the field of dialect languages that are, by the fourteenth century, already vital, mutating, and polyphonic and she makes a profound impress on them by seizing on the critical possibilities of dialects' polyphony. Meera composed her poems in several other dialects like western Rajasthani, Gujarati, Marathi. Some of Meera's padas are in the popular medieval mixture of languages called *"Suddhakadi"* or *"Rekhta"* dialect. The word "Rekhta" means mixture and Rekhta literature is described by the Meera scholar Shabnam as a *khichri* or mixture, which included among others medieval Brajbhasha, Pingal, Khari boli, Persian words brought from Punjabi, Rajasthani, Punjabi and western Hindi used in the Delhi-Meerut area (1976, 115).[16] Traditional literary criticism suggests that the multidialect feature of Meera's poetry is no different from the poetry of her male counterparts, "even Guru Nanak Dev wrote in Persian, in Sanskrit, in Kafi, in Lahndi; even Namdev, Kabir, Raidas and Dadu wrote in Punjabi and Hindui" (Diwana 1969). Meera's polyphonic relation to dialects has been explained by Niranjan Bhagat in terms of two possibilities—either the poems were composed in the language of the region she was traveling through, or Meera's songs were originally composed in her mother tongue of western Rajasthani and her followers translated and adapted her verse into other dialects.[17]

We suggest that the multidialect polyphony in Meera's poetry has distinctive functions. These dialects do not simply map out the regions through which Meera traveled, as Bhagat suggests, they also map out those regions of north India where there was the greatest concentration of infanticidal clans. The patriarchal disciplining of the women of infanticidal clans was through the injunction of silence, isolation of the married woman from her natal home, and seclusion in the Rajput household. It is in this context that we can recognize how the multidialect feature of Meera's oppositional verse was a survival strategy. Meera's versified opposition to court, state, and patriarchal family was orally transmitted to the women and the subaltern classes of several linguistic communities, through generations of street poets, itinerant singers, wandering ascetics, women in the fields or toiling at the grinding stone, or elite women composing verses in the prayer room, and communal singing by the migrant poor. In effect Meera's multidialect poetry creates an alternative community, which is, unlike the male Bhakti poets' alternative communities of bhajniks, woman-centered.

The third feature of North Indian dialects concerns the relation between the category of "literature" and north Indian dialects. The category of "literature" in dialects is not a static, written, and fetishized entity, instead its deployment and modes of transmission continually expand the possibilities and boundaries of that language. The linguistic-literary particularity issues from the historical relationship between Bhakti literatures and north Indian dialects. North Indian dialects received their impetus from Bhakti poets' literary-poetic contributions, which gave an enormous incentive to the dialects in which they composed, the one is inextricably fused with the other. "Literature" is not centered around individual authors in dialect, the reason is that the north Indian dialects were deployed by the Bhakti poets, as well as by their disciples, for the oral-performative elucidations of their teachings *(pravachans)* and compositions. Therefore the linguistic-literary histories of dialects are markedly different from official history precisely because dialects incorporate the spiritual narratives, the experiences of subordination, the metaphors for resistance, the intrareligious borrowings between Sufi saints and Hindu sects, and the everyday practices of creativity by women and subaltern classes. The reciprocal relationship between the two fluid entities, dialects, and Bhakti poetry, is such that Bhakti poetry stretches and actualizes dialect for its very possibilities, and the modes of transmission of dialect extend and enrich Bhakti poetry in turn. This hyphenated entity, dialect Bhakti poetry, keeps alive the borrowings, exchanges, adoptions, negotiations, transferences and connections between communities, religions, and cultures.

It is precisely here, in the literary-linguistic particularity in dialect that Meera is the leader and not a follower. We briefly indicate key features of Meera's poetry in which the possibilities of women's literature in dialect is actualized: subaltern condensation, musical interpretation and the intersubjective "I" in the Meera poem. Subaltern speech in dialect differs from the language of the elite principally in the way an entire life experience, an intergenerational knowledge of subordination, a memory of pain or an oppositional argument is articulated through a condensed phrase. Meera's poetic condensations and tropes from the everyday function in this way.

In Meera's poetry the category of "literature" is fluid rather than static, oral rather than written, and irreverent rather than fetishized because it relies so completely on musical interpretation. Meera's modern critics do not believe that dialect poetry can convey complex arguments, or that Hindi dialects posses intricate conventions for arguments. Contrarily we argue that musical interpretations constitute the traditional interpretive modes for women and subordinate classes. The musical dimension of the Meera lyric was designed to exorcise the power of the ballads that sustained the myth of the Rajput in popular memory. Singers convey the plenitude in the Meera image by the ways they individually interpret, invest, inflect and repeat a refrain, so that the listening audience is attuned to the full range of meaning in Meera's image. For instance Meera's popular pads in Gujarati are called "Meera's *Garbiya*." (Shabnam 1976, 117). Garbiya denotes the *garba* folk dance performed by women in Gujarat, which is associated with *rasleela* or love play between Krishna and the *gopis* or milkmaids. The garbiya songs are short, repetitive, and enjoyable creations where emotions are primary. The lyric remains closed until we hear a bhajan singer open it up, unfold its words, animate it with pulsating emotion, and interpret its meaning. It is only when we listen to the musical interpretations in which the Meera lyric lives and breathes that we realize how Meera draws on the peculiar strengths of dialect.

The intersubjective "I" in the Meera poem is a daring innovation. Hindi dialects contain conventions within which the speaker and addressee are assumed or indirectly indicated. The form of padas that Meera fashions has a poetic signature, "Meera says" in the last line. Meera transforms this dialect convention into a shifting, surprising, and critical assumption of the personal pronoun that is unparalleled in north Indian literature. The bards of Rajasthan interpellated their audiences through digressions and improvisations, Meera goes much further. Modern readers and translators are constantly surprised by the radically aggressive "I" and "You" in the Meera poems. Generally speaking her opening line invokes an interlocutor with whom the poet establishes a range of intimacies—passionate exhortation toward the god Krishna, a tense and defiant address to the male figure of Rana, a gentle inwardness in the invocation of female interlocutors as mother, sister, clanswomen, friend, or fellow victim. Indeed Meera's poetry constitutes the dream possibility in dialect, the possibility that each reader can interpellate herself into the Meera poem by transmitting, translating, adding, and reinterpreting the text. Dialect dreams of becoming the poetic utterance of the collective rather than the individual author. Meera poems realize this dream possibility by making the activity of co-authoring central to the poetic construct.

The fact that dialects are not residual feudal remnants is borne out by the continual transmission of Meera's poetry in new technologies and post-modern cultural forms of filmic music, audio cassette, and compact disc industries, stage shows and dance dramas, painting and sculpture. The continuing political relevance of Meera's dialects can be gauged by the *unbroken continuity* between her preservation in oral traditions and her reincarnation in the industrial technology of mainstream Bombay films.[18] The continuity of Meera's oral tradition over four hundred years is a remarkable achievement for a woman writer. Clearly these are discontinuous continuities, the content of the critique in the Meera poems does not and cannot remain static and continuist. Local, discontinuous, and strategic elements have, at various points in this continuous oral tradition, been added to or subtracted from the Meera poems. It is precisely this critical adaptability that makes the Meera tradition and the author as Meera a vibrant subaltern practice.

English translations of dialect poetry tend toward fidelity to the literal surface of the poem and infidelity to the pleasures and complexities of the dialect. This is certainly true of the translations of Meera's poetry that are available to the English reading public, which reduce the Meera verse into flat and unrecognizable exercises in Orientalist mysticism. The complexities of dialect are rendered opaque or untranslatable in English. For instance in every poem there is an image of plenitude woven around the Krishna figure. The liquid sweetness of the Krishna image is conveyed through Meera's use of dialect. When Meera's Krishna references are translated into English, they have the effect of bathos. In another case a song that is about the injustice done to Meera and her persecution by her family has a refrain, *"Mein sawre ke raang raachi,"* when this refrain is translated into English it reads "I am dyed in the dark one's hue" (Kishwar and Vanita 1989, 79). This translation does not provide any clues about the sweetness and plenitude of the refrain in dialect. English translations can only gesture at these levels of the poems.

As translators we experience the unequal relations of power between dialect (Hindi, Brajbhasha, Awadhi, Bhojpuri, Punjabi, Bengali, Oriya, Gujarati, Marwari) and English not as an external conflict but rather as an intimately lived conflict between our multilingual subjectivity. We negotiate with this vexed issue by positioning criticism as the place where we continually gesture at the untranslatable core of dialect. We live with the unease between Meera's dialect and English translations.[19] For us translation is not a formal, aesthetic activity. Rather the translator/critic deploys criticism to make visible the politics of dialect literatures. Also we draw on our own lived experience with dialect in everyday spoken and written forms in Uttar Pradesh, Madhya Pradesh, and Rajasthan. We are also fortunate to have been able to experience first-hand the performative and enunciatory possibilities of dialect in bhajan mandalis in the aforementioned states. Therefore our own translations signify our participation in this history of female creativity.

Our emphasis as critics/translators is on the manifest meaning of a Meera poem, which we have named the poetic codes that are decoded by Meera's several constituencies of women, migrant poor, lower castes, and Dalits. Meera's chosen poetic genre is a medieval lyric chiefly used by wandering *sants* (spiritual teachers) for spiritual instruction called *padas*. Meera adapts and transforms this short rhyming lyric or pada with aggressive artistry. The ardor and passion of a Meera lyric stands out and imprints the reader /listener. A classic Meera poem contains in all its regional variations certain characteristic political-oppositional features. In our translations and paraphrases we make visible the fact that a Meera lyric is always an oppositional argument explicitly opposing the Rajput patriarchal values.

Meera's Code of Female Renunciation

Meera evolves her own codes for female renunciation. She borrows from the diverse medieval traditions of renunciation that were designed primarily for men. A male contemporary of Meera had the following options if he wished to lead a life of renunciation: there were no social restrictions on his choice of renunciation at any stage of his life; there was no social condemnation for his desertion of responsibilities toward his natal family or his wife and children.[20] Thus the Hindu male was the beneficiary of the productive tension in medieval Indian society between the ideal of the householder or *grihastha* and the ideal of renunciation or *sanyasa*.

The Brahmanical texts posited an ideology of containment for the renouncer. It was an ideology that seduced men with the notion that they could resolve the tension between householder/renouncer by living the middle part of their lives as householder and spend their old age as the renouncer. Meera's male counterpart also benefited from the complicated interdependence between the householder and renouncer, the former considered it his duty to subsidize the latter (alms, land grants, revenues, shops, construction of temples, *maths* or monasteries, gifts or *dana*) and the latter reciprocated by blessing him for the religious merit or *punya* he had earned, or by serving as his political advisor and religious mentor.

If Meera's male counterpart was born in a lower caste, he would find that certain sects closed their doors to a *shudra* (lower caste) ascetic. This problem could be circumvented by the plethora of renunciatory orders like Buddhist, Jain, and Tantric, which did not observe caste exclusion. Thus, the Hindu male had the choice of a life of wandering, or solitary contemplation in a forest or cave, or living with wife and children in a forest. Alternatively he could live on the outskirts of urban centers or near trade routes. He could pioneer a new sect or monastic order. The social acceptance, economic subsidizing and political patronage that male renouncers received had positive and negative consequences. On the plus side male renunciation was socially productive in the creation of monasteries, the survival of traditions, the development of fields of knowledge, and the development of a culture and a social fabric where there was a constant dialogue between nonconformist orders and society. On the minus side male renunciation was so well accepted that its potential for dissent, protest and social change was diffused into, in Romila Thapar's words, a counter culture or parallel society.[21]

We translate this poem as an example of Meera's code of female renunciation:

> Like casting off the veil
> honor, shame, family pride are disavowed
> respect, disrespect, marital, natal home
> renounced in the search for wisdom
>
> people say Meera is maddened
> kinsfolk say she is a family annihilator
> Rana sent a cup of poison
> while drinking it Meera laughed
>
> of father, mother, brother, kinsfolk I have none
> having cast aside familial tyranny
> what people say is of no consequence
> because I sought to keep company with *sadhus*
> people say I have shamed the community's honor

(Chaturvedi 1983, 240)

Society does not allow women to construct a parallel society, the patriarchal order cannot afford the luxury of women's dissent and renunciation because women are essential to the extraction of surplus value in elite Rajput society. In this poem Meera's exclusion from the social privileges for male renunciation becomes her strength. She mocks and disavows the opposition between the male householder and the ascetic. Meera constructs female renunciation within the paradox of the ascetic and the married woman. She turns her marginality into her weapon. Meera's image of female renunciation is a program of opposition to the patriarchal organization of family and society. It is not a social space for a few exceptional women whose spiritual inclinations drive them to choose a life of devotion as an alternative to marriage.[22]

We argue that Meera represents a noninstitutionalized form of dissent. Meera's image of renunciation contains an absolute opposition between her way and the Rajput way. Unlike male renunciatory orders (Buddhist, Jain, Ajivika, Shankaracharya sect, Vaishnavite sects) Meera's renunciation never becomes fully containable or assimilable to patriarchal society. There are no written or oral records that suggest that Meera received or accepted state patronage. She did not woo wealthy patrons. She did not receive land-grants, tax-free subsidies, endowments, or revenue. Temples, resting places, or monasteries were not constructed in her name. That meant for one thing that Meera and her followers were not prey to the problem that plagued male renunciatory orders: the latter courted mainstream society and state; inevitably these processes led to the attenuation of their dissent. Male renunciatory orders could see no way out of this paradox, but Meera did find a way. The survival of her notion of female renunciation did not depend on institutionalizing her teachings into a religious sect, a temple, a deity, or a monastic order. The Meera poems were disseminated by word of mouth. It was through the oral transmission of her poems as well as the additions and extrapolations that a Meera tradition came into being.

Meera's Subversion and Sublation of Marriage Relationship: The Anti-genre

The argument in chapter 3 concerning Rajput hypergamy is a prerequisite for understanding Meera's poetic statements about marriage. There we argued that historically female infanticide appears as the necessary concomitant of hypergamy, exogamy, and vice versa. Both customs constitute gendered violence against daughters: female infanticide is premised on the notion that daughters are of no use to a family and are a threat to family prosperity; exogamy is premised on the notion that daughters should be married into a family that resides at a considerable geographical distance from the natal family and there are no shared relatives between the two clans therefore ensuring that the married daughter will be cut off from her family; hypergamy is premised on the notion that the maximal use should be made of the daughter by marrying her into a family whose wealth and status is greater than the natal family. Whereas the custom of female infanticide presupposes that a daughter is inherently a valueless consumer and therefore easily disposable, in hypergamy the daughter is seen as an extra economic means for accumulation. Both practices come together in instrumentalizing Rajput daughters.

Given the extreme conditions of oppression for women in medieval Rajput society, how did women transact with the roles assigned to them by Rajput patriarchy? We suggest that historically one of the many ways women in India transmit their lived experience and knowledge to other women (daughters, sisters, neices, friends, cousins, and so on) is through narrativizing their lived experience and knowledge in folk songs. In north India songs mark all significant occasions in a woman's life like *bidaai*, *birhaa* (separation from lover, or being cut off from natal home), *Holi* (festival of colors when separated loved ones meet), *Teej* (women's festival when women come to their natal home). We do not know and cannot historically trace the origins of these folk genres. While women compose, sing, and transmit them intergenerationally it is a fact that most often these genres espouse patriarchal patterns of discipline, duty, and punishments for women. That is not to say that there is not an internal tension in these genres but they mainly map women's lives in the set, prescribed ways. Women traditionally used this custom of singing folk songs at various occasions to share survival knowledge with other women within a socially inscribed ritual. Meera's use of women's folk genres as a critical vehicle suggests to us a highly meditated practice.[23]

We have indicated earlier in this chapter that Meera's critique of Rajput patriarchy comes from within the community. Similarly Meera deploys folk forms of women's genres in order to essay a critique of these genres and relocates the affect associated with these genres. Patriarchal ideology and affect are so cathected in these genres that it is impossible to open up the one for investigation without encountering the other. Moreover, this cathexis between ideology and affect becomes sedimented over time by generations of women encoding their experiences in these generic songs. For Meera to ignore the constituency of these songs would be to ignore the very forms in which women have mapped out their understanding and their lived experience. To challenge the ideological content of these genres within the genre itself would be a daring endeavour for any poet. Meera accomplishes this poetic daring, she lays claim to the power of affect in these genres by decathecting it from patriarchal ideology and recathecting it to women's desire.

In order to understand how Meera recodes women's genres we examine the *bidaai* song or the bidaai genre (separation from lover or being cut-off from the natal home). The ideology of this genre naturalizes child marriage, exogamy, treating daughters as temporary residents in the natal home (*beti paraya dhan* or daughters are another's wealth), and the disinheritance of daughters after marriage by the withdrawal of all that is familiar, supportive and nurturing (Leela Dube 1988). Bidaai songs record and memorialize in a highly sentimentalized way the cruelty and detachment with which the girl/woman is made stranger in the only home she has known until that period of her life, including being barred from coming home except on special occasions and by invitation of her natal family and permission of her marital family. The bidaai songs portray this disinheritance, loss, and alienation of the young daughter as the inevitable consequence of a girl's growing up and aestheticize the pain and helplessness of the young girl longing for the carefree days of childhood, the natal family, and the familiar landscape.[24] The interlocutor in the bidaai songs is usually a woman, most often a childhood friend who has been a partner in childhood games, and who, although as yet unmarried faces a similar fate and therefore allows the singer to articulate patriarchal ideology in the form of nostalgia for the natal home.[25]

Meera writes:

Friend from my childhood, I long to be a renunciator
that form which enchants my sahib, that is the form I will keep
friend from my childhood, I long to be a renunciator

at your asking I will dye my sari the color of the kusumal flower
at your asking I will take on saffron robes
friend from my childhood, I long to be a renunciator

at your asking I will fill the parting of my hair with pearls
at your asking I will unbind my hair
friend from my childhood, I long to be a renunciator

my being resides elsewhere, here only the empty husk
like straw in the wind, I have left behind mother father family
friend from my childhood, I long to be a renunciator

(Gulzar's film *Meera* 1979)

The reason that we identify an entire cluster of Meera songs, of which the above is an exemplar, as bidaai songs is that the song follows the rhetorical-affective structure of the bidaai song while critiquing the patriarchal ideology of the genre, which naturalizes daughters as objects of exchange. Meera's bidaai song is addressed to a childhood friend; the first line, which is also the refrain of the song, "Friend from my childhood, I long to be a renunciator," is an entreaty that camouflages an aggressive challenge to the patriarchal ideol-

ogy of these songs. Meera evokes the pathos of the bidaai songs only to audaciously redirect it to the desire for renunciation, thereby surprising the
reader/listener who expects to hear the reiteration of the ideology that senti-
mentalizes the use of daughters as objects of exchange by the natal family. The
use of the rhetorical-affective structure of the bidaai song allows Meera to
articulate two difficult ideas within dialect and the psycho-social experiences
of her female audiences. By expressing the desire for renunciation, she
estranges the ideology of bidaai songs and indicates that the real tragedy is the
treatment of daughters as objects of exchange and their acceptance of such a
status. Meera's desire for renunciation is shocking in its simplicity and directness because Hindu Shastric/Puranic patriarchal injunctions define women as
part of the illusory world: they lack a soul, their *mayavi* (deceptive) nature is
a hindrance to the achievement of renunciation by men and therefore all
women are prohibited from the state of renunciation. According to this tradition, the only way for women to gain access to transcendence is through husband worship and service.[26]

Having subverted Shastric patriarchal injunctions about women and
marriage, the second line of the song, "that form which enchants my sahib,
that is the form I will keep" begins to sketch out Meera's code of the anti-
genre. When Meera defines renunciation as subjugation to her master she
brings together two contraries, renunciation and marriage, and by exaggerat-
ing her master/husband's authority and her own wifely servitude, she animates other significations of marriage than the one prescribed. Her words no
longer refer to her earthly husband and the social-patriarchal marriage forced
upon her by saga alliance politics; they designate her freely chosen immortal
husband Krishna, and her alternate form of marriage to him through renunciation of the world. Meera's description of renunciation as marriage to
Krishna invests the state of marriage with eroticism and spirituality that has
no place in the social-patriarchal marriage relation but that is a large part of
women's spiritual narratives, autobiographies, and folk songs.[27] It is Meera's
articulation of eroticism and spirituality that directly connects her to the
larger community of women. Meera's liberation of herself from her earthly
marriage in order to declare her marriage to Krishna constitutes her dissent
from patriarchal Rajput marriage. The stunning rhetorical consequence of
the poetic enunciation of Meera's marriage to the God Krishna is that she
becomes the sole interpreter of this divine marriage.[28] The marriage allows
her to move out freely in public among men, to converse with them and travel
from place to place.

The next two stanzas of the song maintain the tone of erotic longing
and submissiveness of the opening stanza as Meera details the distinction
between her female mode of renunciation as marriage to Krishna, and male
renunciatory modes. To the traditional signs of male renunciation, saffron

robes and matted hair, she contrasts the red wedding saree and adornment of the parting in her hair, marks of her female sexuality and her married status. The poetic evocation of these symbols of womanhood and marriage reject the male renunciatory mode, which enjoin the forsaking of appearances for spiritual knowledge and yet insist on a prescribed mode of dress. Meera's mode of renunciation through marriage to Krishna is based on sexual difference instead of sexual indifference, it seeks to empower women by incorporating female sensibility where color and ornamentation are important, and in doing so Meera articulates a specifically female mode of renunciation.

The final stanza of the song recalls the critical moment in the rhetorical-emotional enactment of the bidaai song when women singers, married and unmarried, invariably become distraught and cannot continue to sing. It is the moment where the young girl-bride confesses to feeling bereft, unloved and without support amongst strangers. The aestheticized dispossession of daughters in bidaai songs ruptures in performance, and the tears of singers and female audience signify a full understanding of the injustice and indifference visited on daughters by their natal family. Within the horizon of this emotional eloquence Meera issues her final indictment of Rajput patriarchal politics where daughters are sacrificed for political gains, "my being resides elsewhere, here is only empty husk/ like straw in the wind, I have left behind mother father family." The indictment is introduced with a traditional agricultural metaphor for renunciation, the husk/grain contrariety for the body whose soul "resides elsewhere." Meera uses the metaphor to evoke the dispossession of women in the bidaai song, and relocates and connects this female dispossession to renunciation. The ideology of the genre has been subverted by Meera's anti-genre song: a woman's exile from her natal home that is forced upon her by her parents and society becomes in Meera's poem the daughter's renunciation of her natal and marital family. In reconfiguring bidaai as renunciation Meera validates those very experiences in women's lives that in folk traditions are proof of women's weakness and emotional insecurity. She remakes these experiences into transformatory experiences that give women privileged access to renunciation.

The last line of the stanza, "like straw in the wind, I have left behind mother father family," condenses the radical critique of patriarchy that has come to be associated with Meera and serves as her signature. The poem is not signed off in the usual manner with her name. This disavowal of natal kin is a stunning reversal of a genre that celebrates the natal home as the place of refuge and longing, and positions the daughter as the supplicant who seeks the indulgence of her family to permit her to visit the natal home. The repudiation of mother, father, and natal clan serves as the climax of Meera's anti-genre. As Meera's only explicit act of rejection/renunciation, in a poem that narrativizes her desire for renunciation, the poetic line is an indictment of the natal home and family for contributing to, and being part of, the process of the disenfranchisement of women. Meera's abrogation of the natal family points to the fact that the process of disenfranchisement and disempowerment begins at home, through the discourse adopted by the parents toward their daughters where the daughters are treated as strangers in their own home. The natal family, ideally the source of women's nurturing, affective life, and identity, in actuality trains its daughters to accept their disinheritance and disempowerment in their own home, and thereby colludes with the marital home and the community. Whereas bidaai songs sentimentalize this disciplining of daughters by the natal family, Meera's song is a clear and unsentimental condemnation of Rajput patriarchy and community. The song culminates in the refrain ("Friend from my childhood, I long to be a renunciator"), which, as it comes for the last time, has a fullness of meaning that accrues to it. Meera's poem transforms the meaning of renunciation to signify the freedom to dedicate herself to an ideal. It follows that for Meera all women have a right to seek their own ideal, to dedicate themselves to it, a right to their own salvation.

Furthermore, the location of this repudiation of natal kin in a song about Meera's marriage to Krishna shows that the anti-patriarchy code is linked to the code of subversion and sublation of marriage. The links between the two poetic codes are made at three levels: first, she opposes Rajput patriarchal saga alliance politics with voluntary dedication to her chosen husband or ideal; second, she opposes the political advancement of the natal family with her own claim to her own spiritual transcendence; last, she opposes duty and obligation to natal family with duty and obligation to her god/husband. Thus Meera's critique of marriage is a critique of saga alliance politics, which is one of the foundational premises of Rajput patriarchy, and of patrilineal inheritance and the concomitant disinheritance of daughters who must nevertheless serve the political ambitions of the natal family. Meera plays with the traditional ambiguity of defining women both as curse and as the site of religious sanctity; on the one hand she dismantles the definition of women as illusion *(maya)* and objects of exchange; on the other hand she claims on behalf of all women, the right to dedicate themselves to ideals of their own choosing and seek their own transcendence.

Meera and Commodity Fetishism in Medieval Rajasthan: Woman as Fetish Object

Metaphor in dialect poetry functions as a subaltern mode of argument. It is when the subaltern poet cannot locate her claims for mutuality in the material conditions around her that she uses metaphor for a condensed and elliptical gesture toward those possibilities that are outside the idioms and discourses of domination. The metaphors in Meera's poetic code of ecoreciprocity serve as a fine instance of subaltern metaphor, its material determinants as well as the genre conventions through which the material world of the subaltern is mediated and encoded.

The difference between religious and Marxist theories of alienation and de-alienation is that in the idioms of organized religions, the human being conceptualizes de-alienation as a return to some prelapsarian moment of plenitude in human history or mythology; for instance the Edenic paradise in Christianity and Islam, and Brindaban in Vaishnavite sects are the realm of plenitude and self-connection. For Marx there is a kind of alienation that is a necessary part of the human labor process; this necessary alienation occurs when the human being is alienated (separated) from the products of his/her labor. This necessary separation is distinguished from the alienation caused by the structural position of the worker within capitalism, wherein the human being is alienated from nature, other human beings, and from his/her own historically created human possibilities.[29] In Meera's religio-folk idiom de-alienation is not a return to the past but a call for revolutionary change in the present and future.

In telling her women audience that a lifetime's dedication to a self-chosen ideal is the way to counter mediaeval Rajput patriarchal ideology, Meera's poems address the central obstacle to women's radicalization, which is women's alienation from the world they inhabit. In precapitalist feudal-medieval Rajasthan, Meera describes the gender specific self-alienation of the Rajput woman, which should not to be confused with alienation in capitalism. In Meera's medieval vocabulary woman is disconnected because she is alienated from her family, children, the products of her labor, her right to property, her role and abilities as producer, her creativity and productivity, her power to shape and influence the world around her as well as to connect to the social world as agent. Female self-alienation is built into elite Rajput social structures: the Rajput daughter is disassociated from her natal family (exogamy), married to further her father's or brother's political ambitions (hypergamy) without giving her a direct role in the political-economic spheres of society, denied her rights over her female children (female infanticide) as well as prohibited from participation in agricultural production (seclusion and *purdah* in the Rajput *zenana*).

Subaltern understandings of female self-alienation are articulated in the *biraha* (separation) genre. The word biraha denotes the pain and loss experienced in the separation from lover or from god, the genre moves back and forth between the erotic human realm and the divine. Meera reconstellates the biraha genre by linking the religio-folk notion of separation from god/lover to the psychosocial processes of commodification, fetishization, and self-alien-

ation of women in Rajput patriarchy. In the biraha genre the pain of separation culminates in the ecstatic meeting in death with god/lover. Meera sublates this poetic rhythm of separation and ecstatic connection into a this-
worldly materialist conception of woman discovering her connectedness to
the natural world, and through the natural world to the social world. Therefore the end point in Meera's reconstituted biraha genre is the de-alienated
female connecting to herself and apprehending her potentiality and productivity. According to Meera the means by which women can experience connection rather than disconnection is by re-envisioning social relations between
men and women in terms of the reciprocal relations in nature. Meera's poetic
code of ecoreciprocity signifies resistance to women's commodification and
advocates an alternative worldview, a worldview that affirms women's relation
to the divine.[30] In Meera's poetry woman's relation to the divine gestures to the
ways woman can reconnect to her own possibilities as well as to her role as valued producer in society rather than as devalued consumer. Meera writes:

Beloved that which you sever I would not
having severed your love who can I connect with?

if you are a tree I'm a bird, if you are ocean I'm your fish
if you are mountain I'm your shadow, if you are moon I am *chakora*

you are pearl god I am string, you are gold I am *suhaaga*
Meera says god dweller of Braj you are my master I your female slave

(Jafri 1965, 107)

In Meera's poetics Rajput women's self-alienation is described in terms of the
possibility of abandonment by god, she says, "Beloved that which you sever I
would not." The poetic context makes it clear that abandonment by god signifies the human being's estrangement from human connection. That is why
Meera contemplates the severance of god's love as the condition of being
unable to connect with anyone, "having severed your love who can I connect
with?" Instead of obfuscating her train of thought, the religio-folk metaphor
of god's abandonment of women clarifies her thinking about the way out of
self-alienation. Meera suggests that women's relation to the mystical derives
from the reciprocal relations in nature, therefore women cannot be permanently severed from god or from her own powers. The poem describes her
relationship with Krishna as a series of reciprocal relationships grounded in
the laws of nature: bird and tree, ocean and fish, mountain and shadow.

The poem does not directly refer to Rajput women's claim for mutuality but indicates it through the device of linked pairs. A characteristic rhetorical feature of dialect poetry in the biraha genre is auxesis or amplification

through a climactic series of pairs. Meera invests this poetic device with a characteristically subaltern mode of argument in which a series of established pairings—bird/tree, ocean/fish—are enumerated in order to borrow authority of the established pairs for the new pair or new idea. This is a subaltern mode of argument because the versifier cannot locate the subaltern's claim for reciprocity in the material conditions around her; therefore she draws on the interdependent relationships in the natural world and critiques the relations between subalternized women and elite Rajput males through her vision of a complementary universe.

Meera's poem does not directly spell out the relations of subordination and domination between Rajput women and men, although the Krishna/Meera linked pair are a steady meditation on the subject. The significance of enumerating the Krishna-Meera pair alongside the other linked pairs is that the latter are anchored in the material, natural world and are relationships of ecological reciprocity. Meera suggests that if god exists in a tree, ocean, or mountain, she resides in a bird, fish, and shadow. The movement of Meera's poem, from Krishna (the first pada) to the reciprocal relations in nature (second and third padas) back to Krishna (refrain and fourth pada) refers to the social relations between men and women, not as they generally obtain in the world nor even as an other-worldly relation between human being and god, but in terms of the ideal of reciprocity that men should strive for in relation to women.

We have to slow down to unpack the conceit in the next line, "you are pearl god I am string, you are gold I am *suhaaga*." How are we to understand the switch from pairs in the natural world to pairs that are a product of the human imagination and invention: pearl/string, gold/suhaaga? We are given advance notice of the switch by the moon/chakora pairing. The chakora is not a bird that exists in the natural world, but is a bird of legend traditionally associated with the moon.[31] At first glance Meera's naming god as pearl and herself as string may seem like she is adopting the more submissive position vis-à-vis god. However the pearl/string metonymy refers to the reciprocal relationship between part and whole, that the one is incomplete without the other, Meera as string pulls god into signification. In dialect the word for string *(dhaga)* has several sedimented meanings for subaltern artisanal classes; dhaga connotes both the material through which the weaver spins out cloth and the labor of weaving.[32] By emphasizing the basic material of weaving Meera calls attention to the labor process, the work of weaving rather than the commodity of cloth or pearl necklace. By calling herself string, Meera names her poetic labor as akin to that of the weaver. It is her labor as poet that makes god gain in signification and value. Within the rhetorics of dialect both the weaver and the wordsmith are creators; therefore, Meera asserts a relationship of reciprocity with god as fellow creator.

The metaphors in dialect poetry are largely drawn from the labor processes that are a familiar and everyday part of the worklife of subaltern classes in medieval society like molding pots, leather tanning, weaving, spinning, and ferrying. For instance in dialect poetry the boatman who ferries the passengers across the river asserts professional collegiality with god by arguing that his labor is the prototype for god's labor of ferrying human beings from this world to the next. These work processes are undervalued by elite classes, for the subaltern skilled or unskilled worker or craftsman, the work of weaving, tanning, pottery making, ferrying, and jewelry making is not measured in terms of its use or exchange value. Rather work becomes the profound metaphor through which the subaltern worker perceives the world, nature, his/her relationship with other human beings, and god. Work is the central metaphor in dialect poetry, in this way the subaltern poet subverts the caste specific prohibitions on artisans and dalits, and elite shastric prescriptions on learning and knowledge.

Meera's poetic reference to god as gold deserves detailed consideration. Meera's reference to gold signals her critique of the commoditization of Rajput women in hypergamous marriages and Rajput accumulation of land and wealth.[33] In Marx's analysis of the precapitalist world of generalized production of commodities, gold is the universal equivalent form of value because in the production, distribution, and trading of commodities in precapitalist societies gold has "universal exchangeability" ([1867] 1977, 162). Marx holds his profound insight about commodity fetishism in tension between two descriptions, as an "obvious, trivial thing" and as "abounding in metaphysical subtleties and theological niceties." He says there is nothing mystifying about the use value of a commodity or even about the labor that transforms "an ordinary, sensuous thing" like wood into a table. The fetish character of the commodity appears when the table emerges as a commodity transcending its sensuous quality "in relation to all other commodities, it stands on its head, and evolves out of its wooden brain grotesque ideas" ([1867] 1977, 163). According to Marx no matter how one studies commoditization, from the point of view of the raw material used in the commodity or its use value or the labor process, the fact is that the commodity appears as a fetishized object. In the case of gold the fetish character of the commodity is enhanced because gold has universal exchangeability in precapitalist societies.

Meera's conceit about god as gold critiques the way women are positioned within Rajput patriarchy as value-in-exchange only: unless the elite Rajput father could make a politically favorable alliance through his daughter's marriage she had no value and was dispensable. Meera's critique is poised between two significations of gold in folk idioms, gold not only signifies wealth it is also endowed with the properties of auspiciousness, for instance the married Rajput woman's gold jewelry sanctifies *(suhaaga)* her wedded status.[34] Meera engages with these significations while renouncing gold ornaments as marks of feudal wealth and status. Meera's poetic resolution lies in the violent substitution of lust for gold with the search for god. In her pairing of "you are gold I am *suhaaga*" Meera contravenes the notion that it is only the institution of patriarchal marriage through which women gain status and value. She asserts that value and status in the world is gained through daily ethical practice, it is through these daily ethical and reciprocal practices that women give signification to the empty signifier god. In the conventions of Meera's dialect poetry woman's search for god signifies the practice of ethical living and the ethics of reciprocity with nature and other human beings. Therefore value and status cannot be gifted or taken away from women.

Female adornment is a staple trope in subaltern women's idioms. Meera makes a distinction between the fetishized married Rajput woman and women's pleasure in self-adornment. Meera's emphasis on adornment seems to contradict her claim to renunciation, so how are we to understand the references to self-adornment in Meera poems? A number of female saints in the pan-Indian tradition like Mahadevi in the South and Lala Ded in Kashmir have, unlike Meera, left home naked, disavowing the body and the psycho-social restrictions placed on the female body. Alongside female infanticide and woman devaluation in medieval Rajasthan, there exists the religio-cultural tradition of supra-valuation of female beauty and the fetishization of femininity through the marks signifying the married woman.

Few regions in India rival Rajasthan in the elaboration of the married woman's costume.[35] Meera critiques the fetishizing of the married woman in Rajput socio-economic cultural iconography, for instance she says, "armlets and bangles do not please me / nor vermilion in the parting of my hair" (Jafri 1965, 137). Meera describes renouncing as the act of freeing herself from the bondage of the married woman's jewelry, she says, "I gave up all my jewels / unlocking the armlet I freed myself" (Gulzar's *Meera* 1974). In another song Meera says, "I have no use for gold or glitter/ I trade in diamonds" (Jafri 1965, 139). Her poetic references to self-adornment play with these symbols of the fetishized female object by replacing the symbols of the married woman with those of the female renunciator. According to Meera the female renunciator does not disavow her femininity, instead she wears alternate symbols in celebration of her femininity: for example Meera describes the female renunciator's nurture of the self, "rending apart the veil, I wrap myself in a coarse blanket/ removing pearls and corals I string a necklace of forest seeds" (Tewari 1974, 16–19). Through her poetic reference to unbinding her hair and adorning herself with a necklace of forest seeds, Meera makes a statement about female self-nurture that cannot be assimilated into the conspicuous consumption of elite Rajput medieval society.

Meera's Woman-Centered Code of Reciprocity between Nature and Nurture: Resistance to Rajput Accumulation

In her woman-centered code of reciprocity between nature and nurture, Meera challenges certain fundamental metaphors and myths of patriarchally structured agricultural societies that posit the male as the active principle (the seed, the producer) and female as the passive principle (land that is fallow unless tilled and sown). We call these agricultural myths and metaphors fundamental because, as assertions of male supremacy and male primacy, they cut across all classes and castes and structure elite Shastric texts, religion and culture as well as certain modes of subaltern religions, cults and practices.[36] These agricultural myths and metaphors of male supremacy are so deeply ingrained in agricultural societies that they become definitions of nature, assigning the active principle to the male and passive to the female; beyond nature they become defining principles of the universe and cosmos within and beyond human understanding. Their powerful seduction for patriarchal society is such that they even cover over heterogeneous understandings of nature as *prakriti* embodying feminine activity of creation, the earth as mother goddess and women as intimately connected to nature.[37]

In opposition to the myths and metaphors outlined above, Meera offers an alternate vision of woman as sower, planter, and nurturer. A series of poems present the image of a creeper of love or a creeper planted with love *(prem bel)* as an image and metaphor constitutive of women's identity and work in nature. Very often in Meera's poetry the world is imaged as a forest and Krishna is envisioned as the gardener of the forest (Jafri 1965, 117) and Meera names herself as a vine or creeper who is starved of water, that is starved of the love of a reciprocating god (Sekhavat 1974, 154). Not only does Meera call herself a vine in need of love and water, she also speaks of planting a vine of love, thereby recalling and making central women's critical role in the production and reproduction of life and nature. In Meera's vision women are not passive land to be exchanged, bartered, or tilled but rather they share an active relationship of reciprocity with nature. Not only do they plant, but they also nurture the plant until it bears the fruit of bliss. Meera advocates a vision of the world as a forest where there exists ecological harmony and mutual respect between nature and the human world. She says that she will not visit the prescribed holy places in order to gain religious merit, instead she practices her religion daily. She speaks of the deep reverence she feels for the forest trees because she is able to see divinity in every leaf and it makes her worshipful. The respect the tree demands necessitates that she refrain from torturing or misusing any part of the tree (Shekhavat 1974, 165).

When Meera talks about women as producers and reproducers of life in a relationship of reciprocity with nature, she is talking about women's work: women's work that is not only confined to the home but women's work in the world and specifically women's creativity. For Meera a woman tending a plant with her tears is not only the vision of a woman's role as mother and conserver of nature, but of a woman bringing forth and nurturing, with hardship and pain, her creativity. For Meera does not envision intellectual creative work (of song and poem writing) separately from women's other work and life. Therefore in the poem we analyze below a woman's work also refers to a woman's creativity.

> There is no one but *Giridhar Gopal* for me
> my husband is one who wears a peacock crown
>
> love planted this creeper, tears nurtured it
> now this vine of love will bear the fruit of bliss
>
> of father, mother, brother, kinsfolk I have none
> having transgressed clan taboos, what can anyone do to me?
>
> rending apart the veil, I wrap myself in a coarse blanket
> removing pearls and corals I string a necklace of forest seeds
>
> (Tewari 1974, 16–19)

Meera's metaphor for mothering and woman's self-mothering is a woman tending a plant with her tears. We cannot understand the historical-material specificity of the female imagination and the female experience of nurture if we read Meera's metaphor in the male bhakta canon. For male poet-reformers in the medieval Bhakti movement the human experience of nurturing and the nurtured always refers to the human soul that ascends to ultimate bliss or *ananda* only if the body undergoes ascetic austerities. Instead of this male-centered abstraction and universalism, Meera's representation of mothering draws on the historical conditions of medieval Rajput women's lives. Her rhetorical strategy is to take the rich metaphoric folk idiom and alter it ever so slightly. For example female children are often described in folk sayings in the organic metaphor of plants. Meera develops this folk saying into an agricultural metaphor of women as cultivators who sow, nourish, and reap the harvest. Her comparison of birthing to cultivation recalls the historic exclusion of Rajput women from farming and ownership of agricultural property, the disappearance of their role as producers and their seclusion in the Rajput zenana.

Upper class Rajput women are dispossessed outside and inside the household. There is a parallelism between her exclusion from agricultural production and the strict control of her reproductive abilities by the men of her clan. In two separate poems Meera refers tersely to male control of women's womb: the experience of birthing and nurture for a mother of sons is a rise in social status, religious prestige and power in the household (*"putra hetu padvi dayi"* or the high status of being a mother of sons [Shabnam 1973, 461]) while the mother who gives birth to one or more daughters experiences the social ritual of silence, tears, fear, and in many cases the trauma of watching the women of the household kill her infant. Meera's image of the mother crying silently as she gazes at her infant daughter is borne out by numerous British accounts of the Rajput celebration of a male child with festivities, dancing, singing and discharging of rifles, versus the socially ordained silent mourning ritual at the birth of a daughter.

Meera invites women to change the language in which they experience birthing and nurture of daughters. This change in language necessitates a corresponding change in the understanding and perception of the very notion of nurture. The mother's tears, her lived knowledge of the condition of being a woman, nourish the baby girl and make her a fighter and survivor. Meera's verse implies that this maternal transmission of the knowledge of female suffering is as vital a diet for the baby girl as the mother's milk that nourishes the infant's body. Poets raid the limits of speech—silence, sobbing, noise—in order to invest them with meaning in their poetic language. Meera asks women to look at that folk cliché, the cliché that women are passive suffering victims with a child in their arms and tears in their eyes, and read into it the strength of mother-daughter bonding instead of pathos.

In north Indian folk idioms daughters are often referred to as a vine or plant to underscore her difference from her brother who is the clan's hope *(kul deepak, ghar ka chiraag)* and emphasize how daughters are entwined and dependent on parents and brothers and kinsfolk. With poetic economy Meera reconfigures the Rajput devaluation of female children by the phrase *prem bel,* which translates somewhat cryptically as the vine of love. There are several levels of meaning in the phrase: a daughter is the child born in the mother's likeness and with the mother's ethics of love; the little girl entwines her arms and legs on the mother's body in affection instead of dependence; a daughter thrives on maternal love and dedicates herself to the mother's ethics of love, in opposition to the Rajput male child brought up on the Law of the Father in terms of a love of war and predilection for violence.

One of the pleasures of a Meera poem is readerly expectation of the moment of risk in the verse when Meera throws down the gauntlet, rhetorically speaking, to challenge her detractors. Modern Indian feminists find this note of defiance puzzling, perhaps because we are invested in portraying our literary mothers and grandmothers as submissive and ourselves as rebellious; consequently feminists dismiss Meera's poetic defiance as explainable wholly in terms of her class privilege.[38] We argue that class privilege educates women to participate in modes of domination and exploitation and a habit of mind within which their own nonconformism and exceptionalism does not open up liberatory spaces for women of other classes. Far from speaking as a privileged woman when she speaks her defiance, Meera's strategies of resistance are accessible to all women. We can judge this for ourselves in the poem "There is no one but *Giridhar Gopal* for me," which ranks among Meera's most widely known verse. In the second verse defiance fills the mother's heart as she gazes at her grown daughter and realizes that she has survived and is blooming. She does not see the child in the way Rajput patriarchy has taught her: as the bringer of tears, expense, disaster, and as not-son. Meera asks mothers to disbelieve the Hindu Shastric injunction that it is only the mother of sons who has fulfilled her earthly duty and will attain the rewards of the afterlife. Instead, Meera argues, the mother of daughters attains the bliss and spiritual joy of ananda in this life by coming to the understanding that her daughter is a flowering vine who carries forward her creativity and her gift of love and her power to reproduce society. Meera uses the term ananda as social commentary and critique of the traditional dread of misfortune mothers are supposed to feel at the birth of a daughter.

The same verses can be read in terms of a daughter's self mothering. Meera's poetic construction of women's nurture works at two registers: to illuminate woman as mother or spotlight woman as daughter. By the third verse Meera invites daughters to abandon their attachment to the natal family that values her less than her brothers, that reminds her she is fortunate because she was not killed at birth, that marries her for their own advantage. For such daughters Meera constructs her poetics of self orphaning. In the third verse we witness a Shiva-like ecstatic dance of rejection and destruction, a dance in which different parts of Shiva's dead wife are flung in every direction, a dance, which can only end in the world's annihilation. In this terrifying dance the daughter's incantation is, "of father, mother, brother, kinsfolk I have none/ having transgressed clan taboos, what can anyone do to me?" The series of negations are necessary in order that the daughter nurtures herself and by the same token nurtures her creativity. Her girlhood must be spent in rejecting the patriarchal narrative that tells her she has no identity other than as a wife in training. Instead she must nurture her own fantasies of love, her own dedication. We now hear the second verse at two registers and this time it yields a distinct meaning. This time the daughter cries because alone and orphaned, she faces the disciplining and punishment of her natal family and secretly nourishes the fledgling plant of her dedication. With intimate lived knowledge Meera speaks of the moment when the self-nurtured female self comes to the realization that the creeper has become a flowering, mature fruit-bearing vine, which now replenishes her, now parents her.

Meera's woman-centered code of reciprocity between nature and nurture has to be understood in relation not only to female creativity, but also in conjunction with her explicit critique of feudal Rajput conspicuous consumption and accumulation. We differentiate Meera's specific critique of Rajput extravagance from the general critique within the Bhakti movement of the obsession with wealth and the material world. One of the thematics of the Bhakti movement concerns the distinction between the world of appearance and the world of reality based upon the notion that all that appears real is false and transitory and the only truth is god and the human being's relation to god. This thematic even goes so far as to describe the human body in Shastric terms as a set of clothes that must be given up at death to achieve union with god. Within this Bhakti thematic material things like wealth, desire for worldly objects and pleasures are situated as distractions that take one away from the true understanding of the human condition and the purpose of life in this world.

Meera's specific critique of aristocratic Rajput life is aimed at the traditional displays of wealth and ceremony, which was used to establish their right to rule. The Rajput women bore the burden of signifying through their elaborate dress and ornaments the Rajput claim to supremacy. There is a fine irony in the fact that these Rajput women had no rights to property and no part in any real decision making, their movements were restricted by being kept in purdah, they were excluded from any access to production, their marriages were arranged for political convenience, they had no right to bear daughters and only achieved minimal rights when they produced a son. However, for the general populace they embodied a life of untold luxury and consumption. The absolute control of elite Rajput men of their women, the coercive disciplining of the women into consumers, and their erasure and removal from production was discursively referred to as the pampered and protected life of luxury led by Rajput princesses.

Meera mocks this contradiction in a series of poems which are staged as dialogues with her sister-in-law Uda. These dialogues are in the traditional women's genre of daughter-in-law/sister-in-law songs of confrontation where each accuses the other, and which are traditionally sung at festivals and weddings. The daughter-in-law's subject position makes her the rebel who will not give up her difference and mold herself entirely to the demands and dictates of the marital family, while the sister-in-law's subject position makes her the repository of family's values and traditions. Meera sets up this traditional genre by writing into her songs a straw figure of Uda who seems to be more a transmitter of traditional Rajput values and a Sisodiya loyalist than a complex character.

Uda poses a series of questions, along with offering enticements such as a necklace of a thousand chains, jewelry studded with precious stones and ornate silken scarves (Shabnam 1973, 205). The questions ask Meera to account for her aberrant actions in rejecting her princely husband and home, in choosing a life of wandering and poverty over a life of plenty and ease, in her breaking caste taboos by receiving alms from the poor and her adoption of the dress of the poor, in breaking both purdah and caste taboos by associating with all and sundry especially male saints, and in her adoption of the poor. In the poems Uda alternately threatens, shames and cajoles Meera in order to bring her back within the confines of the home, the palace and purdah.

Meera's answers are a series of meditations that are pointedly critical of Rajput values and express concisely her philosophically and spiritually oriented life practices (Sekhavat 1974, 222–223). In one couplet Meera draws a sharp difference between two kinds of human beings: those who nurture themselves and nature by planting a garden, and those who extract a exploitative surplus and then display their wealth by building palaces (Jafri 1965, 117). In the dialogues Meera categorically refuses Uda's enticements, she also sublates the verbal exchange from a confrontation about Meera's rejection of her wifely duties, into an exploration of Meera's need to pursue her vocation, and Meera's need to establishing a separate identity in her work, which is the only way she can hope to meet her lover, Giridhar. She says, "I have an alternate family of *sadhus,* with whom I desire to spend my time in contemplation and composing my poems" (Jafri 1965, 174–177).

In many poems Meera criticizes the Rajput use of saga alliances for political and economic gain and the sacrificing of daughters in saga alliance politics by contrasting saga (economic and political alliance through marriage) with *saancha* (true and real alliance based on love and mutually shared values). In asserting saancha (true relationship based on love) over saga (alliance of families through marriage) Meera is offering a trenchant critique of the way patriarchy positions women as objects of exchange to further family fortunes. As daughters women are neither given love nor affection because they are considered from the beginning as belonging to another family. All that is required from them is that they follow their duty and obligations. In a popular song Meera explicitly calls these relationships of mother, father, extended family, and tribe, as relationships based on patriarchal self-interest (Shabnam 1973, 322). In contrast to these duty-based relationships, Meera offers the saancha relationship, which recognizes and addresses the need of women as human beings to be nurtured and to give as well as receive love. Therefore, the use of the word saancha in Meera's poetry both suggests an abbreviated critique of the place of women within patriarchy and patriarchal affective structures, as well as gestures at an alternative relationship. In another poem Meera says that it is not enough to pay lip service to the concept of love-based relationships while continuing to practice self-interest. She advises women to give up the lover who pretends to love but continues to treat women as objects of exchange (Shabnam 1973, 451). In one of her most powerful statements on the politics of saancha relationship, Meera does not absolve Giridhar because he is god and/or her lover/husband. For Meera

Giridhar too must prove his love and she encapsulates this notion in the phrase, "practice commitment to my love" (Shabnam 1973, 424).

Meera condemns the Rajput martial culture that necessitates the constant search for fresh land to domineer and control, and marginalizes women. The elite Rajput's land-grabbing entails frequent wars with others as well as internecine wars within the family. For Meera the Rajput hunger for land is not complemented by a reciprocal relationship with the land, except by asserting ownership of the land.[39] Meera says that land of one's own, whether fertile or infertile, small or large in size, is perfectly adequate if it provides the human being with enough food to sustain oneself. Working on this land and respecting it is far preferable to nursing hatred and violence and coveting other people's land. This latter route leads to no relationship to real production and land, only to the production of envy (Chaturvedi 1983, 207). Envy causes hatred and wars and has no useful value in terms of sustaining and reproducing life and culture. The full significance of Meera's rejection of Rajput accumulation can be gauged only when we supplement Meera's women-centered code of reciprocity between nature and nurture with her code of the importuning *daasi*. We turn to this in the next chapter.

CHAPTER 7

The Meera Tradition as a Historic Embrace of the Poor and the Dispossessed

Code of Fakiri: Displaced, Dispossessed, Exiled Populations and Meera

Many of Meera's verses prophesy with clairvoyant accuracy the defining twentieth-century experience of indigenous peoples and the poor all over the world—forcibly displaced populations, who are exiled, culturally uprooted, alienated from soil and geographical location, erased, dispossessed, and unable to make claims on the communities of their adopted place. Meera's poetic codes about migration and the community of the migrants, which are absent or unnoticeable in elite decodings of her songs, blaze out in the Meera bhajans that are sung by the poor. This poetic code is not static, rather it is renewed, reinvented, and imbued with historical particularity of meaning every time rural communities experience evacuation and loss.

We name this code in Meera's poetry the code of *fakiri*. Fakiri comes from the Persian word fakir, or a person who cares nothing for material possessions and physical comforts but who wanders in search of knowledge, who is a spiritual seeker.[1] The trope of fakiri connotes two different meanings of the word *faka:* faka literally means fasting due to lack of food, and in its usage as *faka-masti* signifies a carefree and joyous person who despite being deprived of food maintains high spirits. Faka-masti carries with it also a certain connotation of madness, a person is so driven by what she/he are pursuing that they have moved beyond the boundaries of the physical self into the spiritual realm. In Meera's code of fakiri we do not explicitly imply this connotation of madness. However fakiri always carries this meaning at some level. The fakir is one who is not attached to one place, but migrates from place to place and mixes with the populace, offering advice and blessings as a wandering mendicant.

In the code of fakiri we do not romanticize hunger, disempowerment, disinheritance, and the life-threatening conditions imposed through displacement and forcible exile. The plight and terror of such displaced persons can be seen globally: from Africa to Asia, the Middle East and now even in Europe. The fakiri code does not glorify the deprivations and exploitations in poverty,

205

but it does valorize the lives of the poor. Meera's fakiri code also negates the power of the dominant to continue to oppress and coerce the displaced. For obvious reasons we are not advocating through Meera's code of fakiri that children and families reconcile themselves to hunger, poverty, and deprivation. Instead we are paying attention to the acknowledgment and understanding in Meera's poetry that hunger, poverty, and deprivation are widely experienced. Thus Meera says, "*Asal fakiri rurdhi hai* / Actual fakiri is a true tradition" (Sekhavat 1974, 77). She points out that one *can* survive in minimal conditions in the outside world, she who has experienced and partaken of worldly luxuries and pleasure, has chosen to give up material comforts in order to follow her vocation. In doing so Meera aligns herself with the true tradition of fakiri.

Many of the legends around Meera speak of how she is exiled from both her marital and natal home and takes to the life of fakiri. She speaks as one who has had family, home, and country *(desh)*, but by being exiled is now fully dispossessed. Exile is therefore forced on her and she turns the coercion of this enforced exile into her choice by the force of her poetry. However, her poetry does not let the reader and listener forget the harsh and inhuman treatment meted out to her by her family, and the severity of the conditions she has had to endure. Meera rejects Rajput pomp and show in the form of lavish ornamentation and fine silken clothes, for a necklace of wooden beads and the simple cotton clothes worn by the poor because she claims they keep the body comfortable and the spirit and soul free of guilt. She rejects the elaborate food of the palace (56 varieties of dishes) preferring instead poor people's fare (stale dry piece of bread and sour buttermilk) that suffices to keep the body free from hunger. Since Meera does not belong within the palace but has adopted the world, and the majority of people in the world are poor while only the few enjoy wealth, Meera eats and clothes herself like the rest of the world (Chaturvedi 1983, 207). Thus, Meera claims that by adopting and preferring the poor people's clothes and food she keeps herself closely in touch with the reality for the majority.

Meera's poetry holds the code of fakiri in tension with the realities facing a poor, homeless woman in medieval India. Fakiri is at the very limits of life experience, the dominant classes cannot further deprive the hungry, the poor, and the homeless. Meera's poetry focuses on the stratagems by which the hungry, homeless, and exiled person can think through and confront this limit experience. Being at the limits of endurance in terms of hunger and at the mercy of the elements, Meera contends, does not mean that the dispossessed only think through their hunger. It is at the limit experience that the philosophy and practice of fakiri provides the human being with the understanding of the human condition. In asserting the code of fakiri, Meera subverts and challenges elite Shastric and Vedic assumptions about caste *(varna)*, tribe *(jati),* and caste-specific occupation *(vyvasaya),* as well as the universal prejudice that the poor and the hungry, because they are reduced to desiring basic necessities, have neither the desire nor the ability and the wherewithal to lead an ethical, spiritually informed, and philosophically oriented life. In fact she argues that to live through the condition of fakiri—the basic human condition—is to be intimate with philosophy and spirituality.

> Where is the heartache once I have chosen the life of fakiri?
> rapt in contemplation that is how I always wish to be
>
> somedays there is no cart, other days there is no resthouse
> most days the forest gives refuge
> where is the heartache once I have chosen the life of fakiri?
> rapt in contemplation that is how I always wish to be
>
> somedays there is no elephant, other days there is no horse
> most days it is travel on foot
> where is the heartache once I have chosen the life of fakiri?
> rapt in contemplation that is how I always wish to be
>
> somedays a feast on alms, other days simple fare served with love
> and some days cheerful fasting
> where is the heartache once I have chosen the life of fakiri?
> rapt in contemplation that is how I always wish to be
>
> somedays for rest there is a palanquin, other days a hollow ditch
> most days I toss and turn on the hard earth
> Meera says O Savior and Protector of the poor
> to enter this life is to endure what comes your way
>
> (Shabnam 1973, 319)

Meera plays on exile as choice and exile as forced on her, but always exile as the condition of the seeker. In the poem above Meera systematically enumerates the circumstances she has to endure in exile. What is exceptional about this song is that while the conditions of fakiri are presented in all their starkness, there is a reckless joyous abandon in the way the song maps the lack of options in fakiri subversively, as a choice between negatives. The poem plots this lack of choice. For example, the fact that Meera has to travel on foot, and does not have the mode of transport of the rich available to her, is represented so as to suggest "somedays" due to the lack of availability of an elephant or a horse-drawn carriage, Meera chooses to walk on foot because she is determined to be elsewhere. There is self-mockery and self-parody in her adoption of a grandiose manner in dialect, that would be accessible to the poor. Her adoption of a grand style is endearing and faintly comic, and reminds one of Charlie Chaplin dining on shoelaces in *The Gold Rush* (1925) as exquisitely and delicately as if he were dining in the finest of Italian restaurants in Europe. Unlike the Chaplin scene where the hero's poverty is short-lived, Meera sings in the poem about the permanent lack of shelter and therefore having to seek refuge in the forest; the lack of alms and food and therefore having to go hungry; the lack of even the shelter of a tree or a hollow ditch, therefore having to sleep on the hard earth.

The universally relevant aspects of Meera's poetry refer to the experience of exile and displacement from one's desh. In Meera's verses what survives of the hardship of exile is her confrontation and her triumph over the state of exile. She sings, "to enter this life is to endure." The poetic representation of Meera as the high-born Rajput princess adopting and validating the conditions and experiences of the poor, constitutes a unique and remarkable aspect of Meera's poetry. The validation she gives the poor survives, and is reinscribed over time by Meera's poor and dispossessed co-authors. We can only measure the power of this bond between Meera and the poor by the fact that for more than four centuries the code of fakiri survives as a vibrant subaltern tradition.

The way in which we use the term "displaced populations" deserves clarification. Within the terms of our argument, the paradigmatic displaced population is not the upwardly mobile elite classes/families or individuals immigrating from the Third to the First World. Nor are our reference points the exodus of landed gentry to metropolitan centers or the mass migrations from the Old to the New World in search of land and religious liberty. These great historical experiences have given rise to migration myths that continually build on and fictionalize the element of voluntary choice in the decision to leave. By contrast our term "displaced populations" focuses specifically on the *coercive* uprooting of tribal and dalit populations for the sake of misguided development projects in postcolonial India. The elements of coercion permeate the collective experience of forced departure, some of these elements are: loss of livelihood and modes of existence, loss of ancestral history, little or no compensation, undemocratic and nonconsensual political processes by which whole villages and districts are chosen for eviction, repression of collective agitation by the evacuees. Along with this are the experiences of little or no economic resources for travel and amenities, trauma leading to illness and death, fragmentation of family, community, and the wiping out of an entire generation. The populations' relocation signals pauperization due to loss of land and cattle, entry into cheap labor force, cultural alienation and disorientation in a new place, hostility from the settlers in the place of adoption, loss of claim on community, and loss of political rights.[2]

The sheer enormity of the numbers involved gives pause. While Western demographers estimate that the world refugee population increased from

2 million in the 1960s to 15 million in the 1990s (*National Geographic,* October 1998, 998); the ecofeminist Vandana Shiva notes that "fifteen million people have been uprooted from their homelands in India during the past four development decades" (1993, 99). The number of people displaced by development schemes like the Narmada Valley Project not only matches the world refugee population, but is also equal to the total number of people who were displaced in the partition of the subcontinent in the late 1940s. The toll taken by evacuation on such a scale is only now being understood and resisted as ecological and human devastation. For example Shiva argues that in tribal and peasant societies home is not conceptualized in terms of property and land-grabbing but as soil, which is for people the source of sustenance and "the cultural spiritual space which constitutes memory, myths, stories and songs that make the daily life of the community"(102). From the start of the 1990s there have been anti-dam agitations by the Bargi Dam evacuees and the protest against the Sardar Sarovar Dam Project on the Narmada River by ecologists, activists, and affected tribal populations (*Manushi* No. 108; *India Abroad* February 26, 1999). The forms of resistance have been legal, political and cultural-educational, blocking the dam construction through court injunctions and spreading awareness through documentary films by filmmakers like Anurag Singh and Jharana Jhaveri's documentary *How do I Survive, My Friend!* or *Kaise Jeebo Re!* (1998) and the award winning documentary *A Narmada Diary* (1995) by Anand Patwardhan and Simantini Dhuru. There is a specific class content in the migratory consequences of development projects: an overwhelming number of development-induced migrants, almost 80 percent in the case of the Narmada project, consist of tribals and dalits who are the traditionally disenfranchised segments of society in India.

The fakiri code in Meera's poetry can function, and among diverse peasant, artisanal, and dalit communities in northwest India *does function,* as cultural sources for strength, regeneration out of the alienating experience of exile, and collective resistance. In her fieldwork in Rajasthan and Gujarat the Meera scholar Parita Mukta noted the strong correlation between the actual life experience of Rabaris and Ahirs—in their mass migration from Saurashtra to South Gujarat, and from Saurashtra to Okhamandal respectively due to drought and lack of fodder for their cattle—and the specific meanings of Meera as wanderer and exile for them. Mukta notes that in coming to live with their relatives or to a new town for work "they were pointed out [by the townspeople] as those who had a fund of Mira bhajans on their lips" (1994, 11).

The fakiri code functions both as an existing cultural practice and a generalizable possibility for the resistances and daily practices of displaced populations. This is because Meera's poetry speaks directly to specific features of the refugee experience: the crisis for survival; the class specific modes by which an uprooted people name their experience of leaving, traveling, shelter, hunger, and clothing; the cultural ways in which dalits, peasants and artisanal groups salvage and shore up and invent a sense of identity and community; finally, the language and metaphors through which poor people in northwest India piece together and articulate dissent and resistance.[3] Meera's fakiri code is not visible unless we understand and appreciate the rhetorical-performative features specific to the poor people's Meera. Commentators like Hawley have noted that the question of the inauthentic/authentic Meera bhajans can be resolved by seeing the bhajans as having been written by "other Miras" (1988, 123). Mukta also notes how the male bhajniks take on the personae of Meera. She writes that through the "collective singing" of Meera bhajans, "Mira becomes the voice of the oppressed people just as the bhaktas become Mira through their singing" (1994, 87). Through collectively singing Meera bhajans, instead of erasing gender men learn what it is to be woman. The bhajans become a vehicle for the men to experience being a woman. Mukta writes:

> The male bhaktas sing in the *stri vachya* (feminine gender) as in the being of Mira. This is not abstract becoming . . . [but] the living of a woman . . . marked by an active will and an active struggle to grasp the world as she constructs it, and renders it meaningful. . . . When men of a society in which the male consciousness and male constructs are used as yard sticks for the whole of the human experience begin to sing in the stri vachya, then a radical shift occurs in the moral order. It requires a break from and a transcendence of the world created and upheld by men. It requires the recreation of humanity in the female image. The world has to become strimay i.e. the world has to become female. This requires more, much more than an empathy with the female subject. (87)

Harlan (1992) gives a similar if somewhat contorted argument in this context. She writes: "Mira, being female takes on a male role that *reidentifies* her with the female capacity of sexual union with a male lover" (italics ours, 21). We argue that Meera does not have to reidentify herself with her female capacity except when renunciation is made, as Harlan makes it seem, a male preserve and not within the ecofriendly tradition of fakiri.[4]

Nothing so sharply distinguishes the blandness and bourgeoisification of the middle class Meera from the people's Meera than the rhetorical-performative features of the latter, for it is these features that illuminate the emotive and political content of the fakiri code. For instance the artist-audience relationship in the middle class Meera is an orderly, subdued and quietly attentive audience viz-à-vis the singer seated in a room, on stage, at concert recital, or distanced by radio or film. In popular film music an opening line or central metaphor from a Meera poem is appropriated into a film song.

Meera is also appropriated by the burgeoning middle class consumers of "bhajan music" who are targeted by the audio-cassette industry, compact disk technology, and live music conferences. Contrarily the artist-audience relation in the people's Meera replaces passive consumerism with collective participation. The singing is raucous, full throated, and unashamedly emotional. The artist-audience dynamic is analogous to the "call and answer" of gospel singing; the call and answer in Meera bhajans consists of one person beginning, another adding a couplet, a third carrying it forward, while the refrain is sung in unison.

Indeed this is a carnivalesque Meera and the carnival elements of inversion of social hierarchies is evident in a number of ways. For example, in women's bhajan mandalis different women sing, dance, play the *harmonium* (piano like instrument), and *dhol* (drum). Together these poor women evoke the eerily powerful image, always ever-present in the collective Indian unconscious, of a woman with unbound hair and in the *bhagva bhesh* of ascetic dress consisting of coarse cotton, holding an *ektara* (the simple string instrument associated with Meera and represented in calendar art) dancing with anklets on her feet. The middle-class Meera is denuded of many of these features that are so shocking to middle class sensibilities, her dress and posture is made more decorous.

One rhetorical feature that is present both in mixed gatherings and sex-segregated mandalis and is absent in elite interpretations of Meera concerns the multiplicity of voices and interlocutors in the Meera song. Interestingly Meera's interlocutors are generally men, those who represent patriarchal authority at different sites like Rana (Meera's husband and within the poems, the representative of the feudal-military Rajput upper classes), or a representative of the male-dominated spiritual organizations or *sampradayas,* or lower-caste men who are themselves oppressed by the Brahmanical patriarchal order like her guru Raidas.

We can better appreciate the usefulness of multiple voices in subaltern versifying of Meera songs by looking at one of the interlocutors, Meera's husband Rana. In chapter six we theorized the author as Meera, here we note the prolific male appropriations of Meera. Male authors as Meera have composed lyrics for the Bombay film industry right from the inception of the industry to the present.[5] In elite interpretations Rana disappears inside the poem, sometimes as an obscure historical figure, sometimes as an actor in a domestic quarrel, sometimes as the sentient husband bewildered by his wife's moods and wants, passively acquiescent in his wife's preference for the life of an ascetic over the duties of a householder. Poor people are under no obligation to whitewash Meera's marital family, the Sisodiya Rajputs, or uphold the wronged husband. The persona of Rana thus emerge in the bhajniks' construction as the interlocutor who exhorts, shames, threatens Meera and to

whom Meera addresses some of her most defiant and challenging poetic formulations. Meera's poetry comes alive as we understand the venom, the malig-
nant and implacable hatred that is directed at this woman who keeps all the
force of her being directed at the ethics of love. The poor people's Meera questions Rana, "Mewadi Rana, why have you kept up a vendetta against me?"
(Mukta 1994, 103; Alston 1980, 48) or she challenges, "If I incur the Rana's
displeasure, what can he do to me?" (Mukta 1994, 104; Alston 1980, 48) in
another she swears, "Rana, I vow never to drink the water of your land again"
(Mukta 1994, 192). The ventriloquising of the strategies, the power, and the
hostility of the dominant classes attributed to the persona of Rana makes visible, as nothing else can, that Meera is the name not of writing in tranquil
environs but women's writing in the midst of *conflict*. Thus these devices dis-
pel the bourgeois image of a Meera turned inward and lost in spiritual abstraction and replaces it with the poor people's image of a Meera turned outwards
and addressing contentious and contending voices, a Meera who is unregulat-
edly emotional, unambiguously insubordinate and unequivocally militant.

  These rhetorical and performative features inform the structure of the
code of fakiri in Meera's poems. The bhajan singers can, by singing a particular cluster of Meera songs, evoke certain political dimensions in their attention to a particular level of poetic meaning. Meera bhajniks among the poor
continually evoke the "figure" of Meera by tracing and retracing key elements
of her life that contains a special meaning for them. A continual source of
ardent love for Meera lies in the bhajniks' re-imagining of a woman who takes
voluntary exile from Rajput society, who is uprooted from all that she knows
and holds dear, who is shunned and persecuted by her Rajput oppressors.[6]
Many of the songs begin with the moment of Meera's expulsion from home
that she turns into voluntary adoption of fakiri. For instance a popular song
begins, "When she left (was turned out) of the palace she carried the marks of
a married women of status/ having left (been turned out) of her marital home
she also refused her natal home (Merta) and headed as an exile for Pushkar"
(Mukta 1994, 92; Sekhavat 1975, 234). At this level Meera's poetry performs
the function of psychic recall. This recall addresses the psychic need of the
evicted poor to obliquely revisit the scene of eviction, and by revisiting the
scene to understand the reasons for being driven out and wrenched from the
mitti or soil of the homeland. The Meera bhajniks address this collective need
by interpellating themselves into that part of the Meera narrative where she is
turned out of doors by her husband and his family. Looking for work by day
and singing around the makeshift fire by night, the displaced poor give a specific emotive content to Meera's eviction.

  The bhajniks do not erase or even wish to erase the distinction between
their own involuntary eviction and the voluntary exile of a privileged upper
caste woman Meera. While maintaining that distinction they interpret the

scene of Meera's eviction in such a way that forcible eviction is always happening to Meera, in the songs she is forever in the fluid motion of the woman turned out of her own home. The bhajan mandali receives this scene in their nerves and their hearts, and from that receiving flows the singer/listeners' insight—we have been driven out by the same elite classes who turn their own daughters and wives out of doors—an insight that opens up the fissures in elite society and functions as an indictment of that society. Interpreted in this way Meera's eviction opens up a psychic tunnel of collective memory. Their own historical moment of displacement connects to the mass migrations of peasants and artisans in Meera's time, occasioned by the exorbitant taxes levied by Rajput landlords and rajas; the bhajan singers also reconnect to the legions of anonymous tillers of soil in ancient and medieval India for whom, as Romila Thapar notes, mass migration was a traditional form of dissent because it meant the loss of labor force and surplus for the kingdom; the dalit singers recall through Meera that migration was one of the few means of escape from caste oppression and the upper castes' demand for unpaid *(begaar)* services.

Fakiri also deals with that part of the diaspora experience when, having left behind all that is known and dear to the sight, the ear and the mind, the exiled leaps into the abyss. In many mythic narratives this moment in the journey is described as the miracle of the human encounter; for instance Don Quixote meets ordinary people on the road instead of the knights and dragons he expects to find; young Joseph lies naked and injured on the road and the poorest men and women assume the biblical role of the Good Samaritan in Henry Fielding's novel; in a vastly different religio-moral vocabulary the poor in India gesture to this miracle of human connectedness through the aphorism, "Who knows where on the road and in which guise I may meet Narayan (Krishna)." In fakiri the exiled and the displaced reconstellate with harsh self-discipline their nostalgia and its concomitant affect for the lost home and country into hope for the future and the fight for immediate survival. Between this discipline of hope for the future and the fight for survival lies the possibility of human bonding between people.

Meera's poems describe this possibility of human bonding through the meeting between Meera and Raidas or Rohidas, a fifteenth-century tanner who was born around Benaras and traveled all over northwest India spreading his visionary message about God.[7] The meeting between these two human beings constitutes the miraculous, unplanned, and unprecedented aspect of exile. A woman and a man meet in a way that profoundly affects both of them and all those around them. Everything about this meeting is scandalous and subversive. The man belongs among those social groups that are shunned by the upper castes, although the products of his labor are consumed by the elite. The woman who has lived all her life circumscribed by Kshatriya taboos of purity and pollution compounds her impure status as the abandoned wife by going to his house. There are no limits to her self-pollution, she asks the humble tanner to become her guru or spiritual teacher. Meera celebrates her meeting with Raidas by singing, "I met Sant Raidas, adopted him as my spiritual guide and he has profoundly changed my being." In another poem Meera says "My Guru Raidas handed me the sword of knowledge and wisdom which enabled me to cut the hangman's noose that was around my life" (Shabnam 1976, 425, 455).

It is unheard of for a woman in Meera's time to desire her own religious guru and to reject the religion of her marital family. Meera could have gained social prestige by accepting tutelage in an established religious order, instead she audaciously suggests that the lowest of the low in the social order has the spiritual wisdom to become her guru. The function of the meeting between the guru and the initiate is to suggest that migration carries the potential of disestablishing class-caste hierarchies. The dalit singers are extraordinarily moving when they re-envision the meeting between Meera and Raidas as a moment that allows them to relive and inhabit, in the realm of the imaginary, their own lived experience of and their rage at caste oppression. Dalit singers construct the Meera verses as a dialogue between the upper-caste Rajput princess and the lower-caste man: the guru is reluctant, anxious, doubt ridden, and insecure about the wrathful reprisal of the Rajputs; slowly he is won over by the genuine respect, validation, and unreserved trust that Meera offers him; Meera's request to be accepted as a pupil unfolds as a metaphor for caste equality in her complete inversion of her caste superiority through the teacher-pupil relation; in the very hesitations and anxieties voiced by Raidas, dalit singers are afforded scope to express their lived experience of being the untouchable.

The figure of Raidas in Meera's life and poetry and the position she accords him as her Guru is an affirmation for the dalits and the poor of their understanding of the Meera tradition. In the poor people's Meera the political significance of Raidas to Meera's life cannot be underestimated. In postcolonial India the displaced populations that are the poor, the dalit and mainly tribals face the unprecedented challenge of environmental disasters being wrought by a government that is impervious to their needs and committed to implementing development projects under the name of nation building. The very survival of the poor is threatened as the soil, water, and air is contaminated and poisoned by misguided development projects that exclude community and further the global corporate and finance interests. In Meera's time the displaced and the exiled communities still had hope of relocating to a place where at the very minimum there was clean fresh water to drink, clean air to breathe, and land to till. In contemporary India these basic requirements of life are under threat. Meera is relevant for us today because through fakiri she advocates a subsistence lifestyle that the whole world should meditate upon, embrace, and adopt in order to prevent ecological disasters. Through fakiri the Meera tradition teaches the ethics of love and a sense of community with the poor. If we accept the premise of fakiri then we understand that fakiri is a way of being in the world. It is an ethical ontology.

Meera's Code of the Importuning Daasi and Mock Servitude

Modern commentators on Meera contend that she mirrors the Bhakti tradition of glorifying servitude by naming herself Meera *daasi* (female slave) to her god Krishna. These critics argue that the relation between a female poet and her male god contains within it all the hierarchical elements of Rajput patriarchal feudalism such as the subordination of women, children, and the lower classes to the elite Rajput male. Therefore Meera's poetry, these critics argue, reinforces the official Rajput ideology and status quo concerning class and gender.[8]

This specific critique of Meera is allied to the general charge made against the discursive codes of Bhakti by Ranajit Guha. Guha argues that the Bhakti literatures are "an ideology of subordination par excellence" (1989, 259). According to Guha the Bhakti poets, far from challenging the political theories of the Dharmashastras about daasa slavery, in fact adapt the old modes of domination to "the conditions of later feudalism" (1989, 260). In the excerpt below Guha takes the provocative position that *daasatva ras* in Bhakti functions not as dissent from domination, but as the persuasive aspect of domination through the ideology of collaboration:

> those of its cults which were addressed to the religiosity of the lower strata of Hindu society, had it as their function to try and endear the dominant to the subordinate and assuage thereby the rigor of dasya for the latter. It was these that spiritualized the effort, fatigue and frustration involved in the labour and services offered [by the subordinate groups and classes]. . . . In all such instances, Bhakti conferred on the superordinate the sanctity of a deity or his surrogate . . . correspondingly, the latter's submission which rested, in the last resort, on the sanction of force, was made to appear as self-induced and voluntary—that is, as collaboration in short. (1989, 260)

Guha characterizes the deployment of daasatva ras in terms of the hierarchical social ordering prescribed by elite Hindu scriptures. Guha's thesis indicates in a profoundly critical way how the ideology of daasatva functions as an aesthetics (ras); male poets in the Bhakti movement drew on the subject position of the slave or daasa in order to align themselves with the subordinate classes and recruit these classes; the Bhakti poet invites his listeners-participants to take on a feminized and stereotypically passive relationship to god. In Guha's view this aesthetic had less to do with religion and more to do with maintenance of social hierarchy, for it makes the daasa's submission "appear as self-induced and voluntary" and reconciles him to subordination.

In general we are in agreement with Guha's critique because he names an important element in male Bhakti poetry and its nationalist appropriations as well as its deployment by the hegemonic discourse of Hindu fundamentalists.[9] We depart from Guha's general view of Bhakti and daasa ras when it comes to factoring in women poets into the equation. The complexities of women's relation to the systems of subordination means that female servitude is not identical to male servitude and female slaves are not subordinated in the same way as male slaves. Therefore female and male servitude cannot be treated as the same without examining the specificity of how a woman poet activates the poetic code of daasatva. Female self-naming is never a harmonious and tranquil literary exercise, involving as it does the tense and strenuous processes of beating back women's erasure in discourse.[10]

We perceive an element of deliberation in Meera's poetic references to women's servitude, particularly in her self-naming as Meera daasi. Feudal censorship dictated the necessity for encoding mock servitude, a woman invited patriarchal punishment unless she, like Uddyotama Suri's heroine in *Kuvalayamala*, referred to herself as a daasi or servant of her husband.[11] Moreover, there were social sanctions against men and women of subordinate classes who rebelled against the name of servant or slave. In precapitalist feudal societies of medieval India the subordinate classes were regulated, not through the ideology of wage labor or *naukri*, but through a range of Shastric prescriptions concerning the social interactions between subordinate and elite classes. The elite Rajput male saw it as his duty to enforce these prescriptions, for example if he saw an untouchable who did not wear the prescribed marks of servitude on his body or did not display the proper attitude of humility, the Rajput saw it as his duty to severely punish the insubordinate daasa. It is in such a climate that Meera refuses to name herself as daasi of her husband (Rana) but names herself as daasi of Giridhar. Her self-naming as daasi, when she belongs to a princely family and is married to a prince, has to be understood in the specific context of her defiance of class and caste and her open alliance with the poor classes. In naming herself daasi Meera also confronts the irresistible power of patriarchal language to silence her and always already occupy the space between her audience and herself. The poetic effort to locate herself outside the dominant discourses by naming herself daasi can create discord rather than harmony, conflict instead of tranquillity. Meera does not resolve all these tensions in her poetry, rather she keeps these tensions alive making them serve her critique productively.

We call Meera's self-naming the code of mock servitude because Meera lays siege on daasi status and names herself as daasi in order to mobilize critical rejection of the oppression visited upon those who are daasa. Meera transforms the word daasi into a rhetorical strategy. Meera's code of mock servitude in her poems involves a two step process. The first step consists of a distinction between servitude and mock servitude, there is a disjunction between the social ramifications of the word daasi and the range of meanings invested in the word in the Meera poems. Her self-naming as daasi is a feature of a large number of her poems, each time the context of the poem endows the phrase Meera daasi with a new meaning.

As a member of an aristocratic Rajput clan she is not born a slave or servant, in fact her birth in the Merta clan entitles her to be a mistress of servants and slaves. By naming herself as daasi Meera at one stroke disavows her status as a member of the ruling class and therefore entitled to privilege. In many poems Meera as daasi is demanding, importuning, and impatient, her poetic persona is not conducted with the proper marks of servitude. It is precisely in those poems where Meera names herself as servant that the self-naming signals a statement of aggressive insubordination. The religious framework in which Meera calls herself the slave of her god Krishna should not fool us into thinking that this insubordinate female slave is unconcerned with her rights in this world. As daasi she is unreconciled to injustice in the name of God. In effect she takes up daasatva as a rhetorical weapon for making claims and asserting her rights.

The second step in the code of mock servitude consists of unlocking the female slave's understanding of her positioning in the social structure. The importuning Meera daasi is not enough, in itself that rhetorical gesture would merely follow the Bhakti tradition of protest against injustice by deferring justice to the afterlife. In a Meera poem the self-naming as servant unlocks her from isolation and confinement and peoples her universe with all those—peasants, artisans, domestic servants, self-employed in specialist occupations, untouchables and tribals, landless migrant poor—who were referred to as daasa in medieval India and served Rajput elites and sustained their economy. In bhajan mandalis that sing Meera's songs, this code of mock servitude acts as a forum for discussing interactions between subordinate and elite classes; for instance, bhajan mandalis deploy the Meera poems to discuss the ways in which the elite exploit, coerce, and dominate the poor; these discussions facilitate the bhajan mandali members' understanding of how and where the subordinate classes are placed in the social structure. Meera's poems lend themselves to this interpellation, her verses subvert the master-slave dialectic in medieval Rajasthan and radically refuse reconciliation to the oppression of women, children and the lower castes.

We examine Meera's code of mock servitude in one of her famous padas. It is a poem invested with legend. In the folkloric versions of Meera's life it is said that this poem is her last composition, she recited it after years of wandering as an exile in northwest India. Her growing popularity among women and the poor in these wanderings made her a source of political embarrassment to her husband's princely family. They made several attempts to coerce Meera into returning to her marital home, however public opinion made it difficult for the family to remove her by an overt act of violence. Although a Rajput wife in medieval India had no legal rights viz-à-viz her marital family, Meera forged her own protection by transforming herself into a public figure of dissent against elite Rajput norms.

Finally Meera's marital family devised a plan of sending the family priests to coerce her by threatening to commit suicide unless she returned with them. Meera's dilemma was that she was opposed to the Rajput cult of violence and could not contravene her own principles by becoming the cause of the priests' death. There are several folk versions of what happens next. Some claim that Meera retired into the recesses of the temple and was never seen again in human form, others say that Meera escaped from the back door of the temple and walked into the sea behind the temple. Yet others have it that Meera escaped to south India where she lived in anonymity for many years, traveling, and composing wherever she went (Goetz 1966, 33–40; Mukta 1994, 227).

According to legend Meera composes this poem in the throes of her dilemma:

> Hari the oppressed citizenry is in pain
> make their suffering cease
>
> miraculously you protected Draupadi's honor
> draping her with the gift of unending cloth
> Hari the oppressed citizenry is in pain
> make their suffering cease
>
> you appeared as the tiger headed man
> instantaneously destroying evil Hirankashyap for the
>   sake of your devotee
> Hari the oppressed citizenry is in pain
> make their suffering cease
>
> you saved the old elephant from drowning
> by drying the water of the river
> Hari the oppressed citizenry is in pain
> make their suffering cease
>
> you are Lord Giridhar and I am your daasi Meera
> make our suffering cease
> in the misery of oppression there is terrible suffering

(Alston 1980, 59; Subbulakshmi 1986)

In the poetic genres available to Meera women's experience is described by male bards. In order to intervene Meera has to raid male narratives, and draw on popularly available figures and myths from Hindu mythology, which are well known to the poorest members of her audience. For example the bards of Rajasthan often interspersed their ballads or eulogies with a digression into relevant episodes of the religious epics—the *Mahabharata* and the *Ramayana*. A staple of the bardic narrative is the story of Draupadi in the *Mahabharata*. She is a princess married to the five Pandava brothers and she is chiefly remembered for the incident of Draupadi *chir haran* or Draupadi divestment; in a gambling contest with their rival cousins the eldest Pandava loses his kingdom, becomes a daasa along with his brothers and finally gambles his wife, too; despite her class privilege Draupadi is dragged before the court and at the whim of her new masters, stripped of her clothes. What happens next is veiled in the language of miracles, the god Giridhar intervenes and clothes his female devotee until her human oppressors are defeated. Bards inflect the story with a variety of messages—the battle between good and evil, or a homily on divine miracles, or a parable about the villainy of the Kauravas, or a moral about women as the cause of war.

In Meera's retelling of the mythological incident of Draupadi being turned into a daasi, the story is not about men's relationship to each other nor is it about woman as the object of exchange between men. Meera does not spiritualize Draupadi's servitude. Instead Meera reinterprets Draupadi to illuminate the material day to day experience of female servitude. The poem states, "miraculously you protected Draupadi's honor/ draping her with the gift of unending cloth." The phrase *laaj raakhi* or keeping women's honor emphasizes the material experience of women's public humiliation and the continual threat of public dishonor.

As postcolonial woman readers we are left breathless with the way Meera's use of dialect allows her to violently reconfigure patriarchy. Her use of language in dialect is so extraordinary that the contemporary woman understands that language in a nonlinguistic preverbal way. By this we mean that it is only when one repeats words of a Meera song a hundred times, that suddenly the meaning of a line becomes intelligible. Like Freud's notion of condensation in dreamwork, Meera uses the characteric condensed utterance of dialect and combines it with the condensation that is only possible in poetic utterances to accomplish an unprecedented magical condensation, enfolding a code within a code.[12] Within the code of mock servitude Meera unlocks a further code of female empowerment in the phrase *"chat barahyo chir"* or instantly draping her with unending cloth. For us the magic of Meera's poetry lies not in the legends of miraculous events associated with her life that are told and retold in folk tales. For us the magic lies in how she takes the enunciatory possibilities of daasatva and female erasure in discourse and violently brings forth in language the liberatory possibilities in combining the latter with the former. For instance, Draupadi's divestment is referred to in hegemonic language and subaltern dialects as chir haran. In her poem Meera does not refer to Draupadi's divestment (chir haran); instead she celebrates the protection of Draupadi's honor by Giridhar providing her with unending cloth. Therefore, Draupadi's divestment (chir haran) in dialect becomes the magical possibility of Draupadi's endless chir (cloth). In Meera's usage the metaphor of unending cloth signifies that the dignity and humanity that belongs to Draupadi, and by extension to all women, is endless and therefore can never be snatched away from either her or them. In this Meera is reconstellating the traditional understanding of the chir haran from Draupadi's shame into Draupadi's triumph. In the *Mahabharat* this is an instance of a miracle. The magic in Meera's poetry lies in her appropriation and reinscription of this moment in dialect and the making of this moment into a text for the subaltern populace against elite Kshatriya patriarchal interpretation.

Meera's poetic choice of a queen who turns into a daasi drives home the point that women are socially positioned as daasis in potentiality or in actuality. The condition of female servitude can happen even to the most privileged woman, the class and clan privilege of the beloved daughter of a king and the cherished wife of warrior princes can be wrenched away at any point in her life. Draupadi can be gambled or sold as alienable property. As queen turned daasi Draupadi can be dragged in public view and stripped before the family elders. Meera demonstrates to her listeners the power of self-naming; women can name themselves in such a way that they are not isolated in their suffering but connect to others who are in a position of subordination in the patriarchal family. The stripped woman symbolized by Draupadi becomes the stripped child in Meera's reference to the Prahalad story, "you appeared as the tiger headed man/ instantaneously destroying evil Hirankashyap for the sake of your devotee." In this story the evil king Hirankashyap is given a boon that he will not be killed by any man or animal, by day or night. He persecutes his infant son Prahalad because of his piety towards Lord Vishnu (whose incarnation is Krishna) and repeatedly tries to kill him. Finally the god Giridhar takes on the shape of a tigerheaded man and kills the father at dusk.

Meera's poem links the two disparate mythological incidents of Draupadi and Prahalad in order to enlarge the meaning of daasi, the experience of servitude is no longer confined to the adult woman but pervades childhood. We contend that the theme of female infanticide is always a coded reference in Meera's poetry; however here it breaks into the surface of the verse. Meera obliquely gestures to murdered infant Rajput daughters by switching the gender of the child-victim, she speaks with intimate knowledge about the infant who looks into the face of the adult and does not know that he wishes to kill her/him. Meera's reworking of these mythic figures does not seem to fit

Guha's charge of collaborationist assuaging of "the rigour of dasya" by diviniz-
ing the master. The poem steadily redefines the word daasi to connote she
who can be stripped like a slave and she/he who can be killed at birth. The
stripping of Draupadi becomes a metaphor that not only names women's
oppression but also encompasses the stripping of children like Prahalad of
their right to life and their right to parental protection and affection.

Meera's poetic strategies for locating dissent outside the dominant discourses lie in her repudiation of the social identities conferred on her by *kul*
and *varna*. The mythological incidents that Meera picks up have one feature
in common, the violence on the woman and the child is not conducted in the
privacy of the home but in the public realm; for example Draupadi is dragged
before the court and turned into a daasi in full view of the public. The poem
takes another aggressive step forward by shifting the notion of daasi from the
social realm to the political realm. This shift is indicated by the poem's reference to regicide and the poetic tension between *jana*, kul and varna. In the
medieval-feudal political vocabularies available to Meera in the fifteenth century, social stratification and political identity is organized around these terms.
Varna denotes ritual status, hereditary occupation, and social mobility through
the adoption of the insignia of caste sanctions and taboos. *Jati* and kul signify
the socio-economic status of a group, political affiliations, and political rival-
ries based on clan networks, and in Meera's case, the patriarchal Rajput family and extended clan. The third term jana originally signified tribes and tribal
identity but gradually came to mean citizenry.

In the political discourses of the dominant classes in Rajpootana, the
normative relation between caste, clan, and citizenship can be glimpsed
through the processes known as the *Kshatriyization* of Rajput tribes. The
Rajputs Kshatriyized their motley origins, their invader status and military
acquisition of territory by assuming ritual varna status of the Kshatriya or warrior caste. Thus Rajput land grabbing, internecine wars and desire for political dominance was legitimated as the assumption of Kshatriya *dharma* of taking up arms to protect the jana or populace. The caste insignia of Kshatriya
endowed Rajputs with the right to the service of the daasa classes; this relation between varna and jana was further stratified and complicated by the
patriarchal Rajput family and clan organized around the notion of kul, within
which Rajput lineages, crafted with the aid of Brahmins, became the basis of
lineage claims to political dominance.

The code of mock servitude advances its argument by renaming,
Meera's poem subversively reconstellates varna, kul, and jana. Meera repudiates kul identity for women and suggests that women's political identity as citizen can be forged only by rejecting the patriarchal Rajput family. We know
this in a number of ways through Meera's rhetorical strategies of self-namings.
Meera never calls herself Rajpootni in her poems. In many poems Meera

scorns the notion of making affective-familial claims as daughter on kul and *kutumb* (extended family). In this particular poem Meera's critique of women's kul identity consists of recalling, through her rereading of Draupadi, the Kshatriyization of the Rajputs. Meera reminds Rajputs that, given their spurious claims to the varna status of the Kshatriyas and their adoption of Kshatriya values, they would do well to note that even the archetypal Kshatriyas in the Hindu epic *Mahabharata,* the Pandavas, could not protect the honor and dignity of their wife Draupadi. Meera's retelling of Kshatriya failures viz-à-viz their women has the poetic effect of stripping and unmasking, not the hapless Draupadi and her descendants among Rajpootni women, but rather the code of Kshatriya values concerning women and by association the discrediting of Rajput male claims of laying down their lives to protect their women. For Meera women can begin the long process of claiming the political rights and duties of citizenship only by rejecting the patriarchal family.

As yet we have described the negative modes of estrangement from "the universe of dominance" as Guha puts it. In a society where all modes of power and survival of women consist in manipulating their marital-familial and natal-familial rights, the family is both the site of oppression and the only reality women know. There is no outside to the family for women except in the delirium of madness or suicide. Rejecting the family is to literally ask women to jump off the cliff, unless there is an alternate collectivity, a daily practice, a material basis for women's political revolt. In one poem Meera indicates her sense of female community, "you (god Giridhar) appear as one to me, we appear as lakhs and crores of women to you" (Jafri 1965, 129). In other poems Meera's community extends to men and women of the subordinated classes and the dalit castes in northwestern medieval India.

We may now comprehend the ways in which the female dissenter moves outside the patriarchal Rajput discourses, changes the meaning of female servitude by showing women their place in the structure of domination. The poem gestures to the materialist basis for women's politics by establishing a dialectic between the self-naming as jana in the opening line and the self-naming as daasi in the concluding lines of the poem. Meera implies that women earn citizen's right to rebellion, not by their victim status, not even by acquiring consciousness that varna privilege and kul protection does not relieve their conditions of servitude, but by the everyday practices of political identification with the poor and the subordinated. In her rereading of Draupadi Meera abolishes the class difference between underprivileged men and women who are *born* into slavery and are persuaded by the Shastras that their caste identity at birth is that of a slave, and the high born queen whose biological female identity at birth determines that she will either be killed at birth or married to further her father's political ambitions, for both are marked by daasa status at birth.

Perhaps the most effective way in which the poem shows the female subject her place in the structure of dominance is by listing all those who are excluded—women, children, animals, subordinate classes, oppressed citizens—from the Rajput body politic. Meera's listing exposes the fact that the dominant militaristic Rajput patriarchy comprises only a minority of men, female loyalists and collaborators. The more the poem enumerates the list of excluded groups, the more it becomes clear that much of the populace and all living things belong among the daasas. The telos of female self-naming as citizen is Meera daasi. The phrase Meera daasi contains a coded meaning for generations of women, Meera redefines the word daasi to mean, not one who is servant by birth or gender, nor one who accepts her subordinate status, but she who belongs among the subordinate classes. There is an embrace in this self-naming, an embrace of those who are disinherited and dispossessed like her.

The notion of championing the dalits and daasas has a long tradition in the history of dissenting groups in India. Yet Meera's embracing the name of Meera daasi does not quite belong among these traditions of protest. In the poem Meera makes it clear that she is envisioning militant revolutionary struggle to change society rather than issuing a call for a parallel society. We know this because of the way she deploys the word *haro* (forcibly cease) and its variants throughout the poem. The famous opening phrase commands God to take by force the suffering of the oppressed populace. Harior Giridhar is the representation of God Vishnu and Vishnu takes on human and other forms again and again to rid this world of evil and misery. The militancy of haro is maintained in the next couplet which refers to Draupadi's chir haran by the condensed word "chir," which carries the association of haran or abducting women by force. Thus a parallelism is set up between the violence and killing in patriarchy on the one hand, and the militancy of *chat* or instantaneously intervening to put an end to the exploitation of women and children on the other.

We still have to understand how women and slaves can have access to a sense of their own agency for the purposes of resistance. How can a slave who has grown up with intergenerational servitude imagine that she/he can break the chains? How can women who are kept in fear of chir haran/public dishonor break free from the family to which they cling? How can the girl-child who has looked into the face of a killer psychically arm herself with an image of her own agency? As Guha reminds us political dissent can only be short-lived if its images and tropes of human agency are not composed of elements that are "historically antagonistic" to the discourses of domination. According to Guha dissent is not true dissent unless it emerges "from outside the universe of dominance which provides the critique with its object" (1989, 220). Insofar as the tropes, values, and worldview of the dissenter remain within the dominant discourses, the dissenter's capacity to change the world around her is limited. The nonconformist's vision must be located outside and elsewhere, "indeed from another and historically antagonistic universe" (1989, 220).

Meera envisions human agency in a religio-political vocabulary that her lower class audience understands, that her female audiences have decoded for generations. Readers who have had the privilege all their lives to think of themselves as agents, to act, and to be confirmed in their relation to the world as agents, can scarcely imagine the power of the religio-political vocabulary for Meera and her followers. Both the lower class daasa and women are accustomed to being treated as the infinitely exploited body: the slave as beast of burden and the female slave and wife and mother under the double burden of economic and sexual exploitation. That is why the poem gestures in its opening line to bodies in great pain. The citizenry is not described in the bard's panegyric of a happy populace under just rule or *Ram Rajya* (the rule of god Vishnu in his incarnation as Ram) but as *jan ki pir* the suffering of the oppressed citizenry. The next line connects the *pir* or oppression of the populace with the suffering female body: Draupadi standing before the court and witnessing her own body stripped and humiliated. The poetic emphasis on the body in extreme duress is continued by reference to the child's body under threat of murder, and the aged elephant's body.

The body in Meera's poetry is conceived in terms which borrow from the materialist schools of Indian thought as well as from Sufi traditions. In the latter the body in pain is viewed through the tropes of ecstasy, trance, martyrdom; in the former the body is seen as the material vehicle for spiritual knowledge. Meera rejects the idealist conception of the body as that which must be transcended, a conception that belongs to Brahmanical Hinduism and to Bhakti poets like Kabir. Unlike Kabir who sees the *pingla* or skeleton beneath the flesh, Meera's poems speak of the body as that which is adorned, pleasured, and pleasuring, that which experiences the heightened moments of her spiritual and sensual meeting with Krishna, and that which experiences the heightened agony of biraha or separation.[13]

According to Meera, the broken and bruised body of the oppressed slave receives an image of her own agency through the miraculating body. Meera describes two instances when the god Krishna is forced to act, when he drapes Draupadi with unending cloth and when he assumes the form of the tiger-headed man for the sake of the child who may be killed. Most postcolonial scholars take the view that the attributing of one's own political resistance to divine intervention is a symptom of passivity. We argue that for Meera and her bhajan mandali, the religio-political notion of god Krishna's incarnation is not a symptom of passivity, the bhajnik is alienated from his daasa self and gains an understanding of the strategies to oppose the violence inherent in the structures of domination. The agency of an oppressed people is aroused by the notion that God is impelled to assume the body of man in response to the victim's plea. It is a notion radiant with possibilities: if a suffering woman and a child can will God to take on human incarnation, then there are no acts of resistance against patriarchal Rajput society that are beyond the imagination. This imaging of agency and political rebellion in terms of the traffic between the human and divine body can be gauged by Meera's vision of the miraculated female body and the miraculated body of the child. Draupadi's body has become sacralized so that she cannot be divested of her clothes. We can explain this in the language of miracles as God's intervention, or it could signify that there is a limit point when the master cannot further intimidate, disenfranchise and strip the slave, when the master slave dialectic reverses itself and it is the master who is stripped and exposed.[14]

As secular postcolonial subjects we find Meera's image of agency extraordinarily moving because it illuminates the statements of poor women in postcolonial India who try to describe what it is like to kill your own child to journalists. For example, the Uslimapatti woman describes the female infant who survives repeated attempts by her husband and herself to kill her by drawing on the religious vocabulary of the magicalized child's body (Vaasanti 1994). Newspaper stories of children who are found unharmed in hurricanes or landslides or fires, and world religions, which contain parables about the infant protected by nature, gesture at that which cannot be explained by the scientific language of probabilities.[15] Meera's poem describes Prahalad's infanticide as the miraculated child's body that cannot be killed by the parent. In describing the child who will not die in terms of the tiger-headed body, Meera gestures in the language of miracles to the atavistic life principle that rears up and stays the tyrant's blow. It is a notion of agency for the infanticide survivor who must see herself, like Prahalad, as the life principle rearing up with the primordial force and *rudra* (awesome, formidable, fearful) aspect of a tiger springing for the kill.

Meera's code of mock servitude does not advocate political quietism by admonishing women to accept their fate as the daughter who can be killed and the mother who submits to her daughters' killing. At a time when Rajpootni women had no familial, civil, political, economic, or property rights, Meera takes the unprecedented step of envisioning women's claim to a political identity as citizen or jana. Citizenship implies the right to rebellion. Meera says, "make our suffering cease/ in the misery of oppression there is terrible suffering." Through the Prahalad story Meera unambiguously speaks of militant resistance, she names the killing of the infanticidal father not as patricide, but as regicide; Meera explicitly invokes the righteous killing of the unjust ruler who commits infanticide. Thus, Meera situates women's protest against female servitude not in social amelioration, or in women's stoic endurance in this world and recompense in the hereafter, but in political revolution in the here and now.

Meera and Postcolonial Women:
Decoding a Life Encoding Praxis

The final section of this chapter is a tribute to those postcolonial women who innovatively recreate Meera and use her stratagems of survival and resistance to negotiate with their own disempowerment in their daily lives. The women who practice the Meera tradition belong to diverse sections of society and there are myriad ways in which they keep the tradition alive. The following pages can only gesture at these practices. We are not familiar with any of these women in our personal lives, therefore we approach each one of them as a text, and it is as texts that we know them.

Perhaps the most moving of these stories concerns an incident in the life of a poor woman from the dalit castes in Gujarat. It might seem that Meera's poetry is far removed from the practical, day-to-day concerns of a dalit woman in postcolonial India. The dalit communities are the most disenfranchised sections of Hindu communities, traditionally they were regarded as "untouchable" and an elaborate set of taboos were enforced upon them; the ostensible reason for this ostracism was that their occupations (sanitation, cremation, tanning) put them at the lowest rung of the ladder. The dalit woman that we write about is a politicized activist despite her poverty, she joins her community on a train trip to be part of a demonstration for dalit rights. Here is the full anecdote about the dalit woman given in Mukta (1994, 109–10). Mukta writes:

> Nagpur in Maharashtra, is a strong dalit base, being the city in which Dr. Ambedkar had publicly converted to Buddhism as a mark of his opposition to dominant Hinduism. On 6 December 1987, a group of dalits, poor peasants and agricultural workers, forcibly entered the Bombay Express train, in order to be able to make their way to Bombay to celebrate Ambedkar's anniversary. I was on the train and witnessed the episode (Mukta, 19.12.1987:2199). It was an anniversary which was particularly significant, as right wing Hindu organizations were demanding censorship of passages from Ambedkar's *'Riddles of Hinduism'* which had offered a critique of the Hindu pantheon of gods.
>
> The passengers who held reserved seats on this train had colluded with the police in locking all entries into this train, in order to stop the dalits exercising their right to travel to Bombay in time for the celebration of Ambedkar's anniversary. The dalits asserted force in gaining entry, causing anger amongst passengers who held reserved seats. One of them, a Marwari business man, mocked an older dalit woman, addressing himself to the middle class passengers:
>
> They carry their *rotla* with them, he taunted, they'll sleep on the pavements or in Shivaji Park the night before their anniversary! Ha! They'll soon

go running back to their village the next day, as their *rotla* will run out! They
can't afford to buy restaurant food!

At this point, the older dalit woman broke into a Mira song, in
Marathi, about the dignity of eating stale and dry pieces of *roti*, nullifying in
song the grotesque class arrogance of the Marwari businessman. It evoked a
laugh that the businessman had been bested by a poor woman, and it created
respect for the dalit woman who traveled the rest of the journey without
harassment. (1994, 109–110)

The older dalit woman (whose name is not mentioned) is mocked and jeered
at by the male passengers in the train for traveling without a ticket, for being
poor and having the audacity to travel when she is not sure of her next meal.
Train travel is a social space in postcolonial India where class hostilities are
expressed, where violence on women passengers is an ever-present threat.
Train travel is also, ironically, that unregulated social space where the moneyed
classes make reservations and travel inside train compartments that are
divided into first class, second class, and third class, and where the poor traditionally travel ticketless by squatting on the compartment floor of third-
class carriages, or venture into the more hazardous form of sitting on the roof
of the train. Film makers have exploited this feature of Indian railway travel,
for instance Richard Attenborough's film *Gandhi* (1982) has a scene where
having returned from South Africa Gandhi travels through the length and
breath of India in a third-class compartment. Even as late as 1998 the trend-
setting director Mani Ratnam in his film *Dil Se* (From the Heart) picturizes
an entire song sequence, which became extremely popular, where the hero
joins the ticketless travelers on the roof of the train and sings a Sufi-inspired
song and dances on top of the train with the other travelers.

The dalit woman cannot openly challenge upper-caste men in a public
place without fear of retribution. Yet she must speak or the verbal violence
may escalate into physical retribution, she must verbally shame the men into
giving her space in the train compartment. One of the male passengers makes
a derogatory remark about "these people" in which he characterizes their life
from the perspective of the middle class; he says that these people have a pre-
dictable routine, they will travel to a place and when their food supply runs
low they take recourse to begging or return home.

In response to this classist and casteist representation, the dalit woman
sings a line from Meera in which the poetess, as a friend and fellow traveler
of the lower caste men and women and migrant poor of medieval Rajasthan,
says that she rejoices in the fact that she no longer partakes of the rich ban-
quet food that is a regular feature of the elite Rajput household. Meera says
that the rich-man's feast should be thrown away because it is contaminated
with guilt, she would rather share the simple meal of poor people, which is

sufficient for subsistence. The men listening to the dalit woman are shocked into silence and do not trouble her after that.

The significance of this text for us lies in the fact that the disempowered dalit woman makes use of Meera in order to negotiate a social space that is hostile and antagonistic towards her. In our view the dalit woman encodes her praxis—negotiating with the structures of violence—by decoding Meera's validation of the right of the poor to travel. This activity of decoding is performed in a context in which her male fellow passenger deny the right of the poor to travel. The dalit woman also decodes Meera's assertion of the superiority of the ethics of subsistence, eating what is sufficient for human need, over the ethics of luxury and conspicuous consumption. It is a text of praxis because the dalit woman deploys Meera in a situation of class conflict, she strategically makes use of Meera in order to get where she is going without the harassment that would inevitably be part of her journey. The men who are unmoved by her poverty, her age or gender are silenced by her invocation of Meera, even though they can deny the poverty, gender and age of the dalit woman they cannot deny the Meera tradition.

Our second text is Shobhag Kanwar, a rural Rajput woman living and working in the village of Ghatiyali in postcolonial Rajasthan. She is significant for us in two respects. First, she is subject to contemporary Rajput patriarchal injunctions; in spite of these injunctions Kanwar forges a work-related persona that is, we argue, an improvisation from within the religio-cultural idioms of northwest India that resist women's devaluation. Second, the Shobhag Kanwar text is precious to us because we, as postcolonial women, gain access to the Kanwar text from the interpretive and narrative grid of an American feminist anthropologist Ann Grodzins Gold; thus we foreground the relations between center and periphery (see chapters 1 and 2) that are central to the discourses and idioms that circulate around women's devaluation ("Purdah is as Purdah's Kept" 1994, 164–181; "Gender, Violence and Power" 1994, 26–48). Gold's fieldwork on rural Indian womens' subjectivities, histories, gendering and kinship relationships is complex and theoretically informed by postcolonial scholarship. In itself Gold's anthropological work is exciting, challenging, and contentious.

We emphasize the levels of mediation through which the Kanwar text reaches us. Shobhag Kanwar narrates her life story to Gold at the latter's request in the late 1980s. As the subject of Gold's investigation, Kanwar is subject to local Rajput patriarchal injunctions and is inserted into the logic of global capitalist cultural production and scholarship. Kanwar's life story is constructed around a type of female work, and an idiom of female work that is opaque to the secular imagination precisely because it circulates around religious activities. We invite readers to pay attention to the material, social, economic, and cultural-oppositional determinants of Kanwar's religious work, rather than read Kanwar in terms of an essentialist religious identity. Kanwar forges a religio-cultural work-related persona that is apart from her roles as married woman, mother, and daughter-in-law. She accrues social prestige as the unofficial village bard who can recount more stories and folktales than any one else. She is both storyteller and religious worker, the bardic function seeps into and is inextricable from her primary vocation as religious worker. As a result of her religious work, Kanwar does not confine herself to her household duties. This fact gains significance from the argument we made in chapter 3, that the restrictions on women's movement and women's seclusion are the dominant principle in Rajputization. Kanwar is active in the bhajan singing at the Dev Narayan shrine. Her activities at the Dev Narayan shrine are multifarious and extend her social interaction far beyond her marital family; she councils female devotees of the temple, attends bhajan mandalis at other villages, earns a share in the temple earnings and freely mingles with male devotees on the basis of a shared love for religious activities.

Kanwar's worklife is, as Gold notes, a constant reworking of the rules for women in a patriarchal rural Rajput society. As wife, mother, Rajput clanswomen, storyteller, and a working woman who has carved out an unusual life for herself, Shobhag Kanwar becomes the subject of anthropological study by Gold. The anthropologist's First World feminist interpretive grid allows her to decode the fact that Kanwar's "occassionally manipulative behaviour" ("Gender, Violence and Power" 1994, 39) covers over how Kanwar bends the patriarchal rules in the village. Gold notes that Kanwar possesses the ability to negotiate and function within the very society whose injunctions she challenges. It is Kanwar's complex situatedness that generates Gold's fascination as well as distrust.

Gold brings to Kanwar's highly self-conscious self-representation her own feminist agendas and presuppositions, and having done so Gold finds Kanwar lacking in honesty, defiance and open opposition. Gold questions Kanwar's self-constructed narrative of her early dedication to religion, her discovery of her guru in Chand aunty from whom she received religious instruction, her struggle with her husband in the early years of her marriage to follow her chosen mode of worship, the support given by the temple priest who said he had a vision which convinced him that Kanwar is chosen by God and persuaded her husband to allow Kanwar to follow her vocation. Gold finds Kanwar's self-representation—in terms of a series of miracles and fortuitous accidents—problematic and duplicitous.

Gold looks for inconsistencies and contradictions in Kanwar's narrative because she is invested in Kanwar's veracity. The anthropologist wishes to hear from Kanwar the "real" story of her struggle in terms of the First World feminist metanarrative of conflict, transgression and patriarchal punishment for female defiance in an Indian woman's claim to autonomy. Gold is baffled at

Kanwar's implicit refusal to follow this First World feminist script and confess to her occasional drinking, open consorting with men of different castes, and her making money from her religious work. Gold says of Shobhag:

> In the presence of Shobhag Kanwar I always felt myself both favored and manipulated, generously educated and not so subtly mocked . . . [Shobhag] intimidated me with her mixture of honeyed charm, deep knowledge, and occasionally manipulative behavior. ("Gender, Violence and Power" 1994, 41, 39)

At the completion of her research and return to San Francisco in March 1998, Gold receives a letter from her male research assistant in Rajasthan narrating how Shobhag Kanwar was beaten by her youngest son and nephew. The reason for this physical assault is Kanwar's involvement with the Dev Narayan temple, her youngest son even threatens her with the family sword. As a result Kanwar is forced to leave Ghatiyali and live in Kekari in her elder son's home. When Kanwar meets Gold's research assistant she begins "crying hard" and says that she will not live in Ghatiyali. Gold's assistant ends the letter with, "So, Ann, now look what will happen? Will Shobhag Kanwar come back to Ghatiyali or not? Whatever happens, just now she is very sorrowful" (178–179).

It is at this point that the anthropologist, spatially distanced from the site of her fieldwork, introduces her reactions to the violence on Kanwar as a text. Gold experiences, in her own words, remorse and shame and then says, "irrationally, I wondered if it could be my fault, if by analyzing and exposing Shobhag Kanwar's delicate maneuvers to a laudatory audience of Western feminists I had somehow undermined them, leaving her subject to this terrible attack by her drunken son and nephew" (179). Gold goes on to say that her irrational guilt gave way to academic rationalization, and that obviously Kanwar's problem had nothing to do with her. She even confesses to experiencing, although she tried to repress it, "a certain pleasure at receiving the confirmation" ("Purdah is as Purdah's Kept" 1994, 179) of her anthropological theory that Kanwar's lax purdah practices were not simply a privilege of her advancing age; for Gold the incident was proof that Kanwar's freedoms rankled the family men's sense of honor. Gold goes on to analyze the incident in terms of the cultural and iconic value of such terms as "nature of Rajput males" and the "Rajput sword" as a family relic and as the symbol of the glorious Rajput past. Gold ends her analysis of this incident by saying that her research assistant assured her three months later that all was well and that her faith in Kanwar's ability to "manipulate" her social environment was confirmed.

We do not wish to provide a critique of Gold's field work; it is not part of our project in this book to discuss the fact that Gold's temporary adoption of native clothes and food does not automatically give her access to Kanwar's subject-position; it is also not part of our project to express regret at Gold's satisfaction that Kanwar, a respected village elder, is subject to physical violence and disciplining at the hands of her own son. Instead we practice vigilance about the unequal relations that exist between a rural Rajput woman and a First World female academic who can move from a Rajput village to Cornell University at will. These unequal relations between center and periphery have less to do with Gold's First World feminist agenda, her cultural-linguistic knowledge and extensive research, rather the unequal relations inhere in Gold's structural place in the global capitalist exchange relations, a structural location that determines her interpretation of Kanwar's survival strategies as manipulation. Kanwar's resistance to Gold's investigation, indeed Kanwar's refusal to play the naive subject of Rajput discipline and punishment by offering the "real" story of her life, and Kanwar's willed and highly crafted self-representation are interpreted by Gold as duplicitous. Gold finds it duplicitous because it does not fit in with the First World notion of the woman-activist as a defiant, oppositional figure and the rural Third World woman as victim of patriarchal violence and subject to disciplining if she transgresses.

We read Kanwar's narration of her life story in a markedly different way from Gold (her theorizing about Kanwar falls short of her thick description and her own title words, "Purdah Is As Purdah's Kept"). We are interested in Kanwar's self-representation as an agent, not as victim. The protocols of our analysis is to be attentive to Kanwar's self-representation, not in terms of the depth metaphor of the "truth" behind the "manipulation" of truth, but the exteriority of the text in terms of Kanwar's self-conscious *biographing* of her life. We recognize that Kanwar's self-representation is marked by the dictates of censorship, she has to live and work in the village long after Gold is gone, therefore she cannot talk directly of her defiance of the village patriarchal norms.

The genre in which Kanwar mobilizes her work-related persona is the bardic chronicle. This is a genre that contains a concept of historical reality, which is markedly different from the secular modern post-Enlightenment historical imagination. Kanwar configures the key episodes in her life story in the bardic conventions; Norman Zeigler describes these conventions in the following way:

> The Carana was not an "objective" historian (as we understand the term) but a seer, a guardian of legend and a conserver of tradition. As a seer, he was not a conscious manipulator of "truth" or "historical reality," but the preserver of the truth and the reality of what he saw. This truth lay less in the realm of objective fact than in religious values and social ideals, in the means of attaining life and happiness itself. (*History in Africa* vol. 3 1976, 137)

Zeigler illuminates the conventions and the logic of the genre of Kanwar's life story: she focuses on the positing of values through the vehicle of her life story rather than on the objective facts of her life. The exteriority of Kanwar's text is oral-performative and radically participatory. This is borne out by the series of semi-miracles centered around Kanwar's life, which are repeated, added to, enjoyed, and reinscribed in village gossip and popular memory by men, women, and children.

Kanwar innovatively deploys yet another cultural paradigm, one that is woman-centered, in telling her life story. She mobilizes the Meera tradition and amalgamates this tradition to the bardic conventions of history writing. It is this mobilization of the Meera tradition that recasts her life story in a feminist script, albeit a feminist script that emphasizes miracles. In this chapter we have suggested that the language of miracles is a subaltern vehicle for talking about human agency, Kanwar elicits social sanction for the breaking of patriarchal taboos by demonstrating that she has a calling, which is revealed by a series of miracles. Thus Kanwar does not narrate the conflicts and patriarchal violence visited on her as a girl-child in her natal Rajput family and as a young married girl in her marital family, she prefers the language of miracles to describe key episodes of her life. She also does not refer to the devaluation she experienced as a Rajput girl-child or the loneliness and longing of her childhood, she says instead that she was blessed by the discovery of her guru in Chand aunty, from whom she received religious instruction. Similarly she does not directly gesture at the difficulties in her life as a young bride who was not permitted to follow her mode of worship, she describes instead how the men of the village and the temple priest had a vision, which convinced them that Kanwar is chosen by God, and these men persuaded her husband to let Kanwar follow her vocation. In representing these milestones in her life Kanwar is, at one level drawing a parallel between herself and Meera's discovery of her guru Raidas and the miracles Meera is said to have accomplished.

The relationship that Kanwar establishes with Meera is intimate and fraught with danger. As a Rajput woman Kanwar lays claim to a poet who was also born and bred in Rajasthan. This very intimacy means that Kanwar has to step carefully, for there continues to be a tradition of Rajput hostility toward Meera in postcolonial Rajasthan. That may well be the reason that she does not openly tell the American anthropologist that Meera is her point of reference. There is a high degree of self-consciousness in Kanwar's interpellation into the Meera tradition, her narrative implies that just as the medieaval Meera carved out a space for dissent from within the community, she as a postcolonial Meera carves a space for dissent from within her village community. The predominant emphasis in Kanwar's narrative is on a miraculous, continuous series of events that confirm her vocation as religio-cultural worker. For obvious reasons Kanwar steers clear of Meera's aggressive and provocative naming of Rajput tyrannies on her as wife and daughter-in-law. Unlike Meera, Kanwar means to stay within the family fold and make her family and neighbors accommodate her, therefore she stresses those elements in Meera's life that enable her.

The Meera tradition is fluid and heterogeneous, all women do not use Meera's life story in the same way or deploy Meera for a uniform feminist script. Kanwar constructs her own hybridized version, she represents her life story to Gold as a Meeraesque journey of early devotion to the spiritual life, as dedication to her vocation despite familial-male opposition, and as her triumph in being able to finally practice her vocation in her fifties. In deploying Meera Kanwar does several things at once. She culturally encodes her life in indigenous idioms of dissent. In order to do so Shobhag Kanwar also decodes the life and work of a medieval woman as relevant to her own life and work in postcolonial Rajasthan.

The Baee Nathee Case

Selections from the Records of the
Bombay Government Nos. 39–40, 1856

1. The *relevant documents* showing government's action against infanticide of twin
daughters by Baee Nathee.

BAEE NATHEE, Wife of MOHWUR SANGANEEA, age about twenty-four
years, deposes before NURBESHUNKUR HUREESHUNKUR, Attachment Mehta
of Mallia.

On interrogation.—Twin daughters were born to me, and I, *having no wish to
preserve them,* did not suckle them; they survived one day and a half, and then died, and
my husband buried them in the enclosure. My eldest daughter at the time was suffering from the small-pox, and my being unable to take care of her was the cause for my
not preserving them. The girls died one hour after each other. When they were born,
my mother, and Hoora the midwife, only were present. In this there is no doubt and
what I have deposed is correct. I did not adminster opium to the infants, nor did I by
any other means deprive them of life. I denied them suckle, and as it was not my wish
to preserve them, why should I have suckled them?

Neither my husband nor anyone else advised me (to deprive them of life); I did
so of my own wish.

Dated Sumvut 1909, Bhadurwa Vud 5th
(Thursday, 22nd September, 1853).
Mallia.

Witness.	BAEE NATHEE.
CHOWUTTIA BHUTTEE HAJEE.	What is written above is true.
MOHWUR PURBHUT BHODHA.	at the request of
MOHWUR BHARA JOOMLA.	BAEE NATHEE.
JOMA MEPA SOORA.	
MEMAN ALI HUSSON.	

2. The above deposition, having been this day read to Baee Nathee in the presence
of Captain J. T. Barr, Acting First Assistant Political Agent at Camp Balacheree, she states,—

235

These twin daughters were born about three hours after sunrise and on the third day, about midday, they died; in the meantime I suckled them twice or thrice, which not being sufficient, they died. *It was anciently the custom in my caste not to preserve daughters,* but at the present time Infanticide is extinct. My third daughter, who is at present with me, is three years old, and as she suffered severely from the small-pox, my time was taken up in attending upon her; I was therefore unable to suckle my other twin daughters; they consequently died. It was not my intention to destroy them, and, if the Attachment Mehta has above stated so, I am not perfectly aware. My surviving daughter I suckled and ten days prior to the birth of my twin daughters I weaned her. I had not sufficient milk at the time, but to pacify her, I permitted her to suckle, but at present she sufficiently suckled. At the birth of my twin daughters, my mother and a midwife only were present, and when they died no one else besides my husband who buried the four days old baby in a graveyard, therefore none of my caste people or relations attended. The infants are buried in a *Phullia* or enclosure. At the time of my accouchement my surviving daughter was lying on the same cot with me.

This deposition was given before the Mallia Attachment Mehta, and to which *Purbhut Mohwur* and *Mepa Jalim* are witnesses; the latter are called into the presence of Nathee, when they state that they are witnesses to the deposition given by Nathee to Jupteedar, and they call upon her to give a true statement of the case before the Sirkar, when she replies that what she has deposed to in the presence of the Jupteedar is true, and further states,—

It being my wish to preserve my eldest daughter, I suckled her, and not the other infants, when they were born, and consequently they died.

Dated Sumvut 1910, Kartik Shoodh 9th

(Wednesday, 9th November, 1853).

The twin daughters were of the full period, nine months.

	NATHEE MOHWUR,
Witnesses.	Wife of Sanganeea.
ANUNDJEE WULUBJEE	What is written above is true.
MEHTA SUNTOOKRAM MADOWJEE.	MOHWUR PURBHUT,
	MEPA JALIM SOOROO.
	What is written above is true.

On further interrrogation.—After the twin daughters were born, I placed them on a separate small cot, as my eldest daughter slept on the same cot with me; the cots were placed close together. The twin daughters were on one cot, and I constantly looked after them, but my not having suckled them, they died.

I am the married wife of Raja Kajeea, but I deserted him, and live with Sangun, and after my husband's death I returned to Mallia, twelve months ago; until then I kept wandering about.

The daughter now with me, and the deceased twin daughters, are Sanguns. *About five years ago Sangun eloped with me of my own free will.* After the decease of my twin daughters my mother left off visiting my house; she never came when he was present, on account of my elopement with him.

Dated as above

<table>
<tr><td>Witnesses.</td><td>NATHEE</td></tr>
<tr><td>ANUNDJEE WULUBJEE.</td><td>Wife of Sanganeea</td></tr>
<tr><td>SUNTOOKRAM MADOWJEE.</td><td></td></tr>
</table>

3. BAEE HOORA, Wife of Raja MANUK, aged about forty years, deposes before the Mallia Attachment Mehta, NURBESHUNKUR HUREESHUNKUR.

On interrogation.—The wife of Mohwur Sangun is my daughter, and at the time of her accouchement the eldest daughter was lying by her side, and suffering severely from the small-pox. At that time Sangun came to call me, and I went there, after which my daughter was delivered of twin daughters, and seeing that the eldest daughter was suffering, I immediately returned home. This was at midday; and in the evening I went to inquire after them, and found the newborn infants alive. I did not again go there, but I heard in the town that they died on the third day. This much I know.

On further interrogation.—The children were not suckled; they consequently died. I am not positively aware whether they died on the second or the day after birth. I state what I heard rumored in the town.

Dated Sumbut 1909, Bhdurwa Vud 2nd
(Tuesday, 20th September 1853).

<table>
<tr><td>Witnesses.</td><td>BAEE HOORA</td></tr>
<tr><td>MOHWUR PURBHUT BHODHA.</td><td>What is written above is true.</td></tr>
<tr><td>MOHWUR NATHA MERAMUN.</td><td>Written by MHAO HEERA</td></tr>
<tr><td>BHATEE HAJEE KEEMA.</td><td>DEWJEE, at the request</td></tr>
<tr><td>MOHWUR BHARA MERAMUN.</td><td>of the above.</td></tr>
<tr><td>JOMA MEPA SOORA.</td><td></td></tr>
</table>

Baee Hoora is called to the presence of Captain J. T. Barr, Acting First Assistant Political Agent, and the above deposition being read over to her, she confirms it.

On interrogation.—I saw the twin daughters when they were born but I did not see them suckled by my daughter. I went first in the morning and after me came the midwife; but when I went again in the evening, the midwife was not present. Nathee's husband, Sangun, was at home both times I went. The third daughter of Nathee suffered severely from small-pox, and the mother, in the anxiety for her, was unable to attend to the twin daughters, from which they died; but, after giving birth, it is unlikely she would knowingly destroy them. *It was customary in my caste to commit Infanticide,* but from the arrangement made the last twelve months, no one commits the crime. I am not aware who commits it. Would any woman kill her own offspring? All women would not do so. Nathee was married to Kajeea Raja, whom she deserted, and lived with Sangun. I consequently never unnecessarily spoke to them, but their eldest daughter having been very ill with small-pox, I went to see her, but having no wish to remain there, I did not stop to attend upon their eldest daughter. I did not hear my daughter say that she intended to destroy the infants; from her not having suckled them they died.

Sumvut 1910, Kartrik Shoodh 9th (Wednesday, 9th November 1853). Camp Balacheree.

On further interrogation.—Sangun eloped with Nathee while Raja Kajeea was alive, and twelve months after his death Sangun returned to Mallia.

The twin daughters were by Sangun. It is now five years since Sangun eloped with Nathee, and they have now returned. I am not aware who informed me of the death of these two infants. I heard that they died on the third day, at midday. I heard so on the day they died. They were of the full time, nine months. Their birth was not premature.

Witnesses.	BAEE HOORA,
ANUNDJEE WULUBJEE.	Wife of Raja Manuk
SUNTOOKRAM MADOWJEE	What is above written is true.
	J. T. BARR,
	Assistant Political Agent.

On further interrogation.—Both times I went to see the new-born infants they were on a cot, and the cot was close to Nathee's cot.

Dated as above.

Witnesses.	BAEE HOORA,
ANUNDJEE WULUBJEE.	What is written above
SUNTOOKRAM MADOWJEE.	is true.

4. BAEE HOORA, daughter of MUGA BOOSANA, aged about fifty years, inhabitant of Mallia, states before the Mallia Attachment Mehta:—

About one month ago, the wife of Mohwur Sangun Walanee having been labouring in childbirth, I was sent for, and I went, and on examining her found the child was crossways in the womb; but I effected her confinement of twin daughters, and, having put them on a stool, called for water to them, on which the mother said, *"The infants are to be destroyed, therefore do not bathe them."* I then said never to do such a thing, but if so, to give me one, and I would suckle and bring it up, and adopt it as my daughter; but she refused, and I left the house and went away. The next day I went to make inquiries, when she told me *she had destroyed them.* Thus it happened. I am a widow, and a poor woman, and should I openly come forward, it would be difficult for me to live with the Meenas; and such cases happen in many places. In the house of Mohwur Vera's son, *Mala*, about one and a half months ago, and infant daughter met a similar fate. (Statement given on 4.5.1853)

Baee Hoora is this day called into the presence of Captain Barr, Acting First Assistant Political Agent, at Camp Balachereee, and, the above deposition having been read over to her, she states,—That what is written of the infants having been murdered is false, as I did not say that she would destroy them. She told me not to wash them, as she knew what to do with children born to her. So saying, I suspected she would destroy them. *Amongst the Meenas this crime is greatly prevalent, on account of daughters of their own free will eloping with other men; hence the cause of Infanticide.* But since the Government Mehta has come here, all are deterred from committing the crime, and arrangements having been made to prevent the commission of it, it is not now committed.

On further interrogation.—I did not see the woman suckle her infants; the small cot was close to the large one. Knowing the custom of the Meenas, I was suspicious that she would destroy her infants; it was therefore I asked her for one of them, when she replied no one would part with her offspring. When the Jupteedar sent for me, I then became aware that she had destroyed her infants. I forget who told me so. I was ignorant at first as to whether they died, or whether they were destroyed. Not having, according to the custom of the Meenas, allowed the infants to be bathed, I therefore suspect they may have been destroyed. Having confined her of twin daughters, I left them alive, and went home. All do not commit Infanticide, for I have three daughters. They were of the full period, nine months, and their birth was not premature.

Sumvut 1910, Kartik Shoodh 11th (Friday, 11th November 1853).

Witnesses.	HOORA,
SUNTOOKRAM MADOWJEE.	Daughter of Muga Boosana.
MOHWUR PURBHUT BHODHA.	What is written above is true.
JOMA MEPA SOORA.	J. T. BARR,
	Assistant Political Agent.

On interrogation.—Mohwur Sangun was at home at the time of her confinement. At the time of accouchement no male person comes near the cot, but he (Sungun) was in the house.

Dated as above.

	HOORA,
Witnesses.	Daughter of Muga Boosa.
MOHWUR PURBHUT.	J. T. BARR,
NAM MEPA SOORA	Assistant Political Agent.

5. Mr. Anderson's reply to Captain Barr on behalf of Government of Bombay.

POLITICAL DEPARTMENT

From H.L. ANDERSON, Esq., Acting Secretary to Government, Bombay,
To Captain J. T. BARR, First Assistant, Pol. Agent in Kattywar, in charge.

Dated 8th April 1854.

SIR,—I am directed by the Right Honourable the Governor in Council to acknowledge the receipt of your letter, with enclosures, dated the 23rd ultimo.

2. In reply, I am desired to inform you, that as it is essential to the suppression of the crime of Infanticide that every case clearly established should be followed by punishment, His Lordship in Council does not consider it prudent, even under the circumstances explained by you, to extend pardon to the Mohwur female, Baee Nathee.

3. I have therefore to request this female's trial before the Court of Criminal Justice for Kattywar, as directed in Mr. Chief Secretary Malet's letter No. 2892, dated the 6th July last, be proceeded with, and to inform you that, in the event of her conviction before that tribunal, any mitigating circumstances can be considered in awarding punishment.

4. I have further to inform you that after this, and the other case now pending, have been fully disposed of, Government will be prepared to consider the proposal of a reward of Rupees 100 to the Attachment Mehta who discovered these cases of Infanticide.

I have the honour to be, &c.

H. L. ANDERSON,

Dated Castle, 8th April 1854.   Acting Secretary to Government.

Notes

Chapter 1. The Practice of Femicide in Postcolonial India and the Discourse of Population Control within the Nation State

1. For the literature on modern femicide in India see Vimal Balasubramanyam (*Economic and Political Weekly* [henceforth *EPW*] (1982): xvii, 43, 1725; also see her *EPW* (1986): xxi, 2, 69–71; see *India Today,* June 15 (1982): also see *Forum Against Sex Determination and Sex Pre-Selection* (1983); Vibhuti Patel (1984) 1, 2, 69–70; and Radha Balakrishnan (1994). Also see Vaasanti's study of female infanticide amongst the Kallars in Usilampatti taluk, Madurai district of Tamil Nadu for Caritas and the review of her study in *The Hindu* (November 20, 1994) as well as Gita Aravamundan's article on the subject in *The Hindu* (October 16, 1994); also see R. Muthulakshmi's recently published book-length sociological study on the same (1997). For female infanticide amongst the Grounder landowning community in Salem district of Tamil Nadu see R. Venkatachalam and Viji Srinivasan (1993); Sabu George, Abel Rajaratnam and B. D. Miller (*EPW* xxviii, no. 22, May 30, 1992). See also Amartya Sen on missing women, "Missing Women—Revisited," *British Medical Journal,* vol. 327, issue 7427, 2003.

2. The discipline of anthropology has legitimized Third Worldist myths about infanticide and female infanticide. For instance Herbert Aptekar states, "by and large infanticide looms as the primitive population check" (1930, 155). In Aptekar's view infanticide is the paradigmatic behavioral trait of primitive man, "it comes so near to being inherent in the primeval parent-child relationships that one is tempted to say of it: 'Here, if anywhere, is a bit of behavior natural to primitive man'"(157). The flip side of Aptekar's primitivism is the notion that absence of infanticide characterizes the civilized societies of the West, "In Western civilization the practice of infanticide is at present virtually non-existent. . . . As a population check, however, this practice is of little consequence" (155). Aptekar's binaries of non-infanticidal civilized societies of the West versus the infanticidal non-West are revived in the 1970s by Mildred Dickeman who argues that the most effective mode of population control is to reduce the percentage of the population that consists of sexually active fertile females (1975). In effect Aptekar and Dickeman claim that female infanticide is a method of population control in primitive societies. To our knowledge this view has not been challenged on theoretical or empirical grounds, although Barbara Miller expresses dissatisfaction with Dickeman (1981, 56–57).

3. William Tulio Divale and Marvin Harris breathe new life into the anthropological myth that the ignorance of contraceptive devices caused primitive people to take recourse to female infanticide, "We suggest that postpartum selection against female infants is an unavoidable consequence of the absence of effective or safe prena-

tal contraceptives or abortion techniques" (1976, 521–538). We refute Divale and Harris's contention about "the absence of effective or safe prenatal contraceptives or abortion techniques" by pointing to the alternate traditions in homeopathy, Ayurvedic, folk and tribal medicines, and woman healers in India. In many communities women were attuned to their body's rhythms and knew the three days in the month that they were liable to pregnancy. The use of herbs for contraception, pregnancy, and abortion, together with the rhythm method of contraception, were not harmful to women's health. Women also knew that the period of lactation in prolonged breast-feeding functioned as natural contraception. For detailed feminist work on women's traditional knowledge of contraceptive practices see Elizabeth Fisher (1979) and Maria Mies (1988).

4. Historically, female infanticide was a discontinuous practice in India. This feature is borne out in the history of two rural communities in central Gujarat in the period between 1850 and 1890 in colonial India. Both the Lewa Kanbis and the Kolis lived side by side; the former practiced daughter killing while the latter cherished their daughters. The interaction between the communities was conflictual and exploitative; both groups claimed martial traditions and worked on the land; the infanticidal Lewa Kanbis exploited the Kolis by taking over their land, employing them as landless laborers, acting as their moneylenders, abducting and raping their women. The Kolis preserved their tradition of women as producers who worked alongside their men in the fields and never resorted to female infanticide, notwithstanding the loss of land, pauperization, and crimes of violence visited on their women by the Lewa Kanbi landholders or Patidars. The noninfanticidal Koli community bears out our argument that female infanticide was not a universal but rather a discontinuous practice in northwest India. For an excellent analysis of the Lewa Kanbi case see Alice Clark (1989); also see L. S. Vishwanath (2000).

5. Anthropological studies of the infanticidal tribe of Todas in southern India find no conclusive evidence that economic necessity is the prime motive. One study concludes, "At present and during recent times there has certainly been no economic motive for infanticide [among the Toda tribe] and I am doubtful whether it has ever existed" (Rivers). Madhu Kishwar cites a study of two Bengal villages that demonstrates that land reform and relative affluence in one village only benefited male children (1985, 32–33). Infanticidal families tend to use poverty to explain to themselves the economic necessity for killing their daughters; however it is counter-intuitive for students and colleagues to realize that in India a family's prosperity or poverty may only alter the forms in which discrimination toward daughters is practiced.

6. We owe this insight to Mona Eliasson, editor of *Women's Studies Quarterly* (Vol. XXVII [Special Issue] Spring/Summer 1999) where we argued one version of this chapter in our article, "Women Without Choice: Female Infanticide & the Rhetoric of Overpopulation in Postcolonial India." We are grateful for her suggestion that we consider the personal stories of Western women, which underpin their view on reproductive choice.

7. R. Venkatachalam and Viji Srinivasan's study of the incidence of female infanticide in five development blocks in Salem district of Tamil Nadu revealed that

while two-thirds of all the families had more than one male child, only half of the families had one female child. Furthermore only one-sixth of the total sample population had more than one female child. The authors note, "Most of the 83 respondents who had 3 to 5 female children belonged to low income groups, where girls are also accepted as assets, as they start working at a very early age and bring home their earnings" (1993, 38).

8. The historian Romila Thapar's work on traditions of social dissent and the pioneering work by the sociologist M. N. Srinivas on modes of upward mobility challenges the colonialist view of India as a rigidly caste-organized society. Both Thapar and Srinivas emphasize the traditional dynamism, flexibility, and heterogeneity of Indian society. For a fuller discussion of the specific relationship between female infanticide and Indian systems of upward mobility see chapter 4.

9. Vandana Shiva names this collusion in the name of development "maldevelopment" and Maria Mies calls it "the myth of catching-up development." In their book *Ecofeminism* (1993) both authors detail and analyze the damaging consequences of the collaboration between the North and the elites of the South on the environment, the indigenous people and particularly on women. This phenomena has also been referred to as the worldwide feminization of poverty.

10. Bauxite mining in India offers a classic example of how the interests of the indigenous poor are sacrificed for short-term profit-oriented collaboration between international interests and the ruling elite of India. Japan has greatly reduced its aluminum smelting capacity because of the environmental cost of mining and now imports ninety percent of its requirements from poor Third World countries like India. In contrast India has a surplus of aluminum. The Bharat Aluminium Company in collaboration with Japan, planned to mine aluminum reserves in the Gandmardhan forests of Orissa. This will not only destroy the forests, which are a rich water source as well as rich in plant diversity, but it will also mean the displacement of the adivasi population that is dependent on the Gandmardhan forests. Bharat Aluminium Company has already destroyed the ecology of the Amarkantak mountain, which was the source of three rivers, in order to mine small reserves of aluminum. The tribal people of the region organized to resist the company officials as well as the police: they refused bribes of employment that were offered to them in order to secure their consent: instead the tribals asserted their sacred bond with the Gandmardhan hills. For more details see J. Bandyopadhyay (1985). The bauxite mining case is not an isolated example of the conflict between the Indian state and the poor people. There are similar struggles and people's movements at the grassroots level to save the environment and protect traditional modes of reciprocal subsistence living in Chotta Nagpur plateau in Bihar, Garhwal, Bastar region in Madhya Pradesh, and coastal Orissa.

11. By using the term "official version of ecological discourses" we distinguish between the state-sponsored discourse of conservation and indigenous and people-centered ecological movements. The first blames the Third World poor and colludes with multinational industrial interests and refuses to name the extravagant production and consumption patterns of the North and elites in the South as the real cause of environmental degradation. Instead it exploits latent xenophobia by blaming the poor

of the world for destroying the environment. In opposition to this the people-centered ecological movements genuinely address the need for clean water, air, soil, and forests and explore ways to regenerate and conserve the environment.

12. In our view large-scale contraceptive programs in India have three key features: first, there is a massive deployment of untested, unproven, and unsafe contraceptives like the IUD, Copper T, Norplant, laproscopy, tubectomy, and Dipo Provera. One example of India as a dumping ground for unsafe contraception is highlighted by the All India Democratic Women's Association (AIDWA), which successfully campaigned in 1998 against the sale and use of Quinacrine, a drug formerly used to combat malaria, in the Q-method of contraception. Thirty-five hundred women in major Indian cities were not informed about the side-effects of the Q-method like cancer, ectopic pregnancy, and acute body pain. Recently the FDA in the U.S. has banned the sale and use of Quinacrine as a contraceptive.

Second, the vast numbers involved in these governmental programs (e.g. 3,500 women for Norplant alone) effectively removes the capacity and will of medical professionals to inform, counsel, and ensure follow-up care for women patients. Third, when serious side-effects of unsafe contraception for women are brought to the notice of family-planning personnel, for instance women reporting bleeding, anemia, and pain attendant on mass IUD insertions, these agencies treat such reports as part of scientific data collection and refuse postoperative care to the suffering women. The data on damaging side-effects does not result in a policy change and the same cycle is repeated with every new contraceptive invention. To the governmental health-care personnel and policy makers as well as to international pharmaceutical companies, the South is a vast and unregulated laboratory and the women of the South are experimental subjects. For a detailed but biased account see R. H. Cassen (1978, 149–160).

13. We acknowledge the heterogeneous family formations in India like the woman-headed household. We perforce use the term "postcolonial family" in order to account primarily for the historical emergence of the generalized practice of femicide in the 1970s, and to distinguish this postcolonial family formation from the limited and discontinuous practice of female infanticide in colonial nineteenth-century India. In this essay the "postcolonial family" denotes the post-1970s patriarchal organization of the family.

14. We have a collective memory of going to cinema halls in 1985 and being subjected to a slickly produced advertisement for family planning, designed and produced as "public service" by the then CEO of a premier multinational advertising agency, Alique Padamsee. This particular ad stayed in our memory because it brought home to us the indigenous elites' contempt for poor families with many children. The screen fills up with a jar in which two tomatoes are a snug fit. A hand enters the screen and attempts to put a third tomato that presses down and crushes the tomatoes at the bottom of the jar. In the logic of this ad, the country's resources are like a jar in which children are like tomatoes that crush the people below. The ad assumes that Indian people are stupid and illiterate, therefore a visual illustration of a simplified proposition will persuade them better than discussion and debate. The ad typifies the ignorance and prejudice shared by many corporate professional Indians in the 1980s.

15. Artists, intellectuals, and filmmakers—of documentaries as well as feature films—recorded the excesses of the Emergency years. The Theatre Academy, Pune staged plays like *Ghasiram Kotwal* in 1972 as an allegory of Indira Gandhi's reign. The documentary filmmaker Anand Patwardhan's *Waves of Revolution* (1975) documented the Jayprakash Narayan movement in the early days of the Emergency, and the arrest and treatment of political prisoners in those years in *Prisoners of Conscience* (1978). Utpalendu Chakraborty's *Mukti Chai* (1977) was a major documentary emerging from the emergency period. Gautam Ghose's *Hungry Autumn* (1976) about the 1974 Bengal famine faced censorship under the Emergency. Gulzar's *Aandhi* (1975) and Mrinal Sen's *Mrigaya* (1976) were allegories about the Emergency. In 1980 Satyajit Ray made *Hirak Rajar Deshe*, which directly referenced the Emergency of 1975–1977 and in particular Sanjay Gandhi's fascist programmes. There were also crude political satires like Amrit Nahata's *Kissa Kursi Ka* (1977) whose original print was supposed to have been destroyed by Sanjay Gandhi during the Emergency censorship scandal. Also see the 1970s in Rajyadhaksha and Willemen (1999).

16. State complicity in the social sanction for modern femicide can be gleaned from official statements like the one made at a 1974 Stockholm conference by Dr. D. N. Pai, Director of Family Planning Maharashtra State. Pai said that sex-selective abortion is the answer to India's population problem. Post-Emergency official discourse consisted of public commiseration and inaction; for instance the Union Health Minister B. Shankaranand informed the Indian Parliament that even though the commercialized practice of ultrasound technology is "highly unethical, unjust and immoral" no legal action will be taken against the practitioners. Despite growing criticism by women's groups family planning officials continued to argue in a 1984 Bombay seminar that women should have access to sex-selective abortion because population control requires "desperate measures." In 1986 the Minister for State, Margaret Alva, put forward the ingenious argument that governmental ban would be counterproductive because a ban would spread information about this technology to people. The effectiveness of the current governmental ban, instituted as late as 1998, must be evaluated in the context of ultrasound diagnostic equipment becoming the fastest growing industry in India today (*India Abroad* December 19, 1997). For a detailed account about ultrasound technology in India see R. P. Ravinder (1987, 490–492); Indu Agnihotri and Veena Majumdar (1995, 1869–1878).

17. The history of modern femicide is in many ways intimately tied to the history of the women's movements in India. "The press" observes Maria Mies "began to report on the extent and circumstances of female foeticide only after women's groups had started agitating against a threatening tendency towards the extermination of women" (1986, 151). Governmental inaction caused women's groups to formulate, in a meeting in 1982 at New Delhi, a three point position on femicide: the Indian Government was asked to restrict ultrasound technology to research and teaching; the Indian Medical Council was urged to penalize institutions like the New Bhandari Hospital in Amritsar for unethical medical practices; most importantly, women's organizations conceived of their role as one of constant vigilance. For a stimulating discussion of the Emergency and the women's movements, which unfortunately ignores the anti-femicide agitation by women activists see Radha Kumar (1993).

18. The legislation passed by the government continues to get public endorsement from bodies like the AMA (All India Medical Association); effectively it is a failure because it punishes women who take the test along with offending medical practitioners, and makes no provisions for monitoring the use of ultrasound for sex determination and preselection in hospitals. For instance R. Venkatachalam and Viji Srinivasan note that Grounder women in Salem district reported that government medical officials themselves encourage women to have "scans" free of cost in order to abort the female fetus, "The Chief Nurse tried to persuade and pressurize me to have a 'scan' done at her cost when I was pregnant for the third time. She wanted me to be part of her target and have an abortion followed by a tubectomy if it was a girl" (1993, 49). The feminist-activist campaign against amniocentesis and ultrasound in the media—newspapers, magazines, and television—also brought forward the view of many in the female public who felt sex selection was a good decision, that given the position of women they did not want to bring a girl child into the world. Therefore it became clear to the feminists involved with the issue that activism was not enough, that the discourse of women devaluation and women's choice had to be publicly analyzed and debated. For a detailed description of the activities of The Forum Against Sex Determination and Sex Preselection see Nandita Gandhi and Nandita Shah (1991) 128–137; and Raka Ray (1999) 102–109; on similar views expressed by Grounder women in Salem district see R. Venkatachalam and Viji Srinivasan (1993) 48–58.

19. In his anonymously published pamphlet *An Essay on the Principle of Population (1798) (1976)* Thomas Malthus argued that overpopulation causes poverty. Two chilling premises prop up the Mathusian theory; in Malthus's view the Poor Laws should be abolished because the laborer's poverty is fixed and cannot be eradicated, in his own words, "to prevent the recurrence of misery (through poverty) is, alas! beyond the power of man" (v, 44). Together with this classist and anti-poor stance, Malthus posits the relation between nature and man as static. The implication of the Malthusian argument is that the earth's resources are limited and human beings can only relate to the environment in terms of consumption and plunder, not in the reciprocal terms by which indigenous people give back to the environment and thus renew their resources of land, forest, water, and air for subsistence. It is through these classist and anti-environmental premises and implications that Malthus constructs the modern paranoia about overpopulation, a paranoia fed by the seemingly neutral terminology of Malthusian discourse in which people are referred to as anonymous numbers that are fast multiplying and swallowing up the earth's resources.

Malthus was recognized by his eighteenth-century contemporaries as a popularizer, not an original thinker (for a detailed examination of the eighteenth-century context of Malthus's thought see D. V. Glass, (1953) and Michael Turner (1986). Indeed the eighteenth century marks the transition from population conceived under the aegis of mercantilist doctrine as the natural wealth and labor supply of a nation. A new set of crucial distinctions appear in the writings of David Hume, Adam Smith, and William Godwin between the prosperity caused by the "populousness" of ancient Europe on the one hand, and eighteenth-century England's uncertainty regarding the benefits or disadvantages to be derived from the populousness of the English poor and the English colonies on the other hand. Sixty-nine years before the first edition of

Malthus's pamphlet, the imperialist dimension of the idea that overpopulation is the cause of poverty had been savagely satirized in Jonathan Swift's *A Modest Proposal for preventing the Children of Poor People from Being A Burthen to their Parents or Country, and for making them Beneficial to the Publick* (1729). The Swiftian satire unmasks the notion that the colonized Irish people's poverty should be solved, not by ending Britain's economic colonization of Ireland, but by reducing "this prodigious number of children" of the Irish poor. Swift's satirical trope of cannibalism exposes the imperialism in the theory that poverty is caused by overpopulation.

It is accepted academic practice among population theorists to critique Malthusian theory, not so much by textual engagement with his 1798 essay or the revised edition in 1803, but by examining the neoimperialist uses of Malthusian discourse in Third World societies. The definitive work in the postcolonial critique of Malthus is Mahmood Mamdani (1972). For a review of Mamdani's book see Bharat Jhunjhunwala (1974). A trenchant critique of Malthusian imperialism is also made by Debabar Banerji, and Lars Bondestam (1980, 83–102, 1–38).

20. The latest version of the numbers game is demographers' speculation in academic journals and books that early in the twenty-first century, India's population will outstrip China's population. Therefore, unless drastic measures are undertaken, India is becoming the most populous country in the world. The telos of this speculation is to make readers accept phrases like "handling population-related issues on a war-footing" and thereby accept the proposition that India should initiate something like the coercive family-planning model successfully practiced in modern China. The latest figures suggest that the sex ratio of India and China are comparable: 1.07 male(s)/female and 1.06 male(s)/female respectively (*The World Factbook* 2002).

21. R. Venkatachalam and Viji Srinivasan note that the small family norm as well as the gender bias in family-planning technologies serve to exacerbate the incidence of female infanticide amongst the Grounder community in Tamil Nadu: "Paradoxically, the internalization of the small family norm . . . is itself one of the sources of female infanticide . . . fear of tubectomy also results in female infanticide" (1993, 55–56).

Chapter 2. Center and Periphery in British India: Post-Enlightenment Discursive Construction of Daughters Buried under the Family Room

1. Elsewhere, Sleeman had been equally successful in evoking the colonial image of British heroic rescue of India from the criminal Thuggees. Sleeman was widely recognized by Indians and the British as the architect of the anti-Thuggee British police campaign, partly because Sleeman publicized the "rescue from Thugs" motif in books like *Ramaseena, or a Vocabulary of the Peculiar Language used by the Thugs* (1836) and *Rambles and Recollections of an Indian Official* (1844). Sleeman bequeathed to colonialist historiography the pro-annexationist image of the Oudh court overrun by eunuchs and fiddlers. The Sleeman-type figure is often depicted in popular culture of the 1980s and 1990s: in television serials about colonial India such as The *Adventures of Sherlock Holmes* (1986), *The Jewel in the Crown* (1984) and films like *The Deceivers* (1988) starring Pierce Brosnan.

JTKO has an interesting history. It was written by Sleeman during his tour of Oudh in 1849–1850; in 1852 only eighteen copies of it had been printed and distributed to the company officials and his family. Sleeman died in 1856 and JTKO was published and reached the English public in 1858. In this chapter we use both the unabridged edition of Sleeman's writing, *A Journey through the Kingdom Of Oude in 1849–50* Vols. I–II (London, 1858) as well as the abridged version edited and introduced by P. D. Reeves, *W. H. Sleeman in Oude: An Abridgement of W. H. Sleeman's A Journey through the Kingdom Of Oude in 1849–50* (1971).

2. There is an entire context of historical events for Sleeman's text that deserves a brief summary. Sleeman's journal was published and circulated amongst Company officials in the early 1850s, followed by the British annexation of Oudh. The first anti-colonial war of Independence of 1857 was centered around Awadh and was a direct result of the annexation of this province. These bare facts may give some idea of the political nature of Sleeman's text. These large political events were also connected to the colonial documentation of female infanticide in Oudh. In the 1857 war against the British, many British officials who had been active in the infanticide reform were murdered, which is an index of the suppressed anger of rich propertied men who were scolded and shamed by English district officers. Many of the infanticidal families and clans of Oudh were active in the 1857 war. In the post 1857 political climate the British government took over from the East India Company. One of the first administrative actions was to strip the infanticidal clans of their land and property through the euphemism of "confiscations" ostensibly because of their participation in the war of independence. These events suggest that there is a relation between the colonizer and colonized in the sphere of landed property, which has significant bearing on the discovery and naming of female infanticide, which the colonial document suppresses. There is an additional irony here, the English lamented their inability to punish the criminal and protect the girl-child, yet the English moved with swift efficiency to punish the infanticidal men of property when it was a matter of protecting their own economic/political interests.

3. Many of Sleeman's English contemporaries accused him of pro-annexationist bias in his Oudh journal. For example one such critic, "identified Sleeman as no more than Dalhousie's henchman in a pre-arranged plot to annex the kingdom" (Reeves, 1971, 18). By contrast some modern historians and scholars of the Sleeman text argue that Sleeman was not an advocate for the annexation of Oudh. For instance the editor of the abridged volume of *A Journey*, Reeves argues in his introduction to the volume, "Then, to exonerate him [Sleeman] completely, Sleeman's diary [was published in the year after the war of Independence] which showed that he had been all along in favor of an Oudh-based reformed government and strongly opposed to annexation"(18). Reeves goes on to argue that Sleeman's infanticide account is an extended example of how Sleeman appreciated the logic interior to the natives of Oudh. It should be clear that our own reading of *A Journey* is strongly opposed to Reeves.

4. In *The Chess Players* (1977) Satyajit Ray's movie based on the political events in Awadh following Sleeman's tour and report, Ray plays rhetorically with Sleeman's image of the savagery of natives and the civilized Englishman. Instead of Sleeman's

image of savage natives who eat their own children, Ray shows the British as cannibals eating up entire lands and their people with their policy of annexation. See Reena Dube's fothcoming book on this, "Satyajit Ray's The Chess Players and Postcolonial Theory: Culture, Work and the Value of Alterity," 2005.

5. For example, the British Resident at Banaras, Jonathan Duncan, in reporting in 1789 to Lord Cornwallis, the Governor General of India, concerning the practice of female infanticide amongst the Rajkumars noted, "This horrid custom is said to exist also among some other tribes, *more especially in the Vizier's dominions*" (emphasis ours, in Cave Brown, 1857). The "Vizier's dominion" referred to by Duncan is of course the last independent territory of Awadh that was ruled by a Muslim, the Nawab of Awadh.

6. In their provocative book, *The Madwoman in the Attic* (1979) Sandra Gilbert and Susan Gubar put forward the thesis that the recurrent image of confinement, represented in the woman who is declared insane and locked away in some part of the Great House, occurs again and again in the literary imagination of nineteenth-century British women authors. According to Gilbert and Gubar the madwoman in the attic represents the threat of violence to women and functions as the unconscious of the heroine/author. In an analogous fashion we suggest that the murdered girl-child, sister or young first wife, is the unrecorded historical past of families and communities, which haunts the literary imagination of women artists as well as women-centered male texts in India. For Indian writers and filmmakers it is not the image of confinement, but the girl-child or woman who is covered over and buried, unremembered except in whispers, which constitutes the unconscious of the text. Some examples of male film texts are: Himansu Rai's *Achut Kanya* (1936); Kamal Amrohi's *Mahal* (1949); Guru Dutt's *Sahib, Bibi aur Gulam* (1962); and Satyajit Ray's *Pather Panchali* (1955). In the first three films the murdered lover/wife haunts the male protagonists while in Ray's film the girl-child's untimely death haunts her brother.

Some examples of women's texts are: two stories in Mahadevi Varma's memoir, *Atit Ke Chal-Chitra* (1963): in chapter 3 Mahadevi describes a childhood friend who symbolizes the motherless girl-child's death by neglect and beating, in chapter 2 the author describes her childhood trauma of witnessing the beating of a child-widow; Mahadevi self-consciously describes these characters as no-name girls who deeply influenced and constituted her literary imagination and her evolution as a rebellious female artist. The no-name woman haunt the adult Mahadevi's encounters narrated in *Smriti Ki Rekhayen* (1971): in chapter 5 this figure is at the margins of the text, the center-stage encounter occurs between the modern female artist and her alter ego, the traditional bard Thakuri Baba, at the margins of this encounter is a story of Thakuri Baba's first wife who died through starvation. Perhaps the most ambivalent of these figures is in chapter 6 where a young woman called Bibya, who works as a washer-woman for Mahadevi, is persecuted by her brother and husband and finally commits suicide. The figure of the missing woman also appears in Arunajee's film *Rihaee* (1990) in the young wife who is killed by her husband, and the second wife is disciplined and terrorized by the village women who tell her the story of how her husband beat his first wife to death.

7. For an analysis of Orientalist discourses and images see Edward Said, *Orientalism* (1979) and *Culture and Imperialism* (1994).

8. Although L. S. Vishwanath's recent sociohistorical study of female infanticide in western and northern India does not take note of the recurring trope of discovery in histories written of British colonial efforts at suppression of female infanticide, he does observe that "British officials discovered female infanticide by accident" and "the same government took upwards of 30 years to initiate firm action against infanticide" because their policy "was governed by pragmatism" (2000, 150–151).

9. Some examples of administrative travelogues are Bishop Heber's *Narrative of a Journey through the Upper Provinces of India* (1828); James Tod's *Annals and Antiquities of Rajasthan*, vols. I and II (1829, 1832); the travelogues of J. Malcolm, *A Memoir of Central India, including Malwa and Adjoining Provinces* (1832), and Emily Eden, *Up the Country. Letters written to her sister from the Upper Provinces of India* (1937).

10. There are significant consequences that follow from a writer's choice of genre, and the ideology of a genre. Other postcolonial theorists also note this feature of the colonial document: for example Lata Mani's study of British documentation of sati leads her to note that administrators' reports organized their data in order to present a hegemonic model of the practice of sati. Mani suggests that "the insistence on textual hegemony is challenged by the enormous regional variation in the mode of committing sati" but the colonial document ignores the heterogeneity of the practice because "such diversity was regarded as 'peripheral' to the 'central' principle of textual hegemony" (*Recasting Women*, 1990, 96).

11. In contrast in Bram Stoker's *Dracula* (1897) written in the nineteenth-century travelogue genre, the journey is reversed and Dracula travels from the margins of Europe, the Orientalized Transylvania with a population of gypsies, into the heart of Imperial England. See Stephen Arata, "The Occidental Tourist: Dracula and the Anxiety of Reverse Colonization" (1990), 621–45.

12. The contemporary relevance of what we have identified as the post-Enlightenment move to posit a radical and progressive idea at the center by evidence from the periphery can be gauged from the following example. Kate Bornstein, the writer of *Gender Outlaw* and a pioneer in the transsexual movement, made a speech at a 1995 conference at Kansas City. I quote from Barbara DiBernard's unpublished paper, "Transgender Liberation (Ally?), or What's a Nice Lesbian Feminist Like You Doing In a Place Like This" on Bornstein's speech:

> She asked the question of how essential gender is to sexual orientation, and told us about a tribe in western Africa where there are two genders, but a baby's gender is determined not by genitalia, but by the tribe's sense of who is needed. If the person who seems closest to dying is male and a good hunter, the society will declare the next child a boy and hunter (since hunting is a male activity in that culture). There can't even be a gay or lesbian identity in this culture, she pointed out.

Bornstein has made two unexamined rhetorical moves in the above passage. Her reference to Africa as a place of a lost plenitude in notions of gendering reinforces the predominantly male anthropologizing of Africa as the dark continent where Western man/woman can study primitive man. Secondly Bornstein unconsciously echoes the post-Enlightenment move to posit a radical and progressive idea at the center by evidence from the periphery. It is legitimate to ask why the social practices of the periphery must be used in an argument, which is not centrally about the African people. It is also legitimate to ask of Bornstein's text why she cannot draw examples of transsexual identity and gendering from nearer home. Indeed it is vital that we support the feminist agenda of Bornstein while asking her to examine the Third Worldism of her feminist rhetoric. That is one way of making Locke and the Enlightenment, as well as the historical and political contexts of texts in terms of center and periphery, pertinent to postcolonial theory and avant-garde feminist theory. For a contemporary version of how the center and periphery work in representing the Third World woman as victim see Chandra Mohanty's excellent article, "Under Western Eyes: Feminist Scholarship and Colonial Discourses" (1991).

13. For a trenchant contemporary critique of Locke's use of travelogue sources in *An Essay concerning Human Understanding*, particularly in the passages that we have analyzed in some detail, see Edward Stillingfleet, *Three Criticisms of Locke*, 1697 (1987). Locke's own student and protegee, the third Earl of Shaftesbury, contemptuously describes the use of travelogue sources in *An Essay*, "Then comes the credulous Mr. Locke with his Indian, Barbarian stories of wild nations, that have no such ideas (as Travelers, learned authors! and men of truth! and great philosophers! have inform'd him)" (*Several Letters Written by a Noble Lord to a Young Man at the University*, Letter of June 3, 1709). It is noteworthy that Locke refused, despite the barrage of criticism, to disavow his travelogue sources and continued to defend them as valid sources of philosophic evidence. For a brilliant contemporary analysis of the eighteenth-century critique of philosophic and literary use of travelogue sources see Seamus Deane, "Swift and the Anglo-Irish Intellect" (1986, 10).

14. All quotations henceforth from the Locke passage are from the authoritative modern edition of Peter H. Nidditch ed. and intro. *John Locke: An Essay concerning Human Understanding* (1975).

15. This is a crisis that is being constructed in order to evoke the binary of the civilized imperial center and the savage periphery that has fallen so low from basic human standards that they need to be brought back from these depths. The crisis is generated in order to justify the use of force. "A functional change in a sign system" observes Gayatri Spivak, "is a violent event " and therefore "the change itself can only be operated by the force of a crisis" (1985, 331).

16. There are only two exceptions to this, one was the regulations passed by the Bengal Government in the case of the Rajkumars of Banaras (Banaras was under the Bengal Government prior to 1833). In 1795 the Bengal Government passed Regulation XXI by which female infanticide was declared to be murder; Regulation VIII in 1803 repealed the Muhummedan law by which parents/grandparents of a willfully murdered child were spared the death penalty and extended Regulation XXI to the provinces ceded by the Nawab of Awadh. In 1804 Regulation III ordered magistrates to issue proclamations prohibiting female infanticide in all territories under the Bengal Government. Only one case of murder was detected in 1809 but the father was pardoned on the basis that the proclamation had not been circulated in his purgana. By

1856 there had been only three convictions in the Banaras subdivision and even in these three cases the judges had differed as regards the punishment (see J. Harrington in *Hindoo Widows,* 1843, vol. 2, Part I, 9–12). The second exception concerns the investigations and discussions that took place amongst British officials regarding the Anti-Infanticide Act of 1870, when W. R. Moore was appointed to submit a report on female infanticide in the various districts of Banaras division. Moore submitted his report in 1856 and one of his suggestion was that in infanticide cases where no clear proof existed for conviction of murder under British law and there was only circum-stantial evidence available, "Female Infanticide" should constitute a special crime; and the person held responsible in such circumstances should be the child's father as the destruction of the female infant was generally on his orders (1868, 103). This sugges-tion was rejected by the majority of the Infanticide Committee on the grounds that it was against all principles of British law, it was not necessary for the suppression of female infanticide, and such a provision would place the father at the mercy of the midwife or others having access to the female infant.

On the other hand social historians like Lawrence Stone trace the history of modern Anglo-American infanticide law to the Elizabethan period when for the first time in law, premeditated killing of a newborn or an older child was a murder. Lawrence Stone describes the reasoning that lay behind this momentous change in the legal perception of infanticide as a crime that, if concealed, deserved capital punish-ment:

> There is a long history of fairly general infanticide in western Europe going back to antiquity, when it seems to have been extremely common. In the six-teenth and seventeenth centuries, as the Church strengthened its hold over the moral conduct of the population at large and enlisted the help of the state in law enforcement, infanticide became a much more serious offense. Since it deprived an infant of baptism, and so the opportunity for salvation, it now became a crime that carried with it the penalty of death. (1977, 297)

For more detail on Infanticide law in England see Peter C. Hoffer and N. E. H. Hull, *Murdering Mothers: Infanticide in England and New England 1558–1803* (1981).

17. For the purposes of this book, we have decided to examine the East India Company's anti-infanticide measure up to 1857 because once the British Crown and the Parliament take over the administration of the colony, the persuasive aspects of the reformist discourse give way to the discursive and material apparatus of coercion. For example post-1857 the North-Western Provinces are administered by the British under the aegis of anti-infanticide reform efforts like a police state. The Anti-Infanti-cide Act of 1870 was passed and almost the entire preparatory work for framing the law was done by the government of North-Western Provinces and it was introduced principally for the North-Western Provinces including Awadh, Agra, and Punjab. In undivided Awadh (now under British rule) the Act was coercively enforced right up to the early years of the twentieth century. Whole parganas were publicly proclaimed to be "blood red" or especially guilty with regard to the practice of female infanticide. Vil-lage-wise censuses were conducted every year and on the basis of the sex-ratios of the census returns, clans and castes were labeled as progressive, retrogressive, or stationary, and exemptions from surveillance were only given family by family and if members of

other castes from neighboring villages could stand witness and disprove the imputation of guilt. Complex systems of surveillance were established in suspected villages: a messenger was appointed in every village to report on the birth of a girl, in addition the village watchman, midwife, and constable were all separately to report the event to the Police Station and therefore serve as checks on each other; finally on the third or fourth day the midwife accompanied by the policeman and watchman were to visit the family and report on the condition of the child, under the belief that once the child had been breast-fed the family would not, or very rarely, kill it. Civil surgeons were under orders to conduct post-mortems of suspicious deaths in the case of infant girls, new police stations were opened to give greater access to villagers and chowkidars; an Infanticide Catechism was prepared for police officers to ask and record the proper information. In the period between 1871 and 1875, there were 34 convictions. The sentences in these cases was usually fines and a few months or years' imprisonment. Only in one case was the sentence the death penalty and in another, transportation for life. We argue that the elaborate systems of coercion in the North-Western Provinces were devised in the aftermath of the rebellion of 1857, as a direct result of the political events of 1857. Not only did the annexation of Awadh play a major role in fermenting the rebellion of 1857, most of the rebellion took place in the North-Western Provinces of Awadh and Agra and unlike the collaborationist Rajput clans of Punjab or Rajasthan, the wealthy Rajputs of Awadh and Agra participated in the rebellion in large numbers (as a result many of the Rajputs had their lands confiscated by the Government). Furthermore many of the British officers who had been active in the anti-infanticide movement in the North-Western Provinces before 1857 were murdered or died during the rebellion, while those who survived rose to high positions in the colonial Government. For a pro-British account of British anti-infanticide reform measures in North-Western Provinces in the nineteenth century, see Lalita Panigrahi (1976). For a more recent and nuanced reevaluation of British policy regarding suppression of female infanticide in North India including Awadh, see L. S. Vishwanath (2000) 123–149.

18. Here it is instructive to recall Foucault's formulation of power in *The History of Sexuality* as power over life, as well as his discussion concerning the increasing effectiveness of power in inverse proportion to its visibility (137).

19. For a discussion of the discursive reorganization of the public and private sphere by Indian nationalism see Partha Chatterjee, "Their Own Words? An Essay for Edward Said" (1992). In the essay Chatterjee argues:

> A neat separation between a private domain of diverse individuals residing in bourgeois patriarchal families and public domain inhabited by homogenous citizens were not available to Indian nationalism. . . . The [Indian nationalist] strategy, therefore, had to use another distinction—between the spiritual or the inner, on the one hand, and the material or the outer, on the other. The latter was a ground surrendered to the colonial power; the former was where nationalism began to fashion its claims to hegemony. (208)

Commenting on Chatterjee's thesis, Kumkum Sangari and Sudesh Vaid observe:

> The process of the formation of the private sphere as an indigenist alternative to western materialism is, in a sense, instituted at the beginning of the

nineteenth century and comes into its own in nationalist discourses which
sets out to establish, as Partha Chatterjee points out, a series of oppositions
between male vs female, inner vs outer, public vs private, material vs spiritual. (1990, 10)

Our own intervention in this debate in this chapter consists of pointing out that colonialist discourses were actively reconfiguring the public and private sphere in India in
the nineteenth century, although the formulations of Chatterjee and Sangari and Vaid
would suggest that this was a purely nationalist endeavor. Furthermore, we complicate
their analysis of the nationalist discursive binaries by suggesting that British justification for inaction in female infant murder played a major role in what Sangari and Vaid
call "the process of the formation of the private sphere." It is the argument of this chapter that the colonial configuration of the private sphere has the effect of legally and
administratively and discursively endorsing the Indian male householder's right to privacy even if it means that he can kill his infant daughters with impunity.

Chapter 3. Social Mobility in Relation to Female Infanticide in Rajput Clans: British and Indigenous Contestations about Lineage Purity and Hypergamy

1. In 1998 the state of Rajasthan had one of the lowest sex ratios of 913
females per 1,000 males, as opposed to the national average of 929 to a 1,000 males;
for example the Bhati Rajput community of the village of Deora in Rajasthan has practiced female infanticide for 115 years (1883–1998), and it is only now that a few men
from the 150 families are starting the practice of preserving their daughters (*India
Abroad* June 5, 1998, 9).

2. It is worth noting how at the center the joining of mercantile capital with
landed aristocracy is seen as the British compromise, but for that same practice in the
periphery we get racialist theories from the British. The model of a dynamic British
society that allowed traders to buy titles and marry their daughters into the aristocracy
and that allowed penniless Englishmen to make their fortune in the colonies and
return to the home country as a country squire constituted the norm. It is against this
norm that the aberration of the Indian model was defined as a stagnant social formation in which the aristocracy was blocked from reinvigorating itself by intermarriage
and social interaction with other classes, and a man could not move up the social ladder with his hard work and ingenuity because he was trapped in his caste and class
rank. M. N. Srinivas describes how the varna concept of a monolithic and immutable
hierarchy "obscured the dynamic features of caste" (1969, 3) and that the material and
discursive basis of this concept of varna lay in British-colonial institutions "the institu-
ition, which prevailed until 1864, of attaching Brahmins Pandits to British-established
law courts, the presence in every town of a body of Western-educated lawyers who
tried to apply Brahmanical law to all Hindus, the translation of a vast mass of sacred
literature from Sanskrit into English" and orthodox revivalist and nationalist movements like " the rise everywhere of caste sabhas . . . and the growth of a vigorous anti-
Brahmin movement" (1969, 6). Elsewhere Srinivas locates in Louis Dumont's *Homo*

Hierarchicus (1970) the scholarly underpinnings of this concept of varna, "The institu-
ition of varna presents, according to Dumont, the purest example of hierarchy. . . .
While Hindu society is hierarchical, modern Western society is egalitarian and the
dichotomy of hierarchy-equality is part of the larger dichotomy of the traditional and
modern" (1984, 152).

3. Postcolonial scholarship on traditional idioms of social mobility by sociologists, anthropologists, and historians has been pioneering in many respects, and our
own work would not be possible without the groundwork laid out by these scholars.
For the literature on social mobility see M. N. Srinivas's landmark study of the Coorgs
1952; Milton Singer 1964; McKim Marriott 1959; James Silverberg 1968; Milton
Singer and Bernard Cohn 1968; M. N. Srinivas's study 1969; and Romila Thapar
1974, and 1978; M. N. Srinivas 1987; Andre Beteille 1992.

4. Anthropologists and sociologists are primarily concerned with the dynamic,
flexible, localist operation of Rajputization, while historians' primary interest is in the
series of events and struggles that cause the Rajputs to ascend to political power. The
best work done on Rajputization is Surajit Sinha 1962; Richard G. Fox 1971; K. Suresh
Singh 1974; Herman Kulke 1976; B. D. Chattopadhyaya 1976; Herman Kulke 1977;
B. D. Chattopadhyaya 1977; Robert C. Hallissey 1977; and Dirk H. A. Kolff 1990.

5. A corrective to the analysis of women's relation to upward social mobility
was provided by feminist scholars from a variety of disciplines, these scholars enlarged
the field of study of gendered social mobility. Feminists discredits the stereotype that
British colonialism brought emancipation for Indian women through English education, widow remarriage, abolition of sati, and suppression of female infanticide. They
argue that contrary to the stereotype, these reforms were failures and had few real benefits for Indian women (Sangari and Vaid 1989; Kumar 1993). Other feminist scholars have collected data, performed analysis and provided theoretical concepts for
understanding Indian women not as the objects of men's desire for social mobility and
patriarchal constraints, but as subjects through their participation and/or resistance to
social mobility. Some of these studies focussed on the upward mobility of women who,
privileged by class and education and patriarchal benevolence, became the world's
largest labor force of doctors, or the world's first women politicians (Gail Omvedt
1980; Manmohan Kaur 1985; J. Liddle and R. Joshi 1986; Usha Bala and Anshu
Sharma 1986; K. Jaywardene 1986). Some of the important feminist scholarship to
emerge in recent years is on female workers in the context of the increasing feminization of poverty, as well as the feminization of the informal sector of capitalist business
and industry in the periphery, as more and more women are employed on piece-rate
outwork, as casual laborers, migrant coolies, or contract laborers in agriculture, mines,
construction business, domestic servants, etc., and the intervention of global capital
into their lives with micro-credit schemes (M. Meis 1983; K. Bardhan 1986; M. Savara
1986; A. M. Singh and A. Kelles-Viitanen 1987; N. Bannerjee 1991; R. Kalima 1992;
C. Mohanty 1997).

6. See Michel Foucault's *Discipline & Punish* (1979) and *'I, Pierre Rivere.'*
(1982); Ranajit Guha's *Elementary Aspects of Peasant Insurgency in Colonial India*
(1983); and W. H. Sleeman's *The Thugs* (1839) .

7. There is a growing literature in the discipline of sociology concerning field-workers' self-reflexivity and theorizing about the disciplinary tool of fieldwork. See Srinivas's comments on the problems of fieldwork in the discipline of sociology, in Srinivas, A. M. Shah and E. A. Ramaswamy (1979) and Srinivas (1987). We respect this ongoing debate and introspection in the discipline. Our own theoretical interven-tion lies in urging that fieldworkers' data should also be treated as texts that need to be analyzed rhetorically and discursively, and not just by empirical criteria. For example when the fieldworker records the north Indian village women's spoken articulation of the custom of hypergamy and exogamy, the educated fieldworker rarely entertains the notion that her ethnographic subject is capable of reflexive, rhetorically nuanced utter-ance. The assumption is that illiterate women are incapable of moving between several cultural codes in their utterance unlike educated women. A rhetorical-discursive approach allows us to ask: who is speaking and under what constraints, can a daughter-in-law speak her mind before the female or male elders, how might the same utterance be nuanced differently in the natal home or in the marital home. Recent fieldwork that is thoughtful in its investigation of the question of women in Rajput society is Lindsey Harlan (1992) and Maya Unnithan (1995). See also D. Mandelbaum (1988).

8. Racialist arguments were also useful when British officers wanted to justify the preponderance of male children amongst the infanticidal Rajput clans. For exam-ple in the North-Western Provinces, A. O. Hume, the Magistrate and Collector of Etahwa in 1866, expressed the opinion that the the high percentage of boys in com-parison to girls amongst certain Rajput clans was in part due to the fact that they were a healthy and outdoorsy race and as a result produced more male children than other communities in the region (cited in Panigrahi 1976, 131).

9. W. H. Sleeman offers a similar anti-Mughal story about the origin of female infanticide. He reports the views of Lalta Sing of the Nikomee Rajput clan, the latter tells Sleeman "that tradition ascribes the origin of this evil to the practice of the mahommedan emperors of Delhi, to demand daughters in marriage from the Rajpoot princes of the country—that some of them were too proud to comply with the demand, and too weak to resist it in any other way than that of putting all their female infants to death." Sleeman confirms the anti-Muslim sentiment of the native infor-mant by observing, "This is not impossible" (1856, 215). It is an interesting exchange, the native informant Lalta Sing is well aware that the Englishman has traveled to Oudh and is interviewing people all over the Oudh countryside in order to compile evidence to discredit the ruler of Muslim Oudh in particular, and also discredit the East India Company's predecessors, the Mughal rulers, in general. Sleeman is being told what he wishes to hear—the blame for female infant-murder lies neither with the informant, a Rajput, nor with the East India Company—the blame is conveniently placed on the deceased Mughal rulers.

10. The colonial obsession with pure-blooded Indians can be found in the liter-ature of the Raj. For example the colonial writer Jim Corbett writes about the hill region of Kumaon during the British Raj and in his description of the Brahmin village headman's wife, the purity of her lineage plays an essential part, "Daughter of a hun-dred generations of Brahmins, her blood is as pure as that of the ancestor who founded her line. Pride of pure ancestry is inherent in all men, but nowhere is there greater

respect for pure ancestry than there is in India" ("The Queen of the Village" *My India* 1952, 12–13).

11. There is substantial fieldwork that proves conclusively that the term "Rajput" and Kshatriya represents a mode of upward mobility for diverse groups. According to Stein, the medieval period of Indian history is characterized by the fact that "the political units of India were probably ruled most often by men of very low birth" and this "may be equally applicable for many clans of 'Rajputs' in northern India" (1968, 79). Kulke notes that the model of Rajputization was introduced in medieval Orissa after Man Singh, the Rajput general of the Mughal emperor Akbar visited the province; thus the fact that the ruling families of the Garhjat states "claimed to be of Rajput origin" after Man Singh's visit demonstrates that the term denoted their political aspirations and had very little to do with any family connection with the Rajputs (1976, f24). Srinivas states that the Maratha Royal House created fictional genealogies "connecting them to Rajput descent" (10) and in central Gujarat the Koli castes claim Rajput status as a mode of upward mobility (1969, 29). William L. Rowe's study of the census reports of the late nineteenth and early twentieth centuries, as well as his fieldwork with Noniya Cauhans in the village of Senapur, Madhya Pradesh and in Bombay, shows that a segment of the Sudra caste of the Noniyas claimed the status of the Cauhan Rajputs, and consolidated this claim by setting up an organization for caste organization called Sri Rajput Pracarni Sabha (Rajput Advancement Society) in 1898; in terms of our argument about exogamy as part of Sanskritization and Rajputization, it is significant that "for the low status rural Noniyas the average distance from which brides are taken is twelve miles whereas the elite members of the caste invariably report marriage relations at distances of fifty to 300 miles" (1968, 70). In the 1950s David F. Pocock's fieldwork in Gujarat led him to conclude that, "almost every caste in Charottar, (Kaira District, Central Gujerat) including the untouchable Dedh, has in its caste stories and legends a history of warrior and kingly origin" (1957, 24).

12. L. S. Vishwanath provides a interesting counter example to this from amongst the infanticide practicing Lewa Kanbi community of Gujarat. He notes that after the decline of Rajput power as the ruling group in Gujarat in the thirteenth century, the high-status Lewa Patidar lineages who were tax collectors and rulers of villages "started imitating the Rajput style of life and adopted Kshatriya manners and customs" (2000, 3). Vishwanath also notes that the Jats and Ahir castes of North-Western Provinces who practiced female infanticide in the nineteenth century called themselves Rajputs and identified with the Kshatriya ideology (136, 139). Vishwanath identifies female infanticide with Kshatriya martial ideology and caste hypergamous tendencies. He writes that the postcolonial emergence of female infanticide amongst the Grounder community in Tamil Nadu may be related the acquisition of "some kind of martial ideology to justify and legitimise their status as rulers" (160). As a sociologist-historian his perspective is less critical and more explicatory, he attempts to historicize the practice from colonial times to the present day in terms of hypergamous tendencies, the over-population of marriageable women, and high marriage expenses in the upper strata of these castes, and one of the efficacious "solutions" he examines to the problem of female infanticide is the creation of small endogamous caste units amongst the Kanbis of Gujarat called *ekdaas*.

13. The official prestige of Tod's analysis of the practice of female infanticide is evident from the fact that many of the colonial documents cite lines and passages, sometimes by attributing the lines to Tod, and sometimes by recalling from memory, and at other times by fully internalizing the thought expressed by Tod. For instance Sleeman virtually quotes Tod's comment verbatim, "When the aristocracy of Europe buried their daughters alive in nunneries, the state of society was much the same as it is now in Oude" (Tod 1856, I, 232); "Atrocious and cruel as this crime is in Oude, it is hardly more so than that which not long ago prevailed in France and other nations of Europe, of burying their daughters alive in nunneries in order to gratify the same family pride" (Sleeman 1858, II, 60).

14. The gap between traditional sociology and feminist studies can be named, in a sense, as the gap between Srinivas and Singer referring to their disciplinary object of study as Hindu society, versus our own naming of Rajputization as a specific patriarchal formation that is a hybrid product of Hindu-Muslim-tribal cultures. Mary-Searle-Chatterjee and Ursula Sharma also object to the term "Hindu society" and state: "We have deliberately used the term 'South Asian' society wherever possible in this essay. . . . Whether there is such a thing as 'Hindu society' considered as a unity separate from Muslim society or other religious communities in the subcontinent we regard as open to question" (1995, 21). By using the term "Hindu society" the unwitting tendency toward communalizing a secular culture inflects the analysis of cultural concepts. For instance Srinivas tends to see purity and pollution predominantly as a religious distinction, for instance he says that "the concepts of pollution and purity which are central as well as pervasive in Hinduism" (119); moreover, Srinivas states that pollution refers "indirectly even to sinfulness, while purity refers to cleanliness, spiritual merit, and indirectly to holiness" (1969, 120). Contrarily we see these prescriptions as both a religious vocabulary and a secular mode of power. We also argue that these distinctions are not purely Hindu but are a syncretic product of the mixed Hindu-Muslim-tribal culture in a specific community. To be fair to Srinivas, there has been a great deal of spadework that has gone into demolishing misconceptions about the pure/impure in Indian culture. For Srinivas' forceful critique of Louis Dumont's theory of purity and pollution in traditional Hindu society see (1984, 152). For work that follows the Dumont paradigm concerning the Hindu categories of purity and pollution see Ralph W. Nicholas (1982, 367–79).

15. The sites of sati and jauhar are pilgrim sites in Rajasthan and the landscape is dotted with them. The famous Roop Kanwar sati happened on September 4, 1987, in Deorala village, Rajasthan and now the site is a pilgrim center.

16. The nineteenth-century tale of the Sisodhiya Princess Krishna Kumari is worth recounting here as an example of the connection between femicide and saga alliance politics. The ruler of Udiapur as well as the ruler of Marwar both claimed the right to marry the Princess. As a result the forces of Jaipur and Marwar fought each other and although the Jaipur forces were defeated, they refused to give up the claim. According to legend, the solution devised for preserving the honor of all parties was to kill the Princess. Krishna Kumari's brother was sent to stab her but could not do so. Subsequently she was poisoned and died. See Mukta (1994, 152–153) and Tod (1829, I, 539); for a tourism perspective on this tale see *Desh-Videsh* (vol. 4, no. 2, 24–25). For a cinematic version of the same tale see Gulzar's *Meera* (1979).

17. The contemporary relevance of our argument concerning the relationship between social mobility and the policing of caste boundaries can be gauged in the case of the state of Bihar. In early 2000 the television network ABC news program "60 Minutes" carried a news feature on the condition of the dalits in India by Christiane Amanpour. One of the disturbing scenes of the feature showed dalits in a village in Bihar forced to remove their footwear and pass barefoot by upper-caste Rajput landlords, the Rajputs were sitting by the roadside on a raised platform, under a tree. While in the background barefoot dalits walked past the camera, a conversation took place between Amanpour and a Rajput landlord. He points to the fields beyond the camera and says that his crop lies rotting for lack of landless laborers to harvest it, and he is prohibited by his high-caste status from the manual labor of working on the land. Bihar provides an interesting example of our argument concerning Rajputization. Postcolonial Bihar became a test case for the contest between revolutionary change on the one hand (the vigorous Naxalite movement in Bihar carried out by the Maoist Communist Centre, the People's War Group and the Liberation Group of Naxalites) and violent massacres of dalits and landless peasants by upwardly mobile castes in the name of protecting caste boundaries. The seeds of this contest lie in the fact that Bihar was the first state, after the country gained independence, to initiate land reform. The battle began in the 1970s when the wealthy upper caste landlords in Central Bihar—the Brahmins, Rajputs, Kayasthas and other upper castes—formed a private army, comprising mostly of ex-servicemen, the Ranvir Sena, to combat the politicizing of poor landless dalit sharecroppers. In 21 massacres conducted by the Ranvir Sena approximately 336 dalit men, women, and children have lost their lives. Social scientists suggest that in the last 15 years the upper castes have moved into other professions, especially the bureaucracy, and the intermediate castes of Yadavs, Kurmis, and Keons have emerged as the "new Kulaks" who use the Ranvir Sena to preserve their new-found access to political and economic power. Human rights groups in India and the U.S. have called for the Vajpayee Government to disband militias like the Ranvir Sena, and protect the rights of the dalits. The Bihar State Goverment has responded by officially banning the Ranvir Sena (many politicians in Bihar publicly speak against the Sena but use it when the opportunity arises) as well as publicizing administrative shakeups, posting more units of central paramilitary forces and additional director generals of police into the area. The parties of the Left have called for and observed bandhs (lockouts) all over Bihar, and throughout the period of the recent massacres there have been calls for the dismissal of the present goverment in the state by all parties.

18. The British reformist solution to female infanticide, which Tod calls "a fixed nuptial expenditure," was a strange beast called a "sensible marriage." It was not modeled on the marriage dowers in English propertied families in the nineteenth century: a social arrangement by which daughters of English families could lay claim on a provision or marriage portion, which was settled in order that the eldest son's inheritance should not be jeopardized. Nor did reformers' conceptions of a sensible marriage conform to the Rajput model of extravagant marriages with dowries. It was a new social form that entailed little or no allocation of family resources for daughters, negligible expenditure, and no property or inheritance rights for daughters. The consequences of

sensible marriages are not difficult to imagine, it meant the pauperization of daughters and it also made the daughter vulnerable to patriarchal violence in her married home. Within the reformist discourse the parental duties toward daughters consisted of a rational, enlightened disposing of daughters by inexpensive marriage rather than disposing of daughters by killing.

19. The implication of Srinivas' statement is that there is a causal relationship between British colonialism and the ceiling on hypergamy as an upward mobility for the Rajputs. Alice Clark's (1989) analysis of the practice of Jhareja Rajput hypergamy in nineteenth-century colonial Kathiawar is far more aggressive than Srinivas in suggesting a causal relation between British colonialism, Rajput hypergamy, and the Rajput practice of female infanticide. Clark says that the Jhareja clans "were locked into a position under a colonial peace where their status was undermined if they gave daughters to others" and "Thus they practiced wholesale female infanticide." Clark concludes that, "the infanticide of the Jadejas suggests a decapitated and frozen hierarchy of military clans in an age which denied them the opportunity of war " (41).

20. For a textual and shastric view of hypergamy from *The Laws of Manu* and the smriti writers see S. J. Tambiah (1973, 191–229). Irawati Karve notes several curious features of hypergamy in Rajasthan, for instance she notes that "the number of clans from which girls are recieved in marriage is always greater than those to which one gives daughters in marriage" (1965, 167–168). Karve traces this phenomenon to the historical origins of the Rajputs as "mixed origin" and their historical occupation as fighting confederacies, "As warriors they accepted daughters from the conquered group but did not give theirs in return" (169). She concludes that "among the families of the highest status many girls have to remain spinsters" (170), however, she does not connect Rajput hypergamy to the systemic violence on elite Rajput women. For a good treatment of exogamy in north India by using folkloric and popular ritual texts see Leela Dube (1988). Kalpana Bardhan's excellent analysis of the strong connection between exogamy and female child-neglect is worth quoting in full, she states: "The incidence of village exogamy with patrilocal residence, which is far greater in North and West India than in the South, has a lot to do with the level of isolation and desperation of young brides uprooted and placed far away from natal village and kinsfolk, and with the related syndrome of nurturance-deprivation of the female first born in the initial acutely stressful years of marriage" (1986, 9). In order to understand the gendered violence represented by Rajput hypergamy we draw on nonshastric sources like women's songs, bardic literature, and the information provided by native informants to English officers like Charles Metcalfe.

21. The ruling elite of Rajputana have a long history of collaboration with the British. The historian Harbans Mukhia writing about the history of the princely states of Rajashtan, notes that in 1857 while the common soldiers expressed solidarity with the rebels, almost all Rajput princes rushed to the aid of the beleagured British and greeted the suppression of the great rebellion with great satisfaction (1996, 40). Similarly during World War I the Princes expressed their loyalty to Britain by establishing a Chamber of Princes as a bulwark against popular agitations opposing the British presence in India (42).

22. We oppose the shastric textual concept of *kanyadaan* with the lived practices and creative interpretations of this idiom. For a shastric account of the concept of kanyadaan, see Thomas Trautmann (1981). According to Trautmann, "the idiom of kanyadaan is the patrilineal idiom of complete dissimilation of the bride from her family of her birth and her complete assimilation to that of her husband" (291). In contrast to this shastric model of a patrilineal idiom, we posit the text of Mahadevi Varma's autobiographical writings where she describes the creative deployment of the idiom of kanyadaan to end the practice of female infanticide. Varma is a leading figure in Hindi literature (1907–1987) and is described as "easily one of the most distinguished and influential figures in modern India" (Susie Tharu and K. Lalita, 1991, 459). In her autobiography Mahadevi describes, with considerable irony, how her paternal grandfather ended the practice of female infanticide by asserting that he wished to earn the religious merit of kanyadaan for his old age and afterlife, "when a female child had not arrived in the family for a long period, there was concern in the family, for just as a horse is needed for the Ashvamedha ritual, similarly the ritual of kanyadaan is not possible without a girl" (1963, 17). We read this autobiographical text both as the woman writer's courageous acknowledgment of the practice of female infanticide in her natal family, and the savage irony of the female survivor in Mahadevi's Hindi prose, as well as an invaluable glimpse of the indigenous ways in which benevolent patriarchs deployed the ritual of kanyadaan to end the practice in their own family. Mahadevi's American biographer notes the grandfather's use of religion to sacralize the birth of Mahadevi who "was believed by the paternal grandfather to be a boon from the goddess Durga, the family's chosen deity " (Schromer 1983, 157).

23. For an interesting account of the songs sung by peasant women as they do their household work see Poitevin and Rairkar, *Stonemill and Bhakti: From the Devotion of Peasant Women to the Philosophy of Swamis* (1996); also see Kirin Narayan, "Women's Songs, Women's Lives: A View from Kangra" (1994).

24. For an interesting account of sadism as the motor of narrative, see Teresa de Lauretis, "Desire in Narrative" (1984).

25. It is necessary to define the regional specificity of the religious practices of Hindus in Rajasthan from the rest of north-west India. The phrase that has come to be associated with Hinduism in Rajasthan is "Rajput Hinduism." Tod's history suggests that Rajput Hinduism is a pro-violence, martial, and masculinist worship of the god Mahadeo. Contrarily we argue that Rajput Hinduism in Rajasthan is characterized by the following features: while in other regions the Brahmanical model of Hinduism was privileged, in Rajasthan Brahmanical Hinduism was challenged by the privileging of Rajputized Hinduism. Second, the diverse populations of the region, for example the tribals like the Bhils and the Meenas, as well as the sizable Muslim population meant that Hinduism was assimilated and adapted in such a way that there is a great heterodoxy of Hindu sects and local dieties like Ramdeoji, Pabuji, Tejaji, Gogaji, Jambhoji, Dev Narayan and Bhagwati Shri Karniji Maharaj and the Bhakti cults. It is precisely this heterodoxy and localism of religion that creates a space for autonomy and dissent in Rajasthan.

26. The many legends concerning the various attempts at Meera's life and her life-long persecution by her natal as well as marital family has been traced by some Hindi language scholars of Meera to the relatively recent origins of Merta as a dynasty (Chaturvedi 1964, 18). Shabnam (1976) writes that Merta was established in 1518 by Rao Dudaji, Meera's paternal grandfather, when he captured it from the Sultan of Maru (131). Meera was Rao Dudaji's fourth son's only child. Therefore the virulence with which a natal clan persecutes its daughters is in direct proportion to whether or not they are a recently legitimized dynasty.

27. In contrast to the Rajput clan's notion of exogamy is the case of clan exogamy practiced by the Coorgs in Kodagu, South India. The Coorgs or Kodavas are a martial race with distinct ethnic and cultural characteristics. The concept of the clan is a powerful institution amongst them and many credit it with having preserved the Kodava culture for centuries. The clan or *okka* is an exogamous group: marriage within the same okka is considered tantamount to incest. Therefore, the Kodavas practice the cross-cousin marriage system, which is a distinct trait of tribal ethnic communities. Women occupy an exalted place in the hierarchy, and remarriage of widows is encouraged. Many women run coffee estates in the region single-handedly, and local legends often have heroines playing the central role. See Srinivas' *Religion and Society among the Coorgs of South India* (1952).

28. Gloria Goodwin Raheja's anthropological fieldwork in two villages of Pahansu and Hatchoya in the province of Uttar Pradesh shows that women resist exogamy by making complex natal ties in their marital home; for example, they assert a closer kinship with a member of the village who has a kinship tie with their natal village, underlining these closer ties by lax rules of purdah, so that these men and women constitute their support in family and village matters (1994, 73–120).

29. A brief glimpse of the history of the Ranas of Mewar shows how the shaan or honor ideology of the Rajputs worked in the context of saga alliance politics: grandfathers and maternal uncles used a child-king ascending to the throne to rule over kingdoms, they also conspired and intrigued to get their nephews on the throne; sons committed fratricide as well as parricide in order to ascend to the throne and fathers married their daughters to Muslim ruler of neighboring states in order to make peace. For example, Rana Kumbha, who according to Tod was Meera's husband, was killed by his son Udaykarna Uda. Uda is also known to have married his daughter to Ghiyasuddin Khilji, the ruler of Mandu in order to make peace. Uda's own grandfather, Rana Mokal, was murdered by his grandfathers' illegitimate sons. Rana Kumbha himself ascended to the throne in his childhood, so his father's maternal uncle Rao Ranmal Rathore administered the kingdom. The famous Rana Sanga was one of the three sons of Uda's brother Raimal, and at the death of Rana Sanga, his son Ratansingh ascended to the throne amidst bitter internecine warfare between Sanga's seven sons. The maternal uncle of Ratansingh's stepbrothers Hade Rao Surajmal would intrigue for his nephews and as a result, Surajmal and Ratansingh killed each other at a hunt. At Ratansingh's death his stepbrother Vikramaditya ascended to the throne at the age of 14 years, and at 19 was killed by Vanvir, the illegitimate son of his paternal uncle Prithviraj. See Tod, I (1829, 173–252); Dashrath Sharma (1966, I) on the precarious-

ness of Rajput politics based on warfare in medieval Rajasthan; see also Padmavati Shabnam (1976).

30. Alice Clark is one of the few scholars who directly relates female infanticide in northwest India to a power analysis of hypergamy. She writes, "Among the higher castes and dominant castes all over north India there has been a tendency towards hypergamy generally in the north-west" (1989, 40–41). Clark characterizes "true hypergamy" as a "unidirectional hierarchical structure" and an "unequal alliance." She defines true hypergamy as, "the gift of a daughter without return" (41). Our own analysis coincides with Clark in that she too notes that the actual practice of hypergamy was a gendered practice in that only daughters were deployed for marrying into a higher caste or class and not sons. However Clark does not theorize from her analysis of hypergamy that it is not only a gendered practice, but that it constitutes a form of gendered violence on women, even though her research bears this out. Kolff writes, "Women served as pawns given as surety to the allies of their fathers and brothers" (1990, 101).

31. We are indebted to Norman Zeigler's study of the historical chronicles for this remarkable insight. Ziegler noted that bardic writings made a clear distinction between the political value of those familial relationships that were contracted through daughters' marriages on the one hand and a man's natal kinsfolk, "One's saga (those to whom one gave daughters in marriage and from whom one received wives) were obligated to provide support and assistance, and they formed the most important group upon whom one depended outside one's bhaibandhu (lit. 'tie or bond of brothers') or close relations by male blood" (1976, 240). For an excellent analysis of saga alliance politics see Dirk H. A. Kolff (1990). See also Richard G. Fox (1971) and Robert C. Hallissey (1977).

32. Saga alliance played a very important role in medieval Rajput politics. Kolff observes, "Sagai, i.e. the alliance network, represents a mature set of political norms in itself. As an idiom of political behaviour, it played a prime part in pre-Mughal Indian history" (1990, 101). For example in the sixteenth-century Rana Sanga of Mewar married his daughter to the Purbiya Rajput Silhadi in order to engineer the defeat of the Malwa sultanate. But when the bride's father called upon his son-in-law for military aid against the Mughal invader Babar, that claim was refused because the son-in-law did not find it politically expedient; thus the sasur-samdhi alliance on the basis of which Rana Sanga made a bid for the Delhi throne lead to his defeat. As Kolff notes, "But, even if the allies exchanged brides and became each other's in laws or saga, there was really nothing sacred about these co-operative efforts" (1990, 94).

33. R. Venkatachalam and Viji Srinivasan note that dowry demands were on the rise amongst landless agricultural laborers like the Labadis in Salem district, Tamil Nadu. The authors write, "Lambadis never had these customs" I say, "How did female infanticide enter your lives?" "Oh we learnt from the Grounder women!" (1993, 53). L. S. Vishwanath suggests that the dowry problem among the Kallars "got accentuated" with the coming of development projects like the Vaigai dam, which brought irrigation and prosperity to the famers in Usilampatti taluk, and the opening of new colleges and educational institutions in the area (2000, 158).

Chapter 4. A Critical History of the Colonial Discourse of Infanticide Reform, 1800–1854

Part I. Infanticide Reform as Extra-Economic Extraction of Surplus

1. See Gayatri C. Spivak, "History" *A Critique of Postcolonial Reason* (1999) 198–311; Ranajit Guha, "Dominance Without Hegemony And Its Historiography" *Subaltern Studies VI* (1989) 210–309; Lata Mani, "Contentious Traditions: The Debate on Sati in Colonial India" *Recasting Women* (1997) 88–126; and Partha Chatterjee, "The Nationalist Resolution of the Women's Question" ibid., (1997) 233–253.

2. For elaboration and critique of the Marxist concept of economism and the limitations of the economistic approach see V. I. Lenin, *What is to be done?* [1902], 1962; Antonio Gramsci, "Some Theoretical And Practical Aspects Of 'Economism'" [1928–1935] 1971, 158–168.

3. Kanti B. Pakrasi's *Female Infanticide in India* (1970) is by his own admission not an original work but a compilation of colonial documents on infanticide reform in Kathiawar 1800–1854. Therefore we sometimes refer to it as a source and at other times we cite it for easy reference of the reader. Similarly John Wilson's *History of the Suppression of Infanticide in Western India under the Government of Bombay* (1855) is a colonialist history, which includes unedited reproductions of many colonial documents particularly from Kutch. Therefore even while we cite it as a colonialist account of reform in Kathiawar and Kutch, we cite Wilson as a source when we refer to the history of infanticide reform in Kutch.

4. Here it must be noted that although private property did not exist in pre-British India, we name Rajput land grabbing and settlement as land accumulation because while Rajputs did not work on the land or have an intimate involvement with agriculture, land functioned for them as a process of accumulation of wealth.

5. Alice Clark (1989) in her study of female infanticide among the Lewa Kanbi Patidars in nineteenth-century Central Gujarat describes how as the Lewa Kanbi's became wealthy their women stopped performing agricultural work in the fields. Clark suggests that the violence (rape, abduction, etc.) against the lower class Koli women who labored in the fields was one of the direct results of this withdrawal of Kanbi women from agricultural work. See Vishwa Nath (1973) for a description of the Lewa Kanbi houses built in this period that incorporated this seclusion of women as part of their architectural features. Similarly Kalpana Bardhan (1986) attributes the increased violence against laboring women in rural as well as urban postcolonial India to this process of withdrawing upper-class women from the workforce with the coming of prosperity.

6. Nothing better illustrates our differences from linear progressivist socio-historical accounts of British infanticide reform than the argument made in this chapter regarding the interrelationship between British greed for revenue and female infanticide reform. For instance L. S. Vishwanath makes the argument that although the British discovered infanticide amongst the various communities while making revenue settlements, it had no bearing on their strategies or efforts. He writes:

The discovery of female infanticide by the British among the Rajkumar Rajputs in north India and the Jadeja Rajputs in peninsular Gujarat almost at the onset of British rule and the reports of British officials on extensive prevalence of female infanticide in these Rajput groups enables us to surmise that probably British revenue policies did not play a major role so far as female infanticide was concerned. (2000, 13)

For a definition of primitive accumulation see *A Dictionary of Marxist Thought* (1983) 3–4; for an analysis of the continuing processes of primitive accumulation at the periphery see Maria Mies, *The Lace Makers of Naraspur* (1982); we highly recommend Mies' critique of the processes of primitive accumulation under global capitalism in *Patriarchy and Accumulation on a World Scale* (1986) and Vandana Shiva, "GATT, Agriculture and Third World Women" in *Ecofeminism* (1993) 231–245.

7. Samir Amin writes, "The form assumed by peripheral formations will ultimately depend on the nature of the precapitalist formations subjected to attack, on the one hand, and, on the other, on the forms taken by this external attack" (*Unequal Development* 1976, 294). Even though Amin is talking specifically about the economic system, for Amin the economic system of the periphery cannot be understood in itself because its relations with the center are crucial. Similarly the social structure of the periphery, for Amin, is a "truncated structure" (294) that can only be understood when it is situated as an element in a world social structure. The economic and the social are interdependent, and the social is always inclusive of woman. Samir Amin's analysis of the development of underdevelopment and the consequent social formations of the periphery allow us to place the question of British reform of female infanticide and its subsequent positioning of women and daughter rights, in the context of the universalizing tendencies of global capitalism. Historically the fact that the East India Company officers used infanticide reform as an alibi to establish their moral and legal right to police the Jhareja Rajputs and levy fines on them for infringement of the infanticide engagements, has produced for us what Samir Amin calls a truncated structure, which we, as postcolonial feminists, have to unravel in the interests of women's history. This deformed structure of the Company's failed attempts at addressing women's rights through infanticide reform has to be understood within the context of British imperialism's larger project and as an element of the world social structure.

8. The colonial administrator B. H. Baden-Powell in *Land Revenue and Tenure in British India* (1907) describes the *Mevasi* or *Wanta* land tenure systems of the Jhareja Rajputs of Kathiawar, Gujarat at the advent of the British as "curious" because they arose from the disruption of old local chiefships in the wars that followed the last Mughal Emperor Aurangzeb's attempt to conquer the south and after the rise of Maratha power at the close of the seventeenth century. These tenures, according to Baden-Powell were curious because they were "never really under the authority of any Central Government" (114). The conquering power allowed chiefs who held the wilder hill country or outlying territory (like the Kathiawar area) in control of their territories under the usual designation of Taluqdar on payment of tribute. However some of these chiefs were considered too powerful and the Mughals as well as the Marathas would confiscate their estates leaving only a fourth portion to them, thus they were also called Wanta or portions land tenure. A number of these dispossessed Koli chiefs

turned to raiding and levying blackmail and placing under their protection such groups of villages or stretches of territory as could be held from some fort (1913, 113–114). Desai (1948) also calls the land tenure systems held by Koli or Rajput chiefs in the Kathiawar area as *Mevasi*. He explains that these chiefs paid a lump sum in tribute or revenue to the authorities and the difference between what he collected from the inferior occupiers of the lands of his estates and what he paid to the authorities constituted his profit. Both Baden-Powell and Desai describe the *Mevasi* land tenure as resembling the *talukdari* tenure (100).

9. Rajput clans came to Kathiawar as invaders and rose to power by capturing the land of the local inhabitants. Desai describes them as "Rajput chiefs who occupied ruling positions originally or were mere plunderers during the Mughal times" (1948, 100). Therefore tribute collection from the Rajputs chiefs in Kathiawar was no easy matter. The Marathas who were known as keen financiers, became plunderers, using an army to enforce the payment of tribute. R. D. Choksey in *Economic Life in the Bombay Gujarat* (1800–1939) writes that during the first years of the nineteenth century, even the British had "to maintain a regular force to come by the yearly assessment" (1968, 25).

10. Samir Amin defines the tribute-paying mode of production as a precapitalist social formation combining and marked by: 1) the predominance of a communal or tribute-paying mode of production; 2) the existence of simple commodity relations in limited spheres and 3) the existence of long-distance trade relations. He explains that long-distance trade is not a mode of production but the way in which independent formations are linked together (*Unequal Development* 1976, 17). Baden-Powell describes the communal tribute-paying mode of production in Gujarat as including the raiyatwari villages which are also called "sanja =joint or associated," as well as the landlord-villages which are "bhagdari or shared" (75).

11. Jhareja Rajput chiefs of Kathiawar were not proprietors of their *talooks*. The villages included in the *talook* of a chief had strong clan and tribal connections, chiefs had also obtained lordship over various villages or estates made up of parts of villages. The chief was head of the whole but he was not in a position to be dealt with as *Zamindar* or direct landlord of the entire Province. For example, the infanticide document on the trial of the Chief of Rajkot Suraji enumerates his property as the Rajkot *talook*. This consisted of about 55 villages, of which 13 were alienated from revenue charge to Suraji as *Talukdar* (Wilson 1855, 202). The company did not understand the idea of dealing with village bodies, therefore revenue settlements of these villages were made either with the head of family or chief cosharer in the village, or a local merchant who had acquired estates or established chiefship over groups of villages. Interestingly Baden-Powell tells about a report prepared by Jonathan Duncan when he was the Resident of Banaras in 1796 on co-sharing village bodies. In the report Duncan was extremely puzzled by the notion of joint ownership, he could not understand how there could be more than one landlord in a village (Baden-Powell 1913, 161).

12. The Jhareja Rajputs of Kathiawar were known for their rebellious nature. Choksey describes them in these words:

> Rajputs are found all over Gujarat but mostly in Kathiawar. They have lost their purity by marriage with Kolis and Bhils. It is this inter-mixture with

the Bhils that produced one of the most forbidding race called the Gracias. They claim Marwar as their ancestral home. We may perhaps assume they are descendants of Rajputs by Bhil women. Most of these Rajputs are land-lords. Exclusive of the large class of Gracias, who hold estates of varying sizes, on favourable terms, the Rajputs are still the dominant race holding sway over nearly half of the area of Gujarat and over nearly one-third of its people. (1968, 59)

13. In 1752 a treaty was signed between the Gaekwar, the powerful warlord of Gujarat, and the Peshwa by which the Gaekwar ceded one-half of all the parganas held by him in Gujarat to the Peshwa. It was decided that in the peninsula of Saurashtra or Kathiawar the right to send mulkgiri expeditions into the various Jhareja Rajput states was to be defined such that certain territories were reserved for the Gaekwar and oth-ers for the Peshwa. Thus the ruling Rajputs of Kathiawar exchanged imperial Mughal suzerainty for the hegemony and domination of the Marathas. The numerous Rajput dynasties of the region were compelled to pay tribute to both the Gaekwar and the Peshwa. These rights continued with the Poona Government until they were trans-ferred to the Gaekwar and to the British by the Treaty of Poona in 1817, and were finally extinguished with the fall of Baji Rao II in 1818. The province of Gujarat was thereafter divided into two political units, the British districts and the extensive dominions of the Gaekwar of Baroda who shared his tribute with the British, an arrangement that lasted until the great merger of all princely states into the Republic of independent India in 1948. See M. S. Commissariat (1957, vi. 506–507).

14. It must be remembered that tribute was not rent or revenue on lands owned by the Company. Tribute was submission by minor chieftains to the superior military might of the conquering power, and its payment was acknowledgment of inferiority. Yet the British insisted on naming it revenue. Choksey describes the economic depres-sion that characterized the first half century of Company rule as issuing from this rev-enue policy; he writes, "The mischief began with a fundamental error from a revenue point of view which was the confounding of a tribute with the right to a share in the actual produce of the estate" (1968, 71). Writing about British-owned Gujarat, exclu-sive of the Indian states of Kutch and Kathiawar, he writes:

> In a ryotwari tenure land revenue settlement is always subject to revision. In Western India it was at the end of thirty years. This revision was based on top prices which in itself was wholly unjust. At times, even when the eco-nomic history of the tract was against any increase, still in order to get more, the Government, regardless of all survey principles, raised the rates in a large measure even in the poorest of Deccan talukas. This policy had been fol-lowed all along the British rule. Even during their first fifty years which were marked by great all-round economic depression, when they realized that the land revenue was to a considerable extent responsible for the poverty of the ryot, the temptation to try and come by most of the revenue, even in years that followed a famine, they could hardly resist. (1968, 247)

This policy of rack rents followed by the British in these early years reached its zenith when in the 1820s revenue extracted from talukdars and landlords reached 70 percent of the produce and many of them lost their lands to the moneylender with no hope of ever recovering them.

15. Each successive Political Agent fancied himself a historian of the "custom" of female infanticide in Kathiawar. For instance Walker submits four versions of the Jhareja story of the origin of female infanticide: in 1805 based on a native informant Sundarji Sevji's account, another version in 1807 based on the Rao of Kutch's Muslim minister Futeh Mohammad's account, a lengthy report in 1808, and in Walker's second dispatch in 1819 from London where he lived after retirement.

16. The fifty years of infanticide reform in Kutch and Kathiawar are marked by British use of military force to coercively bind the native populations in infanticide engagements. We have already noted the 1807 example of the Chief of Murvi whose attempt to negotiate for the return of the village of Hurralla in exchange for his agreement to sign an infanticide engagement was rejected by Walker. Walker then made the pretense of persuading the Chief's mother to intercede with her son on behalf of the British. When she refused, her son was threatened with coercive action from the Company detail that would soon be passing through Murvi on its yearly revenue collection, and the Chief of Murvi was forced to sign the infanticide engagement twelve months after the incident, in 1808. A second example comes from the last decade of the reform era. In 1841 the Company coercively obtained infanticide engagement with the refractory Hothi tribe in Kutch. The tribe had refused to abide by the engagement signed by the Rao of Kutch in 1819. The Political Agent at Kutch sent letters to the chiefs of the two recalcitrant villages giving them 15 days to leave the province. The report of the Political Agent describes how he achieved his objective:

> I sent these letters by 20 Mausul Swars [horsemen], 10 to each village, thinking it better to avoid by such parties the possibility of the chiefs involving themselves further by resistance, and to show the other tribes the consequences of disobedience to their own Government. I am happy to say that the objects were effected, the Bandara chief repairing to Bhuj the next day and the Tumadi chief the day after. There appeared at Tumadi, at first, a disposition to resist, but it soon evaporated. (Letter of Political Agent of Kutch, Malet, to Bombay Government, September 1841, Wilson 1855, 315)

17. *The Gazetteer of the Bombay Presidency* vol. viii, 1884, 338. The document also notes that in 1800 Walker classified the 193 estates in Kathiawar belonging mostly to the Jhareja Rajput chiefs into three categories: the first category included the large estates of the 13 major Thareja chiefs including Moorvi, Dharol, Gondal, and Rajkot, and they were allowed complete autonomy in management. The second category consisted of smaller 25 estates whose management was shared with the British political agent while the third category included 155 small and petty chiefs and their lands who were managed by the British political agent alone (6–7). Therefore the big estates did not come under the purview of the British Agency and its revenue records were never submitted to the political agent unless it could be proved that there was or had been financial mismanagement. L. S. Vishwanath notes that the Jhareja Rajput chiefs of Kathiawar "retained their estates without much dimunition during Muslim, Maratha

and British rule," and thus "they continued to occupy the pre-eminent position among Rajputs in Gujarat till Independence" (2000, 44).

18. Political Agent of Kathiawar, Carnac, 1811–1816 referred to the Jharejas in the following way, "The Jadejas, though proud, are like, the other natives of India, very avaricious" (Letter of Carnac to Chief Secretary to Bombay Government, Warden, 18 July 1816, *Hindoo Widows 2*, Part II, 97). Alexander Walker's review dispatch in 1819 on reform in Kathiawar after retirement, referred to the nature of the Jharejas as "greedy and necessitous" (July 1819, Wilson 1855, 116).

19. Like in Kathiawar, the British Government recommended to the Jhareja Rajputs of Kutch that they establish an Infanticide Fund. The reaction of the Jharejas is recorded by the Political Agent of Kutch in his report:

> A general marriage fund among the Jadejas was recommended by Colonel Melvill, who hoped to have interested Government in supporting it. This measure, which would have been highly politic and advantageous to the Jadejas, was lost by the passive opposition of that body. It was probably regarded as a *precedent for taxation*, of which they have been ever jealous. The fine fund, which was to have added to the resources of the former one, has up to this hour provided only 1,525 koris. (italics ours, Infanticide Report for 1842 of J. G. Lumsden, Political Agent of Kutch, to Bombay Government, Wilson 1855, 362)

The above extract makes it clear that the Jhareja Rajputs of Kutch had no difficulty in decoding colonial reform measures like the Infanticide Fund as extra economic means of extracting more revenue. However unlike their brethren in Kathiawar, the sovereignty of the Rao of Kutch allowed the Jhareja Rajputs of Kutch to express their opinions and ensure that the fines extracted from infringements were so nominal as to be of no consequence. Nevertheless by 1852, the Infanticide Fund of Kutch was substantial, with Rupees 16, 000 invested in the 5 percent loan, and a balance of Rupees 15, 097 and there being no applications for aid from the Jharejas (Letter of LeGrand Jacob, Political Agent in Kutch, 1853, Wilson 1855, 386).

20. Barbara Miller in *The Endangered Sex* (1981) notes regarding female infanticide in British India that "the historic record contains more anecdotal evidence than quantitative documentation." The preponderance of anecdotes in the colonialist historiography of female infanticide becomes an obstacle to Miller's objective to "partially reconstruct the social context and demographic significance of female infanticide in British India" (50). Contrarily we find the text of the anecdotes extremely revealing of the actual operation and negotiations between the native elite and the Company at the site of infanticide reform.

21. For instance, Sleeman recommends the Bombay reform system for Awadh precisely because the Bombay system made adherence to infanticide agreements the very basis of the sovereignty of the lands of the Jharejas. He writes:

> It might be put down in Oude, as it was put down by Mr. Willoughby, of Bombay, in the districts under his charge, by making the abolition one of the conditions on which all persons of the Rajpoot clan hold their lands, and strictly enforcing the observance of that condition. (II (1858), 39)

22. The Punjab Province, annexed by the East India Company in 1849, was the last province in which female infanticide reform was introduced. The reform measure followed in Punjab typified the misfit between the dimension of the problem of female infanticide and the nature of the solution. The dimension of the problem was far greater than in many other provinces, for Rajput and non-Rajput communities in the province practiced female infanticide. Company officials demarcated the infanticidal communities in the province as the Rajputs (Munha Rajputs, Jammu Rajputs, and Rajputs of Kangra) and non-Rajput communities (Bunjal Khatris, Bedis, Sodhis, Manjha Sikhs, Burar Jats, Lahoree Khatris, Mohyal Brahmins, and Muslim Pathans). The Punjab reform consisted of large-scale meetings, reconciliation between antagonistic branches of the same caste in order to facilitate intermarriage, and the fixing of marriage expenditures. For twenty years the Company made no effort to find out if there was a decrease in the incidence of female infanticide as a result of the reforms. The mobilization of these communities became an end in itself, the implementation of new marriage rules was treated as a sign that reform was successful. Thus marriage reform became a self-sustaining discourse. Therefore the Punjab system of large meetings seems to have been designed more for the mobilization of a people in a newly annexed province under the pretext of reform, rather than a successful demonstration that marriage reform is the solution to female infant killing. For a contemporary critical region-specific analysis of female infanticide in Punjab, we highly recommend Cave Brown (1857), Panigrahi (1976), and Veena Talwar Oldenburg (2002).

23. We go back from the 1850s because this decade has political significance in our account of colonial infanticide reform. Chapter 2 of this book marks the Indian war of independence in 1857 as a watershed; it was the culmination of the hostilities and the resentments generated among the people of North-West India by the reformist campaigns. The 1857 war of independence also marks the end of the era of the British civilizing mission and the beginning of the rule of coercion and administrative control of the colony by the British Crown and Parliament. Therefore we give a nonlinear account of the colonial discourse of marriage reform by beginning at the end of the history of marriage reform.

24. The Muslim rulers of Sind were the result of earlier Muslim invasions and flourished all through the Mughal rule despite having broken down into smaller kingdoms. But by the beginning of the nineteenth century they had been overthrown by the Marathas. Therefore they were no longer eligible partners in hypergamous marriages for the Jhareja Rajputs of Kutch and Kathiawar.

25. In 1816 the Political Agent of Kathiawar, Captain Carnac, had suggested that the Company conduct the marriages of the two daughters of the Raja of Murvi (who had been threatened into signing the infanticide engagement by Walker) who were saved as a result of his infanticide engagements with the British. At the time the Bombay Government had refused saying it would set a bad precedent, which was liable to abuse; instead they requested information regarding marriage expenses of the Jharejas of various classes (Wilson 1855, 97).

26. For instance the Erskine 1837 document begins, "The Jam professes to give his daughters to the Chiefs of the Drangdra family or his eldest son and heir, as head

of the Jhalla tribe,—to no others in Kattywar; but *he has never yet given one*" (italics ours). The document records that in ten generations of the Jam of Nowanugger *one daughter had been preserved* "and she was given to Ramsingjee of Jodhpoor." The two marriages of daughters recorded in the document are marriages of Jhareja daughters to Muslims: the marriage of the daughter of Rao Khengarjee by a concubine, who was married to the Nawab of Joonagur, and the late Jhareja Jyajee's wife's sister who was married to the late Jemadar Futteh Mahomed of Kutch (Pakrasi 1970, 142). Similarly M. S. Commissariat in *A History of Gujarat* notes that the Jhala Rajputs of Kathiawar had maintained "friendly relations with the [Mughal] subahdars of the Province" by giving a daughters in marriage in 1714 to Daud Khan Panni and in 1727 to Sarbuland Khan (1957, 434).

27. Lalita Panigrahi (1976) examining the effect of the passing of the Act of 1870 on the practice of female infanticide in the North-Western Provinces, suggests that the "real" test of change amongst the infanticidal clans was "whether they showed any tendency to relax the rigidity of marriage customs" (184). For her, as for Miller, the change to low-cost marriages is one of the most important solutions to female infanticide. Panigrahi observes that in the 1880s it was reported that some Rajputs of infanticidal clans were now accepting brideprice instead of dowry for their daughters; furthermore an increasing number of dhola marriages and dharam byahs (literally religious marriages but which in practice were, as Panigrahi describes it, the practice whereby the father offered the daughter to whoever would accept her) were being performed all over the North-Western Provinces by Rajputs of infanticidal clans. She calls it a "welcome trend" even as she notes that the dhola marriage system of purchasing wives and dharam byahs were being fueled by economic self-interest of the infanticidal families (182).

28. In a letter from the Political Agent of Kutch Trevelyan dated 9 July 1855, we learn that in recent times both the sister and the daughter of the Jam of Nowanugger were married "by Proxy or Dhola or Khardoo to the Jodhpoor Chief and his eldest son respectively, neither of whom came to Nowanugger to receive and escort them back to the Marwar capital. Swords of State, with a deputation being substituted for the presence of the bridegrooms on those occasions" and that Pudloo or brideprice was not extracted from the either of the bridegroom parties (*Selections from the Records of the Bombay Government* Nos. 39–40, 1856; Pakrasi 1970, 272).

29. In 1845 Political Agent Lang reported that a school had been established at Rajkot with subscriptions from all the chiefs of Kathiawar. The education plan was first suggested by Erskine in 1837. Erskine suggested the plan of national education in Kathiawar for both the natives and the British officers. He suggested that the officers familiarize themselves with Tod's history of the Jharejas as Rajputs who were contaminated by intermarriage with Muslims and unable to find matrimonial alliances amongst the Rajputs of the peninsula of Gujarat. On this basis Erskine asked, "if, therefore, the obstacles to the marriage of females are removed, what can be the operating cause for the crime at the present day?" Ironically for the purposes of guiding the Government's actions in this regard, Erskine drew the Government's attention to the same memorandum concerning intermarrying groups that we have analyzed earlier.

30. Following the example of the Bombay System, as the reform program in Kathiawar came to be known, in the Punjab province before the takeover of the Company by the British Government, large scale meetings became the fashion. In Jullunder a meeting was held for three days in April 1853 between the Bunjal Khatris and the Bedis. The Bedis were the priestly class amongst the Sikhs, and were known as "*Kooree Mar,* or daughter-slayer." The famous Amritsar meeting of October 1853 brought together Rajputs, Bedis, Mohyal Brahmins, Khatris and Muslims, they were assembled for three days and agreements concerning marriage were signed. Similar meetings were organized in Gujranwala, Rawalpindi, Jhelum, Shahpur, Multan, Ambala, and Ferozpur (Cave-Brown 1857, 114).

31. Pakrasi gives an interesting account of this failed meeting at Bhuj. According to Pakrasi, in March 1830 Sir John Malcolm came to Bhuj to address the assembled Jharejas and warned that the English nation would force the East India Company to dissolve all connection with a people who persisted in practicing female infanticide. The assembled Jharejas individually denied committing the crime and at the same time pointed out that they were surprised at such a threat from a government, which at the time was courting friendship with Sind, a province in which female-child murder was carried out to much larger extent and where both legitimate and illegitimate female offsprings of men of rank were put to death (1970, 144).

32. For a post-1857 account of marriage reform as the sole colonial measure used to suppress female infanticide in central Gujarat, see Alice Clark (1989) and L. S. Vishwanath (2000). What is interesting about the case of the Lewa Kanbi Patidars of Charotar area in central Gujarat is that the practice is discovered amongst them in the 1850s, at the precise time when the British reform efforts amongst the Jhareja Rajputs in Kathiawar are winding down. Clark shows that in the case of the Lewa Kanbis the pre-1857 aggressive reform measures taken by the Company in Kathiawar, or the Bombay System, was no longer an acceptable model for the British Government. Vishwanath shows in detail the fact that the Government preferred to follow the route of marriage reform. Clark shows that as a result of following this "moderate " approach, the practice of female infanticide flourished amongst the Kanbis right up to the end of the nineteenth century and the Anti-Infanticide Act of 1870 sanctioning measures to suppress infanticide was rendered "irrelevant." See Oldenburg for a detailed analysis of marriage reform in the post-1857 era in the Punjab (2002).

33. We locate the antecedents of the notion—accepted by Indian nationalists and continued by postcolonial reformers, that all that is needed to address the social violence on daughters is to channel her into a sensible marriage—in the analysis of James Tod who said that the marriage laws of the Rajputs "powerfully promote infanticide." Marriage reform became the central plank of the nationalists' social reform: raise the age of consent so that daughters are not child-brides but marry at a sensible age; educate your daughters so that they have self-respect and the right values and can retain the interest of their educated husbands; teach daughters to magically reform their married households without agitating for their legal-economic-political rights in the home. Indeed an artificial construction of the Hindu married woman and the nationalist ideal of the companionate marriage came to be represented in nationalist novels, plays, pamphlets, speeches, films, and poems.

34. This distinction is particularly important in light of the fact that Miller's North–South dichotomy breaks down when we consider that some of the rural communities in postcolonial Tamil Nadu that practice female infanticide have traditions of cross-cousin marriages and cite their abhorrence of the tradition as one of the cause of the incidence of female infanticide in their communities. See R. Muthulakshmi's study of the Kallars in Madurai district of Tamil Nadu (1997, 22).

Chapter 5. A Critical History of the Colonial Discourse of Infanticide Reform, 1800–1854 Part II: The Erasure of the Female Child under Population Discourse

1. We use the Lacanian term "objet petit a" in reference to our argument that the girl-child functions as a cause in colonial reform discourse, but a cause that is constantly repressed and thereby effects the infinite productivity of census discourse. The objet petit a in the Lacanian lexicon refers to the object that sets desire in motion but is the object that is itself unattainable. Lacan explains that partial objects set drives in motion but the drives can only circle around the partial object, not attain it (*Four Fundamentals* 1977, 179). Inspired by Marx's concept of surplus value, Lacan explains the objet petit a in terms of his formulation of the four discourses. In the discourse of the master, the signifier attempts to represent the subject for all other signifiers and the objet petit a is the inevitable surplus produced. Thus according to Lacan, the objet petit a has no use value but is a surplus of meaning and a surplus enjoyment for the sake of enjoyment or jouissance. Also see Evans, *An Introductory Dictionary of Lacanian Psychoanalysis* (1996) 125.

2. In the 1970s during Prime Minister Indira Gandhi's regime, her son and heir apparent, Sanjay Gandhi tried to make his own as well as the career of the political party launched by him, the Youth Congress, on the bandwagon of population control and sterilization drives. This strategy had nineteenth-century precedent. For example Jonathan Duncan, a civil servant of the Company was Resident of Banaras when he became famous for first discovering the practice of female infanticide among the Rajkumar community of Rajputs in Banaras in the North-Western Provinces in 1789. Duncan was appointed Governor of Bombay from 1795 to 1811, and along with Colonel Walker, directed female infanticide reform in Kathiawar from 1800. Duncan was awarded a knighthood, and when he died in August 1811, the inscription on the monument at his grave at the Bombay Cathedral was inscribed by the following words, "Infanticide abolished in Benares and Kattywar." But in 1816 the Governor-General expressed the opinion that Duncan's agreements with the Rajkumars had "failed to prevent the inhuman practice," and "a greater degree of precaution was observed to prevent detection, there was too much reason to fear that the crime itself had not in any degree diminished" (Wilson 1855, 43).

Alexander Walker, an Army Colonel of the Company forces, spearheaded British reform efforts concerning female infanticide amongst the Jharejas from 1800 to 1809. At his retirement in 1809 he claimed to have devoted his public life to "rescue(ing) a great number of helpless infants from a premature death" (Wilson 1855,

120–121). Bishop Heber writes in his Journal about Walker's departure from Kathi-
awad as if he actually witnessed it:

> previous to his[Walker's] departure from Guzerat he received the most affect-
> ing compliment which a good man could receive, in being welcomed at the gate
> of the palace, on some public occasion, by a procession of girls of high rank, who
> owed their lives to him and who came to kiss his clothes and throw wreaths of
> flowers over him as their deliverer and second father. (1828, chapter xxiv)

Walker continued to keep an eye of reforms from London even when he retired till
1819, through his communications and memorandums because, "I have never been
able to divest myself of care and solicitude for those interests which I left behind me
in India [female infanticide]" (Memorandum of Colonel Walker, July 19, 1819, *Selections* [1856]). The East India Company Court of Directors, as Cave Brown puts it,
"more than once declared their approval and appreciation of his philanthropic zeal; and
shortly after, they still more publicly and substantially recognised his services in India
by appointing him Governor of St. Helena" (1857, 37–38).

3. J. P. Willoughby served as Political Agent of Kathiawar from 1833 to 1835
and was one of the most active agents of the Company and became known amongst
administrators all over India for his strict enforcement of anti-infanticide engagements
amongst the Jharejas. As a reward for his efforts in Kathiawar, he was transferred to
the seat of government of the Presidency of Gujarat in Bombay in 1835. In Bombay
he continued to oversee infanticide reform first as Political Secretary to Government,
then as Chief Secretary; and finally as Member of Council. In effect he continued for
a period of 12 years to be the prime reviewer and director at the seat of authority of all
the anti-infanticide measures followed by the British Government in Kathiawar.

4. For example the Government's letter acknowledging Jacob's 1840–1841
census compared the total number of Jhareja females preserved to the total number
saved in Willoughby's 1834 census and noted their pleasure in the growth in the
female population "an increase of 674 in less than seven years" (Wilson 1855, 274);
Malet's 1843 census was compared to three census of his predecessors including
Willoughby's census of 1834 in order to raise doubts about the disproportion in male
and female births. Perhaps the above instances are partially explained by the fact that
at the time Jacob's 1840 and Malet's 1843 census was submitted, Willoughby himself
was directing infanticide reform in Kathiawar from the Gujarat Presidency in Bombay.
However it is no accident that Lang's 1849 census, which claimed that infanticide had
become extinct in the province of Kathiawar, was noted by the Secretary to the Government of Bombay in the following words, "The foregoing results, I am desired to
remark, are most satisfactory, and show the efficacy and suitableness of the measures
adopted by Government in 1834, at the recommendation of the Hon'ble Mr.
Willoughby" (Letter to Captain Lang, 22 April, 1851, Wilson 1855, 345).

5. The success of the company's infanticide reform efforts in Kathiawar from
1808 to 1833 were established on the basis of informal census-type estimates, which
could scarcely be relied upon. These included four years (1829 to 1833) when there was
no census-type estimates recorded at all in the *Selections from the Records of the Bombay
Government* nos. 39–40, 1856.

6. Willoughby's progressivist history of infanticide reform in Kathiawar has to be appreciated in the context of two texts. The first text is provided by the Bombay Government dispatch of 1816 in reply to Captain Carnac's report on infanticide matters in Kathiawar. The dispatch notes, "Had the annual reports required by the instructions of Government of the 31st of March 1808 been regularly attended to, the chieftains would have observed a continued anxiety on the part of the British Government to enforce the engagements they had contracted" (Wilson 1855, 99). The second text is provided by Colonel James Walker, who in 1819 was living in England, and on receipt from the East India Company offices of all dispatches from Bombay regarding infanticide matters in Kathiawar began his second letter of 27th August 1819, with the acknowledgment that British efforts to suppress female infanticide had flagged in the intervening decade. He writes, "I have found it impossible to suppress the conclusion, that the subject had either been forgotten for years together, or that some impressions and uncontrollable circumstances had rendered our interference utterly impracticable" (Wilson 1855, 117).

7. The 1901 census notes "the neglect of females which is acknowledged as replacing outright infanticide." We agree with Barbara Miller that the censuses in the 1881 to 1901 period erase female infanticide as an explanation for the imbalance in the sex ratio (1981, 65–67). Miller notes that the new acceptable explanation for an imbalanced sex ratio is child marriage. Miller rejects this explanation as implausible. We argue that this new explanation by census analysts manifests the new discursive conjuncture at the end of the nineteenth century between the colonialists and the nationalists, within which female infanticide is shifted under the sign system of marriage reform. See Alice Clark (1989) for a text of this conjuncture in the case of the infanticidal Lewa Kanbi Patidars of Central Gujarat.

8. We draw the readers' attention to the parallel in the post-Emergency period. Once the making of political capital out of sterilization drives by the Congress (I) was rejected by the people through an electoral defeat of the party, two things happened. First, instead of open coercion in the Sanjay Gandhi style, mass sterilizations were done quietly and the issue was removed from public political rhetoric. Whatever the political party in power, the nation state and its policy makers as well as the medical establishment continued to implement the neocolonial Malthusian population discourse. Second, the new subjects of sterilization became woman specially the poor, uneducated women. See our discussion of the 1970s in chapter 1.

9. In the census of 1837 the sex ratios in the various talooks were as disproportionate, they ranged from 547.1 (five males for every female) in Murvi to 236.4 (more than two males for every female) in Dherol.

10. The same problem occurs in Willoughby's 1834 census when it comes to female mortality in general. In 12 of the 28 districts only one or two female children are reported, and in two districts, Veerwa (two males) and Shapoor (93 males) not a single female is on record. Willoughby recounts as a positive achievement of his regime the fact that in nine districts, not a single death of a young female is reported. But a closer look at the figures shows that the number of females in these districts mostly ranged from one to two, and in only two cases were more than two females recorded (six females in Mcngnee and ten in Veerpoor).

11. In 1837 Erskine informed the government that Munshi Gulam Mahommad who had been selected by Willoughby as official censor, had been accused of taking a bribe of Rupees 50/- to hide the murder of a daughter of a Mallia Jahreja. The Munshi admitted to taking the bribe as well as other presents from the Chief of Mallia and so was suspended by Erskine and as a result Erskine wrote, "the census is therefore in a state of abeyance" (Pakrasi 1970, 169). There ensues a gap of four years in census operations in the *Selection of the Records of the Bombay Government* nos. 39–40, 1856.

12. See chapter 1 footnote 19; also see Deepa Dhanraj's documentary film *Something like a War* 1991.

13. The native official who served as the censor and on whom so much of the data collection of the census depended upon, is described in a report by the Political Agent of Kutch, LeGrand Jacob in 1853: "the censors, who went about more as wandering fakirs than accredited servants of Government" (Wilson 1855, 388).

14. While the Jharejas of Kathiawar had been under anti-infanticide engagements to the British since 1808, the Jharejas of Kutch entered into a treaty that included the anti-infanticide provision only in 1820, as part of the treaty signed with the Rao of Kutch whose ascendancy to the throne was engineered with the help of British troops and in whose Regency Council the British Resident had served as president during the minority of the present chief. Therefore while Kutch was a tributary of the British, the Company recognized the sovereignty of the Rao of Kutch.

15. In the census of 1850 there were 193 Jhareja male deaths but only 103 female deaths, in 1851 there were 134 males and 58 females, in 1852 there were 147 males and 90 females, in 1853 there were 158 males and 118 female deaths reported and in the last census recorded in the *Sourcebook,* the census of 1854, there were 190 male and 108 female deaths reported.

16. For instance Lang, the Chief Secretary to Government of Bombay, wrote in his report of 1846 about the "many inaccuracies" in the 1845 census returns:

> the proportion of births of both sexes to the number of married Jharejas appears, generally, to be exceedingly small, and in Veerpoor Khureree, and several of the smaller Talookas, there is not a single birth of either a male or female child during the year under review. The number of grown-up Jharejas in Veerpoor Khureree . . . is sixty-five, and . . . 44 of these are married. It is exceedingly improbable, therefore, that a year should have passed without a single child having been born to any of these . . . there must be some concealment of births that actually take place. (Pakrasi 1970, 225)

17. The number Jhareja infants born in 1847 were 192 female infants and 217 males, but there is an increase of 350 females and 243 males through new arrivals; in the 1850 census there were 267 female infants born in comparison to 292 male infants, and there was an increase of 186 female Jharejas and 149 male Jharejas; in 1852, 180 female infants and 214 male and were born and there was an increase of 88 females and 80 males through new arrivals; in 1853 there were 258 female births and 264 males and an increase of 23 females and 28 males in new arrivals; in 1854, 266 male and 208 female infants were born and there were 111 male and 50 female new arrivals.

18. Our analysis of the Baee Nathee case is, in a sense, a tribute to Ranajit Guha's essay on the tribal woman "Chandra's death," 1997.

19. We present three texts from colonial-reform documents that bear this out. The first text is provided in Walker's report to the Government where he records that the Chief of Rajkot Suraji's father Dadajee, informed him that the mother's wish to preserve her new born daughter "was always subjected to the wish of the husband and/or husband's elderly consangunines and husband's mother" (Report by Walker, 15 March, 1808, *Hindoo Widows* 2, Part II, 31). The second text is Erskine's 1834 report where he informs the Bombay government that it was rumored that the chief informer in the Suraji case, Jhareja Moorjee of the Rajkot clan, had been poisoned by Suraji's mother herself. Pakrasi notes as a postscript that Suraji's mother was later imprisoned for her crime (1970, 121–122). The last text comes from British Resident of Kutch, Pottinger's 1825 letter. He states, "No people appear to have so through a contempt for women, and yet, strange to say, we often see the" dowagers" of households taking the lead in both public and private matters amongst them" (Wilson 1855, 285).

20. Suraji's father had served as a British ally and informer. He had offered the British cantonment facilities in Rajkot (where the headquarters of the Company's Infanticide Agency was situated) when other Jhareja chiefs like the Jam of Nowanugger and Chief of Murvi had refused. He was the first to sign an infanticide engagement with Walker and had preserved a daughter to prove his fidelity to the engagement. In 1826, after the death of his father, "in gratitude" the acting political agent recommended that Suraji be given a loan of Rupees 12, 000 to relieve him of the debts incurred in the marriage of his sister. A similar sum was advanced to Suraji from the Infanticide Fund for the purposes of his own marriage. Ironically Willoughby fined Suraji the identical sum of Rupees 12,000 for his infringement of the infanticide engagement (Wilson 1855, 165).

21. The colonial history of female infanticide written by Cave Brown (1857) shows this bias. The last chapter of his book is devoted to the suppression of infanticide among the "aborigines" tribes of the Khonds of Orissa. Like all colonial writers on the subject, Cave Brown begins by ascribing the origin of female infanticide to a religious legend of the first man Boora and his consort Thari. He imputes the continuation of the practice to "more ordinary work-a-day motives " such as "claims of their purses" (209) and the character of Khond women. Cave Brown takes Tod's "pride and purse" argument a step further by attributing female infanticide amongst the Khonds not to the expensive dowries required for a Rajput daughter's marriage, but to the custom of bride price marriages amongst the tribals. At the same time he is surprised to note that amongst the Khond "their[women's] influence and privileges are very great in public as well as private affairs" (210). He attributes this "remarkable" high status of women among the Khonds not to the women cherishing customs of tribal community, but to the scarcity of women, "The paucity of women renders them the more valuable, and therefore they are not to be obtained in marriage without the payment of a very large sum" (210). Cave Brown completes the picture of the immoral tribal woman by characterizing the freedom of Khond women to marry any man they wish and to leave a marriage as, "in married life their privileges and immunities are preposterous" (210). He underscores this by designating the morals and marriages of Khond women as "most lax" because they have the right to

elopement and divorce, "she may transfer her affections as often as the whim takes her. Few women remain constant; it is no merit to do so" (210).

22. In the Suraji case we see how class and caste operate in the case of midwives. The midwife Ratanbai in the 1834 Suraji case was the wife of a mehta and a friend of Suraji's wife Jethee, so although she executed infant murder at the behest of the wife, she disclaimed all knowledge and stated that she came too late to see the murder. Instead it was the slave girl who became the informer, as she is lower down in the hierarchy of servants. In the Baee Nathee case the midwife Baee Hoora is a tribal woman as well as a widow, therefore she is easily coerced into becoming an informer.

23. In Suraji's trial a slave girl reported that the child was put to death at birth by suffocation and immediately carried away from the room where the mother lay crying (Wilson 1855, 203).

24. The midwife, Baee Hoora is forced to become informer in the Baee Nathee case but she protects herself from colonial law by stating that she herself has three daughters (2nd deposition, November 1853) and was willing to adopt one of the female infants of Baee Nathee (1st deposition, May 1853). This account not only militates against the colonial construction of tribal women as immoral and nonmaternal, it shows the heterogeneity of daughter cherishing customs in tribal families, which is erased in the colonial census and documentation of the tribe.

25. In the colonial documents the irrecoverable victim, the newborn female infant is spoken for by the benevolent British reformer. The rhetorical device by which the East India Company officials represent the subject position of the murdered female infant is ventriloquism. The colonial text ventriloquizes in set pieces like the following:

> How affecting it must have been for him [Alexander Walker] to hear, as he actually did at Dharoal, the tender Rajpoot daughter rescued from the murderous hand of the parental destroyer, exclaim with infantile voice, 'Colonel Walker saved me!' (Heber 1855, 92)

> A common form of speech by a native of Banaras, who desires to say something flattering to a European, is, 'I your slave,—you my god, my father and mother, my Duncan.' (Erskine Perry, *Bird's eye-View of India* 1857, 229)

Notice that the two anecdotes ventriloquize the murdered infant through the grateful natives and the infanticide survivor who has been personally rescued by the British reformer. The ventriloquism is crafted into anecdotes that appear to have been passed down by word of mouth to the native populations, in a concerted attempt to create a folklore of British colonialism. The British reformer is remade into a folk-hero by relaying pictures of popular acclaim that are designed to be a part of everyday speech and popular memory.

Chapter 6. Subaltern Traditions of Resistance to Rajput Patriarchy Articulated by Generations of Women within the Meera Tradition

1. The concept of literature is not pregiven in the postcolonial context of the literatures of India. Rather than presuppose that we already know what is constituted

under the rubric of literature in the Indian context, we suggest that it is necessary to question how and in what way a literature exists as a theoretical object in the history of Indian literatures. Moreover, the cultural productions that come under the category of "Indian literatures" do not have a ready-made historical context by which readers can understand them, contexts that make these literatures intelligible in their own terms. Rather Indian literatures have to be examined in relation to their objective determinations by the development of the culture as a whole. The range of theoretical problems we negotiate with in writing about Meera in a historically and theoretically informed way can be gauged by Aijaz Ahmad's essay "'Indian Literature': Notes towards Definition of a Category" (1992). Ahmad explores the difficulties in constructing the category of Indian literature; he states that the problem of constructing a theory about Indian literatures is far greater "in historical epochs preceding the emergence of the bourgeois nation-state" (244). This chapter negotiates with the kind of difficulties that Ahmad outlines by a self-reflexive protocol of reading; as we execute the reading of Meera we name the particular theoretical issues that undepin each level of our interpretation. We also draw on the arguments of earlier chapters to illuminate Meera; we needed to write a cultural history of heterogenous Rajasthans, to critique British colonial and elite historiographical narratives about Rajasthan history, to re-examine the idiom of Rajputization and the subaltern traditions of dissent in order to provide the historical determinations for Meera's poetry of dissent.

2. Early Indian literature in all languages is almost exclusively in verse and concerned mainly with religious themes. The widespread use of prose for creative purposes follows the arrival of the Europeans into the subcontinent, and the very beginnings of prose cannot be traced back farther than the early decades of the nineteenth century. What is sometimes regarded as the first novel in an Indian language (Bengali) appeared in 1801 (see Asher 1980, viii). Poetry limns new horizons, and we can do no better than to quote two voices on the power of poetry, two voices that have themselves authored new narratives in our time. Jacques Lacan equates poetry with making love, "To make love (faire l'amour), as the very expression indicates, is poetry" (1998, 72). Luce Irigaray calls for a new poetics for a new ethics based on sexual difference. She writes that if sexual difference were to "constitute the horizon of worlds" there would be "the production of a new age of thought, art, poetry, and language: the creation of a new poetics" (1993, 5).

3. In a song recorded by Mukta (1994) sung by peasants in Junagadh district, Saurashtra, Meera's mother asks Meera, "Mira, why did you not come out as a stone from my womb?" (137) While Mukta notes that the question, "'why did you not come out as stone from my womb' can be heard today in many places," is a curse, she does not recognize in this curse of the mother the reference to female infanticide. A common method of killing the female infant was to put a stone in the mouth. Instead Mukta understands it as a mother's way of disciplining her daughter "in a tightly-knit society where the family is the bulwark of social and moral norms" (138).

4. There is much controversy concerning the historical details of Meera's life in the fifteenth–sixteenth century (see Bhati 1964, 18). Only two of her poems are to be found in seventeenth-century literature: one in the *Adi Granth,* and the other in Nabhadas' *Bhaktamal.* Given this lack of material it is worth noting that the particular

legends that are included or excluded, the versions of Meera's life that are chosen by each commentator depends on the theoretical-political agenda of the commentator. For example all commentators acknowledge that there is much confusion about who exactly Meera married. A commentator like Sangari (1990) whose interpretive grid is the elite nationalist paradigm of sati and the Hindu widow, like other commentators (Chaturvedi 1983; Jafri 1965; Sekhavat 1975) chooses to ascribe the majority of Meera's poetic creativity to the period of her widowhood. On the other hand Kishwar and Vanita who emphasize those elements of Meera's biography that lend themselves to women's religious creativity, suggest that in the context of this controversy, Meera may have been either widowed or separated (1989, 75).

5. Kishwar and Vanita (1989) refer to female infanticide in their biographical sketch of Meera, although they make of it only a passing reference within the overall context of the traditionally low status of women and low female sex ratios prevailing in Rajasthan even today. Sangari also only mentions "a high instance" of female infanticide in addition to polygamy and dowry among Rajputs "especially in the upper strata" (1990, 1466).

6. The lack of consistent dates and details of Meera's life, as well as the fact that her compositions cannot be authenticated with certainty, is treated differently by the scholars in Hindi literature as compared to the English-language translations and commentaries on Meera. For instance in his English language translation and commentary, Hawley acutely observes that the paucity of data on Meera's life is a function of her exclusion from the textual tradition of Bhakti which began in the seventeenth century, due to her gender as well as the bias against folk elements in her poetry. He speculates that either, "her poetry, which is definitely closer to the folk idiom than any other we have explored, was regarded as insufficiently 'poetic' to be preserved in writing" or "perhaps the large quantity of poetry now bearing Mira's signature grew up, in the course of time, as a response to the existence of her well-known legend" or even that "they must have been written by other 'Miras' than the original one." But this leads Hawley to conclude that a person like Meera may never have existed at all, "if ever indeed she existed at all" (1988, 122–123).

Although it is true that some Hindi language translators and commentators share Hawley's view (Tewari 1974, 86), others find these very folk elements in Meera's poetry enabling in the absence of verifiable dates, details, or compositions written by Meera. For example, even as Sekhavat acknowledges that the details of Meera's life and poetry are the subject of controversy because of the absence of anthologies of her poems, he writes, "Meera is a folk hero therefore the search for the real Meera must also be undertaken within the arena of the folk." For Sekhavat this arena of the folk includes folk myths, folk dialogues, folk poetry as well as Meera's own poetry, "within" all of which "Meera lives" (1975, 233). Interestingly many Hindi language commentators (Bhati 1964; Chaturvedi 1983; Jafri 1965; Sekhavat 1975) see Meera's taking to renunciation and devoting herself to bhakti of Krishna as in some measure caused by the various deaths in the family. For example Sekhavat notes that Meera's mother died in her infancy (when she was four or five); her paternal grandfather died when she came of marriageable age; after marriage her husband died; then in quick succession her father-in-law, father, and Meera's uncle (father's brother) died. In effect

Meera was a woman without support (244). It would be too easy to dismiss this as the patriarchal bias of male commentators. Instead we see this argument as part and parcel of their access to the folk legend of Meera where they see her as a real person and take account of the ravages of war that Rajput martial valor made its women suffer. We align ourselves theoretically to Sekhavat's position. However for the convenience of our non-Indian readers we choose to follow the general consensus that Meera was born in 1498 and died in 1546 (Shabnam 1976; Alston 1980; Kinsley 1981; Kishwar and Vanita 1989).

7. We don't employ the Bhakti paradigm in our interpretation of Meera, although we do validate the bardic use of religious parable to convey social critique in our forthcoming article in *Subaltern Studies,* vol. xii, "A Poetics of Resistance: Investigating the Rhetoric of the Bardic Historians of Rajasthan." Therefore it is not that we do not respect the key texts of the Bhakti movements. We honor postcolonial reevaluations of the Bhakti movements as social rather than religious movements, as primarily artisanal and peasant modes of organization for social justice, and as articulating a secular and assimilative approach to the co-existence of communities belonging to different religious faiths (see Thapar 1966, 305, 307–308; Mukta 1994, 20, 31–32, 72, 88, 211–223; Lele 1981, and recent work on Kabir). Nevertheless we mark our distance from male-defined social-religious and literary movements, which can occlude rather than illuminate Meera's poetry. The reason that the Bhakti movements have been identified with male poets, followers, and critics is that the Bhakti traditions generated canonical critical approaches in vernacular literatures and the English language. We reject the history of the canonical reception of the Bhakti poets, not the Bhakti poets, movements and followers of these poets.

The traditional canonical location of Meera in the male canon of Bhakti poets measures a woman poet against a standard that is geared for male poets, designed by men and does her a disservice (for an English language version of this see Sangari 1990). Instead we prise apart Meera's poetry from the Bhakti literary canon and see her in her own terms. By doing so we reject Kishwar and Vanita's notion that there is no tradition out of which Meera emerges and there are no female poetic and critical voices before her (1989, 77). Contrarily we argue that the tradition of women's creativity is a more inclusive term in which to situate Meera's creativity. Rather than force her into a narrow, domesticated and male-identified definition of literary or religious creativity we recover the sharpness and difference of Meera's insights and her distinctive female voice. By enlarging Meera's frame of reference and her maternal ancestors, we discover that Meera does belong to and draws from rich and vital traditions of women's creativity in women's traditional role as ecoconservationists, as genetic bankers, as nurturers and transmitters of traditional knowledges.

8. There is no inconsistency in our validation of the bardic use of religious parable to convey their social critique in our forthcoming article in *Subaltern Studies* on the bhats and charans of Rajasthan, and our refusal to see Meera in the Bhakti tradition. We wrest from the canonical approaches to Bhakti, Meera's description of what women's religion means to them (also see our article in *boundary 2,* vol. 31, no. 3, fall 2004, "Meera's medieval lyric poetry in postcolonial India: The rhetorics of women's writing in dialect as a secular practice of subaltern co-authorship and dissent"). We

are by no means supportive of all shades of Hindu religion. We reject Brahmanical Hinduism and nowhere in the book do we endorse it, we reject Rashtriya Sevak Sangh's brand of Hinduvta and the accompanying suggestion that female infanticide was caused by the Muslim invasion of a pure Hindu culture and Hindu fathers' attempt to protect their daughters from the lust of Muslim men by the desperate measure of killing them at birth. We see Hindu religion as plural, dynamically oral rather than text-based, and a flexible medium for social critique. We also make a distinction between the male appropriations of the figures of Shiva (Shaivism) and Krishna (Vaishnavism) and the specifically female interpretation and significance that Meera invests in the figure of Krishna. The reader does not have to be a worshipper of Krishna in order to understand what Meera is doing through the figure of Krishna. We are however implicitly drawing a clear distinction between the marginalization of women's ecofeminist traditions and resistances and the marginalization of indigenous bardic modes of resistance and social critique. The two are not identical. Nevertheless it will be clear to the reader that we are suggesting that there are parallels and that there is a dialogue between the two marginalized traditions in our configuring of the popular.

9. In our focus on Meera as the putative social text of patriarchal critique, we align ourselves with Mukta (1994) and mark our distance from Sangari (1990). Kumkum Sangari's Meera is determined firstly, by her view of Meera through the Bhakti perspective as an "exceptional woman" (1472; in this she follows both Kishwar and Vanita 1989 and Thapar 1966); second, by the privileging of elite decodings of Meera's life and verse (see Mukta's critique 1994, 32, 34); third, by comparison of Meera's bhakti and resistance with a male bhakta like Kabir. Not surprisingly, Sangari's Meera comes off looking like a status quoist. For example Sangari addresses the question of Meera's critique of patriarchy thus:

> The degree of 'real' choice available to Mira is unclear . . . Mira may have chosen to break the feudal relation, she may have been forced to break with it or she may even have felt herself broken by it. Yet if the feudal relation crumbles in her personal practice, in some ways her songs recover it both figuratively and as ideality and so recompose its everpresent 'necessity' as choice. . . . The relation of the female subject to the feudal polity, resisted in practice, is remade in metaphor. (1468)

Notice that in the above extract Sangari poses the question in the western-educated feminist vocabulary of "choice," at the same time she condemns Meera for articulating her critique of patriarchy in the personal, feudal-patriarchal vocabulary of medieval Bhakti of her own time (for a dissenting view see Kishwar and Vanita 1989, 77, and Mukta 1994). Sangari's argument does not pay enough attention to some of her own insights regarding how Meera's verses map ex-centric desire, such as: "she (Meera) constitutes herself as a defiant self-describing subject of Krishna . . . in some ways more a boldly attractive courtesan than a dutiful wife, more immoral than moral" (1472); and, "The spiritual economy of Mira's bhakti may in many ways be homologous with the domestic and political economy of the Rajput state but it is structured as 'uncontainable,' as excessive" (1473). Furthermore the popularity of Meera songs in the feudal-patriarchal vocabulary of medieval bhakti militates against any interpretation of them as conforming to the status quo. Instead their popularity suggests that their interpretations change to reflect the new situation rather than the medieval world. Meera songs are dynamic and ever-changing, as Mukta's field research shows in the folk versions that are in existence and are coming into circulation constantly. The songs are dynamic and ever-changing as the network of social relations that encompasses Meera singers, and their meaning mediates the changes.

10. When Chaturvedi (1983) visited Chittor fort and Udiapur, he was told that Meera was not respected amongst the Rajputs there (cited in Kishwar and Vanita 1989, 92). Mukta tells the story of Chothuji Bhat, an itinerant singer, who was shouted out of a Sisodiya village when he sang a song of Meera; and of Rajput women who will not name their daughters Meera (1989, 95).

11. Parita Mukta's (1994) excellent field work on the subaltern appropriations and creations of Meera's poetry broke the mold of Meera scholarship in the English language. Mukta's work discredited the analysis of Kinsley (1981), Desai (1984), Sangari (1990), and Harlan (1992) by pointing out that there was a subaltern Meera that the above elite interpretations simply did not engage with, for the simple reason that they did not know or care about subaltern classes. We have great respect for the rich source material that Mukta culled in her field work. We also respect Mukta's insistence on the subalternity of the folk, peasant and dalit Meera traditions. Where we depart from Mukta is in her implicit theory of the popular. Mukta's work draws on the elite/subaltern distinction made by Subaltern Studies historians, in this context her pioneering field work lacks a theory of how distinct subaltern groups read the oral performative text, in effect how the members of each group sing, decode, create and interpellate themselves into the Meera song. As a result Mukta narrates and transcribes more than analyzes, consequently the transcribed subaltern text is rendered as a transparent and self-evident text.

In our view Mukta's elite/subaltern distinction needs to be complicated in writing women's cultural history. Mukta explicitly disavows a gendered analysis of the subalterns' Meera, she writes, " the figure of Mira was placed within a subordinated feminized domestic sphere, and Mira's lauded skill in turn was aligned to feminine creativity. This was reduced to one which lacked sophistication or craft, and which was an uncomplicated outpouring of the heart" (29). While Mukta acknowledges that the gendered analysis of Meera gave impetus to the growth of vernacular literature and female creativity, nevertheless she condemns this gendered analysis as a nineteenth- and twentieth-century middle-class domestication of Meera, "The emphasis on Mira as a woman possessed of a pure and simple heart, and the emphasis on a linear progression in history, at one and the same time individualized the figure of Mira, by placing her in the tradition of lone creators—and it granted Mira a constituency only among women confined to the domestic sphere" (italics ours, 29–30).

So while Mukta includes female bhaktas' interpretations and sex-segregated bhajan mandalis, Mukta's approach to the specificity of women's Meera is twofold: first she seems to accept the dalit women's Meera only in so far as the dalit women's oppression coincides with the oppression of the male dalit bhakta; second, she is uneasy about the middle class domestications of Meera by aligning Meera to feminine creativity. Thus Mukta's implicit theory of the popular is gender blind. Women of subaltern classes are acceptable interpreters-creators of Meera because they are just like men of subaltern classes, they share in dalit men's oppression. But middle-class women are despised because the specific oppressions of middle-class women are unexamined by Mukta. Therefore she sees these middle-class women's interpretive-creative traditions as lacking political vigor and lacking the potential for resistance to patriarchal domination. Mukta classifies the latter as the isolating and depoliticizing of Meera by seeing her in terms of "feminine creativity" (29). Mukta is rightly critical of the canonical approaches to Meera as "individualized" (29) and "confined to a domestic sphere" (30). However we depart from Mukta both in our theory of the popular, that is in our acceptance of the middle class Meera, and in our refusal to see the question of female creativity as an entirely bourgeois preoccupation.

12. A pada ascribed to Meera records her noninstitutional status as well as her lack of status in Rajput patriarchy because she did not give birth to sons:

Nam rahego kam se suno sayane log
Meera sut jayo nahin shishya na mudoyo koy.
One's name will live on through one's work, consider this if you are wise;
Meera did not give birth to a son nor did she have any disciples.
(Sekhavat, 1974, 242)

13. Lacan re-reads Poe's story of the letter as "the itinerary of a signifier" (1956, 40), which illustrates the function of Freudian repetition compulsion. He says, "the displacement of the signifier determines the subjects in their acts, in their destiny, in their refusals, their blind spots, their end and fate, their innate gifts and social acquisitions" (60). In an analogous way, we are the beneficiaries of all the "other" Meeras (to borrow Hawley's phrase) that came before us, and just as the displacement of the signifying chain has revealed to us our indebtedness to them, so we hope that all the Meeras to come will reveal to us our refusals, blind spots as well as our gifts, and keep alive the tradition. For Lacan's take on Poe's "The Purloined Letter" see Mehlman 1972; Benvenuto and Kennedy 1986.

14. French feminists began the exploration of the question of feminine ecriture in the late 1970s and have given us some of the most evocative theoretical formulations about women writing about and for women. Helene Cixous (1976) demands that "woman must write woman" (877) because, "Everything will be changed once woman gives woman to the other woman. . . . It is necessary and sufficient that the best of herself be given to woman by another woman for her to be able to love herself and return in love the body that was 'born' to her" (881). Luce Irigaray (1996) also imagines this possibility of establishing love amongst women "for the feminine" through women "double(ing) and play(ing) what we are twice over, lovingly" and thereby fostering the love of the body, "both of that body we give and of that body we give each other back in return" (103). She elaborates this doubling in terms of the need of women for their own language and the ethical consequences of not having gendered speech, "Because women have no language sexed as female, they are used in the elaboration of a so-called neuter language where in fact they are deprived of speech . . . this situation might be analyzed as the female remaining in the plant world without any chance of creating an animal territory for herself. The female world would be paralyzed in its ethical development" (107).

15. It is clear that in defining our position on women's relation to religion, we are operating with an implicit definition of the popular in this book. Our interest is in the dispossessed and marginalized sections of the popular, which include lower caste migrant men and women, folk artists, storytellers, and indigenous historians, itinerant singers and performers. But unlike Mukta (1994) who rejects all lower middle class, urban, vulgar, Bollywood inspired commercial populist versions of the popular and distinguishes these strands from the authentic, rural, noncommercial, politically radical strands of the popular, we do not subscribe to the authentic/inauthentic binary about popular culture, just as we do not subscribe to the debate about the authentic/inauthentic Meera verses. Our focus on the bardic and the ecofeminist has more to do with the lacunae in postcolonial feminist scholarship in the area of women, religion, and popular modes of resistance than with the privileging of the bardic and the folk strands on the grounds of their authenticity. Therefore we select our songs from bardic as well as from Bollywood films, audio cassettes and compact discs of Meera bhajans arranged by both popular singers as well as classical singers, compilations of Meera bhajans by various authors, etc.

16. See Jafri for a similar view on Rekhta (1965, 28). Jafri remarks that Meera's compositions are distinguished by the fact that there is rhythm and appropriateness in them because she was trained in music and dance (29). Chaturvedi (1983) notes that all of Meera's compositions are set to raagas and raaginis (29).

17. Niranjan Bhagat cited in "Mirabai" *Women Writing In India* (Vol. I, 1991, 91). Also see Sekhavat (1974) for a similar view of Meera's language through graphing Meera's life and travels (246–247).

18. Mukta shows that the Meera tradition is an unbroken tradition amongst the peasant, agricultural workers, and dalits in Rajasthan and Saurashtra who sing her songs (1994, 12). In the cities amongst the lower middle-class and the middle-class, the Meera tradition has occasionally been disrupted and had to exist alongside other woman-centered cults like the Santoshi Ma cult whose irruption was occasioned by a B grade movie, *Jai Santoshi Maa* (1975), which became the biggest hit of the year. For a fine analysis of the movie and the cult see Das (1980, 1988). The Vaishno Devi cult is an especially popular cult in the urban centers of north India and each year many thousands visit the Vaishno Devi shrine in Jammu.

Just as there is a cinematic genre in Hollywood of Frankestein films and new interpretations of Dracula, so there is a continuist history of the cinematic genre of Meera films in Bollywood. The Bombay film industry, as Meera commentators have noted (Harlan 1992, 214, note 15; Mukta 1994, 205) is a major source of information about the legend of Meera, and films on Meera have been made since the 1930's in all languages in India: in the silent era Kanjibhai Rathod's version of *Meerabai* (1921); in Tamil Sriram's *Meera* (1922), and Narayanan and Naicker's *Meerabai* (1936); Ellis Duncan made *Meera* (1945) in Tamil/Hindi with the famous south Indian classical singer M. S. Subbulakshmi in the title role; the only Telegu film on Meera was made by B. N. Rao (1940); in Hindi they began with Ramnik Desai's *Meerabai* (1921), then came *Rajrani Meera* with K. L. Saigal in Bengali (1933), and its Hindi version (1945). Other films on Meera were made in Hindi and its dialects in (1940), in Gujarati by Nanabhai Bhat (1947), by Kidar Sharma (1960), in 1976, then by Gulzar (1979), as well as in 1992 and 1995.

19. There are many different English translations of Meera's poems and songs. See S. M. Pandey and Norman H. Zide (1964); Hermann Goetz (1966); Pritish Nandy (1975); A. J. Alston (1980); J. S. Hawley and Mark Juergensmeyer (1988); and Madhu Kishwar and Ruth Vanita (1989).

20. Stories about male bhaktas abandoning their wife and children for a life of contemplation abound in popular memory. The wife of Sant Tukaram of Maharashtra was reputed to have starved to death because of lack of food. The bhakta Narsinha Mehta of Gujarat was believed to have rejoiced at the death of his wife and only son. Mahaprabhu Chaitanya, the famous Vaishnav bhakta-composer from Bengal, is reputed to have married twice and abandoned his second wife and mother to their fate. Also see Mukta (1994) 116–117.

21. See Thapar's "Renunciation: The Making of a Counter-culture?" (1978) as well as her "Householders and renouncers in the Brahmanical and Buddhist traditions" (1982); also see Tambiah's "The renouncer: his individuality and his community" (1982). The difficulties commentators face in accounting for the paradox of Meera's claim to renunciation and claim to suhaagan or married woman status can be guaged by the arguments made by Harlan (1992), Kishwar and Vanita (1989) and Sangari (1990). Harlan argues that by taking up renunciation, "Mira acts like a man" (217), in effect Harlan contends that by taking up renunciation Meera is a woman acting as a man, nevertheless susceptible to the problems women face everywhere. Harlan approaches the conundrum a second way by opposing the pativrata or the ideology that a woman's salvation lies in devoting herself to her husband, with the bhakt-yogi. (222). Harlan's argument is a familiar one, made by Thapar (1966), Kishwar and Vanita (1989) as well as Sangari (1990), viz., by taking recourse to the untheorized concept of the extraordinary woman, they explain away Meera's resistance as the priveledge of a high-born charismatic woman who is able to reconcile the home and the forest. Kishwar and Vanita (1989) pose the question, why did Meera not become a symbol for any self-respect movement amongst women? Their answer is threefold: by repudiating the marital role assigned by society, "Mira gives up much that is very attractive" to ordinary women (91); the ideology of pativrata "comes into active conflict with the ideology of bhakti when the bhakta is a woman" (91); and finally, "Once out of the house, Mira is effectively out of her community" (92). At the core of Kishwar and Vanita's explanation is the untheorized opposition between the renunciator and the suhaagan or pativrata. We see Kishwar and Vanita's portrayal of the conflict between pativrarta and bhakta as reductive and patronizing of the ordinary women's understanding of Meera. We contend that Meera is a renouncer/fakir-suhaagin/pativrata and common people have no trouble understanding her as such (see Mukta 1994). On the question of renunciation Sangari finds that, "in order to do so she (Meera) affirms at figurative and metaphysical levels, some of the structured relations of collective power and some of the very principles of inequality which underlie these systems . . . carry(ing) them well beyond their ascriptive function into the figurative-metaphysical domain . . . governed by faith" (1990, 1469). Sangari's elitist bias does not allow her to see that Meera's adoption of renunciation cannot be seen in the same way as the renunciation of a male bhakta. In contrast we offer an ecofeminist reading of Meera, which recalls and validates women's indigenous traditions of identification and reciprocity with nature,

within which the forest and the household are not irreconciliable opposites. Traditional knowledges survive within which women have learnt how to live at home and in society as a fakir/renouncer, and to dwell in the forest as a suhaagan/pativrata. It is precisely through the adjacency of Meera's code of renunciation and her code of fakiri or mendicancy (the subject of chapter 7) that Meera affirms and aligns herself to the ecoreciprocity of a life of poverty. This mix of renunciation, householder, and ecoreciprocity has been lived by the poor, the dispossessed, the subaltern and dalits all over India for centuries.

22. Kinsley (1981) makes the argument that women saints like Meera exemplify the tension between Bhakti and dharma where their traditional marriages became irreconcilable with their devotion and love for God. Kinsley's Bhakti perspective allows him to come close to our position that Meera articulates her relationship to God as an alternative form of marriage, "devotion to God becomes an alternative to marriage (or an alternative form of marriage), a way of resolving an otherwise impossible situation" (83). However, taking the Bhakti route also leads him to conclude that the irreconciliability of the two is a result of individual "unworthy" men or relatives (92). Kinsley's argument is the complete obverse of our argument that Meera's alternative form of marriage to God is a trenchant critique of Rajput patriarchy.

23. By and large English language commentaries on Meera neither notice nor comment on the use of women's folk genres in her songs. We contend that this oversight issues from the fact that these commentaries privilege the Bhakti mode in which implicitly, Meera's popular songs are compared to the poetry of Kabir, Surdas, or Tulsidas and found wanting in terms of complication of thought and expression. The privileging of Bhakti perspective elides and erases the significance of the feminist rhetorical mode of address in Meera songs. The only exception is J. S. Hawley. Hawley notes this "particularly pronounced" aspect of Meera's poetry, which allows for what he calls an "osmosis" between her poetry and folk poetry of Rajasthan and Gujarat, etc. He observes that this aspect of Meera's poetry is "easy to understand" given the absence of institutional authority around her, yet he displays condescension by characterizing these genres as simplistic. He describes Meera's songs by equating women's songs with simplicity and repetition (1988, 129–130).

24. One of the most moving non-Meera *bidaai* folksongs was made famous by the 1930–1940s singing star, Kundanlal Saigal. *"Babul mora naihar chhooto jai"* from the 1938 film *Street Singer* and has been justly called by Rajyadhaksa and Willamen, "Saigal's all time hit" (1999, 277). Interestingly Saigal had earlier starred in the Hindi/Bengali version of Meera called *Rajrani Meera* (1933). *"Babul mora"* has also been rendered in raag Bhairavi, in the north Indian classical vocal tradition by Girija Devi (1995).

25. Many commentators have noted Meera's conspicuous use of the female form of address in a number of her songs (Kishwar and Vanita 1989, 77, 88). However they do not see it as a characteristic feature of feminine ecriture. Instead they ascribe it to the legend that Meera composed and tried out her songs on her female servant and companion, Lalita.

26. Manu designates women and dalits to the same ritually low status because of sins committed in a previous birth. Both are barred from religious ritual activity such

as the performance of austerities and pilgrimages. They are also barred from taking up renunciation or the fourth and last stage of a householder's life (*Manusmriti*, 133–135, 232–233). The Puranas designate women as maya or illusion and as obstacles in the path of salvation, and advise men to shun them (*Bhagwat Purana*, vol. 5, 1948–1949). Therefore, human beings who have the misfortune of being born a woman or a untouchable can only attain salvation through the performance of her/his duty and service of husband/master as well as brahmins (*Vishnu Purana*, 487–493).

27. Harlan (1992) reports that her upper class Rajasthani women subjects were astute enough to "combine ascetic and bridal imagery in describing Meera" (218). See Harlan's reporting of the complicated way Meera is understood by upper class Rajasthani women surveyed by her (205, 208–209, 211, 218, 220–221 and 222). This is in complete contrast to Kishwar and Vanita's reading where they designate all of Meera's references to *"suhaag"* or marks of a married woman such as jewelry, filling the parting of hair with vermilion and color of clothes as "symbol of delusion and maya" (1989, 86–87). For a slightly different folk version of this particular Meera song see Mukta (1994, 94).

28. Sangari makes an argument concerning Meera's marriage with Krishna that bears examination. At the conclusion of the Meera section of her two-part article on "Mirabai and the Spiritual Economy of Bhakti," Sangari draws a parallel between Meera's enshrining of Krishna in her heart and the "new substantive definition and centrality of the man" as the "'center' of all activity and desire." In other words, Sangari suggests that, "even as god is internalised it becomes possible to internalise specific patriarchal relations—both can be transformed into seemingly 'unmediated' essences and experiences which appear to bypass social institutions" (1990, 1474). Sangari's argument particularizes Meera's approach as internalizing man and thereby patriarchal relations when the same can be said about a male bhakta like Kabir (the focus of part 2 of Sangari's article) or indeed about the Bhakti movements as a whole. But if we do not dismiss Sangari's argument as an anachronistic objection to the feudal-patriarchal vocabulary of medieval Bhakti rather than to Meera per se, and instead take seriously her argument, it would seem that in making her argument Sangari moves too quickly from the idea of Meera's internalization of the figure of Krishna to the internalization of patriarchal relations. She does not take cognizance of the intermediate step where Meera herself takes control of the definition and description of her marriage relationship to Krishna for the simple reason that no one has seen or heard from Krishna himself. Therefore, Meera's marriage to Krishna is her own imaginative creation. It is our recognition of Meera as the sole interpreter of her marriage to Krishna that allows us to see that Meera invests her marriage to Krishna with an eroticism, sensuality, and spirituality that is the realm, in the Lacanian sense, of the "imaginary" and not the "real" of the relationship between the sexes. See Neera Desai (1983, 97–99) for an argument similar to Sangari.

29. It is in the early writings of Marx that we find significant formulations about alienation in the context of Marx's critique of Feuerbach, he says "Every self-estrangement of man from himself and nature is manifested in the relationship he sets up between other men and himself and nature" (*First Manuscript, Economic and Philosophical Manuscripts in Karl Marx: Early Writings* 1975, 331).

30. We make alliances with the French feminist articulation of the mystic as exemplified by Luce Irigaray in *An Ethics of Sexual Difference* (1993). She makes the historically informed argument that women's ancient traffic with knowledge and the divine, as healers and custodians of knowlege about nature, was violently erased in the West through naming the woman healer a witch (114). Irigaray's French feminist understanding of the capacity of women for mysticism comes close to our own ecofeminist understanding of author as Meera.

31. In folk-love legends the chakora is said to yearn for the moon and remain thirsty until the moon rises, then the mythical bird drinks the water, which falls when the moon is in the Swati constellation.

32. Meera's poetic reference to weaving and jewelry-making is grounded in material realities; Rajasthan has long-standing and distinguished traditions dating back to medieval times of artisanal communities of weavers, gem cutters, and jewelry makers.

33. Michael T. Taussig in *The Devil and Commodity Fetishism in South America* (1980) suggests that the devil was brought by European imperialism to the New World where the devil blended with pagan deities. He critically comments on the way in which the proletarianized plantation workers in Western Columbia and miners in the Bolivian tin mines deploy the devil figure to understand their structural location within capitalist production, and mediate the conflict between precapitalist and capitalist modes of objectifying the human condition. A productive critical alliance can be made between the Bolivian miners' deployment of rhetorical figures and fables and Meera's use of images borrowed from religious texts because the critical consciousness produced by these imaginative creations of magic and rite, inspires the subaltern's class struggles, in Taussig's words, "in this [the fight for the miners' rights] they [the workers] have inspired some of the mightiest class struggles and poets of our times" (232).

34. In the context of Meera's subversive use of the traditional notion that the married Rajput Hindu woman is auspicious, it is instructive to recall Dipesh Chakrabarty's examination of the conservative patriarchal discursive construction of the auspicious/inauspicious Hindu woman in nineteenth-century Bengal (1994).

35. Nowhere except in Rajasthan do women traditionally wear ivory bangles from the wrist to the armpit. The intricate jewelry, the *borla* or jewelry worn in the parting of the hair, the *sindoor* (auspicious vermilion in the parting of the hair), the richly embroidered *chunri* or scarf, all denote the fetishized female object, the *suhaagan* or married woman. For a number of Meera bhajans in different dialects that confront this commoditization of women in medieval Rajasthan, see Jafri 1965, 105, 109, 121, 145, 149, 163.

36. Kishwar, in her three-part article "Toiling without Rights: Ho Women of Singhbhum" (1987) notes that the tribal village economy functions primarily on the labor of women. Women and children "perform about 90 per cent of the total labour in villages" (96). Ploughing the field is the only task not performed by women. She writes:

> Among the few tasks that women do not perform is ploughing. They are ritually prohibited from touching the plough. So strict is the taboo that

men do not bring the plough inside the house lest women touch it by mistake. Women are made to believe that their touching the plough will bring ill luck to the whole village, such as drought. Women who dare break the law are fined heavily by the panchayat. In rare cases they could even be stoned to death. Needless to say, the panchayats are composed only of men.

It is often argued that the ban on women ploughing exists because ploughing is a very strenuous activity which women are constitutionally incapable of performing. However, this theory appears unsound because even 12–year old boys manage to use the plough with perfect ease, whereas adult, ablebodied women, who are clearly much stronger are not allowed to do so. The plough used in this area is of a very light variety which makes no more than a two-to three-inch deep furrow. Thus, ploughing would not be a heavier task than many other that women routinely perform, such as cutting firewood and carrying huge headloads from distant forests. (96)

37. In our reading we do not subscribe to the dichotomy that, early Western feminists pointed out, had been so egregious to women's right to equality in the West. The dichotomy is between women's destiny in terms of their biology and thereby the defining of women as nature and therefore passive (Beauvoir 1960, 65) and men as culture and therefore active. For more than two decades now ecological movements have caused Western feminism to revise and rethink this early feminist view. For example see MacCormack and Strathern (1987) and Sidel (1987). Further, as postcolonial ecofeminists we do not adhere to the hegemonic capitalist technological notion of nature as passive requiring 'man's' efforts and productivity to yield its riches. Noncapitalist, nonimperialist cultures have always co-existed alongside imperialist and capitalist cultures and have practiced a respect for nature and shared a reciprocal relationship with nature. These cultures, which have historically been marginalized, do not conceptualize nature and human beings' relationship to nature in terms of activity and passivity. Instead, in these cultures, mainly women but also men, practice frugality of needs and a belief in giving back to nature what they take from it, thus inhabiting a more ecological and spiritual attitude towards nature and the human being's place in history. Therefore, by calling attention to women's intimate connection with nature, we are recalling the ways in which women were respected and accorded status in women-centered agricultural societies as conservers, protectors and guardian producers of nature. Also see Shiva (1988).

38. Kishwar and Vanita (1989) call her "an extraordinary figure" (77); Thapar (1966) calls Meera a "sixteenth-century Rajput princess" (305) an "upper class" woman who "had more freedom" (301); Sangari (1990) calls Meera an "exceptional woman" (1472).

39. By definition Rajputization meant that it was below Rajput dignity to till the soil. Rajputs were typically owners but did not engage in manual labor in the field. They preferred to hire themselves as soldiers than suffer the indignity of tilling the land. Though of course there were always those Rajputs that had fallen on hard times who became peasants. "The martial Rajput," notes John T. Hitchcock, "regards manual labor and field work as unsuitable" (1959, 14).

Chapter 7. The Meera Tradition as a
Historic Embrace of the Poor and the Dispossessed

1. Thapar describes the etymology of the word fakir or faqir in the Sufi movement thus: "Sometimes they formed an order under a *pir* or *shaikh,* the equivalent of the Hindu *guru,* and the members of the order were called *faqirs* (mendicants)or dervishes" (1966, 306). For the purposes of our argument it is clear that Meera was influenced by the Sufi movement as proved by her use of the word "fakiri" and the fact that as Mukta tells, Muslims also sing Meera songs in Jodhpur, Rajasthan (121). Jafri notes in his commentary on Meera, that in Meera's time Rajasthan was well accustomed to the influence of the Sufi's as attested to by the fact that the holy dargaah of Khwaja Moinuddin Chisti had existed and was a popular pilgrimage site in Rajasthan for many hundred years before Meera (1965, 17). Goetz (1966, 38) validates as does Gulzar's cinematic *Meera* (1979) the local legend that Meera shared Akbar's dream of Hindu-Muslim unity in Hindustan. For a postcolonial perspective see Mukta for Gandhi's deployment of Meera to differentiate Muslim aspirations in the Khilafat movement from the Hindu, and focusing Hindus on efforts to save the cow (195, 198). Also see Mukta for a viewpoint on the new crop of commercial Meera bhajan singers who are taking the lead in asserting lower middle class Hindu aspirations against the lower castes as well as Muslims (1994, 203; 1989, 2472).

2. Anuradha Dutt notes that 30 percent of those displaced by the Bargi Dam Project that later came to be called the Avantibai Sagar Dam, are reported to have died of trauma and maladjustment (1998, 41).

3. Mukta notes that there was "acute social differentiation in the feudal social hierarchy, within which distinctions of clothing, ornaments, modes of travel, and differences ascribed by the stigma of poverty (such as the kind of food one ate), symbolized a demonstration of power or lack thereof" (1994, 74). Mukta transcribes another most moving Meera song on fakiri sung by cultivators in Udaipur district in Rajasthan whose refrain is, "My heart lies in *fakiri* / In *fakiri,* in *garibi.* In *fakiri,* in *amiri*" (95–96). Note how with the rhetorical use of enallage, or substitution of one case for another, simply and effectively fakiri is inverted from signifying poverty (garibi) to signifying wealth (amiri). Also see another song on Meera seeking alms (Mukta 1994, 164). Mukta notes that in Saurashtra the figure of Meera shapes up in the nathpanthi tradition of sympathy for the impecunious wayfarer by providing food and shelter to all irrespective of caste or creed (159).

4. In "God and ~~Woman~~'s jouissance" (1998) Jacques Lacan shows how the male can also occupy the place of the mystic through an examination of the difference between men and women. He delineates the experience of the "mystic" (76) as what he calls "another satisfaction," a satisfaction that is the function of speech and "answers to phallic jouissance" (64) but is "more" (74), and not as a complementary to phallic jouissance, but a "supplementary jouissance" (73). Lacan shows that when a speaking being situates themselves under the sign women, she grounds herself as not wholly situated in the phallic function. Lacan makes it clear that mysticism is neither apolitical because it deals with the other world, nor is it the exclusive property of being born female. In

other words men can also be mystics because, according to Lacan, being male does not mean one is "obliged" to situate oneself as man to the phallic function, a man can consent to becoming a mystic by accepting the position of not-whole. Lacan says, "Doesn't this jouissance one experiences and yet knows nothing about put us on the path of ex-sistence? And why not interpret one face of the Other, the God face, as based on feminine jouissance?" (77).

Where we mark our distance from Lacan is, in his implicit theory of the mystic as an exceptional woman or exceptional male. Meera is not an extraordinary woman because millions of women and men all over the world have, and continue to live like her. With all the challenges facing our environment it is important to not see the forest in binary opposition to the home or society, but to recover and recognize subaltern traditions whereby the forest and the home and society are sustained by reciprocity.

5. We contend that all popular love poetry (and in India at present this consists in large part of Hindi film songs) is deeply influenced by the paradigm of Meera's love for Krishna as lover/husband. It would not be advisable, possible, or even desirable to mention all the love songs we offer only a sample of the most obviously influenced lyric writers and songs. The proof that Meera has inspired several communities of male artists is that Hindi film songs, written almost exclusively by male lyricists, have played an extremely important role in keeping Meera and her verses alive. Until the 1940s Meera's songs were popularized through the inclusion of actual Meera bhajans ("*Kit gaye ho khewanhaar/* Where have you gone Boatman" *Achhut Kanya* [1936]; "*Mein to Giridhar ke ghar jaoon/* I will go to Giridhar's house" *Mohabbat* [1943]). From the 1950s Hindi film songs also began to be composed by lyricists like Shailendra, Rajinder Kishan, Hasrat Jaipuri and Shakeel Badayuni, through becoming author as Meera and epitomizing Meera's love for Krishna as the paradigmatic love between lover and beloved. For example: Shailendra's "*Ghar aaya mera pardesi/* My beloved has come home" in *Awara* 1951; Rajinder Kishan's "*Man dole, mera tan dole/* My mind rejoices, my body sways" in *Nagin* 1954; Jaipuri's "*Rasik balma/* Beloved trifler" in *Chori Chori* (1956) and Badayuni's "*Jogan ban jaaongi saiyyan tore karan/* I will renounce the world for you beloved" in *Shabab* (1954) or "*Nagri nagri dware dware dhoondu re sawariya/* From city to city and door to door I search for my beloved" in *Mother India* 1957. At the same time the earlier technique of including a Meera song or Meeraesque bhajan continued (*Jogan* 1950; *Parineeta* 1953; *Reshma aur Shera* 1971; *Julie* 1975; *Ankahee* 1984; *Sur Sangam* 1985).

From the 1960s lyricists like Gulzar, Prem Dhawan, Raja Mehdi Ali Khan, Majrooh Sultanpuri, Neeraj and Anand Bakshi joined Shailendra et al. in composing songs that have a distinct Meera flavor: Gulzar's "*Mora gora ang laile/* Take over my fair body" for *Bandini* (1963); Dhawan's "*Jogi hum to lut gaye tere pyar mein/* Renouncer we have been completely robbed by your love" in *Shaheed* (1965); Mehdi Ali Khan's "*Mein dekhon jis oar sakhiri/* Wherever I look friend" for *Anita* (1967); Majrooh's "*Baiyyan na dharo/* Don't take my arm" for *Dastak* (1970); Neeraj's "*Rangila re/* Multihued beloved" for *Prem Pujari* (1970); and Bakshi's "*Raina beeti jai/* Time is passing" in *Amar Prem* (1971). In the 1980s and 1990s lyricists like Majrooh Sultanpuri, Hasrat Jaipuri and Gulzar continued to write songs that were strongly influenced by Meera: Majrooh's "*Toone O Rangeele kaisa jaadu kiya/* O Resplendent Beloved what magic have you done" for *Kudrat* (1981); Jaipuri's " *Ek Radha, ek Meera, dono ne Shyam ko chaha/* There was one Radha, one Meera, both were in love with Shyam" for *Ram Teri Ganga Maili Ho Gayi* (1985); and Gulzar's "*Kesariya baalma/* Saffron-hued lover" for *Lekin* (1991). Furthermore new lyricists like Sameer, Dev Kohli and Mehboob carry on the tradition of composing Meera type songs: Sameer's "*Mainu ishq da lagya rog/* I am afflicted by love" for *Dil Hai Ki Manta Nahin* (1991); Dev Kohli's "*Mai ni Mai munder pe tere bol raha hai kaga/* O Mother a crow calls out on the balcony" for *Hum Aapke Hain Kaun* (1994) and Mehboob's "*Mujhe range de/* Color me" for *Takshak* (2000).

   Shailendra and Gulzar stand out in this long list of lyricists both because of the lasting influence of Meera verses on their compositions and for the sweetness and enduring appeal of their Meeraesque compositions. Shailendra's songs articulate the folk elements of the Bollywood film scenarios where they are deployed, therefore there is an evocative simplicity, succinctness, ease and suitability of expression in his lyrics that is not found in any other Meera inspired film lyricist. Witness his song in *Bandini* (1963) "*Jogi jab se tu aaya mere dware/* Renouncer since you came to my door"; or his compositions in *Madhumati* (1958): "*Aa ja re pardesi/* Do come stranger," "*Bichhua/* Scorpion" and "*Julmi sang aankh lari/* My eyes entangled with my pitiless beloved"; his song for *Guide* (1965) traces the barahmasas or twelve month poems composed by Meera, "*Piya tose naina laage re/* Beloved since our eyes entangled." After the untimely death of Shailendra, Gulzar, now one of the premier Bombay film industry lyricists who is also a well known poet in his own right, followed in the footsteps of Shailendra to whom he is often compared in his facility with the north Indian folk idiom. Gulzar considers his most favorite composition in a long and illustrious career to be the first song he ever composed for a film, a song which he writes as a poet as Meera, "*Mora gora ang lai le*" from the film *Bandini* (1963).

   6. We concur with Mukta's (1994) view of the figure of Rana in Meera songs. Mukta writes, "It is highly significant that the Mira bhajans do not flout the authority of a particular historical Rana by name, but seek to revel in the shame incurred by a feudal power who symbolizes the authority of kingship. Mira thus emerges from the bhajans not as a figure of rebellion against one particular Rana, but as someone who despised and condemned the essential embodiment of Rajput kinghood" (84). See Mukta for folk versions of Rana poems (94, 96–97, 102–103, 144, 160, 166).

   7. See Chandrikaprasad Jijnasu (1969). See Mukta (1994) for songs composed by Raidas that are sung by dalits, peasant and agricultural communities (110).

   8. For example Sangari writes that Meera's servitude "is obedient not to the mere letter of feudalism but to its 'spirit,'" and thus "Mirabai, by replenishing the reciprocity structured into an 'ideal' feudal relation, replenishes that relation, turns it into unmitigated excess" (1990, 1472). Also See Kishwar and Vanita (1989) for a short discussion of daasatva (88).

   9. We contend that the Gandhian nationalist appropriation of Meera is one of the many appropriations of Meera. In this section we analyze a specific Meera bhajan that Gandhi appropriated for the nationalist movement and that was made famous by the south Indian Carnatic music singer, M. S. Subbulakshmi. We offer an alternative feminist subaltern reading of the bhajan. For a detailed exploration of the Gandhian

nationalist appropriation of Meera, see Mukta (1994) who devotes two chapters of her book to it ("Incorporation" 173–77, "A Nation Cleaved" 182–200). Also see Kishwar and Vanita (1989, 86–87) for another brief treatment of the same issue.

10. In poem after poem Meera speaks of being so maddened with love she cannot keep quiet (the refrain of one of her most famous songs is, "O friend, I am love maddened, nobody understands my pain," Alston, 1980, 70). She cannot be silenced, she must speak, call out, express herself by clapping and dancing with bells on her feet, she beats the drum, laughs and goes wherever she wants to without any restrictions. In a poem Meera says, "Put a curtain up in your house, I am a weak woman, and *deranged*" (Bhati, 1964, 26). In another she sings, "There is no one to stop you, rapt Meera walked away/ she swept away all thoughts of chastity shame honor of the family" (Jafri, 1965, 163). In another she says, "Some say Meera has gone mad" (Chaturvedi, 1983, 164), or "People may approve or reprove, I walk my inimitable walk" (Jafri, 1965, 81) Many of her poems end with phrases such as, "Meera says" (Chaturvedi, 1983, 85) or "Meera calls out" (Jafri, 1965, 167) or "so says Meerabai" (Bihari, 1961, 162). Another song begins with, "Mira *danced with ankle-bells* on her feet./People said Meera is *mad;* my mother-in-law said I ruined the family reputation./ Rana sent me a cup of poison and Mira drank it *laughing*" (Bhati, 1964, 18). In this context it is instructive to recall what Cixous says about the power of feminine writing which breaks the silence and consensus with laughter. She writes:

> A feminine text cannot fail to be more than subversive. It is volcanic; as it is written it brings about an upheaval of the old property crust, carrier of masculine investments; there's no other way. There's no room for her if she's not a he. If she's a her-she, its in order to smash everything, to shatter the framework of institutions, to blow up the law, to break up the "truth" with laughter. (1976, 888)

11. Cited in Sharma (1966) vol. I, 455.

12. We also read Meera's poetry in terms of Julia Kristeva's formulation concerning the nonverbal in maternal language. In "Sabat Mater" (1987) Kristeva announces her program of "herethics" which, taking into account the demise of the Virgin Mary cult and women's religion in the West, addresses the need for a discourse of motherhood and death. She arrives at a description of maternal language through the analysis of the Virgin Mother's recurring image of the body with tears in her eyes and exposed breast. Kristeva writes, "what milk and tears have in common; they are the metaphors of nonspeech, of a "semiotics' that linguistic communication does not account for" (370). She relates the nonverbal maternal language to the notion of death by suggesting that man conquers "the unthinkable of death" through "postulating maternal love in its place" (372) recalling the early identification of the mother, Kristeva says, as the first shelter of the newborn. According to Kristeva, this maternal love "of which divine love is merely a not always convincing derivation," surges at the precise moment of death when, "The possibilities of communication having been swept away, only the subtle gamut of sound, touch, and visual traces, older than language and newly worked out, are preserved as an ultimate shield against death" (373). She implies that no one escapes being subject to this fiction, "except perhaps the saint, the mystic,

or the writer" (373). The writer, the saint, and the mystic are the exception because they understand the fiction and by understanding and identifying "with love itself" they must speak in a fire of tongues and exit from representation. Kristeva defines her proposal for herethics in terms of the processes of life that make the notion of death tolerable. She writes, "if ethics amounts to not avoiding the embarrassing and inevitable problematics of the law but giving it flesh, language, and jouissance—in that case its reformulation demands the contribution of women . . . an *herethics*, is perhaps no more than that which in life makes bonds, thoughts, and therefore the thought of death bearable,: herethics is underneath *[a-mort]*, love" (380).

13. The Kabir bhajan, "*Ye tan mundla re mundla/* This body is bones only bones" has been sung by the noted Indian classical vocal singer, Pandit Bhimsen Joshi (1989). Many Kabir poems state the same idea in different ways. For example the song, "*Jhini chadriya/* See-through body/blanket " sung by another classical vocal singer Pandit Kumar Gandharva in his collection of Kabir bhajans (1998). See these poems in printed form in Sukdev Singh (1972). Also see David N. Lorenzen (1987, 281–303).

14. Mahasweta Devi powerfully textualizes and dramatizes the political valence of Draupadi's divested and sacralized body through her short story, "Draupadi" (1988). The context of the story is the Naxalite uprisings by the landless peasants and tribal cultivators in West Bengal in May 1972 and the state's military and police action against the insurgents during these uprisings. The story is about a Santhal tribal woman Draupadi who is being hunted by the army for her role in the uprising. The story ends with Draupadi's capture and torture. She tears up her cloth and naked, confronts Senanayak, the military's expert on tribal insurgent tactics and her captor and torturer. Devi writes:

> Draupadi's black body comes even closer. Draupadi shakes with an indomitable laughter that Senanayak simply cannot understand. Her ravaged lips bleed as she begins laughing. Draupadi wipes the blood on her palm and says in a voice that is as terrifying, sky spitting, and sharp as her ululation, What's the use of clothes? You can strip me, but how can you clothe me again? Are you a man?
>
> She looks around and chooses the front of Senanayak's white bush shirt to spit a bloody gob at and says, There isn't a man here that I should be ashamed. I will not let you put my cloth on me. What more can you do? Come on, *counter* me—come on, *counter* me—?
>
> Draupadi pushes Senanayak with her two mangled breasts, and for the first time Senanayak is afraid to stand before an unarmed *target,* terribly afraid. (196)

15. All of us have heard news stories of babies found unharmed nestled in a tree after a tornado. On Thanksgiving Day, November 25, 1999, Elian Gonzales, a six-year-old Cuban boy was found at sea two days and nights after his mother, step father and ten others on the boat sank, trying to come to the U.S. from Cuba. The expatriate Cuban community in Florida dubbed Elian the miracle child and fought long and hard for seven months to keep Elian in the U.S.

Among the popular hunting stories of the colonial writer Jim Corbett is the story of the miraculous discovery of two infants, Putali and Punwa from the jungle which Corbett writes "to my certain knowledge" contained apart from animals harmless to human beings, five tigers, eight leopards, four sloth bears, two Himalayan black bears, a number of hyenas, a pair of wild dogs, numerous jackals and foxes and pine martens, a variety of civets and other cats, two pythons, many kinds of snakes, eagles and hundreds of vultures. Corbett describes the discovery of the infants thus:

> Two-year-old Putali and three-year-old Punwa were lost at midday on Friday, and were found by the herdman at about 5 p.m. on Monday, a matter of seventy-seven hours. I have given a description of the wild life which to my knowledge was in the forest in which the children spent those seventy-seven hours, and it would be unreasonable to assume that none of the animals or birds saw, heard, or smelt the children. And yet, when the herdsman put Putali and Punwa into their parents' arms, there was not a single mark of tooth or claw on them. ("The Law of the Jungle" *My India* 1952, 76)

Bibliography

Original Documents

Alha-Udal. ed. Syamsunderdas. Allahbad, 1919, *The Lay of Alha.* Trans. William Waterfield. Oxford: Oxford University Press, 1923.

Baden-Powell, B. H. *A Short Account of the Land Revenue and its Administration in British India; with a Sketch of the Land Tenures.* 2nd edition. Oxford: Clarendon Press, 1913.

Bardai, Chand. *Prithviraj Raso.* Ed. A. F. Rudolf Hoernle. Calcutta: Bibliotheca Indica, 1886; M. Y. Pandya and Syamsunderdas version (Banaras [1888–1904]); B. P. Sharma (Chandigarh [1962]).

Bhandarkar, R. G. "Why Social Reforms?" Address at the Ninth Social Conference, 1895. K. P. Karunakaran, *Religion and Political Awakening in India.* Delhi: Meenakshi Prakashan, 1965, 159.

Bombay Gazetteer. Gazetteer of the Bombay Presidency, vol. 5, 1880, vol. 8, 1884, and vol. 9, 1901. Bombay: Government Central Press.

Bombay Government Records. Repression of Female Infanticide in the Bombay Presidency. H. R. Cooke. No. XLVII (New Series). Bombay: Government Central Press, 1875.

Bombay Secretariat Record Office. Political Department, vols. 4 (no. 2014 and 2181, 1848), vol. 61, 1855, and vol. 86, 1856.

Bombay Secretariat Record Office. Judicial Department, vol. 15 (no. 237, 1849), vol. 21, 1849, 1851, and Judicial Department [Police], vol. 31, 1853.

Brown, John Cave. *Indian Infanticide: Its Origins, Progress, and Suppression.* London: W. H. Allen and Co., 1857.

Burnes, Alexander. "On Female Infanticide in Cutch." *The Journal of the Asiatic Society of Great Britain and Ireland,* ser. 1, vol. 1, 1834, 285–289.

Census of India (1875). Census 1872 General Report. London.

Eden, Emily. *Up the Country. Letters written to her sister from the Upper Provinces of India.* Oxford, 1937.

Elphinstone, Mountstuart. "The Minute [1824]" *Gazetteer of Bombay Presidency,* vol. 5, 1880, 107–264.

Harington, J. H. "Analysis of Bengal Regulations" *Hindoo Widows,* vol. 2, 1843, part 1, 9–12.

Heber, Bishop. *Narrative of a Journey through the Upper Provinces of India (1828): Selections from Heber's Journal.* Ed. M. A. Laird. Cambridge: University Press, 1971.

Hindoo Widows. Vols. 1 and 2. India: Bombay [1843]. These include papers relating to infanticide (Part I, II, III [1789–1820]) and extracts from the *Records of the Bombay Government* until 1843.

Indian Political and Foreign Consultations, 1843–1858 (relevant volumes).

India Political Consultations, 1836–1843 (relevant volumes relating to infanticide operations in Rajputana).

India Legislative Proceedings, 1861–1871. Range 208 (vol. 6–11), range 436 (vol. 53–57, vol. 709–710).

Kaye, J. W. *The Administration of the East India Company,* n.p., 1853 [reprint]. Allahabad: Kitab Mahal Pvt. Ltd., 1966.

Malcolm, J. *A Memoir of Central India, including Malwa and Adjoining Provinces.* London: 1832.

Montgomery, Robert. *Minute.* 16 June 1853. *Selections from the Public Correspondence, Punjab,* 1853, vol. I, 6.

Moore, W. R. *Papers on the Subject of Mr. W. R. Moore's Investigation and Report Regarding Female Infanticide in the Benaras Division.* Calcutta: A. Dozey, Home Secretariat Press, 1868.

Nabhadas. *Shri Bhaktamal,* with the *Bhaktirasabodhini* commentary of Priyadas. Lucknow: Tejkumar Press, 1969.

Pakrasi, Kanti B. *Female Infanticide in India.* Calcutta, 1970.

Parliamentary History of England 17, 1771–1774, London, 1813.

Parliamentary Papers on Female Infanticide in India No. 264 (1912–1913); No. 426 (1824); No. 548 (1828); No. 613 (1843); and No. 62 (1865).

Report on the Political Administration of the Rajputana States [1865–1867], Bikaner, Rajasthan.

Selections from the Records of the Bombay Government, No. 37 (new series), No. 167 (new series), No. 296, 436, 1856.

Selections from Records of Bombay Government .Measures Adopted for the Suppression of Female Infanticide in the Province of Kattywar. Bombay: Education Society Press, 1856.

Shaftesbury, Third Earl of. *Several Letters Written by a Noble Lord to a Young Man at the University,* Letter of June 3, 1709.

Sleeman, W. H. *A Journey Through The Kingdom Of Oude,* in 1849–1850, vols. I and II. London: Richard Bentley, 1858.

———. *W. H. Sleeman in Oude: An Abridgement of W. H. Sleeman's A Journey through the Kingdom of Oude in 1849–50* [1858], P. D. Reeves. ed. and "Introduction" Cambridge: At The University Press, 1971.

———. *The Thugs or Phansigars of India comprising a History of the Rise and Progress of the Extraordinary Fraternity of Assasins, and a Description of the System which it Pursues, and of the Measures which have been adopted by the Supreme Government of India for its Suppression.* Philadelphia: Carey and Hart, 1839.

Swift, Jonathan. *A Modest Proposal for preventing the Children of Poor People from Being A Burthen to their Parents or Country, and for making them Beneficial to the Publick* (1729).

The Local Muhammedan Dynasties: Gujarat, 1886. Trans. Edward Clive Bayley. Delhi: Nagendra Singh, 1970.

Tod, James. *Annals and Antiquities of Rajasthan,* vol. I and II, 1829, 1832.

UNICEF. *Children and the Environment,* 1990.

Vasudevsaran, Agarwal, ed. *Padmavat by Mallik Muhammad Jaysi.* Jhansi: Sahitya Sadan, 1972.

Walker, Alexander. "Report on Resources etc. of the Districts of Nariad, Matur, Mondey, Beejapur, Dholka, Dhandodka and Gogo, the Tuppa of Napar and the Kasba of Rampoor in Gujarat" [1804]. *Selections from the Records of the Bombay Government,* no. 39, Part I.

———. "Report on Infanticide in Kattywar [1808]." *Selections from the Records of the Bombay Government* (1856), 325–340.

Wilson, John. *History of the Suppression of Female Infanticide in Western India.* Bombay: Smith, Taylor, and Co., 1855.

Newspapers and Journals

Economic and Political Weekly (1970–2004)

Illustrated Weekly (1960–1980)

India Abroad (1998–2004)

India Today (1986–2004)

Manushi (1979–2004)

The Hindu

Times of India

Works Cited

Acharya, G. S. *Bhakt Mira.* Chittorgarh: Vijay Prakashan, 1983.

Adi Sri Guru Granth Sahib, 4 vols. Lucknow: Bhavan Vani Trust, 1978–1982.

Agnihotri, Indu and Veena Majumdar, "Changing Terms of Political Discourse: Women's Movement in India, 1970–1990," *Economic and Political Weekly,* July 22, 1995, 1869–1878.

Ahmad, Aijaz. *In Theory: Classes, Nations, Literatures.* London: Verso, 1992.

Alston, A. J. *The Devotional Poems of Mirabai.* Delhi: Motilal Banarsidas, 1980.

Amin, Shahid. "Gandhi as Mahatma: Gorakhpur District, Eastern UP, 1921–1922," *Subaltern Studies III: Writings on South Asian History and Society.* Ed. Ranajit Guha. Delhi: Oxford University Press, 1984, 1–61.

Amin, Samir. *Unequal Development: An Essay on the Social Formations of Peripheral Capitalism.* Trans. Brian Pearce. New York and London: Monthly Review Press, 1976.

———. *Class and Nation: Historically and in the Current Crisis.* Trans. Susan Kaplow. New York and London: Monthly Review Press, 1980.

Aptekar, Herbert. *Anjea: Infanticide, Abortion and Contraception in Savage Society.* Westport, Connecticut: Hyperion Press Inc., 1930, 155.

Arata, Stephen D. "The Occidental Tourist: Dracula and the Anxiety of Reverse Colonization," *Victorian Studies* 33, 1990, 621–645.

Aravamundan, Gita. "Whose Baby is She Anyway?" *The Hindu,* Oct. 16, 1994.

Asher, R. E. "Introduction," *"Me Grandad 'ad an Elephant!" Three Stories of Muslim Life in South India by Vaikom Muhammad Basheer.* Edinburgh University Press, 1980, vii–xviii.

Bala, Usha and Anshu Sharma. *Indian Women Freedom Fighters, 1857–1947.* New Delhi: Manohar, 1986.

Balakrishnan, Radha. "The Social Context of Sex Selection and the Politics of Abortion in India," *Power and Decision: The Social Control of Reproduction.* Ed. Gita Sen and Rachel C. Snow. Harvard University Press, March 1994.

Balasubramanyam, Vimal. "Medicine and the Male Utopia," *Economic and Political Weekly* (23 October 1982): xvii, 43, 1725.

———. "Towards a Woman's Perspective on Family Planning," *Economic and Political Weekly* (January 11, 1986): xxi, 2, 69–71.

Banerjee, Anil Chandra. *The Rajput States and the East India Company.* Calcutta: A. Mukherjee and Co. Ltd., 1951.

Banerji, Debabar. "Political Economy of Population Control in India." In *Poverty and Population Control.* Ed. Lars Bondestam and Staffan Bergstrom. London: Academic Press, 1980, 83–102.

Bandyopadhyay, J. "Havoc," *Illustrated Weekly of India,* December 13, 1985.

Bannerjee, Nirmala, ed. *Indian Women in a Changing Industrial Scenario.* New Delhi: Sage Publications, 1991.

Bardhan, Kalpana. "Women: Work, Welfare And Status. Forces of Tradition and Change in India," *South Asia Bulletin,* vol. VI, no. 1, Spring 1986, 3–16.

Bardhan, Pranab K. "On Life and Death Questions," *Economic and Political Weekly*, vol. ix, no. 32–34. Special Number, 1974, 1293–1304.

———. "Little Girls and Death in India," *Economic and Political Weekly*, vol. xvii, no. 36, September 4, 1982, 1448–1450.

Benjamin, Walter. "The Flaneur: The Paris of the Second Empire in Baudelaire." In *Charles Baudelaire: A Lyric Poet in the Era of High Capitalism*. Trans. Harry Zohn. New Directions Publishing, 1973.

Benvenuto, Rice and Roger Kennedy. "The Purloined Letter (1956)," *The Works of Jacques Lacan An Introduction*. London: Free Association Books, 1986, 91–102.

Beteille, Andre. "Caste and Family in Representations of Indian Society," *Anthropology Today* 8, I, 1992, 13–18.

Bhagwat Purana. Trans. Ganesh Vasudeo Tagare, 5 volumes (1976). Rpt. Delhi: Motilal Benarsidas, 1979.

Bhati, Desarajasingh. *Mirabai aur Unki Padavali*. Delhi: Ashok Prakashan, 1964.

Bhatnagar, Rashmi Dube, Renu Dube, and Reena Dube. "Dissent in the Oral-performative Bardic Literatures of Rajasthan: Erased Traditions of Oppositional Rhetoric and History," forthcoming article in *Subaltern Studies*, vol. XII. Ed. Shail Mayaram. Delhi: Oxford University Press, 2005.

———. "Meera's Medieval Lyric Poetry in Postcolonial India: The Rhetorics of Women's Writing in Dialect as a Secular Practice of Subaltern Co-authorship and Dissent," *boundary 2*, vol. 31, no. 3, fall 2004.

Bihari, Bankey. *Bhakt Mira*. Bombay: Bhartiya Vidya Bhavan, 1961.

Bondestam, Lars. "The Political Ideology of Population Control." In *Poverty and Population Control*. Ed. L. Bondestam and Staffan Bergstrom. London: Academic Press, 1980, 1–38.

Bornstein, Kate. Speech at a 1995 conference at Kansas City quoted in Barbara DiBernard's unpublished paper, "Transgender Liberation (Ally?), or What's a Nice Lesbian Feminist Like You Doing In a Place Like This?"

Bottomore, Tom, ed. *A Dictionary of Marxist Thought*. Cambridge, Massachusettes: Harvard University Press, 1983.

Cassen, R. H. *India: Population, Economy, Society*. London: Macmillan Press, 1978, 149–160.

Chakravarty, Dipesh. "The Difference-Deferral of a Colonial Modernity: Public Debates on Domesticity in British India." In *Subaltern Studies VIII: Essays in Honour of Ranajit Guha*. Ed. David Arnold and David Hardiman. Delhi: Oxford University Press, 1994, 50–88.

Chakravarty, Uma. "The World of the Bhaktin in South Indian Traditions: The Body and Beyond," *Women Bhakta Poets Manushi*, 50–51–52, January–June, 1989, 18–29.

―――― and Kumkum Roy. "In Search of Our Past: A Review of the Limitations of the Possibilities of the Historiography of Women in Early India," *Economic and Political Weekly,* April 30, 1988, WS-2–WS10.

Chatterjee, Partha. "Their Own Words? An Essay for Edward Said." In *Edward Said: A Critical Reader.* Ed. Michael Sprinker. Cambridge, Massachusets: Blackwell, 1992.

―――― . "The Nationalist Resolution of the Women's Question." In Kumkum Sangari and Sudesh Vaid, eds., *Recasting Women: Essays in Indian Colonial History.* New Brunswick, New Jersey: Rutgers University Press, 1997. 3rd edition. Orig: New Delhi: Kali for Women, 1989, 233–253.

Chattopadhyaya, B. D. "Origin of the Rajputs: The Political, Economic and Social Processes in Early Medieval Rajasthan," *The Indian Historical Review,* vol. III, 1, 1976, 59–82.

―――― . "State and Economy in North India: Fourth Century to Twelfth Century," *Sidelights on History and Culture of Orissa.* Ed. Manmath Nath Das. Cuttack: Pitamber Misra, 1977, 104–114.

Chaturvedi, Parasuram, ed. *Mirabai ki Padavali.* Allahabad: Hindi Sahitya Sammelan, 1983.

Chodorow, Nancy. *The Reproduction of Mothering: Psychoanalysis and the Sociology of Gender.* Berkley: University of California Press, 1979.

Choksey, R. D. *Economic Life in the Bombay Gujarat (1800–1939).* Bombay: Asia Publishing House, 1968.

Chowdhry, Prem. "Marriage, Sexuality and the Female 'Ascetic': Understanding a Hindu Sect," *Economic and Political Weekly,* August 24–31, 1996, 2307–2321.

Cixous, Hèléne. "The Laugh of the Medusa." Trans. Keith Cohen and Paula Cohen. *Signs,* 1976, vol. 1, no. 4., 875–892.

Clark, Alice. "Limitations on Female Life Chances in Rural Central Gujarat." In *Women in Colonial India: Essays on Survival, Work and the State.* Ed. J. Krishnamurty. Delhi: Oxford University Press, 1989, 27–51.

Commissariat, M. S. *A History of Gujarat Vol. II The Mughal Period: From 1573 to 1758.* Bombay: Orient Longmans, 1957.

Corbett, Jim. *My India.* Delhi: Oxford University Press, 1952.

Coward, Rosalind. *Female Desires: How they are Sought, Bought, and Packaged.* New York: Grove Press, 1985.

Dabbe, Vijaya and Robert Zydenbos. "Akka Mahadevi," *Women Bhakta Poets. Manushi* 1989, 39–44.

Das, Veena. "The Mythological Film and its Framework of Meaning: An Analysis of Jai Santoshi Maa," *India International Centre Quarterly,* vol. 8, no. 1, New Delhi, March 1980.

―――― . "Shakti Versus Sati—A Reading Of The Santoshi Ma Cult," *Manushi,* no. 49, Nov.–Dec. 1988, 26–30.

Deane, Seamus. "Swift and the Anglo-Irish Intellect," *Eighteenth Century Ireland* (1986).

de Beauvoir, Simone. *The Second Sex.* Trans. H. M. Parshley. London: Jonathan Cape, 1953.

Dehejia, Vidya. *Antal and Her Path of Love: Poems of a Woman Saint from South India.* New York: State University of New York Press, 1990.

Desai, M. B. "Land and Its Problems," *The Rural Economy of Gujarat.* London: Oxford University Press, 1948, 96–107.

Desai, Neera. "Women and the Bhakti Movement," *Samya Shakti,* vol. 1, no. 2, 1984, 92–100.

——— and Maithreyi Krishnaraj. *Women and Society in India.* Delhi: Ajanta, 1987.

Desh-Videsh. "Indian Destinations: Jaipur, Jodhpur, Udaipur," vol. 4, no. 2, 19–25.

Detha, Vijayan. *The Dilemma and Other Stories.* Trans. Ruth Vanita. New Delhi: Manushi Prakashan, 1997.

Devi, Gayatri, of Jaipur and Santha Rama Rau. *A Princess Remembers: The Memoirs of the Maharani of Jaipur.* Philadelphia and New York: J. B. Lippincott Co., 1976.

Devi, Mahasweta. "Draupadi." Trans. Gayatri Chakravorty Spivak, *In Other Worlds.* New York: Routledge, 1988, 187–96.

Dhavamony, Mariasusai. "The Sanskrit Term Bhakti." In *Love Of God: According to Saiva Siddhanta.* Oxford: Clarendon Press, 1971, 13–23.

Dickeman, Mildred. "Demographic Consequences of Infanticide in Man," *Annual Review of Ecology and Systematics* 6:107:137, 1975.

Divale, William Tulio and Marvin Harris. "Population, Warfare, and the Male Supremacist Complex," *American Anthropologist* 78, 1976, 521–538.

Diwana, Mohan Singh. "Indian Sociolinguistic Background." In *Language and Society in India.* Simla: Institute of Advanced Study, 1969.

Dube, Leela. "On the Construction of Gender: Hindu Girls in Patrilineal India," *Economic and Political Weekly,* April 30, 1988.

Dube, Reena. "Satyajit Ray's The Chess Players and Postcolonial Theory: Culture, Work and the Value of Alterity." MacMillian-Palgrave, 2005.

Dube, Renu and Reena and Rashmi Bhatnagar. "Women Without Choice: Female Infanticide and the Rhetoric of Overpopulation in Postcolonial India," Teaching About Violence Against Women. Ed. Mona Eliasson. *Women's Studies Quarterly,* vol. XXVII (Special Issue), Spring/Summer 1999.

Dumont, Louis. *Homo Hierarchicus.* Gallimard, 1967, London: Wiedenfeld and Nicholson, 1970.

Dutt, Anuradha. "The Meek Shall Inherit the Earth?" *Manushi,* no. 108, Sept.–Oct. 1998, 41.

Enthoven, R. E. *The Tribes and Castes of Bombay,* vol III. Government of Bombay, 1922.

Evans, Dylan. "objet (petit) a," *An Introductory Dictionary of Lacanian Psychoanalysis.* London and New York: Routledge, 1996, 24–25.

Everett, Jana Matson. *Women and Social Change in India.* New Delhi: Heritage, 1979.

Fisher, Elizabeth. *Women's Creation.* Garden City, New York: Anchor Press, Doubleday, 1979.

Forum Against Sex Determination and Sex Pre-Selection. "Campaign Against Sex Determination and Sex Pre-selection in India: Our Experience" (Bombay), 1983.

Foucault, Michel. *Discipline and Punish: The Birth of the Prison.* Vintage Books, 1979.

———, ed. *"I, Pierre Rivere, having slaughtered my mother, my sister, and my brother . . .":
A Case of Parricide in the 19th Century.* Trans. Frank Jellinek. Lincoln, Nebraska:
University of Nebraska Press, 1982.

Fox, Richard G. *Kin Clan Raja and Rule: State-Hinterland Relations in Preindustrial
India.* Berkeley: University of California Press, 1971.

Gandhi, Nandita and Nandita Shah. *The Issues at Stake: Theory and Practice in the Contemporary Women's Movements in India.* New Delhi: Kali for Women, 1991,
128–137.

George, Sabu. Abel Rajaratnam and Barbara D. Miller, "Female Infanticide in Rural
South India," *Economic and Political Weekly* XXVIII, no. 22, May 30, 1992.

Gilbert, Sandra and Susan Gubar. *The Madwoman in the Attic: The Women Writer and
the Nineteenth-Century Literary Imagination.* New Haven: Yale University Press,
1979.

Glass, D. V., ed. *Introduction To Malthus.* New York: John Wiley and Sons Inc., 1953.

Goetz, Hermann. *Mira Bai: Her Life and Times.* Bombay: Bhartiya Vidya Bhavan,
1966.

Gold, Ann Grodzins."Purdah Is As Purdah's Kept: A Storyteller's Story," *Listen To The
Heron's Words: Reimagining Gender and Kinship in India.* A. G. Gold and Gloria
Goodwin Raheja. Berkeley: University of California Press, 1994, 164–181.

———. "Gender, Violence and Power: Rajasthani Stories of Shakti," Nita Kumar, ed.,
Women as Subjets: South Asian Histories. Charlottesville, Virginia: University Press
of Virginia, 1994, 26–48.

Gramsci, Antonio. "Some Theoretical and Practical Aspects Of 'Economism'"
[1928–1935], *Selections From The Prison Notebooks.* Ed. and trans. Quintin Hoare
and Jeoffrey Nowell Smith. New York: International Publishers, 1971.

Guha, Ranajit. "Dominance without Hegemony and its Historiography," *Subaltern
Studies IV: Writings on South Asian History and Society.* Ed. Ranajit Guha. Delhi
and New York: Oxford University Press, 1989, 259.

———. *A Rule of Property For Bengal: An Essay on the idea of Permanent Settlement.* 2nd
ed. New York: Apt Books, 1982.

———. *Elementary Aspects of Peasant Insurgency in Colonial India.* Delhi: Oxford University Press, 1983.

———. "Chandra's Death," *Subaltern Studies V.* Delhi: Oxford University Press, 1987,
135–165.

Gulzar, S. S., Dir. *Meera* (1979). Original film soundtrack recording, Suchitra International Productions, Polygram CDNF 292.

Hallissey, Robert C. *The Rajput Rebellion Against Aurangzeb: A Study of the Mughal empire in Seventeenth Century India.* Columbia: University of Missouri Press, 1977.

Harlan, Lindsey. *Religion and Rajput Women: The Ethic of Protection in Contemporary Narratives.* Berkeley: University of California Press, 1992.

Hawley, John Stratton. "Mirabai," *Songs of the Saints of India.* Trans. J. S. Hawley and Mark Juergensmeyer. New York: Oxford University Press, 1988, 118–140.

Hitchcock, John T. "The Idea of the Martial Rajput." *Traditional India: Structure and Change.* Ed. Milton Singer. Austin: University of Texas Press, 1959, 14.

Hoffer, Peter C. and N. E. H. Hull. *Murdering Mothers: Infanticide in England and New England 1558–1803,* 1981.

Irigaray, Luce. *This Sex Which Is Not One.* Trans. Catherine Porter and Carolyn Burke. Ithaca, New York: Cornell University Press, 1985.

———. *An Ethics of Sexual Difference.* Trans. Carolyn Burke and Gillian C. Gill. Ithaca, New York: Cornell University Press, 1993.

Jacobson, Doranne and Susan Wadley. *Women in India: Two Perspectives.* Delhi: Manohar, 1977.

Jafri, Sardar, ed. *Prem Vani: Mirabai ke Ek Sau Padon ka Sankalan.* Bombay: Hindustani Book Trust, 1965.

Jayawardena, Kumari. *Feminism and Nationalism in the Third World.* London: Zed Books, 1986.

Jhunjhunwala, Bharat. "Population and Poverty," *Economic and Political Weekly,* July 6, 1974: ix, 27, 1059–1061.

Jijnasu, Chandrikaprasad. *Sant Parivar Raidas Sahab.* Original edition 1959. Revised edition. Lucknow: Bahujan Kalyan Prakashan, 1969.

Kabeer, Naila. *Reversed Realities: Gender Hierarchies in Development Thought.* London: Verso, 1994.

Kabir. *Kabir-Bijak.* Ed. Sukdev Singh. Allahabad: Nilam Prakashan, 1972.

Kalima, Rose. *Where Women are Leaders: The Sewa Movement in India.* New Delhi: Vistaar Publications, 1992.

Karve, Irawati. *Kinship Organization in India.* New York: Asia Publishing House, 1965, 167–168.

Katiyar, T. S. *Social Life in Rajasthan: A Case Study.* Allahbad: Kitab Mahal, 1964.

Kaur, Manmohan. *Women in India's Freedom Struggle.* New Delhi: Sterling, 1985.

———. *Role of Women in the Freedom Movement, 1857–1947.* Delhi: Sterling Publishers, 1968.

Kinsley, David. "Devotion as an Alternative to Marriage in the Lives of Some Hindu Women Devotees." In Jayant Lele, ed., *Tradition and Modernity in Bhakti Movements.* Leiden: E. J. Brill, 1981, 83–93.

Kishwar, Madhu. "Introduction," *Women Bhakta Poets Manushi,* 1989, 5.

———. "Toiling without Rights: Ho Women of Singhbum," *Economic and Political Weekly,* vol. xxii, no. 3, January 17, 1987, 96.

——— and Ruth Vanita. "Poison to Nectar: The Life and Work of Mirabai," *Women Bhakta Poets Manushi* 1989, 74–93.

———. "The Continuing Deficit of Women in India and the Impact of Aminocentesis," *Man-Made Women: How New Reproductive Technologies Affect Women.* Ed. Gena Corea and others. London: Hutchinson and Co., 1985, 32–33.

———. "Rethinking Dowry Boycott," *Manushi,* no. 48, Sept.–Oct. 1988, 10–13.

———. "Dowry—To Ensure Her Happiness Or To Disinherit Her?" *Manushi,* no. 34, May–June 1986, 2–13.

———. "Dowry Calculations: Daughter's Rights in Her Parental family," *Manushi,* no. 78, Sept.–Oct. 1993, 8–17.

Kolff, Dirk H. A. *Naukar, Rajput and Sepoy: The Ethnohistory of the Military Labour Market in Hindustan, 1450–1850.* Cambridge: Cambridge University Press, 1990.

Kristeva, Julia. "Sabat Mater," *In the Beginning Was Love: Psychoanalysis and Faith.* Trans. Arthur Goldhammer. New York: Columbia University Press, 1987.

Kulke, Hermann. "Kshatriyaization and Social Change," *Aspects of Changing India: Studies in Honour of G. S. Ghurye.* Ed. S. Devadas Pillai. Bombay: Popular Prakashan, 1976, 398–409.

———. "Early State Formation and Royal Legitimation in Late Ancient Orissa," *Sidelights on History and Culture of Orissa.* Ed. Manmath Nath Das. Cuttack: Pitamber Misra, 1977.

Kumar, Radha. *The History of Doing: An Illustrated Account of Movements for Women's Rights and Feminism in India, 1800–1990.* London: Verso, 1993. Orig: New Delhi: Kali for Women, 1993.

Lacan, Jacques. "God and ~~Woman~~'s jouissance," *The Seminar of Jacques Lacan.* Book XX: Encore 1972–1973. Ed. Jacques-Alain Miller. Trans. with notes by Bruce Fink. New York: W. W. Norton and Co., 1999, 61–77.

———. *On Feminine Sexuality: The Limits of Love and Knowledge.* Book XX. Encore 1972–1973. Trans. with notes by Bruce Fink. New York: W. W. Norton and Co., 1998, 64–77.

———. "Le seminaire sur 'La lettre volee.'" Trans. J. Mehlman. *Yale French Studies* 48, 1972, 38–72.

———. *Four Fundamental Concepts of Psycho-Analysis.* Ed. Jacques-Alain Miller. Trans. Alan Sheridan. New York and London: W. W. Norton and Co., 1981.

Lauretis, Teresa De. "Desire in Narrative," *Alice Doesn't: Feminism, Semiotics, Cinema.* Bloomington: Indiana University Press, 1984, 103–157.

Lenin, V. I. *What is to be done? [1902].* Trans. Joe Fineberg and George Hanna. London: Penguin, 1962.

Levi-Strauss, Claude. *Structural Anthropology.* Trans. Claire Jacobson and Brooke Grundfest Schoepf. New York: Basic Books, 1963.

Liddle, Joanna and Rama Joshi. *Daughters of Independence: Gender, Caste and Class in India.* London: Zed Books, 1986.

Locke, John. *An Essay concerning Human Understanding* (1689). In Peter H. Nidditch, ed. and intro., *John Locke: An Essay Concerning Human Understanding.* Oxford: Clarendon Press, 1975.

Lorenzen, David N. "The Kabir Panth and Social Protest," *The Sants: Studies in a Devotional Tradition in India.* Berkley: Berkley Religious Studies Series, 1987, 281–303.

MacCormack, Carol and Marilyn Strathern, eds. *Nature, Culture and Gender.* Cambridge: Cambridge University Press, 1987.

Malthus, Thomas. *An Essay on the Principle of Population* (1798). Ed. Philip Appleman. New York: Norton, 1976.

Mamdani, Mahmood. *The Myth of Population Control: Family, Caste and Class in an Indian Village.* London: Monthly Review Press, 1972.

Mandelbaum, D. *Women's Seclusion, Men's Honour: Sex Roles in North India, Bangladesh and Pakistan.* Tucson: University of Arizona, 1988.

Mani, Lata. "Contentious Traditions: The Debate on *Sati* in Colonial India." In *Recasting Women: Essays in Indian Colonial History.* Ed. Kumkum Sangari and Sudesh Vaid. New Brunswick, New Jersey: Rutgers University Press, 1990. Orig. 2nd edition: New Delhi: Kali for Women, 1989, 88–126.

Manu. *Manava Dharma Sastra* or the *Institute of Manu.* Trans. G. C. Haughton, ed. Rev. P. Percival, preface by William Jones 1825, 4th edition 1863, rpt. Delhi: Asian Educational Services, 1982.

Marglin, Frederique Apffel. "Types of Sexual Union and Their Implicit Meanings," *The Divine Consort: Radha and the Goddesses of India.* Ed. John Stratton Hawley and Donna Marie Wulff. Berkeley: University of California Press, 1982, 298–315.

Marriott, McKim. "Interactional and Attributional Theries of Caste Ranking," *Man in India,* xxxix, 1959, 92–107.

Marx, Karl. "First Manuscript": Economic and Philosophical Manuscripts in *Karl Marx: Early Writings.* Trans. Rodney Livingston and Gregor Benton. New York: Vintage Books, 1975, 331.

———. *Capital. A Critique of Political Economy.* I [1867]. Introduced by Ernest Mandel. Trans. Ben Fowkes. New York: Vintage Books, 1977, 162–163.

Mathur, P.C. "The People of Rajasthan," *Insight Guides: Rajasthan.* Ed. Samuel Israel and Toby Sinclair. Boston: Houghton Mifflin Co., 2nd edition, 1996, 57–66.

Mies, Maria. *Lace Makers of Naraspur: Indian Housewives Produce for the World Market.* London: Zed Press, 1983.

———. *Patriarchy and Accumulation on a World Scale.* London: Zed Books, 1986, 151.

———. "Social Origins of the Sexual Division of Labour," *Women, the Last Colony.* London: Zed Books Ltd., 1988, 74–78.

Miller, Barbara D. "Female Neglect and the Costs of Marriage in Rural India," *Contributions to Indian Sociology* (NS), vol. 14, no. 1, 1980, 95–129.

———. *The Endangered Sex: Neglect of Female Children in Rural North India.* Ithaca: Cornell University Press, 1981, 56–57.

Mishra, Bandhu. *Meera Bhajanawali.* Delhi: Hari Darshan Prakashan Mandir, n.d.

Mohanty, Chandra T. "Under Western Eyes: Feminist Scholarship and Colonial Discourses." In Chandra Talpade Mohanty et al., eds., *Third World Women and the Politics of Feminism.* Bloomington: Indiana University Press, 1991.

———. "Women Workers and Capitalist Scripts: Ideologies of Domination, Common Interests, and the Politics of Solidarity." In M. Jacqui Alexander and Chandra Talpade Mohanty, eds., *Feminist Genealogies, Colonial Legacies, Democratic Futures.* New York: Routledge, 1997.

Mukhia, Harbans. "History Wrapped in Legend's Colors," *Insight Guides: Rajasthan.* Ed. Samuel Israel and Toby Sinclair. Houghton Mifflin, 1996.

Mukta, Parita. "Mirabai in Rajasthan," *Manushi,* nos. 50, 51, 52, 1989, 94–101.

———. *Upholding the Common Life: The Community of Mirabai.* Delhi: Oxford University Press, 1994.

Muthulakshmi, R. *Female Infanticide: Its Causes And Solutions.* New Delhi: Discovery Publishing House, 1997.

Nandy, Pritish, trans. *The Songs of Mirabai.* New Delhi: Arnold-Heinemann, 1975.

Narayan, Kirin. "Women's Songs, Women's Lives: A View from Kangra," *Manushi,* no. 81, March–April 1994, 2–10.

Nehru, Jawaharlal. *The Discovery of India.* (1946). Delhi: Oxford University Press, 1985.

Nicholas, Ralph W. "Sraddha, Impurity, and Relations Between the Living and the Dead," *Way of Life: King, Householder, Renouncer Essays in Honour of Louis Dumont.* Ed. T. N. Madan. Delhi: Vikas Publishing House, 1982, 367–379.

Oldenberg. Veena Talwar. *Dowry Murder: The Imperial Origins of a Cultural Crime.* New York: Oxford University Press, 2002.

Omvedt, Gail. *We Will Smash This Prison.* London: Zed Press, 1980.

Pandey, S. M. and Norman H. Zide, trans. "Poems from Mirabai." Chicago: University of Chicago, 1964.

Panigrahi, Lalita. *British Social Policy and Female Infanticide in India.* New Delhi: Munshiram Manoharlal, 1976.

Pant, Sumitranandan. *Pallav,* n.p. 1967, 22.

Patel, Vibhuti. "Aminocenteses and Female Foeticide—Misuse of Medical Technology," *Socialist Health Review,* September 1984, 1, 2, 69–70.

Pocock, David F. "Inclusion and Exclusion: A Process in the Caste System of Gujerat," *Southwestern Journal of Anthropology,* vol 13, no. 1, Spring 1957.

Poe, Edgar Allan. "The Purloined Letter," *The Tell-Tale Heart and Other Writings.* New York: Bantam Books, 1982, 108–125.

Poitevin, Guy and Hema Rairkar. *Stonehill And Bhakti: From the Devotion of Peasant Women to the Philosophy of Swamis.* New Delhi: D. K. Printworld (P) Ltd., 1996.

Raheja, Gloria Goodwin, and Ann Grodzins Gold, eds. "On the Uses of Irony and Ambiguity: Shifting Perspectives on Patriliny and Women's Ties to Natal Kin," *Listen to the Heron's Words: Reimagining Gender and Kinship in North India.* Berkeley: University of California Press, 1994, 73–120.

Rajadhyaksha, Ashish and Paul Willemen. *Encyclopedia of Indian Cinema.* Delhi: Oxford University Press, revised edition, 1999.

Ramanujan, A. K. "On Women Saints," *The Divine Consort: Radha and the Godesses of India.* Ed. John Stratton Hawley and Donna Marie Wulff. Berkley: University of California Press, 1982.

———. "Talking to God in the Mother Tongue," *Women Bhakta Poets, Manushi,* 50, 51, 52, January–June, 1989, 9–17.

Ravinder, R. P. "Struggle Against Sex-Determination Techniques: Unfinished Battle," *Economic and Political Weekly,* March 21, 1987, 490–492.

Ray, Raka. *Fields of Protest: Women's Movements in India.* Minneapolis: University of Minnesota Press, 1999, 102–109.

Rivers, W. H. R. *The Todas.*

Rowe, William L. "The New Cauhans: A Caste Mobility Movement in North India," *Social Mobility in the Caste System in India.* Paris: Mouton and Co., 1968, 66–77.

Rudolph, Susanne Hoeber et al., eds. "Notes About My Cousin's Marriage," *Reversing the Gaze: Amar Singh's Diary: A Colonial Subject's Narrative of Imperial India.* Boulder, CO: Westview Press, 2002, 362

Said, Edward W. *Orientalism.* New York: Vintage Books, 1979.

———. *Culture and Imperialism.* New York: Vintage Books, 1994.

———. *A Critical Reader.* Ed. Michael Sprinker. Cambridge: Blackwell Publishers, 1992.

Sangari, Kumkum. "Mirabai and the Spiritual Economy of *Bhakti* Part 1," *Economic and Political Weekly,* July 7, 1990, 1464–1475.

———. "Mirabai and the Spiritual Economy of *Bhakti* Part 1," Part 2: *Economic and Political Weekly,* July 14, 1990, 1537–1552.

—— and Sudesh Vaid, eds. "Recasting Women: An Introduction." In *Recasting Women: Essays in Indian Colonial History.* New Brunswick, New Jersey: Rutgers University Press, 1997. 3rd edition. Orig: New Delhi: Kali for Women, 1989.

Savara, Mira. *Changing Trends in Women's Employment: A Case Study of the Textile Industry in Bombay.* Bombay: Himalaya, 1986.

Schromer, Karine. *Mahadevi Varma and the Chhayavad Age of Modern Hindi Poetry.* Berkeley: University of California Press, 1983.

Searle-Chatterjee, Mary and Ursula Sharma, eds. *Contextualizing Caste.* Oxford: Blackwell Publishers, 1995.

Sekhavat, Kalyansingh, ed. *Mirabai ka Jivanvrtt evam Kavya.* Jodhpur: Hindi Sahitya Mandir, 1974.

——. *Meera Brihapadavali,* vol. 2. Jodhpur: Rajasthan Oriental Research Institute, 1975.

Sen, Amartya. "Missing Women—Revisited," *British Medical Journal,* vol. 327, issue 7427, 2003.

Shabnam, Padmavati. *Mira: Vyaktitva aur Katitva.* Lucknow: Hindi Pracharak Sansthan, 1976.

Shah, A. M. and R. G. Shroff. "The Vahivanca Barots of Gujarat: A Caste of Genealogists and Mythographers," *Traditional India: Structure and Change.* Ed. Milton Singer. Philadelphia: The American Folklore Society, 1959.

Shiva, Vandana. "Terra Mater: Reclaiming the Feminine Principle," *Staying Alive: Women, Ecology and Development.* London: Zed Books Ltd., 1988, 218–224.

—— and Maria Mies. *Ecofeminism.* London: Zed Books, 1993.

Sidel, Ruth. *Women and Children Last.* Harmondsworth: Penguin Books, 1987.

Silverberg, James, ed. *Social Mobility in the Caste System in India.* Paris: Mouton and Co., 1968.

Singer, Milton, ed. "The Idea of the Martial Rajput," *Traditional India: Structure and Change.* Philadelphia: The American Folklore Society, 1959, 16.

Singh, Andrea Menefee, and Anita Kelles-Viitanen, eds. *Invisible Hands: Women in Home-Based Production.* Delhi: Sage Publictions, 1987.

Singh, K. Suresh. "A Study in State Formation among Tribal Communities," *Indian Society,* 1974, 317–336.

Singer, Milton. "The Social Organization of Indian Civilization," *Diogene,* vol. 45, winter 1964, 84–119.

—— and Bernard Cohn, eds. *Structure and Change in Indian Society.* Chicago: Aldine Publishing Co., 1968.

Sinha, Surajit. "Early State Formation and Rajput Myth in Tribal Central India," *Man In India,* vol. 42, no. 1, January–March 1962, 5–80.

Spivak, Gayatri C. "Subaltern Studies: Deconstructing Historiography," *Subaltern Studies 1V.* Delhi and New York: Oxford University Press, 1985.

——. "The Rani of Sirmur: An Essay in Reading the Archives," *History and Theory* 24, no. 3, 1985.

———. "History," *A Critique of Postcolonial Reason.* Cambridge, Massachusetts: Harvard University Press, 1999.

Srinivas, M. N. *Religion and Society Among the Coorgs of South India.* Oxford: Oxford University Press, 1952.

———. *Social Change in Modern India.* Berkeley: University of California Press, 1969.

———. "Some Reflections on the Nature of Caste Hierarchy," *Contributions to Indian Sociology,* vol. 18, no. 2, July–December 1984, 152.

———. A. M. Shah and E. A. Ramaswamy, eds. *The Fieldworker and the Field: Problems and Challenges in Sociological Investigation.* Delhi: Oxford University Press, 1979.

———. "Village Studies, Participant Observation and Social Sciences Research in India," *The Dominant Caste and Other Essays.* Delhi: Oxford University Press, 1987, 175–192.

Stein, Burton. "Social Mobility and Medieval South Indian Hindu Sects," *Social Mobility in the Social Mobility in the Caste System in India.* Paris: Mouton and Co., 1968, 79.

Stillingfleet, Edward. *Three Criticisms of Locke* (1697). New York: Georg Olms Verlag, 1987.

Stone, Lawrence. *The Family, Sex and Marriage in England 1500–1800,* 1977.

Tambiah, S. J. "The Renouncer: His Individuality and His Community," *Way Of Life: King, Householder, Renouncer. Essays in Honour of Louis Dumont.* Ed. T. N. Madan. New Delhi: Vikas Publishing House Pvt. Ltd., 1982, 299–320.

———. "From Varna to Caste through Mixed Unions." In *The Character of Kinship.* Ed. Jack Goody. Cambridge: Cambridge University Press, 1973, 191–229.

Taussig, Michael T. *The Devil and Commodity Fetishism in South America.* Chapel Hill, North Carolina: University of North Carolina Press, 1980.

Tessitori, L. P. "A Progress Report on the Work Done During the Year 1916 in Connection with the Bardic and Historical Survey of Rajputana," *Journal of the Asiatic Society of Bengal,* N.S. 13, 1917.

Tewari, Bhagwandas. *Mira ki Pramanik Padavali.* Allahabad: Sahitya Bhavan, 1974.

Thapar, Romila. "Assimilation on Trial C.A.D. 1200–1526," *A History of India, vol. I.* New York: Penguin Books, 1966, 289–320.

———. "Social Mobility in Ancient India," *Indian Society: Historical Probings in Memory of D. D. Kosambi.* Ed. R. S. Sharma. New Delhi: People's Publishing House, 1974, 94–123.

———. "Renunciation: The Making of a Counter-culture?" *Ancient Indian Social History: Some Interpretations.* Delhi: Orient Longman, 1978, 63–104.

———. "Social Mobility in Ancient India with Special Reference to Elite Groups," *Ancient Indian Social History: Some Interpretations.* Delhi: Orient Longmans, 1978, 122–151.

————. "Householders and Renouncers in the Brahmanical and Buddhist Traditions," *Way of Life: King, Householder, Renouncer. Essays in Honour of Louis Dumont.* Ed. T. N. Madan. Delhi: Vikas Publishing House, 1982, 273–298.

Tharu, Susie and K. Lalita, eds. *Women Writing In India: 600 B. C. to the Present,* vol. I. New York: The Feminist Press, City University of New York, 1991.

Tiwari, R. C., R. S. Sharma, and Krishna Vakil. *Hindi-English Dictionary.* New York: Hippocrene Books, 1994.

Tewari, Bhagwandas. *Meera Ki Pramanik Padavali.* Allahabad: Sahitya Bhavan, 1974.

Trautmann, Thomas. *Dravidian Kinship.* Berkeley: University of California Press, 1981.

Turner, Michael, ed. *Malthus and His Time.* London: Macmillan, 1986.

Unnithan, Maya. "Girasias and the Politics of Difference in Rajasthan: 'Caste' Kinship and Gender in a Marginalized Society," *Contextualizing Caste.* Ed. Mary Searle-Chatterjee and Ursula Sharma. Oxford: Blackwell Publishers, 1995.

Varma, Mahadevi. *Atit Ke Chal-Chitra.* Allahabad: Bharati Bhandar, 1963.

————. *Smriti Ki Rekhayen.* Allahabad: Bharati Bhandar, 1971.

Vaasanti. Study of female infanticide in Usilampatti taluk, Madurai district for Caritas and the review of her study in "Born to Die: Tragedy of the Doomed Daughter," *The Hindu,* November 20, 1994.

Venkatachalam, R. and Viji Srinivasan. *Female Infanticide.* New Delhi: Har-Anand Publications, 1993.

Vishnu Purana. Trans. H. H. Wilson (1840). Rpt. Calcutta: Punthi Pustak, 1961. Intro. by R. C. Hazra.

Vishwanath, L. S. *Female Infanticide and Social Structure: A Socio-Historical Study in Western and Northern India.* New Delhi: Hindustan Publishing Corp. (India), 2000.

Zeigler, Norman. "Marvari Historical Chronicles: Sources for the Social and Cultural History of Rajasthan," *The Indian Economic and Social History Review,* April–June 1976, vol. xii, no. 2, 219–250.

Zwingle, Erla. "Women and Population," *National Geographic,* Millenium Supplement, October, 1998.

Index